CAMBRIDGE STUDIES IN
INTERNATIONAL AND COMPARATIVE LAW

General Editors:
C. J. HAMSON AND R. Y. JENNINGS

IX
THE THEORY AND PRACTICE OF DISSOLUTION OF PARLIAMENT

THE THEORY AND PRACTICE OF DISSOLUTION OF PARLIAMENT

A comparative study with special reference to the
United Kingdom and Greek experience

BY

B. S. MARKESINIS

D.IUR.(ATHEN.), M.A., PH.D.(CANTAB.)
of Gray's Inn, Barrister-at-Law
Fellow of Churchill College, Cambridge

Forword by C. J. Hamson
Professor of Comparative Law in the
University of Cambridge

CAMBRIDGE

AT THE UNIVERSITY PRESS

1972

Published by the Syndics of the Cambridge University Press
Bentley House, 200 Euston Road, London NW1 2DB
American Branch: 32 East 57th Street, New York, N.Y.10022

© Cambridge University Press 1972

Library of Congress Catalogue Card Number: 70–189592

ISBN: 0 521 08524 1

Printed in Great Britain
at the University Printing House, Cambridge
(Brooke Crutchley, University Printer)

TO MY FATHER

CONTENTS

FOREWORD

This book makes an unusual and valuable contribution to comparative studies, and it is not easy to give an adequate account of it in a foreword.

Basically the author offers to provide in Parts II and III a historical survey of the United Kingdom and Greek experience in the matter of the dissolution of Parliament over the period of the past hundred years or so, and more particularly during the twentieth century. And simply as a historical survey the book has considerable merit. In the Greek part (Part III) Dr Markesinis makes available unpublished material from some of the protagonists in the more recent crises and also provides for the first time a lawyer's interpretation as well as a new insight into events more canvassed by historians, such as the two dissolutions of 1915. Principally however, he gives a coherent, informed and most commendably dispassionate account of the actual operation in Greece of a political institution – the power of dissolution – which has been the storm-centre of the troubled course of Greek affairs. Because of the involutions of the story and because of the condensation which has been necessary, the narrative requires to be read with close attention; but it is rewarding and it has the additional topical interest of putting the present Greek situation into a proper perspective.

The United Kingdom scene (Part II) is necessarily more familiar to an English reader, though I doubt that the book will have English readers only. But even the English constitutional lawyer will gain advantage from the new matter which Dr Markesinis has found in unpublished Cabinet and other papers, and from his Chapter 7 on 'Dissolution today', where the opposing views are discussed with modesty and discrimination, and not without an element of originality. The foreign reader will greatly benefit from the lucid survey of the English precedents, and it may be specially recommended to politicians, Greek and others, who are apt to quote and to misquote those precedents.

The book however is not by a historian but by a lawyer, and by a widely informed and intelligent comparative lawyer. It is this quality which gives it its special character and its specific value. Into the narrative of the events Dr Markesinis introduces an account of the opinions which are expressed by the actors and others about the institution (opinions which were often weapons for use in the political struggle), and an analysis and appraisal of those opinions. He thus succeeds in accumulating an orderly and most impressive mass of legal and historical information about the institution, the true nature of which depends not so much from its formal definition as from its actual operation in a constantly changing social and economic environment. He is at pains to emphasise the importance of this changing environment, and of the correspondingly varying set of political axioms and assumptions associated with it, in determining the nature of the institution itself. By this insistence he also succeeds in making into a truly comparative study what might have become, in view of the extreme difference of the political situations in Greece and in the United Kingdom, a mere catalogue of wholly disparate events. And he adds a further dimension to his enquiry by setting out in Part I the technical provisions concerning the power to dissolve to be found in continental Constitutions as well as the highly formal and abstract discussions of the topic favoured by continental political scientists little known in this country.

Dr Markesinis has in a relatively very small compass produced a full and most instructive study in depth of an institution which is commonly regarded as a critical feature of parliamentary government, which historically has played an important part in the development of our political societies and which, though changing in its role, is likely to remain as important and as critical in the future.

It is my privilege as one of the General Editors of the series to have this opportunity of commending to the reader a work of great intrinsic merit to which the 1971 Yorke Prize was awarded by the Cambridge Faculty Board of Law.

June 1972   C. J. Hamson

ACKNOWLEDGEMENTS

In writing this book, I was fortunate enough to be greatly assisted by a number of extremely well-informed people. Much as I should like to thank them all, I feel I have to limit myself to only a few.

I am grateful to H.E. Mr Stephanos Stephanopoulos, former Prime Minister, for the use of his unpublished papers which deal with two highly controversial periods of modern Greek history. I must also thank H.E. Mr George Athanasiades-Novas, former Prime Minister, and Admiral John Toumbas, former Minister of Foreign Affairs, for the use of his private papers and his valuable assistance covering his last term in office.

Special thanks are also due to Professor Theodore Angelopoulos, formerly of the Council of State and head of the late King George II's political bureau, for allowing me to consult some of his private papers and also for his willingness to provide further information; Mr Charilaos Mitrelias, Honorary President of the Greek Council of State and Chairman of the 1967 Constitutional Committee originally entrusted with the task of drafting a new Constitution; Professor John Triantaphyllopoulos of the University of Athens, former Minister of Justice, for allowing me to consult and eventually to publish some of his private papers and letters covering his period in office, and General Thrasyvoulos Tsakalotos, formerly Chief of the Army Staff, for valuable information. Finally, my thanks are due to Mr Kyros Kyrou, editor of the oldest Athens daily, *Estia*, for the use of the paper's archives.

The author and publisher are most grateful to the following for permission to reproduce in the Appendix their letters to *The Times*: Lord Chorley, Lord Shawcross, Q.C., Lady Simon of Wythenshawe (for two letters of the late Lord Simon of Wythenshawe), Sir Eric (now Lord) Fletcher, M.P., Sir Alan Lascelles, the Rt. Hon. Roy Jenkins, M.P., Mr R. G. Paget, M.P., Q.C., Mr Ian Gilmour, M.P., Professor Max Beloff, and Professor S. A. de Smith. Thanks are also due to *The Times* for permission to reproduce the editorial article of 15 April 1969.

I have also been helped and encouraged by a great many people. I feel I should first thank H.E. the former British Ambassador to Athens, Sir Michael Stewart for his interest and advice concerning English history. More specifically, I am grateful to the Rt. Hon. Lord Justice Roskill for kindly reading my English chapters and drawing my attention to certain omissions. I am particularly indebted to Professor Stanley de Smith of

Fitzwilliam College, Cambridge, for reading the entire manuscript and making invaluable comments. I was also assisted by Mr D. G. T. Williams of Emmanuel College, Cambridge, who most kindly read several chapters and helped me in many ways. I would also like to thank Dr J. K. Campbell, of St Antony's College, Oxford, for his help and advice concerning my Greek chapters.

I have left until last Professor Charles John Hamson of Trinity College, Cambridge. My indebtedness to him is in more ways than one immeasurable. He most kindly read my chapters several times and spent a considerable part of his precious time discussing them with me and correcting errors of fact and judgement. Had it not been for his unfailing assistance and guidance this work would, perhaps, never have been brought to an end. His many pupils, who have benefited from his guidance, will, I am sure, realise the extent of my indebtedness.

Finally, I would like to thank my own father, Spyros B. Markesinis, who kindly allowed me to use some of his private papers and who also initiated me into the intricacies of Greek politics – by any standards a most confusing topic.

I should also like to take this opportunity to express my sincere thanks to the Master and Fellows of Churchill College, Cambridge, for electing me in May 1970 to a Gulbenkian Research Fellowship and for assisting me in many ways in completing this work. I would also like to thank the British Council for kindly financing the initial phase of my research.

Thanks are also due to the Public Record Office for allowing me to consult the Cabinet Papers and the Foreign Office Papers; the Cambridge University Library for the use of the Stanley Baldwin Papers; the Librarian of the London School of Economics Library for the use of the Hugh Dalton Papers and all those who assisted me in the Greek Parliament Library and the Bibliothèque de la Faculté de Droit in Paris.* I am grateful also to the Syndics and staff of the Cambridge University Press for the interest they have shown in my book.

I hope I have made clear how much I owe to all the above-mentioned. Needless to say, however, for the little that is left, I alone should be held accountable. Last but not least, I also thank my wife for her patience with me and my book.

October 1971

B.S.M.

* In writing this book I was obliged to make frequent references to a great many books, articles, private papers, etc., all of which appear in the footnotes of the text. I feel, however, I have to mention five books in particular which, in more ways than one, have greatly assisted me in my research. These are: Sir Ivor Jennings' *Cabinet government*; Dr E. Forsey's *The royal power of dissolution of Parliament*; J. Velu's *La dissolution du Parlement*; Sir Harold Nicolson's *King George V*, and my father's *Political history of Modern Greece, 1827–1920*.

CONSTITUTIONAL TEXTS*

---

* Most of the texts can be found in the following books: F. R. Dareste and P. Dareste, ʹLes *constitutions modernes*, 4th ed. by J. Delpech and J. Laferrière, Paris, 1928–34; M. Duverger, *Constitutions et documents politiques*, 5th ed., Paris, 1968; B. Mirkine-Guetzévitch, *Les constitutions européennes*, Paris, 1951. The Greek Constitutions can be found in the Government Gazette and are reproduced in E. Kyriakopoulos, *The Greek Constitutions* (in Greek), Athens, 1960.

INTRODUCTION

This book focuses its attention on the theory and practice of dissolution of Parliament in two European monarchies – the British and the Greek. However, in order to formulate more general conclusions on the institution of dissolution, Part I has been added. It consists of three chapters containing comparative material based on a large number of European constitutions, old and new. Naturally, these chapters are not as complete on the subject as the British and Greek chapters would like to claim that they are. An exhaustive description of the theory and practice of dissolution in every European country would need not one but many volumes.

The information contained in these first three chapters also serves an additional purpose: it reveals how European legislators have tackled the more or less similar and persisting problems to which the right to dissolve Parliament usually gives rise. Questions such as which state organ should exercise the right of dissolution, what are the appropriate limitations to avoid abuses of the right and, finally, on what grounds should dissolution be advised, are treated more extensively, since they are extremely important for the understanding of the institution. All this is done – wherever possible – in conjunction with the constant evolution of the parliamentary form of government.

Parts II and III deal with the theory and practice of dissolution in the United Kingdom and Greece. The purpose is that of all comparative studies, namely, to

bring into an approximately sensible juxtaposition at least two systems of laws as systems, as entireties, and within the measure of the possible (and of the author's capacity), to see in each something of its own native quality; without seeking to attribute praise or blame . . . and, indeed, without predetermined ulterior purpose saving only that of knowledge and understanding.[1]

One may ask, however, why these two countries in particular?

The answer is simple. Both these countries seem to place considerable emphasis on the institution and both have an interesting – though different – past as regards this subject. Yet neither of them has produced an extensive, detailed, up-to-date work on dissolution that would attempt to bring together historical and legal material already published and, at the

---

[1] C. J. Hamson, *The law: its study and comparison* (inaugural lecture, Cambridge, 1955), pp. 28–9.

same time, would also take into consideration Cabinet Papers, private papers, diaries etc., recently made accessible. As far as Greece is concerned, unpublished private papers unknown to foreign and Greek readers alike were kindly given to me. I hope the importance of this material – which I intend to publish and edit one day – will not pass unnoticed. Lawrence Lowell has emphasised the fascination, but above all, the difficulties of a study of contemporary politics. 'The forces to be studied,' he wrote,[1]

do not lie upon the surface, and some of them are not described in any document or found in any treatise. They can be learned only from men connected with the machinery of public life. A student must, therefore, rely largely upon conversations which he can use but cannot cite as authorities, and the soundness of his conclusions must be measured less by his references in footnotes than by the judgement of the small portion of the public that knows at first hand the things whereof he speaks.

As I said, I have relied on such information which I obtained from the political protagonists of the recent Greek crises and, I may add, was particularly fortunate to have been given the right to quote the sources. It goes without saying, however, that all necessary cross-checking of the available material was carefully done in order to minimise the chances of possible error. But there was a further reason that led to the present attempt to examine in some depth the experience of these two particular monarchies.

The United Kingdom, of course, is always an obvious choice and little need be said on this. The Mother of Parliaments, with dissolution still playing an interesting and at times controversial part, is an excellent topic for a comparative lawyer. It is here that the pure doctrine of the institution can be found, and by comparison its deviations in other countries can be made obvious.

The second country ought to be a monarchy in order to aid possible comparisons. Of the few remaining European monarchies, Greece seemed the best choice. One reason for this has already been mentioned: the available material was interesting and unexploited. The second reason is that Greece has always attached considerable importance to the right to dissolve Parliament and in fact has an extremely interesting past on this issue. In the Scandinavian countries, on the other hand, and to a lesser extent in Holland and Luxembourg, dissolution has practically fallen into disuse. This leaves only Belgium as a possible alternative for comparison. But Greece was chosen instead for the additional reason that the Greek Constitution of 1844 (and all subsequent constitutions that were based on it) owed a great deal to the Belgian Constitution of 1831. It would

[1] *Government of England* (1917 edn), I, vi.

thus make an interesting study to see how more or less similar constitutional texts were operated and have developed in entirely different environments. In any case, a number of books have been written concerning the Belgian theory and practice of dissolution and it seemed purposeless to cover the same ground even if I might occasionally have – and indeed do have – differing views from those expressed by more competent Belgian colleagues.

To summarise: the title of this work indicates where the main emphasis lies, i.e. the detailed examination of the precedents in the United Kingdom and Greece in the late nineteenth and twentieth centuries. But the scope of the research is not limited to these countries alone, nor is its purpose purely descriptive. Its aim is more ambitious: namely, to describe and examine in some depth the institution as part of the parliamentary form of government. It was therefore necessary to include comparative material so as to present a complete picture, as far as possible, of how the institution was originally devised, and how it has actually functioned. And, it seems to me, the extensive reference to European constitutions, coupled with the more detailed analysis of the British and Greek practice, make the final conclusions more sound and, at the same time, relate the practice of dissolution to the general theory of parliamentary government in our times.

A few words still remain to be said on the method of treatment of the subject. Basically, this study raised two problems. The first was related to the non-legal aspects of the subject. It is obvious that the study of a particularly important institution of public law would be incomplete, indeed even defective, if it were restricted to purely legal material and ignored the socio-economic and historical background within which the institution was practised. As the well-known Belgian Professor Ganshof van der Meersch has wisely observed:[1] 'Une coupure opérée de manière trop nette entre le droit public et la science politique conduirait à une vue incomplète, voire fausse de cette procédure constitutionnelle.' The introduction of other material, mainly political and historical, was therefore essential and hence research was also conducted in historical subjects. This is particularly true as regards the Greek chapters, since contemporary Greek history is little known, even though Greek politics frequently make the front pages.

The second difficulty was closely linked with the method of treatment of the subject. The terms 'theory' and 'practice' offer a significant indication of what has been attempted in this work. The examination of the 'pure doctrine', even if related to a specific institution of a specific country

[1] Introduction to J. Velu's *La dissolution du Parlement* (1966), p. viii.

is, by its nature, a more appropriate subject for Continental lawyers accustomed to dealing with abstract notions. The Continental way of treating legal subjects lends itself to more abstract, theoretical and philosophical analysis which, even if it occasionally arouses the suspicion of the common law lawyer, can further in its own way the understanding of the legal structure, accentuate the differences between legal systems and finally help to reveal the variation between theory and practice. As far as the actual practice is concerned, the successful English historical method was applied. Instead of arguing which method is preferable, I have attempted to combine them. Thus, Part I has basically followed the continental method, whereas the study of the actual historical precedents in Parts II and III made the adoption of the English method highly desirable. It is in these chapters that the historical, political and sociological material was mostly used.

So much then for the subject and the method of its treatment. One further point, however, should be borne in mind by the reader. In the words of the well-known French author Benjamin Constant, a nation's institutions are stable so long as they correspond to its ideas.[1] But ideas and societies change – and in our days much faster than they did in the past – and hence so do their institutions. Dissolution has not escaped this rule. What characterises the institution is that during the last hundred years or so it has served a variety of purposes, thus demonstrating a remarkable degree of flexibility.

Dissolution is linked through parliamentarism with the representative system of government which, in this country, can, in a sense, trace its origins as far back as the Magna Carta and the Model Parliament.[2] But it was not until the seventeenth century that Parliament began to be convened at regular periods and later, by the Septennial Act 1716, was given a maximum term of years.[3] This was a crucial development for dissolution because only if Parliament has a given term of years can a premature ending (through dissolution) be conceived. Most important, however, the seventeenth-century crises in England opened the way for the subsequent gradual development of modern constitutional concepts.

---

[1] *Des réactions politiques*, in *Cours de politique constitutionnelle* (1820), II, 71.

[2] See for instance: T. P. H. Taswell-Langmead, *English constitutional history from the Teutonic conquest to the present time*, 11th edn, ch. 6; A. F. Pollard, *The evolution of Parliament*, 2nd edn (1964); G. O. Sayles, *The medieval foundations of England*, 2nd edn (1950).

[3] By the First and Second Triennial Acts (1640, 1664) and the Meeting of Parliament Act (1694): see W. C. Costin & J. S. Watson, *The law and working of the constitution*, 2nd edn (1961–4), I, 33–4, 79–80. The Bill of Rights, ibid., pp. 67–74, established that the King reigns solely with and by the consent of Parliament. This gradual development of the British form of government can find a parallel only in ancient Rome, equally conservative in temperament and eager to preserve traditions. Cicero, *De Republica*, II.1 (ed. Lipsiae, 1823).

After a brief flirtation with the doctrine of separation of powers which was adopted by the Instrument of Government (1653),[1] England's first and only written constitution, the idea of a mixed constitution and the necessity of an effective system of checks and balances gained ground and finally led to the nineteenth-century model of classical parliamentarism.

Following the Napoleonic wars the English form of government was increasingly used as a model in one way or another. Even France, which had elevated the separation of powers to the heights of a religious doctrine and thus had no use for dissolution,[2] soon followed the English pattern and included the institution in the 1814 (art. 50) and 1830 Constitutions (art. 42).[3] After a brief lapse – in 1848 – dissolution was re-introduced by the 1875 Constitutional Laws (art. 5),[4] this time making France the first Republic ever to accept the institution. Her example was later followed by the Weimar Constitution (1919) (art. 25) and the post-World War One constitutions which also subjected its exercise to legal rules.

Parliamentarism thus spread through Europe and with it came dissolution, which provided the means for solving conflicts between the Executive and the Legislative, while paying tribute to the supreme powers of the electorate. Its advantages dazzled observers and made it attractive to constituent legislators even after the socio-economic conditions that had produced it had changed or even disappeared. The growth of the modern political parties in particular was something that was bound to have a great impact on dissolution, as indeed it did. But, once again,

---

[1] Sir D. Lindsay-Keir, *The constitutional history of modern Britain, 1485–1951*, 5th edn (1957), pp. 226–7; M. J. C. Vile, *Constitutionalism and the separation of powers* (1967), pp. 47–8. For the seventeenth-century dissolutions see F. W. Maitland, *The constitutional history of England* (1908, repr. 1965), pp. 292–7.

[2] Art. 16 of the *Declaration des droits de l'homme et du citoyen*, 16 August 1789, in M. Duverger, *Constitutions et documents politiques*, 5th edn (1968), p. 4.

[3] Dissolution appears for the first time in the Senatus Consulte Organique of the 16th Thermidor of the 10th year (1802) of the Revolution. It was exercised once after Napoleon's return from Elba. For the decade see E. Ferrus, *Le droit de dissolution* (1935), pp. 45–55; R. P. Voinesco, *De la dissolution des assemblées législatives en France, en Angleterre et en Belgique* (1896), pp. 59–74. Paradoxically, the 1814 Constitution, though it included dissolution (art. 50), ignored the political responsibility of the Government towards the House. Despite the eloquently expressed views of Chateaubriand, *De la Monarchie selon la Charte* (1816), ch. 15, and Benjamin Constant, *Principes de politique* (1815) and *Réflexions sur les constitutions et les garanties, avec une esquisse de constitution* (1814) in *Cours de politique constitutionnelle*, vol. 1, political responsibility was not introduced until the Martignac Government was sworn in in January 1828.

[4] For details see Y. Haikal, *La dissolution de la chambre des députées* (1935), pp. 9–27; M. D. Alexandrakis, *De l'exercice du droit de dissolution par le pouvoir exécutif* (1937), pp. 119ff. For the background see Sir Denis Brogan, *The development of modern France* (1967), pp. 77ff. and J. Gouault, *Comment la France est devenue républicaine* (1954).

dissolution survived the change in the environment. Just as in the nineteenth century it had liberated itself from the monarchical elements of the past, so in the twentieth century it became an effective party weapon. Certain minor exceptions apart, this book deals with the evolution of the institution during the last hundred years and with its effects on the parliamentary form of government.

PART I

THE GENERAL THEORY

═══

Chapter 1

THE INSTITUTION OF DISSOLUTION

A: DEFINITION AND VARIOUS KINDS OF DISSOLUTION

Dissolution in its broadest sense means decomposition, disintegration, undoing a bond. In a broad sense – the constitutional – it implies the dismissal of an Assembly. In its narrow sense, in which it will be used in this book, it indicates the lawful act of the Executive[1] to put an abrupt end to the life of Parliament.

Thus dissolution is an act of the Executive which dismisses the legislative body, and refers a disputed case to the electorate, the supreme arbitrator of the State; it is lawful, in the sense that it is exercised according to the Constitution, the laws and the conventions of the country, and is not a product of power (e.g. revolution, etc.); and it prematurely ends the life of Parliament.

Classifying dissolution into various categories has been a subject of controversy between constitutional lawyers. This theoretical endeavour is not entirely without practical significance. For example, in certain countries such as Belgium, it is normal constitutional practice to ask the Conseil d'Etat for its opinion about an intended dissolution. Naturally, however, this does not apply in the case of an automatic dissolution (*dissolution de plein droit*).

But is such a categorisation possible and can it ever be complete? Some authors take the view that it is not feasible to attempt to classify the various kinds of dissolution.[2] Others,[3] using as a criterion the state organ

---

[1] Whenever the term Executive is used without further qualification it refers to the function of the State concerned with government and executing laws as contrasted to the Legislative and the Judiciary. Accordingly it may refer to the Head of State (King or President) or the Government or both.

[2] P. Matter, 'La dissolution des assemblées parlementaires' (1898), p. 10.

[3] C. Schmitt, *Verfassungslehre* (1928), pp. 353ff.; E. Gordon, *Les nouvelles constitutions européennes et le rôle du chef d'état* (1932), p. 280; S. Markesinis, *The Head of State in modern*

vested with the authority to dissolve, distinguish between monarchical, presidential, ministerial, self-dissolution and revocation of the mandate by the people. Finally, a third group[1] uses the legality of the act as a criterion and hence describes dissolution as being legal, illegal, voluntary and natural.

None of these views seems totally satisfactory. Matter's view, according to which a distinction is not feasible, has been proved wrong by the mere fact that numerous distinctions have been made. Similarly, the other categorisations mentioned occasionally overlap. For example: a monarchical (or presidential) dissolution can be either legal or illegal. Furthermore, to take Schmitt's theory, a monarchical (or a presidential) dissolution can at the same time be a ministerial dissolution as in the case of Belgium or France during the Fourth Republic.

There exists, however, one common element in all the cases mentioned in the previous paragraph. Be it the Monarch, the President or the Cabinet that decides on dissolution, the basic fact still remains that the Executive is interfering with the work of the Legislative, by determining its life span. Therefore, it is perhaps preferable to lay the emphasis elsewhere: namely on whether the power of dissolution is bestowed on the Executive, on the Legislative or on the people themselves.

In accordance with the above, dissolution, in its broad sense, can fall under any of the following categories:

(a) Natural

This occurs when the life of Parliament expires, usually four or five years from the time of the previous election.

(b) Automatic or constitutional (dissolution de plein droit)

Under rather special and usually rare circumstances, certain constitutions require an immediate – or automatic – dissolution. Elections follow and, of course, a new Parliament is summoned within a fixed period of time. The two most common causes for such an automatic dissolution are: vacancy of the throne,[2] and revision of the constitution.[3] In Belgium

---

democracies (in Greek) (1935), p. 155; P. Couzinet, *La dissolution des assemblées politiques et la démocratie parlementaire* (1933), p. 39. Prevost-Paradol's distinction (*La France nouvelle* (1894), pp. 148ff.) refers only to a parliamentary form of government.

[1] E. Pierre, *Traité de droit politique, électorale et parlementaire* (1902), p. 333; H. Zengelis, *Parliamentary law* (in Greek) (1906), I, 409ff.

[2] See for example art. 85 of the Belgian Constitution of 1831, which, nevertheless, was never used in practice. The text can be found in B. Mirkine-Guetzévitch, *Les constitutions euro-péennes* (1951), vol. I. In the U.K., until the passing of the 1867 Representation of the People Act, the death of the Sovereign always involved the dissolution of Parliament.

[3] Art. 131 of the Belgian Constitution; art. 107 of the Greek Constitution of 1864; art. 108 of the Greek Constitution of 1911.

alone the second reason has resulted in five dissolutions (1892, 1919, 1954, 1958, 1965). The essential characteristic in both cases is that dissolution occurs without the intervention of the Executive.

(c) *Revocation of the mandate by the people (Abberufungsrecht)*

Dissolution in this case results from the doctrine of popular sovereignty.

(d) *Voluntary or self-dissolution*

This originates from Parliament itself,[1] and is common with constitutions which recognise the complete preponderance of the legislative body. A Constituent Assembly, being a sovereign body, decides on its own when to end its existence. Lastly,

(e) *Dissolution in its narrow context*

I.e., the lawful act of the Executive that prematurely ends the life of the Legislature.

The above types of dissolution, if exercised according to the constitution, the laws and the conventions of the country, are legal or, in a broader sense, constitutional. The dissolution of a legislative body by means of force (*vis absoluta*), e.g. revolution, cannot and will not be discussed since it is outside the field of the various positive legal systems. Consequently it is more a problem of political science. It may be noted nevertheless, that from a strictly legal point of view, the question of whether a revolution creates law largely depends on the success of the revolution.

Dissolution as a separate and distinct institution of constitutional law falls into the last category (*e*), and it is in this sense that it will be referred to in this work.

B: DISSOLUTION OF A CONSTITUENT ASSEMBLY AND OF A REVISIONAL PARLIAMENT

It is difficult to say whether dissolution can be exercised indiscriminately against an ordinary House, a Revisional Parliament and a Constituent Assembly.[2]

---

[1] A typical example can be found in art. 79, para. 3 of the Greek Constitution of 1927. The present German Constitution of 23 May 1949 affords an example of a constitution that does not recognise the right of self-dissolution. See Th. Maunz, *Deutsches Staatsrecht*, 11th edn (1962), para. 32, no. 7, p. 297, and below, chapter 3.

[2] The discussion in the text naturally refers to countries with rigid constitutions which establish special and, as a rule, complicated revisional procedures. For a different and

Referring to a Constituent Assembly, one must, I believe, distinguish whether it derives its powers to draft a constitution from the people (i.e. through a revolution etc.) or not. In the former case, dissolution of a Constituent Assembly can be either the product of power (successful revolution as, for example, in 1922 in Greece)[1] or a decision emanating from the body itself if it considers that its task has come to an end (as, for example, in 1864 in Greece).[2] In the latter case, the Constituent Assembly drafts the constitution in collaboration with another, distinct, State organ and within certain limits, which are as a rule precisely defined. This is usually the case of the so-called constitutions – contracts (*constitutions octroyées*)[3] between the Monarch and his people. Under these circumstances, the Monarch is considered a constituent factor and collaborates with the representatives of the people in drafting the constitution,[4] which he has been obliged, by the force of events, to grant to his people.

It becomes obvious from the above that such an assembly, far from being sovereign, can be dissolved, though such a decision usually entails serious political – not legal – difficulties. Experience has shown that European rulers of the nineteenth century proved capable of delaying, but not preventing, democratic government by obstructing or delaying constitutional innovations. It should be noted, however, that the above applies to the constituent work of the assembly. If the assembly undertakes ordinary legislative work, then there is no reason to treat it differently from an ordinary Parliament. A Revisional Parliament is subject to dissolution since its revisional character does not alter in any respect its nature as a deliberative and representative body.

It is occasionally argued that a Revisional Parliament cannot be dissolved by the Head of State when the latter is not a constituent factor as, for example, in all the Greek constitutions since 1864. The adherents to this view maintain that the dissolution of a Revisional Parliament by the Head of State constitutes a serious intervention and may jeopardise its work. This, however, is not generally accepted, as a dissolution may delay but not prevent the revision of the constitution, since the next Parliament will usually continue the task of its predecessors. Greek constitutional practice offers three examples of the above (1910, 1935 and 1950).[5] Thus a Revisional Parliament can be dissolved regardless of

---

probably more important use of the terms 'rigid' and 'flexible' constitution see Sir K. Wheare, *Modern constitutions* (1966), pp. 16ff.

[1] Below, chapter 10.　　　　　　　　　　　[2] Below, chapter 9.

[3] The preamble of the 1814 French Constitution offers a typical example.

[4] This, for example, is the case in Belgium in the event of a revision of the Constitution; see art. 131, para. 3.

[5] Below, chapters 10, 11 and 12.

whether it is an ordinary Assembly with revisional powers or whether it is a Revisional Assembly, summoned *ad hoc* to undertake this particular task, in which case it may consist of double the usual number of members.[1] The criterion whether an Assembly is Revisional or Constituent, is difficult to define and usually depends on a number of factors and, of course, on the specific provisions of the constitution concerned. Needless to add, all provisions that apply to the dissolution of an ordinary parliament are also applicable to the dissolution of a Revisional House.

Dissolution of a Revisional Parliament is more complicated in countries with two Houses both of which collaborate in the revision of the constitution. In most of these countries only the Lower House can be dissolved (as in France during the Third Republic or in Greece under the 1927 Constitution). This problem is more extensively treated in chapter 12 of the present work. Here it will suffice to note that the Lower House can be dissolved, in which case the revision comes to a halt until a new House is elected and continues the revisional work with the Upper House.

C: THE ESSENTIAL FEATURES OF THE INSTITUTION

It is evident from the preceding paragraphs that the exercise of the right to dissolve Parliament presupposes certain conditions; these are: first, the existence of a representative body, which is the object of dissolution; second, an act of the Executive, which implies a separate and distinct state organ, vested with the right to dissolve; and third, the summoning of a new Parliament. The general elections that follow a dissolution of Parliament represent an important safeguard against an abuse of the right. But though an appeal to the electorate is always regarded as proper, excessive use will undoubtedly tend to defeat its purpose. These three essential characteristics of dissolution now deserve some consideration.

By representative body we mean a periodically elected number of citizens who are vested collectively (and not independently) with a certain function – mainly the legislative – for a limited period of time. If the members of the body are chosen by the Head of the Executive or if they are elected to perform a specific function, they can be discharged, but not be dismissed or dissolved in the technical sense of the word.

If this basic element, i.e. the periodic election by the people, is preserved, it is of no significance whether the representative body consists of one

[1] A. Svolos, *The revision of the constitution* (in Greek) (1933), pp. 55ff.; Alexandrakis, *Dissolution*, pp. 16ff.

or two Houses (Upper and Lower House). Dissolution is usually exercised against the Lower House,[1] but can also be exercised against the Upper House[2] in so far as it is elective and not formed on a hereditary basis. Lastly, certain constitutions demand a simultaneous double dissolution.[3]

Naturally, dissolution presupposes the object of dissolution, i.e. Parliament. Yet, a certain ambiguity exists, as to the exact moment when Parliament comes into existence. This ambiguity is caused by the interim period that elapses between the dissolution of the previous Parliament (and more precisely, election day) and the official opening of the new Parliament, during which time Parliament technically does not exist. Thus the question arises: Can Parliament be dissolved immediately after the elections or must it start formally functioning before it can be dissolved?

Simple as it may seem, it is a problem of practical significance. It has arisen in the past and was one of the primary causes of the Revolution of 1830 and the dethronement of Charles X. Ever since, it has concerned constitutional lawyers in Europe, and it therefore merits a few lines.

Most of the Governments of Charles X were formed in defiance of the opinion of Parliament. The Polignac government (8 August 1829) proved the last straw. To a wave of national discontent, Charles reacted with threats which, in an unprecedented way, he included in his speech from the Throne (2 March 1830). On 16 March, his Government was defeated in the House, which also passed a resolution declaring that: 'Le concours permanent des vues politiques du gouvernement royal avec celle du peuple, condition indispensable à la marche régulière des affaires publiques, n'existe pas.'[4] Two days later, a printed document embodying the above resolution was handed to the King. Yet the Government remained in office until 16 May, when Parliament was dissolved. In the subsequent elections and despite the King's personal intervention in favour of his followers, his opponents increased their number of seats in Parliament from 221 to 270 out of a total of 430. King Charles was

---

[1] See for example art. 5 of the French Constitutional Law of 25 February 1875; art. 79 of the Greek Constitution of 1927; art. 12 of the French Constitution of 1958, etc.

[2] Art. 71 of the Belgian Constitution of 1831 as amended in 1921; art. 22 of the Danish Constitution of 5 June 1915 as amended on 10 September 1920; art. 75 of the Constitution of Holland of 30 November 1887; art. 108 of the Constitution of Sweden of 6 June 1809 as amended by the *loi organique* of the Riksdag of 22 June 1866 (art. 3, 5 and 36); art. 88 of the Constitution of Italy of 1 January 1948, etc.

[3] This was the rule in Germany before 1871. See H. Zöepfl, *Staatsrecht. Gründsätze des Gemeinen Deutschen Staatsrecht* (1863), II, 320ff. See also art. 26 of the Polish Constitution of 1921.

[4] See Ferrus, *Dissolution*, p. 90.

determined to use force to make his views prevail. On 25 July, he had recourse to article 14 of the Constitution, obtained extraordinary powers, suspended all press liberties and dissolved the newly elected Parliament. On 27 and 28 July the Revolution broke out with the cry, 'vive la Charte, à bas les Ministres'.[1]

The King's right to dissolve Parliament at such an early stage was seriously challenged by Casimir-Perier, and the latter's views were further elaborated and supported by Rossi.[2] In Rossi's opinion, dissolution must be preceded by the official opening of Parliament. During the interregnum – the period between elections and the opening of Parliament – certain elements of it exist – i.e. M.P.s who will form it – but not Parliament itself.[3] The speech from the Throne and the election of a Speaker usually mark the formal beginnings of the functioning of Parliament. Dissolution at an earlier stage would mean annulling the elections rather than dissolving something that does not exist. 'Dissoudre la Chambre avant que la Chambre soit constituée en corps délibérant, c'est anéantir les élections, mais non dissoudre ce qui n'existe pas.'[4]

The opposite view was supported by Professor Anschütz,[5] according to whom Parliament exists immediately after the elections and hence can be dissolved from that point onwards. This theory no longer prevails on the Continent, and one should add that it is probably politically unwise to proceed to a second dissolution within such a short period of time. Such a premature dissolution would directly challenge the supremacy of the electorate – particularly if one party has claimed victory over the other – and would increase instead of decrease the chances of a major political crisis.[6]

It is perhaps relevant to note that the same view is taken in the United Kingdom. As Dr Forsey maintains:

---

[1] For further details see Ferrus, *Dissolution*, pp. 89–94; Matter, *Dissolution*, pp. 25, 79; L. Radenac, *De la dissolution des assemblées législatives* (1897), pp. 142ff.; Voinesco, *Dissolution*, pp. 42ff.; Velu, *La dissolution du Parlement*, pp. 206ff.

[2] P. Rossi, *Cours de droit constitutionnel* (1877), IV, 44ff.

[3] 'Qui dit chambre, en effet, dit assemblée, dit corps politique délibérant; or qui dit corps dit nécessairement une organisation, une constitution de ce corps. Avant l'organisation, il y a les éléments de ce corps, mais pas le corps lui-même.' Rossi, ibid.

[4] Rossi, *Droit constitutionnel*, IV, 26. The declaration of 27 July 1830 was in accordance with the above.

[5] See G. Anschütz, *Die Verfassung des Deutschen Reichs, vom 11 August 1919* (Vierte Bearbeitung, 14 Auflage, Berlin, 1933), pp. 196ff. saying: 'Mit der Wahl, nicht mit dem ersten Zusammentritt, beginnt seine Wahlperiod.' Also E. Walz, *Das Staatsrecht des Grossherzogtums Baden* (1909), p. 87.

[6] See also L. Duguit, *Traité de droit constitutionnel* (1924), IV, 577; J. Barthélemy & P. Duez, *Traité de droit constitutionnel* (1926), p. 691; N. N. Saripolos, *Constitutional law* (in Greek), I, 3rd edn (1915), 526; D. Kyriakos, *Interpretation of the Greek Constitution* (in Greek) (1904), I, 350; Zengelis, *Parliamentary law*, p. 459.

The new Parliament must be allowed not only to meet and elect a Speaker, but also to proceed to the transaction of the ordinary business of the session. Neither the Government which has had the previous dissolution, nor a new Government, has a right to dissolve a new Parliament immediately after the election of the Speaker, or immediately upon the adoption of the Address. Even if the Government is dependent in critical divisions on the Speaker's casting vote, and is therefore in a position to claim that effective legislation is difficult to the verge of impossibility, it would not, at this stage, be entitled to a dissolution unless it had at least made a serious attempt to get Supply voted.[1]

Practice seems to agree entirely with Dr Forsey's views. For example, on 21 April 1950, Sir Alan Lascelles placed before the King a memorandum in order to assist him in the event of Mr Attlee advising an early dissolution. In it he stated that,

if the King decided to grant a dissolution, he should certainly not do so save on the condition that it should not become operative until Parliament has done its duty of making at least a minimum provision for the national finance . . . Consequently the King would be bound to insist that the dissolution asked for by Mr. Attlee should not take effect until Parliament had dealt with a Minimal Finance Act and an Appropriation Act.[2]

Once Parliament has been formally opened, it can be dissolved whether it is in session or not.[3]

The state organ vested with the right to dissolve Parliament must express its will to do so, in a manner which accords with the constitution, laws and conventions of the country. On the Continent this is usually achieved by an act of the Head of State taking the form of a Royal (or Presidential) Decree countersigned by the Cabinet, or by the competent Minister, usually the Minister of Interior or by the Prime Minister himself. Dissolution can also be announced in a presidential message, as for example in Poland under the 1926 Constitution. In the United Kingdom it takes the form of a proclamation under the Great Seal and writs of summons calling a new Parliament. Since 1818 no sovereign has dissolved the House in person[4] and it is the usual, though not invariable, practice to prorogue and dissolve Parliament on the same day.[5]

---

[1] *The royal power of dissolution of Parliament in the British Commonwealth*, 2nd edn (1968), pp. 261–2.

[2] Quoted by J. W. Wheeler-Bennett, *King George VI; his life and reign* (1958), p. 774. See also Turkish Constitution of 1876, art. 102, para. 2, and Serbian Constitution of 1903, art. 174, para. 2.

[3] Matter, *Dissolution*, p. 27; P. Laband, *Staatsrecht des Deutschen Reichs* (1876), I, 558.

[4] But more or less similar proceedings occurred in 1831, 1837 and 1847. See Erskine May's *Treatise on the law, privileges, proceedings and usage of Parliament*, 17th edn (1964), p. 36.

[5] Prorogation and dissolution took place on the same day in 1857, 1865, 1874, 1880, 1892, 1910, 1923, 1924, 1929, 1931, 1935, 1945, 1955, 1959. Dissolution followed prorogation in

The above is the second necessary condition for dissolution to be lawfully exercised. The details – as noted above – will of course vary according to the diverse legal systems. It is essential, however, to note that from the moment dissolution was incorporated in parliamentary government it adapted itself to certain democratic principles, one of these being that it falls to the Cabinet or the Prime Minister to countersign the relevant act thus assuming responsibility. Who in particular undertakes this responsibility will be discussed later. Here it is sufficient to note the underlying political responsibility. Hence, nowadays old theories, regarding dissolution as a royal prerogative independently exercised by the Monarch, are obsolete and inconsistent with present political realities.

The last prerequisite is that elections follow the dissolution, and a new Parliament is summoned within a reasonable period of time. As Matter correctly observes,[1] if the Head of State can dissolve without being obliged to summon a new Parliament, we are confronted not with a representative or parliamentary form of government but with a particular type of Etats Généraux. Whether the summoning of the new Parliament is done by the same act that dissolves the previous one or by a subsequent act, or whether this is done by law or convention, is of no importance. The essential factor still remains that a new Parliament is summoned and the routine of parliamentary government is not seriously disrupted.

D: EFFECTS OF DISSOLUTION

The premature interruption of the life of Parliament has numerous results which affect the Assembly as a body, as well as its individual members; likewise its work is also abruptly ended by dissolution. And it is only natural that greater disruption may occur and problems can be more complex, wherever the two-House system prevails. Furthermore, the political nature of the institution is bound to exercise a profound influence on the political events in the country concerned, and at times has a certain impact on international affairs as well.

The primary consequence of dissolution is that Parliament legally ceases to exist and cannot perform its legislative functions. This occurs immediately after the Royal Decree dissolving Parliament is published in the Government Gazette or is orally announced in Parliament by the Speaker, depending on the specific provision of the various constitutions. If dissolution is pronounced while the House is in session, the Speaker is

---

1859, 1886, 1895, 1900, 1906, 1910, 1918, 1950, 1951. May, *Parliamentary practice*, p. 36, nn. (*p*) and (*q*).　　　　　　　　[1] *Dissolution*, p. 29.

obliged to adjourn immediately and, if he refuses to do so, it occurs automatically. Any further meeting of the ex-members of Parliament is considered an ordinary meeting of citizens and not an official session of Parliament in its legislative capacity.[1] Most of the constitutions provide little guidance if any on this subject. It is generally acknowledged, however, that the main effect of dissolution is the termination of the life of Parliament. Nevertheless, a comparative study of the subject reveals that there exist, in certain countries, interesting though relatively minor deviations from the above rule which have led several authors such as Alexandrakis,[2] Berlia,[3] and Blamont[4] to maintain that dissolution is completed only with the election of the new Parliament. The most striking example is provided by article 29 of the Austrian Constitution which provides that even in the event of dissolution the legislature carries on until the meeting of the new Parliament. Examples of lesser importance can be found in article 35 of the Greek Constitution of 1927, inspired by article 35 of the Weimar Constitution (1919); this provided that a special parliamentary committee for foreign affairs should carry on after dissolution and until the meeting of the new House. Finally, in the United Kingdom dissolution does not hinder the work of the special committee dealing with private bills affecting Scotland.[5] However, the above examples – and one could mention many more – are not sufficient to justify the view that dissolution does not put an end to the life of Parliament. Furthermore, these cases should not be confused with the possibility of reviving a dissolved Parliament which, though rare, is more interesting.

Thus, the problem posed is whether Parliament can meet after it has been dissolved. The answer, I believe, is in the affirmative on condition that the constitutional text specifically provides for this. The opposite has also been maintained for cases of extreme necessity and emergency. But can expediency produce such important results? As has been observed, dissolution marks the death of Parliament; and no living creature ever vanquished death. No political expediency can adequately justify an exception to a constitutional rule of such grave importance. If such an expediency exists it is the duty of the constituent legislator to

[1] Matter, *Dissolution*, pp. 32ff.; Anschütz, *Verfassung des Deutschen Reichs*, p. 196; Laband, *Staatsrecht*, I, 558; Alexandrakis, *Dissolution*, p. 23.

[2] *Dissolution*, pp. 21ff.

[3] 'La dissolution et le régime des pouvoirs publics', *Revue de droit publique et science politique* (1956), pp. 130–41.

[4] 'La dissolution de l'Assemblée Nationale de décembre 1955', *Rev. dr. publ. sc. polit.* (1956), pp. 119–24. Contra to the above, Velu, *Dissolution*, pp. 201ff.

[5] May, *Parliamentary practice*, p. 1058, n. (*q*).

incorporate it in the constitution and not leave its interpreters to decide upon such a delicate matter. A precedent supporting this view can be found in Belgium in 1870. A week after dissolution was announced the Franco-Prussian war broke out (15 July). The King summoned a Crown Council to decide whether, in view of the grave circumstances, Parliament should be revived. The council finally agreed that the elections should take place as originally decided and Parliament was not reconvened.

Several constitutions, however, contain provisions regulating a possible revival of Parliament. These provisions usually fall under two categories, the first of which deals with the event of the death of the King whereas the second refers to martial law. Thus, article 79 of the Belgian Constitution and articles 50 and 51 of the Greek Constitution of 1952 provide for a revival of the dissolved House in the event of the death of the King. In practice this never occurred in Belgium and it occurred only once – in 1920 – in Greece. Under the second category one could place article 77 of the Italian Constitution of 1948 and article 91 of the Greek Constitution of 1952. Both provide that the government can adopt exceptional measures to meet a state of emergency. If, however, this is done the government is obliged to re-convene Parliament even if dissolved – and obtain its approval for the measures.[1] Lastly one could mention the illegal revival of the 1915 Parliament in Greece which was accomplished under pressure from the French and British Governments in 1917.[2]

The second effect of dissolution is to deprive members of Parliament of their title and parliamentary privileges and rights. As J. Barthélemy notes, 'la dissolution équivaut à la révocation en masse de tous les membres de l'assemblée'.[3] A vigorous campaign lies ahead and for many what will remain is a memory of the past and the title of former members of Parliament.

With the title, other more substantial assets are lost. The salary, the special privileges and members' inviolability. They can no longer claim parliamentary immunity from arrest or imprisonment, but they can be held politically responsible only for the actions they took and the statements they made in their official capacity.

In addition to the above, dissolution terminates all legislation pending in Parliament. This is justifiable both logically and politically. Logically, because the new Parliament cannot inherit and cannot he held responsible for the activities of its predecessor to which it has not contributed at all.

---

[1] See also art. 83 of the Greek Constitution of 1927 providing for a revival of the dissolved Parliament if war were to be declared. Article 16 of the 1958 French Constitution is discussed more fully in chapter 3.   [2] Below, chapter 10.   [3] *Droit constitutionnel*, p. 685.

Politically, because it is believed that the unfinished work of the previous House may run counter to the national feeling expressed in the new Parliament. It is only fair that the new House be given the opportunity to decide on what subject it will legislate.

Yet, the above is a generalisation that varies from country to country. The extent to which the new Parliament is committed as regards the work of the previous one depends on the stage this work has reached at the time of dissolution. What happens to legislation which has been completed by Parliament but which still has to receive the royal assent? The answer may differ from country to country. Thus it may be that the Sovereign can give his assent after dissolution or – most probably – that he cannot. Provided that the new Government agrees with the legislation, it is perhaps theoretically advisable to accept the first view, since the Sovereign nowadays has usually no right to refuse his assent; it would thus be a waste of time to delay legislation for no apparent reason.

A different solution is appropriate if a two-House system exists and the Upper House has not finished with a bill at the moment dissolution occurs. The reason is that unlike the Monarch's role in the previous case, the role of the Upper House is not independent. On the contrary it has to be conducted in relation to and in co-operation with the Lower House. They conduct discussions on bills at different times yet the one presupposes the other's existence, as can be realised by the fact that a bill can always be sent back to the Lower House for further amendments. Occasionally – according to certain constitutions – it is possible that a joint session is required by the two Houses for a bill to be enacted, which of course requires the simultaneous existence of both Houses. Thus, if not otherwise stipulated by the constitution, a bill that has not been passed by both Houses before dissolution occurs must start again from the beginning.

It was noted above that dissolution can also be exercised against a Revisional Parliament. What in that case is the fate of the revised articles? One must, I believe, distinguish between the fate of the revision as such and the revisional work already completed.

The revision is not affected, since the next Parliament usually also has a revisional nature. On the other hand as regards the revisional work done by the previous Parliament, the new one is not bound by it unless the whole revision is completed. The reason is that the revised constitution comes into effect from the moment it is promulgated as a whole and not after each article is independently revised. If, however, the whole revision is completed, but the King's assent has not been obtained when dissolution occurs, all that has been previously maintained could be applied *mutatis mutandis*. Nevertheless it must always be borne in mind that the above solutions may vary according to the different constitutions and to the position of the Head of State within this framework.

Whenever dissolution of the Lower House does not necessarily imply a dissolution of the Upper House as well, it results in its temporary adjournment. Whether this is obligatory or not depends on the constitution of the country concerned. But if this does happen then all pending legislation in the Upper House must be re-introduced. In its new session the Upper House cannot continue the work it left unfinished in its previous session.

Certain constitutions provide that the Upper House may sit as a judicial body to judge cases of ministerial responsibility. In this capacity the Upper House may continue its work and is not interrupted by a dissolution of the Lower House.[1]

But dissolution also has political results that can only be discussed very briefly here.

If the government that conducted elections is a caretaker government, then it must hand over its office to the party with an absolute majority. If no party has obtained an absolute majority – whether it is workable or not is immaterial – it must usually wait until the election of the Speaker. The party that elects the Speaker is assumed to possess a majority of votes in the House.

If, on the other hand, it is a political government, it may remain in office only if it has won the elections. If it is defeated the best course seems to be to resign without waiting to appear in Parliament.[2]

The Head of State may constitutionally refuse dissolution to a Prime Minister who has been defeated at a general election and then requests another immediate dissolution; but the Crown's refusal will usually depend on the possibility of an alternative government.

Dissolution gives the electorate the opportunity to decide on issues of

---

[1] Matter, *Dissolution*, p. 40.

[2] Disraeli was the first to do this in 1867 and it became the usual, though not entirely invariable practice. Thus, see Lord Salisbury's resignation on 11 August 1892. R. Jenkins, *Asquith* (1967), p. 62; Sir Robert Ensor, *England 1870–1914* (1966), p. 208. The same thing occurred in 1923. Mr Baldwin wanted to resign immediately after the elections and thus avoid a defeat in the House. The King, however, persuaded him not to take this step asserting that: 'The Sovereign ... ought not to accept the verdict of the polls, except as expressed by the representatives of the electorate across the floor of the House of Commons.' Sir H. Nicholson, *King George V* (Pan Piper edn, 1967), pp. 494ff. In the Cabinet Papers (P.R.O. CAB 23/46, 58 (23) of 11 Dec. 1923) one finds the following interesting piece of information: 'The P.M. mentioned to his colleagues that he had met Mr. Asquith at his club, and had told him confidentially of the decision taken by the Cabinet that morning' (i.e. not to resign before encountering defeat in the House). 'Mr. Asquith replied that, so far as he was concerned, it was a perfectly correct decision.' In 1929, both the King and Mr Baldwin took the opposite and what seems to me to be the correct constitutional view. Nicholson, ibid. pp. 559ff.

conflict. It is argued that often mere numbers (votes) can decide difficult theoretical questions in a fairly adequate manner. This, of course, presupposes that the results of the election are not the consequence of force and fraud. A fraudulent result usually brings a chain of unpleasant events and finally political chaos. It may also question the motives for the dissolution. These, however, are problems of political science rather than of law, and hence cannot be examined here.

Chapter 2

DISSOLUTION AND THE VARIOUS FORMS OF GOVERNMENT

A: DISSOLUTION AND THE DOCTRINE OF SEPARATION OF POWERS

Perhaps the most interesting feature of the institution of dissolution is the fact that it represents an intervention of the Executive in the field of the Legislative. It is thus fundamentally linked with the evolution of the principle of separation of state functions.

The doctrine of separation of powers is most elusive; often it is also difficult to give it a precise meaning. It can mean separation of organs or functions or both; it can refer to the lack of accountability of one branch of government (in the broadest sense) to another or conversely it can refer to the existence of some system of mutual checks and balances. Assuming, as we shall in this chapter, that a separation of organs and functions exists, the question that follows is whether there should be grounds for mutual influence and control.

The possibility of mutual check has been argued to be both compatible and incompatible with the doctrine of separation of powers. In the sphere of Executive–Judiciary and Legislative–Judiciary relationships the different attitudes can be found in the controversy over the need for judicial invalidation of legislative or administrative action. The one extreme can be found in the U.S.A., where in the celebrated case of *Marbury* v. *Madison* Chief Justice Marshall elaborated the arguments of the first school of thought. 'The Constitution', he said, 'is either a superior paramount law, unchangeable by ordinary means, or it is on a level with ordinary legislative acts ... if the former part of the alternative be true, then a legislative act contrary to the Constitution is not law: if the latter part be true, then written Constitutions are absurd attempts ... to limit a power in its own nature illimitable.'[1] This reasoning inevitably leads to the conclusion that the Courts must control the constitutionality of ordinary legislation. In the words of the famous Chief Justice, 'If, then, the Courts are to regard the Constitution, and the Constitution is superior to any ordinary act of the legislative, the Constitution, and not

[1] *Marbury* v. *Madison* (1803), 1 Cranch, 175.

such ordinary act, must govern the case to which they both apply.'[1] In this sense, judicial review is a guarantee and not an affront to the doctrine of separation of powers.[2] In France, on the other hand, judicial review of the legislative or even administrative action seems an 'obvious encroachment upon the principle of separation of powers'.[3]

Dissolution is connected with a different interrelationship, namely that which exists between Executive and Legislative, and luckily in this field both English and French parliamentarism (and their various offshoots) recognise the need of interaction and mutual influence. The differences, wherever they exist, refer to the degree of mutual control and not the principle itself which is broadly acknowledged by all types of parliamentarism.

Having established the particular aspect of separation of powers which we propose to deal with, we must now point out that the question of the proper interrelationship of state functions has occupied political scientists from the days of Aristotle to our times as its solution has been linked with the preservation of a set of values such as liberty, justice, equality, law and order and sanctity of property, which ancient and western thinkers alike have carefully developed through the ages. Consequently, the brief sketch that follows is only meant to show how dissolution came to play the important role classical parliamentarism ascribed to it.

Aristotle's famous triple distinction and classification of the various functions of the State[4] is, undoubtedly, the first scientific approach of the ancient world.[5] Unfortunately, however, it was only partly elaborated by subsequent political theorists. The emphasis was laid on the separation

---

[1] Ibid.

[2] Even in England, where judicial review is unknown in the typically American sense, the administration is controlled by the ordinary Courts of the land. The French administrative Courts, on the other hand, are not constitutionally part of the Judiciary.

[3] H. Kelsen, *General theory of Law and State* (Engl. trans., 1961), p. 269. For an interesting new criticism of the doctrine of separation of powers, see G. Marshall, *Constitutional theory* (1971), pp. 97–124.

[4] *Politics*, 1297b (ed. Loeb), pp. 37ff.

[5] His terminology of course must always be regarded in reference to the political framework of the ancient city state (πόλις–κράτος) and in connection with the particular philosophical and political attitude of the ancient world. For example, legislating (νομοθετεῖν) was a rare rather than an everyday procedure as it is with modern Parliaments. Once a set of laws was put into force, their amendment was undertaken infrequently and with great caution, due in particular to the deep respect Ancient Greek legislators such as Lycourgos, Drakon or Solon enjoyed. Hence Aristotle's 'law giving' body does not always correspond exactly to the concept of modern Parliament. But these differences should not result in underestimating the importance of the contribution of the ancient world to political science. The sovereignty of law, the theory of mixed government and the doctrine of a mild separation of powers are few but characteristic cases. See, for example, K. v. Fritz, *The theory of mixed constitution in antiquity* (1954); Sir P. Vinogradoff, *Outlines of historical jurisprudence* (1922).

rather than the interaction of functions. Yet, Aristotle had hinted[1] that the interaction of functions was necessary and had maintained that it is 'expedient [for each function] to be in a state of suspense and not to be able to do everything exactly as seems good to one, for liberty to do whatever one likes cannot guard against the evil that is in every man's nature'.

The Aristotelian theories were partly adopted by the Romans[2] and the later mediaeval philosophers such as Marsilius Patavinus,[3] though the latter's work is still cast in a somewhat mediaeval mould. By the sixteenth and seventeenth centuries, however, political thinkers such as Machiavelli,[4] Bodin,[5] Puffendorf[6] and Grotius[7] have a more crystallised view of the separation of functions though once again the emphasis is on the separation rather than the fusion of powers. But the greatest impetus to further development was given by the English Civil War which provided a favourable background for the evolution of what was now developing into a doctrine of separation of powers. The dissatisfaction with a predominant King or a predominant Parliament resulted only temporarily in a complete separation of function and persons adopted by the Instrument of Government in 1653. But this, too, soon proved unworkable in its extreme form and was abandoned before the formal end of the Protectorate. A compromise solution had to be found.

By the time John Locke wrote his two famous treatises on government, the doctrine of separation of powers and the ancient theory of mixed government were fairly widely accepted by English political thinkers. Hence, certain authors[8] argue that Locke's great contribution lies primarily in incorporating the doctrine in his work and thus placing the great weight of his own influence behind it.

It is important, however, to note that though Locke's work emphasises the essential elements of the doctrine of separation of powers, it never takes them to extremes. Locke's main problem seems to have been the reconciliation of the doctrine of separation of powers with the principle of

[1] Ibid. 1318*b*, pp. 39ff.
[2] Cicero, *De Republica* (ed. Lipsiae, 1823), 1.31: 'Sunt enim expertes imperii, consilii publici, judicii delectorum iudicium.'
[3] *Defensor Pacis* (Fröben, Basle, 1522), prima dictio, cap. xii, and English trans. A. Gewirth (1951), ii, 45.
[4] *Discorsi sopra la prima deca di Tito Livio*, i, 2.14, and English trans. by L. Walker, *The discourses of N. Machiavelli* (1950), i, 214.
[5] *Les six livres de la République* (ed. Jacques du Puys, Paris, 1583), liv. i, ch. x, mentioning six functions.
[6] *De officio hominis et civis juxta legem naturalem* (Cantabrigiae, 1682), lib. ii., cap. vii, distinguishing seven 'partes potentiales summi imperii'.
[7] *De iure belli ac pacis* (Amsterdam edn, 1653), lib. i, cap. 3, para. 6.
[8] Vile, *Constitutionalism*, p. 58. The reader is also referred to von Fritz's *The theory of mixed constitution*, which presents a scholarly analysis of the problem in the ancient world.

legislative supremacy. He seems to have solved it – to some extent at least – by two means. First, the supremacy of the Legislature must be interpreted as the supremacy of law to which of course the Executive branch is also subject. Thus, in this sense, the Executive ultimately depends on the Legislative, since 'What can give laws to another, must needs be superior to him.'[1] But this does not mean that the Executive is 'completely subordinated to the Legislative *in the exercise of its own functions*'.[2] Second, according to Locke, the role of the Executive in relation to the Legislative is a negative one, in the sense that it can only veto legislation. Hence, Locke's theories embodied a basic division of functions leading towards the pure doctrine of separation of functions, though never actually achieving it. Nevertheless, this opened the road to a more positive relationship between the Executive and the Legislative which was eventually further expounded by Montesquieu.

The work of Montesquieu is the next important step. His theories, though occasionally contradictory and at times an amalgam of previous ideas, nevertheless hold a predominant position in the history of political theory, owing to their direct influence on the American and French Revolutions. Even though it has been said[3] that Montesquieu's 'influence . . . cannot be ascribed to his originality . . . but rather to the manner and timing of the doctrine's development in his hands', his contribution must not be underestimated. His elaboration of Locke's thesis – though it misinterprets contemporary English government – is nevertheless a lucid and ingenious analysis. Montesquieu, like Aristotle, firmly believed that he who possesses power tends to abuse it, and the only way to prevent this is for one function to check the other. 'La Démocratie et l'Aristocratie', he wrote, in the eleventh chapter of the famous *Esprit des Lois*,[4] 'ne sont point des états libres par leur nature. La liberté politique ne se trouve que dans les gouvernements modérés . . . il faut que par la disposition des choses le pouvoir arrête le pouvoir.' Despite his aphorism that 'tout serait perdu si le même corps des principaux ou des nobles ou du peuple exerçait les trois pouvoirs: celui de faire les lois, celui d'éxécuter les résolutions publiques, et celui de juger les crimes ou les differends de particuliers',[5] Montesquieu was never an advocate of the pure doctrine of separation of powers; quite the opposite. In contrast to Locke's 'negative' system of checks and balances, he was the first, in modern times, to advocate positive checks of bilateral control between Executive and Legislative. Montesquieu particularly stressed what he called the 'faculté d'empêcher'

---

[1] *The second treatise of government* (ed. Laslett), ch. XIII, para. 150.
[2] Vile, *Constitutionalism*, p. 63.   [3] Vile, ibid. p. 76.
[4] *L'Esprit des Lois* (ed. Flammarion), liv. XI, ch. IV.   [5] Ibid. liv. XI, ch. VI.

which he defined as 'le droit de rendre nulle une résolution prise par quelque autre'.[1] But his views went even further as he laid down the theoretical basis of dissolution as the means of checking the powers of Parliament. 'Si la puissance exécutrice n'a pas le droit d'arrêter les entreprises du corps législatif, celui-ci sera despotique, car comme il pourra se donner tout le pouvoir qu'il peut imaginer, il anéantira toutes les autres puissances.' So, Montesquieu continues, 'il faut ... que se soit la puissance exécutrice qui règle le temps de la tenue et de la durée de ces assemblées, par rapport aux circonstances qu'elle connaît.' But, on the other hand, 'la puissance législative ... a le droit, et doit avoir la faculté d'examiner de quelle manière les lois qu'elle a faites ont été exécutées.' So he concludes: 'Voici donc la constitution fondamentale du gouvernement dont nous parlons. Le corps législatif y étant composé de deux parties, l'une enchaînera l'autre par sa faculté mutuelle d'empêcher. Toutes les deux seront liées par la puissance exécutrice qui le sera elle-même par la législative.'[2]

B: THE DEVELOPMENT OF THE PARLIAMENTARY FORM OF GOVERNMENT

Despite the above, however, Montesquieu was misunderstood both by the American and French revolutionaries[3] who transformed the principle of separation of powers into a rigid dogma. In a way, of course, the times favoured such a misunderstanding, since it was believed – to a certain extent quite rightly – that such separation was the only effective means of controlling the royal powers. But the French, like the English a century before, very soon found out that a rigid separation of state functions was unworkable and nowadays it is undoubtedly unacceptable.[4] A complete separation of functions comes into direct conflict with the element of unity that characterises the theory of the modern state. This element is disrupted if three different and independent powers exist instead of one, which at times may be exercised by different organs. It is also *de lege lata* wrong to refer to three distinct functions, since most contemporary constitutions expressly provide that all power flows from the people. Separation of functions thus cannot, in the present circumstances, be considered a dogma of political science but merely a principle of con-

---

[1] Ibid. liv. xi, ch. vi.   [2] Ibid.
[3] See, for example, art. 16 of *La déclaration des droits de l'homme et du citoyen* of 26 August 1789.
[4] For a summary of modern views see M. Duverger, *Institutions politiques et droit constitutionnel* (1968), pp. 176–81.

stitutional art (*Ein Verfassungs technisches Prinzip*) that directs rather than rigidly binds the constituent legislator.

But to return to Montesquieu, his idea of checks and balances contains two elements: a mild separation of functions as well as the possibility of interaction amongst state organs. In other words, though Montesquieu was against the Legislative and the Executive each exercising the whole power of the other, he did not oppose the idea of mutual influence and control. In this set-up dissolution clearly had an important part to play.

This notion of co-operation and interaction of functions was adopted and further developed by parliamentarism. Naturally in the beginning – in England early in the eighteenth century and in France from 1814 to 1830 – the Crown remained in the very centre and exercised considerable powers (including the right to dissolve Parliament) despite important constitutional laws that provided some control. But one of the results of the Industrial Revolution, first in England and later in France and other European countries, was to strengthen the middle classes and indirectly to increase the powers of the elective House.

After Parliament had asserted its exclusive right to legislate, it gradually increased its powers of control and criticism and in the end the Executive could not govern without the support of Parliament. As long as the Sovereign was still the Government, to hold him responsible for any possible mistake was incompatible with the doctrine of royal immunity. So the Cabinet, which gradually emerged in the eighteenth century, became responsible for the acts of the King. Executive dualism thus became a political reality. Theoretically it combined the advantages of permanency (in the person of the King) and responsibility (in the body of the Cabinet). In practice it reflected the new political situation, namely, that the Government had become dependent on and accountable to Parliament.

But the bourgeoisie – which by now was forming its own ideology of economic and political liberalism – though strong, was not strong enough to dominate completely the political scene through Parliament. So during the first half of the nineteenth century, in theory as well as in practice, the ideal form of government could be found in a balanced constitution – a notion which bore an interesting resemblance to the ancient Greek theory of mixed government.[1] With the veto to all

[1] Plato in his *Laws*, III, 683ff., 691dff., VI, 756e, 757a, was the first to treat this subject systematically. He was followed by Aristotle, *Politics*, 1266a, 4ff., 1294b, 14ff. and 34ff., 1294a, 30ff. See also *Diogenes Laertius* (ed. Loeb), VII, 1, 131; Stobaeus, *Florilegium* (ed. Lipsiae, 1838), MΓ, 92.134. Polybius, *Fragmenta*, Libri VI(ed. Lipsiae, 1866). On the theory of mixed constitution in Antiquity see Fritz, *The theory of mixed constitution*, pp. 76ff., 155ff. 184ff. On the evolution of the theory in England see Vile, *Constitutionalism*, pp. 98ff.

intents and purposes obsolete, the only effective check against Parliament was dissolution.

Hence at a certain stage of its development parliamentarism idealised the notion of complete equilibrium between the Executive (Crown and Government) and the Legislative.[1] Further, the relationship between the two Houses as well as that of Crown and Government also relied on this idea of balance. Thus, on the one hand the Government was responsible to Parliament but the Crown played a major part in its appointment; on the other hand, Parliament always ran the risk of being dissolved if it defeated the Government. In this set-up the theoretical justification for dissolution – perhaps the only one the institution ever had – was obviously to maintain the equilibrium of functions and powers.[2]

But parliamentarism was essentially an oligarchic form of government that had emerged from the socio-economic conditions that prevailed at a certain stage of the development of most European states. Further, in most cases it achieved its classical form before the introduction of universal suffrage.[3] For a long time, however, the constitutional texts did not reflect this change even though it represented, from a purely sociological point of view, a dramatic development by bringing into the political arena new vital forces – workers and farmers. Modern political parties also owe their existence to universal suffrage. Towards the end of the century the socialist parties had emerged in many European countries (for example the Italian Socialist Party in 1892, the British Labour Party in 1899, etc.) and their political as well as financial existence increasingly relied on massive recruitment. Faced with such competition and with the new political realities many old bourgeois parties – notably

---

[1] From the vast bibliography on the subject, R. Redslob's *Die Parlamentarische Regierung in ihrer wahren und in ihrer unechten Form* (1918), is still considered a classic. See also Duverger, *Institutions*; P. Lalumière & A. Demichel, *Les régimes parlementaires européenns* (1966); W. Hasbach, *Die Parlamentarische Kabinettsregierung* (1919); G. Burdeau, *Le régime parlementaire dans les constitutions d'après-guerre* (1932); Burdeau, *Droit constitutionnel et institutions politiques* (1969); Melot, *L'évolution du régime parlementaire* (1936); H. Laski, *Parliamentary government in England* (1968); H. van Impe, *Le régime parlementaire en Belgique* (1968); R. Fusilier, *Les monarchies parlementaires* (1960); B. Waleffé, *Le roi nomme et révoque ses ministres* (1971); N. N. Saripolos, *The system of parliamentary government* (1921) (in Greek); A. Svolos, *Problems of parliamentary democracy* (1931) (in Greek). Further bibliography is provided at the relevant points.

[2] Duguit, *Droit constitutionnel*, IV, 581; M. Hauriou, *Précis de droit constitutionnel*, 2nd edn (1929), p. 459; Esmein, *Droit constitutionnel*, pp. 175ff.; Radenac, *Dissolution*, p. 3; E. Taron, *Du droit de dissolution des assemblées parlementaires spécialement en Belgique* (1911), pp. 7ff.; Constant, *Cours de politique constitutionnel*, I, 31.

[3] According to Duguit, ibid., II, 817, parliamentarism in its classical form operated in France only between the years 1830 and 1848. Professor Crick, *The reform of Parliament* (1968), p. 20, maintains that this applies to the United Kingdom for the years 1832–67. In Belgium the years are 1846–1916 and in Greece 1875–1911.

the British Conservative Party – met this challenge and re-organised themselves along similar lines. The old loose connection between members of Parliament with a common ideology was replaced by strict party disciplines and organisation. Wherever this happened – and the United Kingdom offers a unique example – the change favoured the Government. Professor Mackintosh, for example, maintains[1] that already by the beginning of this century 'the Cabinet dominated British Government. The House of Commons still exercised a strong influence, but it did so more as an indicator of public opinion than as an authority that might dethrone the Cabinet or reverse its policies,' and the two World Wars strengthened this trend. Nearly a century earlier Chateaubriand had prophetically written:[2] 'Les Ministres sont ... maîtres des chambres par le fond, et leurs serviteurs par la forme.' The effect this change had on the exercise of dissolution is discussed later[3] and need not occupy us at this stage.

But not all countries had the same development. In many, parties never approached, even remotely, the above-mentioned degree of organisation and coherence and basically the political battles were still fought around and influenced by personalities. Strong local M.P.s were elected on the basis of their own popularity rather than because of the support of their party, and in France they retained this independence to a great extent until the period of General de Gaulle, when the 'personnalisation croissante du leader national' resulted in the 'dépersonnalisation du candidat local'.[4] In these countries – and one could mention as examples France under the Third and Fourth Republics and Austria under the Constitution of 1 October 1920 – the influence of Parliament became predominant. With the Head of State reduced to the role of figurehead (and not even enjoying the advantages of permanency) and with excessive use of ministerial responsibility it soon became clear that the real source of authority was the elective House.

But many authors and politicians, particularly during the period of the Third French Republic, expressed their frustration at the shrinking power and influence of the President and the Government. President Millerand, who had experienced the difficulties of dealing with Parliament in 1924, had eloquently expressed the belief, shared by many, that dissolution alone could restore the balance of powers.

Pour que soit pleinement assuré l'équilibre de pouvoir qui est nécessaire dans l'intérêt

---

[1] *The British Cabinet* (1968), p. 174.
[2] *De la Monarchie selon la Charte*, p. 19. R. Muir, in his introduction to *How Britain is governed* (1940), vigorously attacks the notion of the Cabinet as a committee of Parliament.
[3] Part II.   [4] M. Mabileau, *La personnalisation du pouvoir et ses problèmes* (1964), p. 18.

de la liberté de la Nation, de la souveraineté du peuple, il faut qu'en face du pouvoir dont dispose le législatif, l'exécutif ait aussi une arme, et l'on n'en voit pas d'autre que l'appel au peuple souverain, que le droit de dissolution.[1]

But the general climate was unfavourable and dissolution was never used. Thus, in this form of impure parliamentarism the balance was heavily shifted in favour of Parliament.

Impure or unbalanced parliamentarism developed yet another variant and in this case the scales were tipped in favour of the Head of State. This preponderance of the Head of State is counterbalanced by the fact that he is held responsible for his acts. This, however, presupposes that the Head of State is elected and holds office for a limited period of time. Parliamentary government, with a preponderance of a hereditary Head of State (King) is an historical anachronism, not least because the King would be allowed a personal policy for which he would not be held responsible. Examples of this type of impure parliamentarism can be found in the Weimar Republic and the Fifth French Republic.

Dissolution in the Weimar Republic would make in itself an interesting subject of research.[2] In this chapter, however, one must be content with a few general remarks.

The Constitution of Weimar (1919) was by no means unambiguous on the question of dissolution of the Reichstag. Hence, one might possibly object to classifying Weimar in this category. The manner in which dissolution was actually exercised during the years of the Republic is the basic reason for its inclusion here. More specifically, dissolution was transformed, particularly during the last phase of the Republic, into practically a presidential prerogative, which furthermore was clearly abused. The last five dissolutions (1930, 1932, 1932, 1933 and 1933) out of a grand total of eight, surely prove the point.

Article 25 of the Weimar Constitution stipulated that the President of the Reich can dissolve the Reichstag but the Presidential Decree should be countersigned by the Chancellor or the competent Minister.

The preparatory debates reveal that three different opinions were held on the matter.[3] The extreme right believed that dissolution ought to be a presidential prerogative and that dissolution need not be countersigned

---

[1] Quoted by Duguit, *Droit constitutionnel*, IV, 584.
[2] Above all one should mention: Anschütz, *Die Verfassung des Deutschen Reichs*, art. 25, pp. 195ff.; E. Vermeil, *La Constitution de Weimar et le principe de la démocratie allemande* (1923); H. Oppenheimer, *The Constitution of the Weimar Republic* (1923); H. Pohl, *Die Auflösung des Reichstags* (1921); H. Esche, *Die Auflösung der Volksvertretung im Deutschen Reich und in seinen Ländern* (1930). E. Eyck's *A history of the Weimar Republic* (1962–3) provides interesting information on the historical background.
[3] Vermeil, *Constitution de Weimar*, pp. 153ff., provides a full account.

by a minister. The Social Democrats took the exact opposite view and maintained that the President should be allowed to dissolve only on the recommendation of the Cabinet – a system resembling that of the Fourth French Republic. Finally, the moderate elements took the middle path, maintaining that a ministerial signature was necessary but that of a ministry ad hoc would also do.

It was the second view, held by Professor Hugo Preuss, the eminent author of the Constitution, that finally prevailed – in theory at least. In practice, however, the President's right to appoint a Chancellor ad hoc was maintained. There was little doubt that the Constitution favoured a strong Executive and in fact was the first to grant exceptional powers to the President in the event of an emergency.

The rise of the Third Reich cannot be discussed here. Nevertheless, it is undisputed that from the moment Brüning was appointed Chancellor (March 1930) five dissolutions took place, all of which reflected President Hindenburg's personal policies. Under these circumstances dissolution totally failed to produce any results. Similarly, the limitations imposed by the Constitution proved unable to prevent abuse. Parliament found itself more divided after every dissolution and with the Communist vote continuously increasing.[1] The electoral law and the existence of fundamentally anti-democratic parties in a highly divided country finally gave Adolf Hitler the opportunity which he did not hesitate to seize.

The Constitution of the Fifth French Republic is an even clearer and more obvious example of this category. Article 12 of the 1958 Constitution ascribed to the President in no uncertain terms the right to dissolve the Assemblée Nationale and article 19 stipulates that the Presidential Decree need not be countersigned by any Minister. Dissolution is thus one of the many and important prerogatives that belong to the President in person.

The 1958 Constitution can and should be regarded as a document embodying in many respects General de Gaulle's personal views and opinions expressed in a period of over twelve years and advocating the need for a strong Executive.[2]

A presidential dissolution thus fitted in with De Gaulle's concept of 'parliamentarism', characterised by 'Un Président de la République désigné par la raison et le sentiment des Français pour être le Chef de l'Etat et le guide de la France'.[3] To what extent, of course, the above are

[1] See K. Loewenstein, 'Réflexions sur la valeur des constitutions dans une époque révolutionnaire', in *Revue française de science politique* (1952), pp. 313–14.

[2] See his 'Discours de Bayeux' in *Rev. fr. de sc. pol.* (1959), pp. 188ff.

[3] *Le Monde*, 22 September 1962. Also 5 October.

compatible with the classical concept of parliamentarism is a widely debated matter.

But despite the President's and M. Debré's[1] efforts to convince the critics that the new constitution established parliamentarism, it remains a fact that the new system has nothing in common with the classical concept.[2] Perhaps the classical concept is obsolete. It had certainly failed to produce any results in France. But this does not alter the fact that the manner in which dissolution was regulated by the constitution had nothing or very little in common with parliamentarism proper.

But, to return to dissolution, the only limitation imposed on the President was that he had to obtain his Prime Minister's view before dissolving. But this did not bind him in any way.

C: POSSIBLE ALTERNATIVES TO PARLIAMENTARISM

Co-operation of state functions is not the only possible form of government and a few words should be added on the other possible alternatives. But it must be noted from the outset that dissolution, if it is recognised at all, plays a quite different part in these set-ups.

System of concentration of functions

In this system, all powers are vested in the hands of either (*i*) one man (e.g. absolute Monarch by Divine Right); (*ii*) a dictator, acting or pretending to act in the best interest of the people – this can also be achieved with a façade of popular approval, usually by means of a referendum (Caesarism, Napoleon III);[3] (*iii*) a privileged class, oligarchy (party) or aristocracy; (*iv*) the electorate which, in this case, possesses both legal and political sovereignty (Ancient Greece, Rome).

The system of parliamentary preponderance (*système conventionnel, gouvernement d'assemblée*) is usually included in this category, since it is characterised by a centralisation of all political activity in the National

---

[1] 'La nouvelle constitution', in *Rev. fr. de sc. pol.* (1958), pp. 7ff.
[2] The Constitution was in this respect seriously criticised by G. Burdeau, 'La conception du pouvoir selon la constitution française du 4 Octobre 1958', *Rev. fr. de sc. pol.* (1959), pp. 87ff.; M. Duverger, 'Les institutions de la Cinquième République', *Rev. fr. de sc. pol.* (1959), pp. 101ff.; G. Berlia, 'Chronique constitutionnelle française', *Rev. fr. de sc. pol.* (1959), pp. 71ff. Also G. Berlia, 'Le Président de la République dans la Constitution de 1958', *Rev. fr. de sc. pol.* (1959), pp. 71ff.; A. de Laubadère, 'La Constitution française de 1958', in *Zeitschrift für ausländisches öffentliches Recht und Völkerrecht*, vol. 20 (August 1960), 520.
[3] Constitution of 14 January 1852, in Duverger, *Constitutions*, p. 104.

Assembly.[1] The Assembly legislates and also supervises the execution of the laws by means of an executive committee (the Cabinet) which can be relieved of its functions whenever the Assembly deems it necessary. In this form of government dissolution originates only from the Assembly (self-dissolution), either because it may consider that its work has come to an end, or because it may decide that it is in disagreement with public feeling. Yet this system of government rarely exists in its pure form. Theoretically, of course, the government can always be dismissed by the Assembly. In actual practice nevertheless this does not often happen. Furthermore the judicial function always commands an independent position. Hence, it is preferable to include this form of government in the third category (preponderance of one function).

This concentration or 'fusion' of powers in the hands of one man or one assembly can occur in either an absolute or a relative form. In the first case only one governmental organ exists, vested with all three functions. All the other state organs are purely administrative. In the second case a number of State organs exist and co-operate closely with each other, one being responsible to the other. In actual fact, however, one of them possesses all effective power, whereas the others are established to preserve appearances. The Italian Parliament and the German Reichstag under the pre-war Fascist and National Socialist forms of government respectively are excellent examples.

System of complete separation of powers

In this system – democratic by nature – the different functions are vested in separate and independent organs. It is of course obvious that a system such as this ignores the principle of ministerial responsibility and naturally of dissolution. The government of the United States of America amply illustrates the case. Introduced in the United States because of empirical and historical reasons, this form of government places all three functions of the State at the same level. The President, chief of the Executive, governs with secretaries, responsible only to him. Congress is vested with the legislative function while the Judiciary is left to the Supreme Federal Court of the U.S.A.[2] Yet, a degree of co-operation does in fact exist, the Presidential veto, the Senate's executive functions (ratifying treaties, etc.) and the Judicial control of the Supreme Court being the most notable examples.

[1] See art. 71 of the Constitution of Switzerland of 29 May 1874.
[2] Articles 1, 2 and 3.

System of complete preponderance of the executive function

This system, giving the leading role to the Head of the Executive function, also entrusts him with the right to dissolve Parliament.

Constitutional Monarchy (*monarchie limitée ou constitutionnelle*) is usually included in this category. Though the rules of parliamentary government do not apply in this case, democratic appearances are duly preserved.

Constitutional Monarchy is in theory based on a system of separation of the various State functions, since it was devised to limit the powers of the Monarch. The lack of reciprocal action between the executive and the legislative functions was devised in order to protect Parliament from royal interventions. In most European countries, limited Monarchy by means of a constitution was the intermediate phase between absolute Monarchy of the seventeenth and eighteenth centuries and parliamentary government as established approximately by the middle of the nineteenth century. Yet in certain countries – Germany more notably – this intermediate phase was prolonged until the First World War.[1]

In reality, nevertheless, all powers lay in the hands of the King. He appointed and dismissed his Ministers, who usually countersigned his acts but were not responsible to Parliament. The Ministers collaborated with Parliament in the making of laws and could also initiate legislation. The assembly was elected by universal or restricted franchise – usually secret – for a certain number of years. It is obvious that the right to dissolve this assembly lay within the powers of the King and was used to obtain an obedient and docile House. One such example can be found in the Othonian Constitution described in chapter 8. Another can be found in Germany between 1871 and 1919.

The Constitution of the German Federation (1871) gave the Emperor the right to adjourn the Reichstag and even dissolve it with the concurrent opinion of the Bundesrat.[2] Elections were to follow within sixty days, and the new Reichstag would be summoned within ninety days of dissolution. Since, however, Prussia controlled the necessary number of delegates in the Bundesrat, the King of Prussia could dissolve practically as and when he chose. In actual fact, most dissolutions that followed were caused directly or indirectly by the reluctance of Parliament to increase the expenditure on armaments in the Federal Budget. It is characteristic,

---

[1] Seydel, *Constitutionelle und Parlamentarische Regierung* (1893); J. Barthélemy, 'Les théories royalistes dans la doctrine allemande contemporaine', *Revue de droit public et de la science politique* (1905), pp. 717–58.

[2] Articles 24, 25 of the Constitution of 16 April 1871. For the analysis of the text consult the classic work of Paul Laband, *Deutsches Reichsstaatsrecht*, 7th edn (1919), pp. 81ff.

however, to note that Tirpitz's famous Naval Acts, damaging as they
proved to be to Germany's foreign relations, particularly with Great
Britain, were never rejected by the Reichstag, probably because of the
great popular support behind them. Thus, a German author correctly
described the Emperor's right to dissolve in the following words: 'The
right includes a declaration of the Crown that the House does not express
the national feeling and therefore the electorate is summoned to express
its disapproval of the behaviour of its representatives.'[1]

[1] Quoted by Ferrus, *Dissolution*, p. 8.

Chapter 3

DISSOLUTION: THE RIGHT TO APPEAL TO THE ELECTORATE

A: REASONS THAT LEAD TO DISSOLUTION

Sir William Anson maintains that the Prime Minister's advice for dissolution should, as a rule, be accepted. But he then proceeds to mention when such a request is constitutionally proper.[1] In his view the reason which *par excellence* justifies dissolution is that the electorate is at variance with Parliament, a fact usually indicated by by-elections, the adoption by the Government of a new controversial issue of policy etc. He considers that variance between Parliament and the electorate is so important that it can justify a forced dissolution, even if this will necessarily lead to a dismissal of the ministry in office.

Most authors, both in England and on the Continent, would nowadays agree that the Government's discretion to dissolve is extremely wide and not limited to the basic reason Sir William Anson suggests. Therefore, it is no longer necessary to list the proper reasons for a dissolution. Yet, it is still interesting to attempt a classification of the dissolutions of the past under various headings. Because different pretexts were used at times and, by following the changing pattern of reasons that cause dissolution, one can trace the changing purposes fulfilled by the institution.

When, then, is dissolution advised? The question has two aspects. The first is concerned with the reasons that lead to a dissolution; they will be discussed in this section (A). The second aspect deals with the limitations affecting the exercise of the right and will be examined in the next two sections (B and C).

It was the French constitutionalist Rossi who once declared that: 'dissoudre une chambre ce n'est pas satisfaire un caprice, c'est faire un appel au pays'. This also seems to have been the unanimous opinion of British statesmen during the nineteenth century. A few examples will suffice to prove the case.

In 1846 Sir Robert Peel declared in Parliament[2] that:

I do not think a dissolution justifiable for the purpose merely of strengthening a party.

[1] *Law and custom of the constitution*, I, 4th edn (1911), 306–7.
[2] *Parliamentary Debates*, 3rd series, LXXXVII, 1043.

The power of dissolution is a great instrument in the hands of the Crown; and it would have a tendency to blunt the instrument if it were employed without grave necessity.

In 1852 Lord John Russell endorsed Peel's doctrine and summarising the position of previous statesmen on the subject, stated:[1]

They have thought, when there was a great question depending, upon which no satisfactory conclusion could be obtained in this House – when the House and the Ministers of the Crown were decidedly at variance ... that the solution of any such question should be sought in an appeal to the electors of the United Kingdom. But it is quite another matter when the question is whether a particular Prime Minister or a particular party should remain in office.

In 1858 Lord Aberdeen maintained[2] that: 'A Minister would not advise Her Majesty to take such a step unless he thought it was for the good of the country'. In 1868 Gladstone maintained in Parliament that,

There are two conditions, as it appears to me, which are necessary in order to make an appeal to the country by a Government whose existence is menaced a legitimate appeal. The first of them is that there should be an adequate cause of public policy; and the second of them is that there should be a rational prospect of a reversal of the vote of the House of Commons ... I entirely question this title of Governments, as Governments, to put the country as a matter of course to the cost, the delay, and the trouble of a dissolution to determine the question of their own existence.[3]

Similar arguments were put forward by politicians and lawyers in other countries during the nineteenth century. The result was that resignation in the event of defeat was usually preferred to dissolution.[4] Gladstone's opinion that governments should not have recourse to dissolution in order 'to determine the question of their own existence'[5] was closely followed.

During the nineteenth century (since 1868) the United Kingdom, Belgium and Greece – to take three characteristic examples – offer only three clear examples[6] of a dissolution caused by what we would describe today as party politics. During these years a conflict between the Government and Parliament was one of the reasons that most frequently led to a

---

[1] *Parliamentary Debates*, 3rd series, CL, 1076.
[2] *Letters of Queen Victoria*, 1st series, III, 359, 363–5, 367.
[3] *Parliamentary Debates*, 3rd series, CXCI, 1712–13.
[4] During the nineteenth century (i.e. 1834–1900) the Government, in the United Kingdom alone, was faced fifteen times with the alternative of resignation or dissolution. In ten cases (1839, 1846, 1851, 1852, 1855, 1858, 1866, 1873, 1885 and 1895) it chose to resign. In the remaining five it dissolved Parliament (1841, 1857, 1859, 1868 and 1886).
[5] *Parliamentary Debates*, 3rd series, CXCI, 1713.
[6] United Kingdom: 1880; Greece: 1885 and 1890 (that is not counting the 1847 dissolution), below, chapters 8 and 9.

dissolution. In the three countries mentioned, out of a total of twenty-five dissolutions[1] eleven resulted from conflict between the Executive and the Legislative.[2]

In 1900, however, Gladstone's doctrine was flagrantly violated by an old colleague of his. Joseph Chamberlain's notorious 'khaki elections' made it abundantly clear that dissolution could be used as an effective political weapon against the Opposition. Mr Lloyd George's 1918 dissolution – highly criticised at that time – was another example of the new trend.

With the growth of political parties a defeat of the Government became less likely and dissolution was frequently used for party purposes. The trend became in the course of the twentieth century the new reality. Out of a total of sixty-two dissolutions in the United Kingdom, Greece and Belgium, thirty, nearly half, were caused by party politics.[3] It seems reasonable to assume that the prevailing party system has deprived the Peel–Russell–Aberdeen–Gladstone doctrine of most of its significance and prestige.

This of course does not mean that dissolution *ex definitione* is advised only for party reasons. For the last one hundred years or so various reasons for dissolution have been invoked. Some of them are more characteristic of nineteenth-century conditions, others were firmly established during the twentieth century. Dissolution in the United Kingdom, Belgium and Greece – and indeed in all other European countries – falls under one of the following headings.

(a) Automatic dissolution (dissolution de plein droit)

Strictly speaking this does not fall within the scope of the present work. Its essential feature is that it takes place automatically on the occurrence of a certain event and without the intervention of the Executive. The typical example is a decision to revise the constitution which automatically leads to elections for a Revisional Parliament.[4] No precedent exists in the United Kingdom but there are five precedents in Belgium (1892, 1919, 1954, 1958 and 1965) and one in Greece (1910).

---

[1] United Kingdom: 1868, 1874, 1880, 1885, 1886, 1892 and 1895; Belgium: 1870, 1884, 1892, 1894; Greece: 1868, 1869, 1872, 1872, 1874, 1875, 1879, 1881, 1885, 1886, 1890, 1892, 1895, 1898.

[2] United Kingdom: 1868, 1886, 1895; Greece: 1868, 1869, 1872, 1873, 1874, 1875, 1887, 1895.

[3] See Appendices 1.4, 1.5.

[4] Art. 131 of the Belgian Constitution 1831 and art. 107 of the 1864 Greek Constitution and 108 of the 1911 Constitution.

(b) Conflict between the two Houses

The 1911 Parliament Act amply illustrates this case. It is well known and need not be discussed here. In the rare circumstances that such a conflict becomes possible in our times it is expected that the Upper House will give way to the opinion of the representative House.

(c) End of life of Parliament approaching

Few parliaments cover their full life span. At the end of this period the House usually does not represent the electorate's opinion as it did at the beginning of the first session. Dissolution in this case is constitutionally welcome, particularly if important legislation is imminent.

In England, according to G. Burdeau:[1] 'le cas le plus fréquent est celui où elle est utilisée pour mettre fin au mandat de la Chambre des Communes lorsqu'approche son terme légal'. His opinion, however, does not seem to correspond to reality. Out of seven dissolutions between 1867 and 1900 only one, that of 1892, occurred solely for this reason, whereas the exact date of the 1880 dissolution was determined according to party politics. Similarly, between 1900 and 1970 out of eighteen dissolutions, six can be said to be influenced by this reason (1906, 1918, 1929, 1945, 1950, 1964), though other reasons were also taken into consideration in determining the exact date of the elections. Moreover, it seems that this reason was used more frequently in the twentieth century than it was in the nineteenth.

(d) Conflict between Government and Parliament

During the nineteenth century this was one of the most important and frequent causes of dissolution. The term is broad and includes a direct conflict between the Government and Parliament which results in a parliamentary defeat, as well as any form of ministerial instability. The latter is more frequent in countries (such as France, Belgium, Italy and Greece) where the multi-party system usually prevents the formation of strong governments. The typical example is, of course, France under the Third and Fourth Republics.

It is this conflict that dissolution is meant to solve by referring the dispute to the electorate. But as France once again shows, dissolution in itself cannot provide a solution and must be aided by the electoral law in order to produce the desired results. The growth of modern political parties has diminished the possibilities of such conflicts. But they may still

---

[1] *Traité de science politique* (1949–57), VII, no. 131, 340.

occur, particularly in multi-party countries where strong majorities are the exception rather than the rule.

(e) Conflict between the Head of State and his Government, supported by Parliament

In modern times this is restricted to presidential and parliamentary democracies like France under the 1958 Constitution; the typical example is the dissolution by President de Gaulle on 6 October 1962.[1] While this was also the rule with constitutional monarchies in the early nineteenth century, it is now highly unlikely that it could occur without seriously endangering the position of the Crown.

In the United Kingdom the last incident was in 1834, in Holland in 1853, in Belgium in 1857 and in Denmark in 1920. In the twentieth century Greece is the only European country that offers examples of open interventions by the Crown.[2]

(f) Parliament does not represent the electorate

Dissolution in this case would usually emanate from the Head of the Executive (President or King) on the advice, however, of the Prime Minister. This may happen either because of acquisition of new territories which must be represented in the House (as for example in Greece in 1882) or because of the extension of the suffrage as a result of an alteration of the electoral law. Belgium offers three precedents of this category (1848, 1894, 1900). Finally by-election results may create the impression that Parliament does not reflect public opinion. There are two precedents in Belgium (1870, 1884), two in Greece (1936, 1963) and two in the United Kingdom (1885, 1922). Contemporary practice in the United Kingdom indicates that it is unlikely that any Prime Minister will advise dissolution because of unfavourable by-election results. Favourable by-election results, however, may lead to a dissolution if the Prime Minister interprets them as a sign of an 'electoral swing' towards his Government.

(g) Party politics

As a reason leading to dissolution party politics were practically unknown in the nineteenth century. With the emergence of modern political parties, however, they became increasingly important and nowadays

---

[1] On 3 October 1962 a Presidential Decree was published calling for a referendum to revise the Constitution. It was based on article 11 of the Constitution thus by-passing the procedure laid out by article 89. Parliament was outraged and defeated the Pompidou Government. M. Pompidou had warned Parliament that a defeat would lead to a dissolution (*Débats de l'Assemblée Nationale*, 4 October 1962, 3254). Dissolution was pronounced two days later.

[2] For the two dissolutions of 1915 see below, chapter 10.

they are the most important single cause for dissolution. Since 1900 there have been sixty-two dissolutions in the United Kingdom, Greece and Belgium. Of these, thirty were caused by party politics.[1]

Party politics as a reason for dissolution is a wide term. Basically it encompasses two possibilities. In the first, dissolution is used as a weapon against the Opposition. The Government has the right to choose the appropriate moment to go to the country, thus gaining considerable advantage over its opponents. This is the typical case in the United Kingdom. In the second case, dissolution is once more caused by party politics. This time, however, it is the result of a split in a coalition which is unable to form a viable Government and is obliged to go to the country. The typical example of this category is Belgium which, since 1919, has been ruled, practically without exception, by coalition governments.

(h) *Major political issue at stake*

Any government is justified in appealing to the electorate and asking for a fresh mandate if an entirely new and unexpected political issue arises or if it decides to embark on a new and important foreign or domestic policy on which the electorate's opinion is not clear. Dissolution in this sense replaces the referendum procedure which, as a rule, is not accepted by the parliamentary form of government. According to Asquith himself this was one of the reasons for which he advised a second dissolution in 1910.[2] In 1913 the Conservatives pressed the Liberals unsuccessfully to advise dissolution and allow the electorate to decide on Home Rule. This reason has frequently led to a dissolution in the United Kingdom and, in several cases, it was the predominant reason. One could quote as examples the 1910, the 1923 and 1931 elections.[3] In Greece the electorate was indirectly asked to decide on an important issue of foreign policy in 1915.[4]

(i) *Dissolution by force or threat of force*

Greece offers four examples all of which took place in politically anomalous years. This category does not fall within the scope of the present work.

(j) *Other reasons*

One could mention the end of the work of the Revisional Parliament as the most important in this category.

---

[1] See Appendices 1.4, 1.5.   [2] *The Times*, 19 December 1923.
[3] Below, chapter 6.   [4] Below, chapter 10.

B: LIMITATIONS TO THE RIGHT TO
DISSOLVE PARLIAMENT

As already stated the vast majority of European constitutions allows the Executive a wide discretion regarding the right to dissolve Parliament. Though in theory one can conceive of dissolution with or without limitations, in practice various restrictions have been imposed in order to secure the proper functioning of the institution. These limitations, usually found in conventions are, by their nature, vague and vary from country to country and era to era according to the prevailing constitutional and political ideas. But despite their ambiguity and their great variety they all share a common aim, namely, to prevent an abuse of the right. One further point should be made at this stage. The post-World War One constitutions meticulously defined the rights and duties of the various state organs and transformed many of their conventions into written provisions in an attempt to increase their sanctity. Experience, however, shows that rules such as the above are not observed merely because they are backed by constitutional sanctions. In the words of Sir Paul Vinogradoff: 'we must remember that sooner or later we come to a point where law is obeyed not on account of material compulsion, but for other reasons – in consequence of reasonable acceptance, or instinctive conformity, of habit, or absence of organised resistance'.[1] Parliamentary government is, perhaps, the only form of government that has been built upon conventions and requires political ethics and maturity of a very high standard; and if these do not exist, no legal rule can guarantee its preservation.

The control of the act of dissolution can be legal or political. Legal control is, perhaps, theoretically preferable but in practice meets with great difficulties when it is related to political institutions such as dissolution. One way of exercising such control is through the Conseil d'Etat and this is discussed later. Political control on the other hand can be exercised either before the act is put into effect or afterwards. The *a priori* political control can be achieved by obliging two or more State organs to co-operate in order to make dissolution legal. The *a posteriori* control can be exercised by the electorate. In Professor Wigny's words: 'If public opinion has penetrated the spirit of the constitution sufficiently deeply ... it will react violently against anything that constitutes an attempt to violate the spirit of the fundamental law.'[2]

One of the main objects of these restrictions is to avoid a frequent

---

[1] *Common sense in law*, 3rd edn (1959), p. 39.
[2] P. Wigny, *Droit constitutionnel* (1952), I, 187.

exercise of the right. The constitutions one could mention as examples are numerous. We shall briefly examine three, namely, article 51 of the French Constitution of 27 October 1946, article 88 of the Italian Constitution of 1 January 1948, and article 12 of the French Constitution of 9 October 1958.

Article 51 of the French Constitution of 1946 reads as follows:

Si, au cours d'une même période de dix-huit mois, deux crises ministérielles surviennent dans les conditions prévues aux articles 49 et 50,[1] la dissolution de l'Assemblée Nationale pourra être décidée en Conseil des Ministres, après avis du Président de l'Assemblée. La dissolution sera prononcée, confermément à cette décision, par décret du Président de la République.

Les dispositions de l'alinéa précédent ne sont applicables qu'à l'expiration des dix-huit premiers mois de la législature.

The first limitation concerning the time of dissolution is found in the second paragraph of the article. Its purpose is obvious. In the mind of the French constituent legislator of 1946 an early dissolution would only encourage ministerial instability. It must also be noted that this eighteen-month period represents a compromise between two opposite views.[2] The supporters of the first view advocated that dissolution ought to be capable of being exercised at once and therefore opposed this limitation. The opposite opinion[3] prohibited dissolution during the first thirty months. The Constitution finally adopted the above-mentioned, compromise attitude.

After the first eighteen months had elapsed, Parliament could be dissolved only if two ministerial crises took place within the next eighteen months. Furthermore, and this made the exercise of dissolution practically impossible, the two crises should be caused by a vote of no-confidence or a motion of censure (articles 49 and 50). Thus ministerial crises provoked by voluntary resignations or refusal to accept the appointed Prime Minister were not included in articles 49 and 50 and hence could not lead to a dissolution.[4] It is therefore easy to understand why dissolution was exercised only once (1955) during the life of the Fourth Republic.

---

[1] Articles 49 and 50 deal with a defeat of the Government, the first as a result of a vote of no confidence, the second as a result of motion of censure.

[2] See the reports of M. Coste-Floret of 2 August and 26 September 1946 (*Assemblée Nationale Constituante*, no. 11-350, art. 37 and 11-1075, art. 37).

[3] This was adopted by the draft of 19 April 1946, art. 84, para. 2. See Duverger, *Constitutions*, p. 133. It was changed in the final text.

[4] Duverger, *Institutions politiques et droit constitutionnel*, p. 474; G. Vedel, *Manuel élémentaire de droit constitutionnel* (1949), p. 473. The Constitution's main preoccupation was to avoid abuses of the right to dissolve: J. Laferrière, *Manuel de droit constitutionnel* (1947), p. 1111, and Vedel, ibid. p. 472.

Article 88 of the Italian Constitution gives the President the right to dissolve both Houses or either of them after consulting their Speakers. But he cannot exercise this right during the last six months of his tenure of office. The reason for this prohibition is not given but seems to be obvious. The President is elected by the two Houses in a joint session and it is considered improper for him to be able to influence them indirectly by threatening dissolution. A similar provision was made by article 31 of the Constitution of Czechoslovakia of 20 February 1920.

Finally, the slightly different provision of article 81 para. 3 of the Spanish Constitution of 1931 must be mentioned. According to this article dissolution can be practised twice at the most during the President's term.

The 1958 French Constitution seems equally anxious to avoid successive dissolutions. Its relevant provisions, however, are infinitely more lenient than those of its predecessor. Thus, it contains only two provisions relating to the time of dissolution. The first is found in article 12 para. 4 which stipulates that: 'Il ne peut être procédé à une nouvelle dissolution dans l'année qui suit les élections.' The second is found in article 16 para. 5 which provides that the President cannot dissolve Parliament 'pendant l'exercise des pouvoirs exceptionnels'.

In the first case dissolution is prohibited within the year following the general elections. This contingency very nearly occurred during the summer of 1969. When General de Gaulle resigned in April 1969 elections followed for a new President. The main contestants were M. Poher, Speaker of the Senate, and M. Pompidou. In the event that M. Poher won he would have wished, or even been obliged, to dissolve the Gaullist Assembly. Nevertheless, he would have had to wait until the end of June because of the above-mentioned article 12. The general purpose of article 16[1] is equally plausible though much more vague than article 12 para. 4 and to this extent dangerous. Thus, the French press expressed concern about its possible application by maintaining that the President could – in theory – have resort to article 16, then revert to normal so as to dissolve Parliament, and then once again fall back on article 16. Theoretically possible as this may be, it would put unbearable stress on the institutions and hence it is unlikely that it could ever occur.

Two further possibilities, however, are not met by the article though the chance of their occurring is considerable. In the first place, the constitution makes no provision for the possible expiration of Parliament during

---

[1] An extensive analysis of the article can be found in M. Voisset, *L'article 16 de la constitution du 4 Octobre 1958* (1969), and especially pp. 95–100.

this critical period. Perhaps the best solution is to allow Parliament to continue to exercise the functions until the end of the emergency period.

The second possibility is that Parliament has been dissolved and article 16 subsequently put into force. If this can happen, then the President can always dissolve first and then have resort to article 16. This has led lawyers to suggest that article 16 cannot be applied after dissolution. Article 3 of the law of 3 April 1878 provided for such contingencies and forbade the President to assume exceptional powers during the period in which Parliament was dissolved. But no such provision can be found in the 1958 Constitution and to apply it through analogy would only defeat the purposes of article 16.

So it seems that the President cannot be prevented from applying article 16 if Parliament is already dissolved. Considering that the President has no power – in theory at least – to postpone the elections this, in effect, means that he is given complete and absolute powers for a period of forty days. This also means that the electoral campaign would take place in a disturbed atmosphere and with the emergency powers in force. But this has happened in the past – in 1961 – and for lack of a better solution it could happen again in the future.

Dissolution of Parliament must be followed by a general election. During the period of absolute monarchy, delaying the elections and the summoning of the new Parliament was the usual way of violating the electorate's rights. The act of dissolution must always specifically provide for elections and a date for the new Parliament. The period that elapses between dissolution and the summoning of a new Parliament varies from country to country, though it is generally accepted that it must be as short as possible in order not to disrupt normal political life and State activity.

Thus the Japanese Constitution[1] provided for a five-month period before the new Parliament met. The Abyssinian Constitution[2] provided a four-month period. According to the Egyptian Constitution,[3] elections ought to be held within three months and Parliament ought to meet within four months from dissolution. The Bulgarian Constitution[4] provided for two months and four months respectively, and the Constitution of Saxony[5] provided for the new Parliament to meet within six months. In other constitutions three months and occasionally two months

---

[1] Of 11 February 1889, art. 45, F. R. Dareste & P. Dareste, *Les constitutions modernes* (1928–34), V, 559.

[2] Of 16 July 1931, art. 40 (Dareste, V, 477).

[3] Of 22 October 1930, art. 38.3 (Dareste, V, 446).

[4] Of 28 April 1879 as revised in 24 July 1911, art. 137.

[5] Of 4 September 1931, art. 116.3.

are required for the new Parliament to meet. The former is the case in Holland[1] and Rumania,[2] the latter in Belgium.[3] The German Constitution provides for elections within two months and the meeting of Parliament within three months from dissolution. Finally, the Italian Constitution provides a maximum of seventy days during which elections must be held. A further twenty days are allowed until Parliament meets.[4]

Occasionally the constitution provides for the elections, and the meeting of Parliament is regulated by another statute but the delay does not exceed two months, as for example in the Constitutions of Weimar,[5] Spain,[6] Lithuania,[7] Czechoslovakia,[8] and the Third French Republic.[9]

C: LIMITATIONS (CONTINUED)

Only two contemporary European constitutions give the Head of the Executive the right to dissolve Parliament without requiring the co-operation of another State organ. Thus, article 19 of the French Constitution of 1958 provides that 'Les actes du Président de la République autres que ceux prévus aux articles 8 (1er alinéa) 11, 12 (dissolution) 16, 18, 54, 56 et 61 sont contresignés par le Premier Ministre et, le cas échéant, par les ministres responsables.' It is interesting to note at this point that the *avant-projet* of the constitution prepared by the government (art. 17) did not include article 12 (dissolution)[10] and hence the Prime Minister's signature was also necessary for dissolution to be valid.

Similarly, article 63 para. 4 of the German Federal Law[11] provides that in the event of the President's nominee failing to obtain the required majority and the Bundestag also being unable to elect a Chancellor, a new ballot takes place. This time, however, the person that obtains the largest number of votes is elected and no absolute majority is required. Nevertheless, 'if the person elected did not receive this (absolute) majority, the Federal President must, within seven days, either appoint him or dissolve the Bundestag'. The President is thus not obliged to appoint the minority Chancellor. If he chooses not to appoint him he is obliged to dissolve the House and his decision does not have to be countersigned by any Minister.

[1] Art. 75. Elections within forty days (as revised in 3 December 1922 and 3 September 1948).
[2] Of 29 March 1923, art. 90.6. Elections within two months.   [3] Art. 71.
[4] Art. 61.   [5] Art. 25 para. 2.   [6] Art. 81.5.
[7] Art. 53.   [8] Art. 31.   [9] Art. 5 para. 2.
[10] See Duverger, *Constitutions*, p. 164.
[11] A detailed analysis of the article and relevant bibliography can be found in J. Amphoux, *Le chancelier fédéral dans le régime constitutionnel de la république fédérale d'Allemagne* (1962), pp. 30ff. and especially pp. 84ff.

But in most other constitutions, including the present German Constitution (except for the case of article 63, para. 4) the right to dissolve Parliament is subject to the control of one or more State organs even though this control is in many cases fictitious. In these cases, the validity of dissolution depends on the concurrence of another State organ. To put it in a different way: two, usually 'simple' or independent State organs have to combine their actions in order to achieve the total function, i.e. dissolution. Thus, the partial functions of the two (or more) organs compose the total function of dissolution of Parliament.[1] Historically speaking, this limitation originated in England and was based on the concept that the co-operation of two organs instead of one acting independently is a greater guarantee for the functioning of any particular institution.[2] Thus, the first known precedent was that of the Long Parliament.[3]

The State organs that are most frequently expected to co-operate are the Head of State (King or President) and the Cabinet. In this category one can today place Italy, Ireland and Iceland. Several African states have also followed this structure.[4]

Italy   Article 88 of the 1948 Constitution provides that the 'President of the Republic may, after having heard the advice of the Speakers of the two Houses, dissolve either House or both of them'. According to article 89 his decision must be countersigned by the competent Minister.

It is generally agreed that the President may refuse a dissolution to his Prime Minister. It is debatable, however, whether he may dissolve with a Government appointed for this purpose only, as the President, according to article 92 para. 2, has merely the right to appoint and not dismiss the Prime Minister in office.[5]

Ireland   Article 13 para. 2.1 of the Constitution of 29 December 1937 provides that the President can dissolve the Dail Eireann only on the concurring advice of the Prime Minister. However, according to article 13

---

[1] Kelsen, *General theory of Law and State*, pp. 195–6. Also Svolos, *Constitutional law*, pp. 224ff.

[2] Lord Bryce, *Modern democracies* (1929), II, 428ff.

[3] The abuse of dissolution during the early part of the seventeenth century led, as might be expected, to the opposite extreme – the impossibility of using it at all. On 17 May 1641, the Long Parliament enacted a Bill which provided that the Commons' own approval was necessary if the Monarch contemplated dissolution. Parliament was finally dissolved in 1660. See F. W. Maitland, *The constitutional history of England* (1965 edn), pp. 294–5.

[4] Thus Constitution of Sierra Leone of 14 April 1961 (art. 55), Constitution of Uganda of 9 October 1962 amended on 9 October 1963 (art. 60 para. 2), Constitution of Federal Nigeria of 1 October 1963 (art. 68) in D. G. Lavroff & G. Peiser, *Les constitutions africaines* (1961), II, 302, 304ff., 225, 228ff. and 144, 145ff. respectively. For Greece, see Part III.

[5] For further details see F. Mohrhoff, *La dissolution des assemblées législatives dans les constitutions modernes* (Rome, 1953), pp. 87ff., cited by Velu, *Dissolution*, p. 414.

para. 2.2, the President may refuse the advice of the Prime Minister to dissolve if the latter does not command the confidence of the House.

Iceland According to article 24 of the Constitution of 17 June 1944 the President may dissolve the 'Althing' but his act must be countersigned by the competent minister (art. 19).

The German Constitution of 1949 Perhaps at this stage one should also mention the present German Constitution. The reason is that in many ways it is a remarkable text which, on this topic, successfully attempts to achieve some degree of balance and co-operation between President, Chancellor and Bundestag while allowing the final word to rest with the elected body. The interesting system of checks and balances which it adopts deserves discussion in some detail.

Article 67[1] is one of the most important of the new Constitution. In effect, it states that the Bundestag can censure the Chancellor only if it simultaneously appoints his successor. Article 68 deals with the question from the Chancellor's point of view. He can ask for a vote of confidence which can be accepted or rejected. If it is rejected one of the following may happen: the Chancellor may advise a dissolution; the President may or may not accept his advice; the President may be prevented from dissolving if the Bundestag elects, in the meantime, a new Chancellor; or provided all relevant conditions are satisfied, the emergency powers may be invoked by the President. It must be noted, however, that the above may happen only in the event of a defeat of the Chancellor in a vote of confidence (art. 68) and not in a vote of censure (art. 67).

Whether the defeated Chancellor advises the President to dissolve or to have recourse to the emergency powers he may still retain his post. This is because the German Constitution adopts the so-called creative vote of censure (*Konstruktives Misstrauensvotum*) requiring the simultaneous appointment of his successor (art. 67). This, however, cannot be the case in article 68 because article 67 presupposes a vote of censure and not a vote of confidence in the terms of article 68.

The President is not bound to accept the Chancellor's advice and dissolve, though he has to make up his mind within twenty-one days starting from the moment the advice was tendered. But the initiative may be taken from the President's hands if, during the above period of

[1] For a translation of the articles mentioned in these paragraphs see Appendix 3. For detailed discussion consult: Th. Maunz & G. Dürig, *Kommentar zum Grundgesetz* (1964), I, art. 63; Maunz, *Deutsches Staatsrecht*, para. 32. The official translation of the entire Constitution is included in Andrews' *Constitutions and constitutionalism*, pp. 100–51.

twenty-one days, a new Chancellor is accepted by the Bundestag, or the defeated Chancellor succeeds in a second vote of confidence.

The right to dissolve the Bundestag is recognised in one more case (art. 63). We have already seen that if no candidate can be elected Chancellor by an absolute majority of the Bundestag, the President may appoint as Chancellor the candidate who obtained a relative majority or he may dissolve. But here again the President must exercise his option within seven days from the last vote and if he fails to do so then the candidate with most of the votes becomes Chancellor.[1] Thus, the President may dissolve only in the case of article 63 or article 68 and no further initiative is permitted to him.[2]

One final question remains to be discussed, namely whether the President can be obliged to dissolve, because, as already stated, neither article 63 nor article 68 oblige him to do so. The question is not an easy one to answer not only because is there no relevant provision in the text but equally because a continuous refusal of the Chancellor's advice would inevitably lead to accusations of lack of impartiality.

It is clear from all relevant articles of the Constitution that the constituent legislators, haunted by the Weimar experience, were unfavourably disposed towards dissolution. This is clear from both articles 63 and 68 which do not oblige the President to follow the Chancellor's advice and dissolve but, on the contrary, allow him a free hand and encourage him to attempt to appoint a new Chancellor from the existing House. Further, it is generally accepted that self-dissolution is not recognised[3] and hence the Bundestag cannot, on its own, decide to end its own life prematurely. These considerations could suggest that the President is free to oppose the majority's wishes and refuse to dissolve the Bundestag. So it would seem that if a majority Chancellor advised dissolution, the President would be free to refuse his advice and, pursuing the procedure of article 63, attempt to appoint a new Chancellor.

It is submitted that the opposite view is correct. If the Chancellor remains resolute in his decision for a dissolution and continues to enjoy the support of the majority, it is difficult to see how the President can continue to refuse his advice. So, the following seems to be an accurate description of the President's rights on this subject. The President is free to refuse his Chancellor's advice for a dissolution and may proceed according to article 63. But if he fails and the majority still backs the Chancellor in his decision to dissolve then we are faced with a lacuna in

---

[1] Maunz & Dürig, *Kommentar*, art. 63, no. 9.
[2] Ibid. art. 63, no. 12.
[3] Maunz, *Deutsches Staatsrecht*, para. 32, no. 7, 297.

the Constitution which must be solved through interpretation. In this case the fundamental principle of the Constitution, that in the event of a conflict between various State organs the elective body must have the final word, would be applied and would determine the question in favour of the Chancellor and the majority.[1]

It is conceivable that another organ apart from the Cabinet must also concur for dissolution to be valid. This may be the second House, the Conseil d'Etat or finally any other high-standing State organ, as for example the Council of the Nation under the present Greek Constitution.

A typical example of the first case can be found in the Third French Republic. Article 5 of the Loi Constitutionnelle of 25 February 1875 provided that the Senate's approval was necessary for the President to dissolve the Lower House. This limitation was established because of fear of abuses; also because Field-Marshal MacMahon insisted on sharing the responsibility for such a grave decision. He himself had maintained that: 'L'usage de ce droit extrême serait périlleux, et j'hésiterais moi-même à l'exercer si, dans une circonstance critique, le pouvoir ne se sentait appuyé par le concours d'une assemblée moderatrice.'[2]

A similar provision was made by article 79 of the Greek Constitution of 1927, and by article 26 of the Polish Constitution of 1921 (abolished in 1926) which, in addition, required a majority of three-fifths of the Senate before dissolution could be exercised. In all the above cases the Senate's approval did not substantially alter the President's right, as he still retained the initiative.

A typical example of the second case can be found in recent constitutional practice in Belgium. Thus the Decree of the Regent of 19 May 1949 which dissolved Parliament was made 'vu l'avis du Conseil d'Etat' and the same procedure was followed in the 1950 and 1961 dissolutions. As J. Velu notes: 'Dans la pratique administrative, le gouvernement aussi bien que le Conseil d'Etat admettent l'obligation pour le premier – hors le cas d'urgence – de soumettre à l'avis du second, les projets d'arrêté de dissolution.'[3] But this practice is not only impossible in urgent cases; it also faces the difficulty of demanding that a judicial body decide an essentially political question. But the *a priori* control should not be confused with the ex post facto interference of the Conseil d'Etat, the wisdom of which seems even more doubtful.

---

[1] This would be in accord with the diminished position of the President in comparison with the Constitution of Weimar. On this see Maunz, *Deutsches Staatsrecht*, para. 34, pp. 312ff.

[2] A. Esmein & H. Nézard, *Droit constitutionnel* (1928), II, 168; also, S. Markesinis, *The Head of State* (1935), pp. 152–3.   [3] *Dissolution*, p. 117.

Giving such powers to the Conseil d'Etat would mean that dissolution would be looked upon as a 'fonction administrative' and not an 'acte de gouvernement' in the broadest sense, which, in my opinion, it is. This can perhaps be argued only for countries like Belgium, where no provision exists similar to the well-known article 26 of the French law of 24 May 1872 which establishes the fundamental distinction made by the French *droit administratif* between 'actes de gouvernement et d'administration'. Furthermore, what would the Conseil d'Etat be called upon to decide? Whether the decree was countersigned by all the members of the Cabinet or whether it fixed a date for new elections? These are the necessary minimum requirements dissolution has to fulfil and no government would violate. If, on the other hand, the Conseil d'Etat were asked about the advisability of a dissolution then the character of dissolution would be fundamentally altered: it would be transformed from a political to a judicial decision. Finally one could mention borderline cases to illustrate the difficulties that a judicial body would have to face. An interesting example is offered by constitutions forbidding dissolution twice for the same reason. In this case the Conseil d'Etat could be called to decide on the constitutionality of the second dissolution. Experience has shown that this problem is fundamentally political and its solution is finally determined by politicians and not lawyers.[1] As a result it was abandoned by more recent constitutions.

Finally, dissolution may be controlled by another State organ such as the Council of the Nation under the 1968 Greek Constitution.

Parliament is always dissolved by an act of the Head of State – royal or presidential decree or royal proclamation. But where the concurrence of another State organ is required it is interesting to note whether the opinion of the concurring organ is binding or not on the Head of State.

In certain rare cases the President may dissolve and the concurring organ merely offers its opinion. In such cases dissolution is at the President's discretion and his act need not be countersigned by the Cabinet or the Prime Minister. Article 12 of the 1958 French Constitution offers an ideal example. Here the President has to consult the Prime Minister and the Speakers of the two Houses, but he is not bound by their recommendations. Similarly, according to article 58 of the present German Constitution the Federal President's act dissolving the Bundestag under article 63 para. 4 need not be countersigned by the Federal Chancellor.

In other cases the Head of State can only dissolve with the concurring opinion of another State organ. Article 5 of the Loi Constitutionnelle of 1875 allowed the President to dissolve Parliament only 'sur l'avis

---

[1] Below, chapter 10.

conforme du Senat' and a similar provision can be found in article 79 of the 1927 Greek Constitution.

Finally, in many constitutions the Head of State has merely the right to refuse a dissolution and, in certain constitutions, his part is little more than a mere formality. This is the case in most constitutional monarchies of our time where the real power has shifted to the Cabinet or the Prime Minister. In a Republic a typical example of this category can be found in the 1946 French Constitution. In the Fourth French Republic the President merely pronounced dissolution but had nothing to do with the decision which lay with the government. This was made quite clear in 1955 when M. Robert Schuman, then Minister of Justice and Garde des Sceaux, alluded to the 'travaux préparatoires' of the Constitution and maintained that the President had no responsibility whatsoever for the dissolution of Parliament.[1]

The real power lay in the hands of the Cabinet. The Constitution provided for a special procedure which the Cabinet had to follow in order to obtain dissolution. The Cabinet, under the chairmanship of the President of the Republic, first met and discussed the possibility of a dissolution. At this stage the advice of the President of the Assemblée Nationale should be obtained but no definite decision could be reached. The decision could be taken only at a second Cabinet meeting which took place only after the President of the Assemblée Nationale had communicated his written opinion on dissolution to the President of the Republic. His opinion, however, was not binding on the Cabinet. The final decision was taken on a majority vote in which the Prime Minister's vote was equal to that of his colleagues. Ministers who did not expressly disagree were held equally responsible.[2]

Finally it is interesting to see how article 45 of the 1968 Greek Constitution will be interpreted in practice. The wording of the article is vague and it could suggest that the role of the Council is purely an advisory one.[3]

---

[1] *Le Monde*, 1 December 1955. For views expressed in the national press, see Velu, *Dissolution*, p. 444, n. 2. See also J. Reis, 'Dissolution-sanction et mort du parlement', *Revue socialiste* (1955), pp. 481ff., arguing that dissolution was incompatible with the prevailing form of parliamentarism.

[2] Art. 48. M. Duverger, in *La Cinquième Republique* (1963), p. 37, had maintained that it was the Prime Minister who decided on dissolution. But on 29 November 1955 the French Cabinet met to decide dissolution and the opinion of M. Edgar Faure, the then Prime Minister, counted as one vote. The result of the ballot was nineteen for and five against dissolution and President Coty signed the Decree, 'conformément à la décision prise par le Conseil des Ministres'.

[3] Thus see C. Georgopoulos, *Elements of Greek constitutional law* (in Greek) (1968), p. 153. Professor Triantaphyllopoulos expressed grave doubts concerning this new institution. His views are contained in an illuminating and as yet unpublished letter to the Prime Minister of 6 July 1968. Triantaphyllopoulos Papers.

In my opinion this will not be correct. The diminished position of the King in the new Constitution and the unfortunate experience of dissolution in Greece make it highly unlikely that the constituent legislator wished to allow the Crown a free hand in the matter of dissolution. This spirit is obvious in the rather carelessly and quickly printed minutes of the Cabinet meetings covering the drafting of the Constitution. It is even more apparent in the hitherto unpublished letter of the Minister of Justice, Professor Triantaphyllopoulos, who was the responsible Minister at that stage and who is known to have taken a firm stand on this point. Finally, the composition of the Council of the Nation, which, in effect, is likely to be a puppet of the Prime Minister in office, makes it probable that in the final outcome it will be the Prime Minister who will make the decision.

D: THE EFFECT OF LIMITATIONS

The limitations and restrictions imposed upon the exercise of the right to dissolve are obviously numerous and, at times, quite complicated. But one often wonders whether they have always produced the desired results. Unfortunately, it is practically impossible to draw general conclusions on how various limitations actually worked in practice. The difficulty lies in the fact that the way dissolution was practiced by the various European countries depended largely on their political and socio-economic conditions rather than on the constitutional texts themselves. In many countries, various limitations were adopted for historical reasons or on the basis of theoretical concepts but were not based on practical experience. This is particularly true with many post-World War One régimes that copied the French and Weimar Constitutions without really making a serious effort to adapt them to their own conditions.[1]

One would expect that the various limitations and restrictions would prevent frequent dissolutions but this is not necessarily so. The Weimar constituent legislators were clearly haunted by the Bismarckian *Konfliktszeit* and wished to avoid frequent dissolutions. In practice this was not the case. Within a period of practically thirteen years (1919–32) dissolution was exercised eight times (1924, 1924, 1928, 1930, 1932, 1932, 1933, 1933) and seventeen Prime Ministers took office. The last five dissolutions demonstrated an abuse of the right as a result of President Hindenburg's personal policies. The division of the parties, the electoral law and extreme passions kept the Reichstag divided and prepared Hitler's

---

[1] The constitutional texts can be found in B. Mirkine-Guetzévitch, *Les constitutions de l'Europe nouvelle* (10th edn, 1938). *Les nouvelles tendances du droit constitutionnel* (by the same author, 1936), is an interesting study of the aims of constitutional law between the two wars.

amazing rise to power. Similarly, by her 1927 Constitution Greece imposed severe limitations on dissolution but these too failed to produce any results. Between 1927 and 1935 four dissolutions took place (1928, 1932, 1933, 1935) two of which were closely linked with the interests of one party.

If one compares these two examples with the practice in the United Kingdom and Belgium one realises that the frequency of dissolution does not necessarily depend on the existing limitations in the text. Neither the United Kingdom nor Belgium imposed any legal limitations on dissolution, and yet had no more – and in fact had less – dissolutions in the same number of years.[1] Clearly in the case of Germany and Greece, the limitations were unable to produce results due to the prevailing economic and political conditions. The Weimar Constitution, though drafted by eminent scholars and with the best of intentions, through its continuous attempts to reconcile conflicting principles and ideas, proved incapable of preserving internal stability and unity. Of course, it cannot be denied that international political and economic problems were also responsible to a great extent for its final collapse. Similarly in Greece mere constitutional provisions were unable to overcome the immense problems the Asia Minor disaster had created.

At times, however, numerous restrictions may lead to a more or less complete atrophy of the right. Despite the fact that the French constituent legislators of 1946 regarded dissolution as 'une des clefs de voûte principales de tout le système [parlementaire]',[2] the right was so severely restricted that the conditions under which it could be exercised arose only once during the lifetime of the Republic.

Perhaps one conclusion can be drawn from the above: the political environment determines the way dissolution functions more than the texts themselves. Parliamentary government is an exceedingly delicate form of government and can function properly only if backed by tradition, political self-restraint and a highly developed sense of fair play. Legal institutions can survive only within a favourable environment. The best example again comes from the Weimar Republic. Professor Vermeil prophetically emphasised the important role these factors would play in the collapse of the Weimar Republic:

Un peuple qui n'a jamais été souverain ne le devient pas d'un jour à l'autre; ... passant brusquement de l'autocratie monarchique à la démocratie pure en évitant le parlementarisme autocratique et plutocratique qui a eu en occident une si grande tradition, l'Allemagne fait le 'salto mortale' qui peut la briser ou la regénérer.[3]

The rise of the Third Reich proved the correctness of his opinions.

[1] United Kingdom: 1922, 1923, 1924, 1929, 1931; Belgium: 1919, 1921, 1925, 1929, 1931.
[2] *Assemblée Nationale Constituante*, no. 11-350, 14.   [3] *La Constitution de Weimar*, pp. 374, 431.

PART II

DISSOLUTION OF PARLIAMENT IN THE UNITED KINGDOM

Chapter 4

ENFORCED DISSOLUTION AND DISMISSAL OF THE GOVERNMENT

A: DISSOLUTION AS A ROYAL PREROGATIVE

Dissolution, in law, is a prerogative of the Crown that has frequently given rise to heated controversy.

Dicey's definition[1] of the royal prerogative as the 'residue of discretionary or arbitrary authority, which at any given time is legally left in the hands of the Crown', has been criticised at times, particularly for the use of the term 'arbitrary',[2] but it has also frequently been approved by the Courts,[3] and thus can be taken as a starting point in the present chapter. Its value, I believe, lies primarily in the flexibility of the masterly phrasing. Thus, the words: 'at any given time' and 'authority . . . legally left in the hands of the Crown', undoubtedly underline the importance of time and the evolution of the position of the Crown within the framework of the constitution. This is particularly apparent if one compares Dicey's definition of the royal prerogative with that of Blackstone[4] which emphasises the 'special pre-eminence which the King hath, over and above all other persons . . .' The following chapters will try to clarify the effect of time on the use of the prerogative of dissolution.

But, to return to Dicey's definition, the prerogative is also 'discretionary' in the sense that the Courts can determine its existence but cannot

---

[1] A. V. Dicey, *Introduction to the study of the law of the constitution*, 10th edn (1967), p. 424.
[2] O. Hood Phillips, *Constitutional and administrative law*, 4th edn (1967), p. 241; R. F. V. Heuston, *Essays in constitutional law* (1964), pp. 58, 64ff.
[3] Cited by Lord Dunedin in *Attorney-General* v. *De Keyser's Royal Hotel Ltd.* (1920), A.C. 508, at p. 526. For a most interesting historical summary of the evolution of the royal prerogative see Sir D. L. Keir & F. H. Lawson, *Cases in constitutional law* (1967), pp. 73ff.
[4] *Commentaries of the laws of England*, 7th edn (1775), I, 239.

control the manner in which it is exercised. It is, however, in the exercise of the prerogative that lie the dangers it may entail.

Among the most important 'political prerogatives' enjoyed by the Crown is the right to dissolve Parliament. A sentence such as the above, however, suffers from lack of precision. The question that must be asked here is whether the Crown can dissolve without or even against the advice of its Ministers.

The growth of parliamentary and cabinet government, and the doctrine of ministerial responsibility in particular, have considerably reduced the value of the royal prerogative today.[1] It is fair to say that the origin of most parliamentary conventions can be traced to the manner in which the prerogative can and will be controlled and, as a result, 'there are very few occasions nowadays when the Queen can act without or against the advice of her Ministers . . .'[2] Dissolution is thus a prerogative in the sense that it is an 'act which the executive government can lawfully do without the authority of the Act of Parliament'.[3]

A dissolution of Parliament, on the Prime Minister's advice, is a very serious and important decision. In the words of Harold Laski:[4] 'Dissolution is an invaluable mechanism . . . but it is, of course, an exceedingly delicate instrument, about the uses of which there are grave differences of opinion.' Thus dissolution shortens[5] the life of the existing Parliament and plunges the country into the tumult and turmoil of elections which are bound to disrupt its normal activities. Furthermore, elections are costly, and frequent elections can be detrimental to the national economy. The situation is even more precarious if a dissolution follows a dismissal of H.M. Government. The Crown will find itself involved in political controversy of the highest order and that is certainly the last thing it can afford.

Two basic questions arise from the exercise of the prerogative. First: can the Monarch dissolve Parliament without advice? (viz. royal dissolution or forced dissolution). This is bound to be connected with a forced resignation of the Ministry. Second: if advice is deemed necessary, whose advice may it be and is it binding on the Monarch? The first of these questions is examined in this chapter, while the second is the subject under discussion in the next chapter.

---

[1] G. Marshall & G. Moodie, *Some problems of the constitution* (1967), p. 43.

[2] Hood Phillips, *Constitutional law*, p. 242. As Heuston, *Essays*, puts it, 'to the normal practising lawyer today the common law powers of the Crown are of little importance'.

[3] Dicey, *Law of the constitution*, p. 425.   [4] *A grammar of politics*, 5th edn (1967), p. 342.

[5] With the exception of 1910 and 1935, when Parliament was prolonged because of the World Wars up to 1918 and 1945 respectively, few Parliaments have exceeded a four-year period. In 1923, 1924, 1931 and 1935, Parliaments were dissolved long before their normal periods expired.

B: THE RIGHT TO DISMISS A GOVERNMENT
AND ENFORCE A DISSOLUTION

Technically speaking, in the United Kingdom a dissolution necessitates an Order in Council, the Lord President accepting responsibility for summoning the Council. It also necessitates a Proclamation and writs of summons under the Great Seal, for which the Lord Chancellor is held responsible. It is therefore obvious that dissolution cannot originate only from the King.

From the constitutional and political angle it also appears to be universally accepted[1] that the Monarch may never use the prerogative power relating to a dissolution of Parliament in an arbitrary way, entirely on his own responsibility. There must always be a Minister willing and prepared to assume responsibility for the Monarch's act and thus shield him from attack, should there be any. Sir Robert Peel, when Lord Melbourne's Government was dismissed by King William IV, shielded the Sovereign by declaring in a hostile House of Commons that: 'I am, by my acceptance of office, responsible for the removal of the late government.'[2] In 1913, when King George V asked Lord Esher for his advice, the latter replied: 'Ministerial responsibility is the safeguard of the Monarchy. Without it, the Throne could not stand for long amid the gusts of political conflict and the storm of political passion.'[3] Thus the King needs advice, in order to dissolve Parliament and if his Ministers refuse it he can only dismiss them and try to find others who will agree with him.[4]

But can the King dismiss his Ministers? It is obvious that one can dismiss a person whom he has chosen but not someone who has been imposed on him. The answer therefore to the question is closely related to the King's right to choose his political advisers. For this reason it is desirable to dispose of this problem before endeavouring to give an answer to the first question.

Legally speaking the King appoints his Ministers; they depend on him and remain in office until they are dismissed or allowed to resign. The Prime Minister on the other hand merely nominates his Ministers.

[1] Sir Ivor Jennings, *Cabinet government*, 3rd edn (1961), p. 417; Anson, *Law and custom of the constitution*, I, 306; Hood Phillips, *Constitutional law*, p. 106; E. C. S. Wade & A.W. Bradley, *Constitutional law* (1970), p. 120; Forsey, *The royal power of dissolution*, p. 258; Marshall & Moodie, *Some problems of the constitution*, p. 44; E. Campbell, 'The prerogative power of dissolution', *Public Law* (1961), p. 165.

[2] Hood Phillips, *Constitutional law*, p. 285; J. Harvey & L. Bather, *The British Constitution* (1966), p. 194.

[3] *Journals and letters of Reginald, Viscount Esher* (1934–8), III, 126–9. See also Lord Haldane's answer to King George V, quoted by Nicolson, *King George V*, p. 379.

[4] Jennings, *Cabinet government*, p. 413.

In actual fact, nevertheless, the Ministers – including members of the Cabinet – depend primarily, if not wholly, on the Prime Minister.[1] This does not necessarily imply that the Sovereign does not occasionally exercise some influence in selecting the Ministers. But if the King disagrees with the Prime Minister, he must either give way, or find another Prime Minister, which is not always easy to do and is nearly always a dangerous step.

A careful study of the influence of the Monarch in choosing his Ministers reveals a gradual but steady decline. This, no doubt, is the result of the gradual abandonment of real and effective power in order to adapt to a continuous flow of social changes unprecedented in the past. As H.R.H. the Duke of Windsor wisely stated: 'If the British Monarchy can be said to have demonstrated one outstanding quality, it has been its capacity to adapt itself to a social change.'[2]

It was Queen Victoria's practice to demand – as her predecessor William IV had done – a list of the future Ministers to be submitted to her for her approval.[3] Through this procedure many an eminent British politician was denied a Cabinet position or prevented from attaining one, solely through the whim of the Queen. No Prime Minister dared after 1851 to suggest Lord Palmerston for the Foreign Office, because of her well-known 'personal feelings' regarding the 'dangerous qualities of Lord Palmerston'.[4] The Queen, in fact, insisted that 'she must reserve to herself the unfettered right to approve or disapprove the choice of a Minister for this office' (Foreign Office).[5]

Others, Sir Charles Dilke for instance, one of the most able and clearsighted politicians of the nineteenth century, were denied further advancement, chiefly because of personal antipathy rather than disagreement with their policies.[6] And the Queen's personal objections became more frequent after the second Reform Act.

Unfortunately the Queen was not always the only one to blame. Mr

---

[1] Jennings, ibid. p. 61; Marshall & Moodie, *Some problems of the constitution*, p. 41; J. D. B. Mitchell, *Constitutional law* (1964), p. 162; P. Gordon Walker, *The Cabinet* (1970), pp. 82–3.

[2] *The Crown and the people, 1902–1953* (1953), p. 4.

[3] In 1841, Lord Melbourne advised 'the Queen to adopt the course which King William did with Lord Melbourne in 1835 viz. asking him to send a list . . . and the King having them all before him expressed his objections to certain persons which Lord Melbourne yielded to'. *Letters of Queen Victoria*, 1st series, I, 339.

[4] *Letters of Queen Victoria*, 1st series, II, 447.   [5] *Letters of Queen Victoria*, 1st series, II, 415–16.

[6] Gladstone had proposed Dilke first as Chancellor of the Duchy of Lancaster and then President of the Board of Trade. The Queen objected to both. She would allow Dilke to become president of the local government board, but only if 'he should give a written explanation or make one in Parliament on the subject of his very offensive speeches on the Civil List and the Royal Family'. Dilke had previously attacked a dowry of £30,000 voted by Parliament to Princess Louise and £15,000 granted for Prince Arthur, later Duke of

Disraeli, for one, though an ingenious, able and gifted statesman, through his constant flattery of the Queen was not always the ideal parliamentary adviser. He once wrote to her:

If your Majesty's government have from wilfulness, or even from weakness deceived your Majesty, or not fulfilled their engagements to their Sovereign, they should experience the consequences of such misconduct, and the constitutional, and becoming, manner of their punishment is obvious. They cannot with their present parliamentary majority in both Houses, and their existing difficulties, as men of honour, resign, but Your Majesty has the clear, constitutional right to dismiss them.[1]

Very strong wording indeed, or as Jennings argues, 'rhetorical flourish' which offered no solution as to the course to be followed if Mr Disraeli's parliamentary majority were to be dismissed.[2]

Queen Victoria's death marks an important change in the relations of the Monarch with his Ministers. The few and unimportant examples that exist – or more precisely that have been revealed – clearly suggest that the choice and the final word lie within the Prime Minister's powers. But then, does the Queen still choose the Prime Minister?

Disraeli and Gladstone were the first to give the office of Prime Minister its special pre-eminence and prestige. Since then the evolution has been continuous and authors have described the British form of government as prime-ministerial.[3] Nowadays the office itself carries immense powers though the way they are exercised still depends largely on the personality of the holder.

In spite of this pre-eminence, the Prime Minister, particularly in the past, relied on the King who had the power to appoint him should the office fall vacant. It was perhaps the only prerogative that was exercised at the discretion of the Crown, and for practical reasons was not the responsibility of the Ministers. This prerogative whenever exercised,[4] though not always without discontent and political turmoil, was generally accepted as being exercised well. This, of course, is understandable

---

Connaught. See S. Gwynn & G. Tuckwell, *The life of the Rt. Hon. Sir Charles Dilke*, 2 vols (1917), pp. 492–5; R. Jenkins, *Sir Charles Dilke – a Victorian tragedy* (1965); S. Markesinis, 'Charles Dilke – a sincere Philhellene', *Historia*, August 1968.

[1] W. F. Monypenny & G. E. Buckle, *The life of Benjamin Disraeli, Earl of Beaconsfield* (1910–20), VI, 246.   [2] Jennings, *Cabinet government*, p. 407.

[3] R. Crossman, Introduction to Bagehot, *The English Constitution* (1968), p. 51. For a challenge of this view see Gordon Walker, *The Cabinet*, pp. 85ff. See also: R. W. K. Hinton, 'The Prime Minister as an elected monarch', *Parliamentary Affairs* (1960), pp. 297ff.; G. W. Jones, 'The Prime Minister's powers', *Parl. Aff.* (1964–5), pp. 167–85; D. J. Heasman, 'The Ministerial hierarchy', *Parl. Aff.* (1962), pp. 307–30, and 'The Prime Minister and the Cabinet', *Parl. Aff.* (1962), pp. 461–84; D. N. Chester, 'Who governs Britain', *Parl. Aff.* (1962), pp. 519–27; F. W. Benemy, *The elected monarch* (1965).

[4] In the twentieth century it was exercised in 1923, 1931, 1940, 1957 and 1963. The 1931 exercise of the prerogative was particularly controversial.

once one has studied the cases when it was exercised. If we take the Conservative Party leaders[1] since Mr Disraeli's death in 1881, the Crown actually had a choice five times,[2] notably: Lord Salisbury, Mr Baldwin, Sir Winston Churchill, Mr Macmillan, and Sir Alec Douglas Home. If one disregards Lord Salisbury's appointment, since it was taken under circumstances that no longer exist,[3] one realises that the Crown was called upon to exercise this prerogative only four times in the last ninety years. And even in these four cases the King exercised the prerogative on the advice of senior party statesmen and at times on material evidence of the party's preferences based on soundings[4]. In fact it is known that twice at least (in the cases of Lord Curzon and Lord Halifax) the King followed the advice of the above in spite of his own personal feelings.[5]

In all other cases, the elected leader was the 'natural' or 'evident' leader, and stood uncontested.

Nevertheless, because of the political unrest that occasionally followed when the King exercised the prerogative power to appoint a Prime Minister, constitutional lawyers, Keith the most notable of them, argued[6] that the Monarch, although culpable was not constitutionally ac-

---

[1] Salisbury, Balfour, Bonar Law, Baldwin, N. Chamberlain, Churchill, Eden, Macmillan, Douglas Home and Heath. A. Chamberlain served as its leader for eighteen months in 1921–2, but was never formally elected to that office because he never served as Prime Minister. Mr Heath cannot be included since he was chosen under a new electoral process.

[2] Lord Rosebery's appointment as leader of the Liberal Party in 1894 instead of Sir William Harcourt was probably the last creative choice, though in this case too it seems that the Queen acted in conformity with the wishes of the majority of the Cabinet.

[3] Furthermore, by 1885 Lord Salisbury had firmly established his own claim. Thus the Queen's selection was accepted 'not only with unanimity but as a matter of course'. R. Mackenzie, *British political parties* (1968), p. 26.

[4] Mackenzie, ibid. pp. 21–54 and pp. 586–90.

[5] Thus, on Tuesday 22 May 1923 Lord Stamfordham visited Lord Curzon and informed him of the King's decision to appoint Mr Baldwin as Prime Minister. The former recorded this meeting in a memorandum to the King (quoted by Nicolson, *King George V*, p. 488) in which he writes 'His Majesty, after due consideration, felt compelled, though with great regret, to ignore the personal element, and to base his choice upon what he conceived to be the requirements of the present times.' On 29 May the King saw Lord Curzon and expressed to him his 'deep regret' for having reached such a decision so painful to Lord Curzon 'whom he had known for some 35 years and regarded as an old friend, while his personal acquaintance with Mr. Baldwin was that of having met and spoken to him on a few recent occasions', ibid. p. 490. The King's decision was based on soundings and the opinions of senior statesmen. Mr Bonar Law was also reported to have said that if he were asked he would also have recommended Mr Baldwin. See G. M. Young, *Stanley Baldwin* (1952), p. 48; A. W. Baldwin, *My father* (1955), p. 121. See also L. S. Amery, *Thoughts on the constitution* (1964), pp. 21ff. In Sir Winston Churchill's case it is known that both the King and Mr Chamberlain preferred Lord Halifax. But at the dramatic meeting that took place on 10 May 1940 between the P.M., Lord Halifax and Mr Churchill, it soon became clear that Mr Churchill was the only one that could undertake the task. See Wheeler-Bennett, *King George VI; his life and reign*, pp. 440–7; Sir Winston Churchill, *The Second World War*, 1 (1950), 596–601.   *The British cabinet system*, 2nd edn by Gibbs (1952), p. 277.

countable for the exercise of the prerogative. Keith's view is an obvious attempt to revive the doctrine of ministerial responsibility and divert attention and criticism – if there be any – from the Monarch. But, as Marshall and Moodie argue,[1] the doctrine in this case did not 'have this protective effect in 1931, when the King was criticised rightly or wrongly for his part in the selection of Ramsay MacDonald to head the National Government', and is 'pure fiction'.

Nowadays it is doubtful – especially after Mr Heath's election in 1964 – whether the Queen still possesses this prerogative.[2] Even if she does, there is little chance that she will be given the opportunity to exercise it, or even that she would wish to do so.

But as it has been stated, even before the Conservatives altered their method of electing a leader (1964), the parties, and indirectly the electorate, had a very strong voice in choosing the next Prime Minister. To take a recent example Mr Macmillan in 1957 had a strong following within his party and can hardly be described as 'the Queen's choice',[3] and it is significant that in 1963 Sir Alec Douglas Home kissed hands as Prime Minister twenty-four hours after he had been commissioned to try to form a Government. Twenty-four long hours that Sir Alec – capable as he proved himself to be – had to use to win over Mr Butler, Mr Hogg and Mr Maudling, in order to secure his party's support. It can be said, without being far from the truth, that he became Prime Minister through his colleagues' tolerance rather than through his ex-leader's preference. In any case, the Queen's selection was highly controversial and constitutes an intriguing constitutional dispute, which undoubtedly must have had its effect in the subsequent alteration of the system of choosing a leader which the Conservative Party introduced.[4]

On the other hand, the electorate – through the parties – has gained

---

[1] *Some problems of the constitution*, p. 51.

[2] This, of course, is assuming that one party commands the majority in the Commons. In the unlikely event, however, of no party having an overall majority in the House, the situation may be different.

[3] Mackenzie, *Political parties*, p. 592, appears to have serious doubts whether the Queen was faced with a real choice. Contra, Jennings, *Cabinet government*, p. 28. It appears that Mr Butler's legitimate claims to the premiership as a senior and proved statesman were jeopardised primarily by right-wing Conservative backbenchers, who were opposed to his progressive views on domestic social policies (Mackenzie, ibid. pp. 590–1). Subsequent events seem to have justified Mr Butler in many of his views. In any event Mr Macmillan's firm leadership (see *Economist*, 14 March 1959) proved in many respects successful. The so-called 'Iremonger correspondence', published in the *Daily Telegraph*, 12 January and 18 January 1957, is enlightening on the backbenchers movement.

[4] On the subject consult: R. Churchill's *The fight for the Tory leadership* (1964); I. Macleod, *Spectator*, 17 January 1964; M. Redmayne in the *Listener*, 19 December 1963; and Mackenzie, ibid. pp. 594b–594h.

considerable powers in this field. Recent statistics and opinion polls have
indicated to a great extent 'the fairly narrow limits of the rational element
in voting behaviour'. The support electors give to a party 'is linked, not
with "issues", but with much broader general "images" with which the
party is associated'.[1] To these images the character and the personality
of the leader contribute to a varying but usually great degree. One could
perhaps say that 'the only mandate given by the electorate to an M.P., is
to support his leader'.[2] In fact the importance attached to the party
leader is such that it could be argued that to a great extent the electorate
chooses between personality images.[3] The result is that his position is
secure and normally he can be sure that his party will back him. This
being so, if his party wins the elections, he will necessarily be the next
Prime Minister. There seems to be no doubt that nowadays little margin
is left for the Queen to exercise the 'residue' of her original powers to
appoint a Prime Minister, and a 'King of great sagacity would want
nothing more'.[4]

The conclusion of this very brief analysis is that the Monarch's powers
to choose his advisers have in recent times been seriously curtailed, and
have been transferred to the Prime Minister. Consequently, the Sovereign's power to dismiss Ministers has equally disappeared. In actual fact
it has not been practised since 1834.

C: THE PRECEDENTS

The last time dissolution resulted from a forced resignation of the Government was in 1834. But this does not mean that the Sovereign can act
proprio motu.[5] Even if the King forces a dissolution or dismisses his
Ministers, the new Government must assume responsibility for his action.
This has happened three times in the recent history of Great Britain: in
1783, 1807 and 1834. The events of 1783 and 1807 are too remote to have
any bearing whatsoever on the present conditions. But until fairly recently 1834 was looked upon as an influential precedent. It is therefore
important to establish if the last crisis of 1834 is a precedent capable of any
influence in our times.

[1] J. Blondel, *Voters, parties and leaders* (1967), pp. 81–4.
[2] Jones, 'The Prime Minister's powers', *Parl. Aff.* (1964–5), p. 168.
[3] The outcome of the 1970 General Election can challenge this statement. During the campaign Mr Heath trailed badly behind his opponent but his Party finally won.
[4] Bagehot, *The British Constitution* (Fontana edn), p. 111.
[5] William III seems to have been the last monarch to dissolve Parliament on his own responsibility in 1701: Anson, *Law and custom of the constitution*, I, 304.

In 1834, Lord Grey resigned his Premiership. His Government had been in office with various minor alterations since November 1830 and had borne the burden of passing the first Reform Act. When he failed to secure Lord Althorp's support on an Irish Coercion Bill, he found this a plausible excuse and retired. Lord Melbourne succeeded him after the King failed to persuade the politicians of the necessity of a coalition government. Lord Melbourne, the most conservative Whig of his time, did not seem particularly interested in the appointment. It is said that he once told his private secretary: 'he thought it a damned bore' to be a Prime Minister.[1] However, once he took office he obviously thought otherwise. All this is particularly significant in connection with his dismissal.

From the outset, the Government was faced with great difficulties. Owing to internal disagreement, it was deprived of many eminent members.[2] Lord Althorp's withdrawal to the House of Lords in November 1834 was the *coup de grâce*.[3] His support was a sine qua non for the government, owing to his great influence in the House of Commons. Lord Melbourne took the case to the King. He suggested Lord John Russell as Lord Althorp's successor, and expressed his confidence that he would retain the majority in the House of Commons. In what would seem today an unprecedented and unconstitutional step the King turned him down. He would not even hear of 'the dangerous little radical' because he 'would make a wretched figure opposed by Sir Robert Peel and Mr. Stanley'.[4] So Lord Melbourne offered to resign and although he considered the meeting with the King (14 November) 'as very painful' he 'asserted his strongest personal attachment' and declared he would not 'venture to pronounce that he (the King) was wrong'. The fact that Lord Melbourne 'offered' his resignation and adopted a moderate attitude in his dealings with the King, has made historians believe that it was not unlikely that he wished the King to come to this decision.[5] It certainly makes it very difficult to pronounce in clear-cut terms whether his government was dismissed, 'turned out neck and crop' as Lord Palmerston put it, or forced to resign. Whatever the verdict may be, the case still cannot be considered as an influential precedent, mainly because the circumstances

---

[1] Quoted by Sir Llewellyn Woodward, *The age of reform* (1962), p. 98.
[2] Graham, Stanley, Ripon and Richmond resigned after disagreeing with Russell who insisted on raising in the Commons the question of the appropriation of surplus revenues of the Irish Church to secular purposes.
[3] In November Lord Spencer died and Lord Althorp succeeded him in the House of Lords, thus vacating his place as Leader of the House of Commons.
[4] Quoted by J. A. Farrer, *The monarchy in politics* (1917), pp. 154–5.
[5] Woodward, *The age of reform*, p. 101.

in which it took place are unlikely to arise again. As Sir Ivor Jennings argues, 'whether the case was good or bad, justifiable or unjustifiable, the conditions cannot be repeated today and it cannot be regarded as a precedent'.[1] Lord Melbourne was succeeded by Sir Robert Peel who dissolved Parliament and lost the subsequent elections.

The fact, however, that Lord Melbourne took a moderate line, made things easier for the King to recall him after Sir Robert Peel's defeat at the elections. The King's language on the other hand was so harsh and absurd, that even Peel was obliged to warn the King's secretary to advise the King against the risks of using violent language about his Ministers. As Sir Llewellyn Woodward correctly points out, 'Here, rather than in the circumstances of Melbourne's dismissal, was the danger of a constitutional dispute of the first order',[2] illustrating the dangers of a political system which places too much power for obstruction in the hands of a Monarch.

Even Sir Robert Peel, who publicly shielded the King, thought that 'it is obvious that His Majesty's case was a bad one'. And Mr Gladstone, Britain's leading parliamentarian, condemned the incident as 'harsh and hard to justify'.[3]

Regardless of the position one takes on the constitutional issue, there is little doubt that rarely has the British Monarchy reached such a low ebb, particularly after the King was obliged, to his embarrassment, to recall Lord Melbourne to form a new Government.[4] Thus, apart from the 1807 resignation of the Whigs, it can be concluded that no Government has been dismissed by a Monarch since that of Lord North in 1783.

In 1913, Home Rule stirred up a serious constitutional crisis which was linked to dissolution and dismissal of a Ministry. Its importance makes it worthy of detailed analysis. However, the more one examines the 1913 crisis the more one comes to the conclusion that the extremes it reached were caused largely by irrational and at times fanatical party controversy, which can be partially attributed to the impatience of the Conservative Party which had been out of power for seven years.

With today's political ethics, any attempt to drag the King into party politics seems inconceivable, to say the least. One might add perhaps that it was thanks to the First World War that the constitutional issue was

---

[1] Quoted by Jennings, *Cabinet government*, pp. 403, 405.

[2] Woodward, *The age of reform*, p. 102. The King's words were: 'Mind me . . . the Cabinet is not my Cabinet; they had better take care, or by God, I will have them impeached.'

[3] Quoted by Jennings, *Cabinet government*, p. 405.

[4] The Duchess of Gloucester described the King as being, 'in the most pitiable state of distress, constantly in tears and saying that he felt his Crown tottering on his head'. Quoted by Farrer, *The monarchy in politics*, p. 158.

abruptly ended. In the words of Robert Blake,[1] 'Between 1910 and 1914 the British Constitution and the conventions upon which it depends were strained to the uttermost limit; and paradoxically, it was the outbreak of the First World War which although it imperilled Britain's very existence, probably alone saved Britain's institutions from disaster.' Ironically, the issue is practically unknown to the great majority of people today.

No sooner had the 1910–11 crisis ended, than King George V was confronted with a new crisis.

The Liberals and the Irish Nationalists[2] were determined to pass a Home Rule Bill, aided by the recent Parliament Act of 1911, regardless of the opposition in the two Houses. This would undoubtedly end a political issue that had been troubling the country for well over a century. Yet the Bill and all its predecessors made no provision for the exclusion of Ulster. On 11 April 1912, Home Rule was introduced in the House of Commons.

The Conservative Party and of course the Liberal Unionists, formally fused in 1912, would not accept this and argued – to a certain extent correctly – that the Government lacked a popular mandate to force such a law through the two Houses, aided by the Parliament Act of 1911, since the last elections had been fought on a completely different issue.[3] On 27 July 1912, Mr Bonar Law, in his famous Blenheim speech, flung down the gauntlet of defiance and proclaimed that 'I can imagine no length of resistance to which Ulster will go, which I shall not be ready to support and in which they will not be supported by an overwhelming majority of the British people.'[4] In Mr Asquith's opinion, this speech provided for the future 'a complete grammar of anarchy';[5] it nearly did.

But the Conservatives were a minority party and their last chance to

---

[1] R. Blake, *The unknown Prime Minister. The life and times of Andrew Bonar Law, 1858–1923* (1955), p. 121; G. Wilson, *Cases and materials on constitutional and administrative law* (1966), p. 28.

[2] The strength of the political parties was then in the House of Commons as follows: Liberals 272, Conservatives 272, Irish Nationalists 84, Labour 42. The Irish Nationalists had voted with the Liberals in the passing of the Parliament Act and in exchange for their support the Liberals would introduce Home Rule.

[3] This is only partly true, since Mr Redmond had made it clear as early as 1910 that his Irish Nationalists would support the Government only if it undertook the obligation to introduce Home Rule after the Parliament Act was passed. See Gwynn, *The life of John Redmond*, pp. 166–7; I. Colvin, *The life of Lord Carson* (1934), II, ch. 2.

[4] Quoted by Nicolson, *King George V*, p. 269. Blake, *The unknown Prime Minister*, pp. 130–1, maintains that 'such a tone had not been heard in England since the debates of the Long Parliament and it certainly sounded strangely from the lips of a leader of the party which

[5] traditionally stood for law and order'.

On 5 October 1912. See Asquith, *Fifty years of Parliament* (1926), II, 136.

prevent the enactment of Home Rule was that the King would refuse his assent to the Bill and oblige the Liberals to resign. The first stage of the constitutional battle was thus linked with the veto powers of the Crown.

Sir Austen Chamberlain relates[1] that on 3 May 1912, Mr Bonar Law told the King that if Mr Asquith did not resign voluntarily, then the King should either accept Home Rule and the possibility of civil war, or dismiss his Ministers: 'In either case, half your subjects will think you have acted against them.' And Mr Bonar Law concluded: 'They may say that your assent is a purely formal act and the prerogative of veto is dead. That was true, as long as there was a buffer between you and the House of Commons, but they have destroyed this buffer and it is true no longer.' In this Mr Bonar Law seemed to have had Sir William Anson as an ally, since the latter in a letter to the King's Private Secretary stated: 'That the King undoubtedly possessed according to the law of the Constitution, the "discretionary power" to refuse his Assent to a Bill' and 'the abolition of the powers of the House of Lords did not', in Sir William Anson's opinion, 'affect the constitutional right of the King to exercise his ultimate veto, but it might suggest reasons which did not exist before for the assertion of that right.'[2] Yet, on 26 March 1913, Mr Bonar Law wrote to Dicey saying: 'I do not think that it is a question of using the Veto; but in my own view the one constitutional right which the sovereign undoubtedly still possesses is that if Ministers give him advice of which he does not approve, he should then see whether he can get other Ministers who would give him different advice.' Dicey replied deprecating any revival of the Royal Veto, but adding: 'I entirely agree with your view of the King's constitutional position.'[3] Whether Mr Bonar Law's advice to the King was different from what he privately believed, or whether he changed his mind since his first talk with the King in which he had recommended the use of the Royal Veto, it is hard to decide, particularly because of lack of evidence. Perhaps the latter seems more probable. In any case Mr Bonar Law finally decided to insist on the King's right to dismiss his Ministers.

Mr Bonar Law's opinions on the Royal Veto and the effect that the Parliament Act had upon it, today seem highly questionable if not

---

[1] *Politics from inside; an epistolary chronicle, 1904–1914* (1936), pp. 486–7.

[2] But Nicolson, *King George V*, p. 169, comments: 'Such an opinion, although doubtless incontestable in law, does not appear to be equally sound as a matter of practical politics.' Blake also agrees that some of Bonar Law's views expressed in this memorandum, 'may well seem open to some doubt on constitutional grounds'. Asquith himself, *Fifty years of Parliament*, gives a brief and a surprisingly dispassionate account of events.

[3] Quoted by Blake, *The unknown Prime Minister*, p. 152. Yet Dicey took the opposite view regarding the veto power in his letter to *The Times* of 15 September.

extremely dangerous. It is hard to perceive how the Parliament Act had the effect on the Royal Veto that Mr Bonar Law implied, as it was primarily a measure towards establishing a more democratic process, by giving the lead to the elective House. It certainly was not conceived as a step backwards, as it would be, if it revived the King's powers.

As stated above, Mr Bonar Law modified his opinions, and in a memorandum submitted to the King,[1] emphasised the latter's right to dismiss his Ministers. In it he argued that:

The King not only had the constitutional right but that it was his duty before acting on the advice of his Ministers to ascertain whether it was not possible to appoint other Ministers who would advise him differently and allow the question to be decided by the country at a general election.

In public he continued to encourage Ulster's resistance. The constitutional battle thus entered its second phase and the problem of the dismissal of the Ministry in connection with a forced dissolution arose.

In the autumn, Mr Bonar Law wrote to Lord Stamfordham hinting that if Home Rule was enacted a civil war might break out and continued:

If it is in our power to prevent it, we shall not permit this; and sooner or later, if the tension does not come to an end in some other way, we shall have to decide between breaking the Parliamentary machine and allow the terrible results to happen. When faced with the choice of such evils as these, we shall not, I think, hesitate in considering that the injury to the House of Commons is not so great an evil as the other.[2]

Mr Bonar Law was directly implying that 'the opposition might be forced to resort to violent obstruction'. In a meeting with Churchill a year later he frankly stated that the Unionist Party would not hesitate to encourage the army officers to refrain from obeying orders if Home Rule was enacted.[3]

On 31 July 1913, Mr Bonar Law and Lord Lansdowne in a joint memorandum to the King elaborated the Conservative thesis and insisted that the King should dismiss Asquith if he did not advise a dissolution. By autumn 1913, staunch and eminent Conservatives, such as Sir William Anson and Professor A. Dicey were openly drawn into the dispute, a dispute which – by today's standards at least – seemed from the very beginning pointless.[4]

---

[1] Quoted by Blake, ibid. p. 150.
[2] Quoted by Nicolson, *King George V*, p. 272.
[3] In a letter to Lord Lansdowne, quoted by Blake, ibid. pp. 155–7. See also the correspondence with Dicey in Colvin's *Lord Carson*, II, ch. 16.
[4] Sir William Anson letter to *The Times*, 10 September 1913. Professor Dicey's letter was published on 15 September. Also, Lord Hugh Cecil, *The Times*, 10 September 1913.

Detailed consideration of their argumentation is, I believe, necessary, because it proves that, regardless of its value at that time, today it cannot and should not be considered as persuasive.

Mr Bonar Law's argument, quoted above, is indeed a very dangerous one. It encourages the King to participate actively in political affairs. He can disregard his Prime Minister's advice – in fact, according to Mr Bonar Law, it is his duty to do so – and follow a different policy. This different policy can be either his own or that of the Opposition. It is certainly not the majority's policy on a given problem. In this way the King ceases to be impartial, as the British Constitution has always wished him to be. He becomes a party leader, and hence ceases to be unaccountable. The maxim 'Rex nec potest peccare' obviously ceases to apply, because the King can do no wrong only if he 'reigns and does not rule' or in Bagehot's wise words, 'if he follows a well-considered inaction'.

According to Lord Esher, the King himself had always in the past reacted against the theory that he has to take decisions and not his Ministers. Lord Esher recorded[1] that the King 'is properly disturbed by a speech of Mr. Bonar Law's in which he throws the onus on H.M. of "deciding" whether the Royal Assent is to be given to the Home Rule Bill, on H.M.'s own initiative, whatever the advice of his Ministers may be'. The King rightly protested against 'this new departure in doctrine'.

Sir William Anson slightly alters Mr Bonar Law's strong phrasing. He does not say that the King has the 'duty' to try another government or hold elections. He leaves this alternative for the King to decide and if in the 'interest of the country he should decide to take a course which his Ministers disapprove of, he must either convert his Ministers to his point of view or before taking action must find other Ministers who agree with him'. This is a very careful statement, though it has a weak point which must not pass unnoticed. Why should the King's decision be better than the government's? After all, most of the vital information he needs to form an opinion he obtains through his Ministers. In fact most of his actions are decided on their advice and put into effect on their responsibility. Why should he suddenly consider the Opposition's advice preferable? With political life becoming more and more complicated and sophisticated, it is doubtful whether the King – commanding at the most a very general knowledge of the situation – should undertake such initiatives.

In his letter to *The Times*, Dicey mentioned the 1783 and the 1834 'precedents' as conclusive and added rhetorically: 'No statesman would be ashamed to follow the example of Pitt or Peel.' The 1834 'dismissal'

---

[1] Quoted by Nicolson, *King George V*, p. 270.

has been examined and was not considered as a precedent at all. The 1783 dismissal is too remote and the circumstances too different to be considered as having any bearing on the subject.

Pitt and Peel were eminent British statesmen, who undertook responsibility for the Monarch's action, *after* he had acted and in order to shield him from a hostile House of Commons and angry public opinion. They offered themselves as scapegoats in order to save the Monarchy from the disastrous effects the King's action had produced, just as any statesman would have done if he believed in the survival of the Monarchy in Great Britain. But this does not imply that they approved of the King's action politically and constitutionally, as Dicey suggests. Peel's reaction was mentioned above and he also had maintained that 'His Majesty's case was obviously a bad one.' Yet Dicey was now suggesting that the King follow this unhappy precedent and dismiss his Ministers on the advice and responsibility of the Opposition.

It is universally accepted today, that precedents before 1832 'must be used in rare cases only, for the Reform Act of 1832, altered the fundamental assumption of the Constitution'.[1] Furthermore a well-known political scientist has argued that 'the principles underlying contemporary politics only really began to operate after the second Reform Act of 1867 had had its effects'.[2]

The principle that the Crown must never enter into direct conflict with the majority of the people was strongly advocated by a leading article in *The Times*.[3] The Conservative proposition was dismissed as 'originating in irresponsible quarters and betraying its amateur origin in a complete ignorance of our legal and constitutional usage'; 'A dissolution of Parliament as an exercise of the Royal Prerogative proprio motu Regis, might be followed by a vindication at the polls of the very Ministers whose advice has been laid aside.'

Asquith's memorandum was the last to reach the King; in a letter drafted in his own handwriting and handed to the Prime Minister on 11 August 1913 he had asked Mr Asquith for his advice. In it the King noted among other things that, 'Whatever I do I shall offend half the population.' The Prime Minister's memorandum (September 1913) was one of the most successful documents he ever drafted and in Professor Wilson's words contained 'the orthodox view of the position of a constitutional Monarch in the twentieth century'.[4]

---

[1] Jennings, *Cabinet government*, pp. 7–8; Marshall & Moodie, *Some problems of the constitution*, p. 37.
[2] Mackintosh, *The British Cabinet*, p. 19.
[3] 8 September 1913.   [4] *Cases and materials*, p. 28.

After admitting that the

Sovereign undoubtedly has the power of changing his advisers but it is relevant to point out that there has been during the last 130 years, one occasion only on which the King has dismissed the Ministry which still possessed the confidence of the House of Commons, [he continues:] Nothing can be more important, in the best interest of the Crown and the Country, than that a practice, so long established and so well justified by experience, should remain unimpaired. It frees the occupant of the Throne from all personal responsibility for the acts of the executive and the legislature. It gives force and meaning to the old maxim that 'the King can do no wrong'. So long as it prevails, however objectionable particular Acts may be to a large section of his subjects, they cannot hold him in any way accountable. If, on the other hand, the King were to intervene on one side, or in one case – which he could only do by dismissing Ministers in de facto possession of a Parliamentary majority – he would be expected to do the same on another occasion, and perhaps for the other side. Every Act of Parliament of the first order of importance, and only passed after acute controversy would be regarded as bearing the personal imprimatur of the Sovereign. He would, whether he wished it or not, be dragged into the arena of party politics; and at a dissolution following such a dismissal of Ministers as has been referred to, it is no exaggeration to say that the Crown would become the football of contending factions. This is a constitutional catastrophe which it is the duty of every wise statesman to do the utmost in his power to avert.[1]

In an impressive answer to his Prime Minister, the King, among other things, wrote 'I am most grateful to you for your very clear and well reasoned memorandum' (22 September 1913). There is no reason to tire the reader with all the details of the Home Rule Bill. The King finally decided not to oppose his Prime Minister and in a letter (31 July 1914) which, however, was never despatched in view of the imminence of war, stated that, 'the extreme course should not be adopted in this case unless there is convincing evidence that it could avert a national disaster or at least have a tranquillising effect on the distracting conditions of the time. There is no such evidence.'[2] As Mr J. A. Spender noted, the King possessed an excellent gift for ignoring bad advice,[3] and proved this by refusing to adopt Mr Bonar Law's views.

The Conservative thesis, according to which the King could dismiss the Liberal Government if Mr Asquith refused to advise a dissolution is, as previously stated, constitutionally questionable. Even if the King possessed and still possesses today from a purely legal point of view the right to dismiss his Minister, it is politically unwise to exercise it. To revive a right which has been dormant for about a hundred years and

---

[1] Spender & Asquith, *Life of Lord Oxford and Asquith*, II, 29–31.
[2] Quoted by Nicolson, *King George V*, p. 313.
[3] Nicolson, ibid. p. 270.

which had only been successfully exercised before the 1832 Reform Act and against an entirely different background, would be extremely dangerous.

It is extremely fortunate that the United Kingdom had at that time a sagacious Monarch, who, faced with two major political crises in the first years of his reign, was able to demonstrate successfully that he realised that the constitutional position of the Monarch in the twentieth century had changed.

The 1913 constitutional crisis has been discussed up to this point in relation with royal power to dismiss a Ministry. As stated, however, the Conservatives originally held the view that the King could refuse his assent to the Home Rule Bill. It was subsequently decided to insist that the King should dismiss the Liberal Government if it refused to advise dissolution and allow the electorate to decide on the Bill. Clearly, what the Conservatives were asking the King to do was to force dissolution on a reluctant Liberal Party. The political crisis was thus further complicated by the confusion of different constitutional issues.

The King's right to dismiss his Ministers has been examined above. The so-called forced or penal dissolution,[1] closely linked to the dismissal of a Ministry still remains to be briefly discussed.

Mr George Cave, in a letter to *The Times*,[2] was willing to admit that the Crown had an independent right to dissolve in order to ascertain whether the House really represented the opinion of the electorate. Professor Keith was also among those who were willing to grant that the Crown had the right to force a dissolution, if necessary by dismissing a Ministry. 'The right', according to Keith, 'exists for wise employment in grave circumstances.' This, for example, could happen if it was 'necessary in the public interest' or, 'necessary for giving the will of the people its just course' or, if the necessity arose from some 'vital' and 'irreparable decision on foreign policy' or 'serious . . . domestic strife'.[3]

Keith's doctrine, mainly through the vagueness of its terms, is so dangerous, that it can be easily dismissed. Keith himself had pointed out the weaknesses of his theory in one of his earlier works. In 1916 he wrote

---

[1] Forsey, *Dissolution of parliament*, p. 80, considers as a penal dissolution, an appeal to the electorate by a defeated Government. In this sense dissolution is the counterbalance of Ministerial responsibility. In the text, however, the term is used as a synonym to a Royal or forced dissolution and a variant upon the dismissal of Ministers. See Laski, *Parliamentary government*, p. 412.   [2] 6 September 1913.

[3] *The King and the Imperial Crown. The powers and duties of His Majesty* (1936), pp. 140, 178; Anson, *Law and custom of the constitution*, I, 309. Also Dicey, *The law of the constitution*, p. 433. But, as Dr Forsey, *Dissolution of parliament*, p. 128, observes, 'It can never be equally clear that a Cabinet which, ex hypothesi, has a majority in the assembly, has no, or insufficient, popular backing.'

'it is, and must always be, a matter of the most grave difficulty to decide whether the people really approve or not the existing government, and it is not desirable that the Crown should be involved in action which must rest on doubtful calculation, and which in any case at once submits the person of the Sovereign to the bitterness of political discussion'. He further admits that if Asquith's advice had not been accepted, 'the position of the Sovereign would have been gravely affected'.[1] Keith's doctrine thus imposes a heavy burden upon the Monarch, or 'whatever informal advisers he chose to rely on ... since his formal advisers, the Cabinet of the moment, would ex hypothesi be unavailable'.[2] In Laski's words it 'places upon the King the grave onus of deciding what "critical circumstances" are; and this raises the problem, once more, of whether he is to rely upon his own judgement or to take counsel other than that of his official advisers. The latter course is patently unconstitutional.'[3] Nor can the electorate with its subsequent verdict provide the answer. If the party with which the King associated himself is defeated, his position is precarious. If, on the other hand, it is victorious, then a dangerous precedent – open to wide interpretation – becomes established, i.e. that the King may compel a dissolution whenever he thinks fit.

Forsey, Evatt, Laski, Wilson, Keith, Morgan and Jennings[4] all agree that a forced dissolution would have resulted in a dismissal of the Liberal Government in 1913 which would have been extremely dangerous to the Crown.

Professor Morgan's letter to *The Times* stressed the fact that a forced dissolution would inevitably be considered as equivalent to a dismissal and lead to a direct confrontation between the Monarch and his people. He concluded that: 'The right of dissolution, regarded as a ministerial right, owes its existence to a general recognition of the Sovereign's immunity for responsibility for its exercise.'[5]

The King thus needs advice – and advice in this sense can only come from his Government.

[1] *Imperial unity and the Dominions* (1916), pp. 87–8.

[2] Forsey, *Dissolution of Parliament*, pp. 97ff., 121–3 and n. 1; Keith, ibid. p. 86.

[3] *Parliamentary government*, p. 413. Professor Anson, in his letter to *The Times*, 10 September 1913, directly stated the opposite. Forsey, *Dissolution of Parliament*, p. 82, takes the opposite view: 'Advice unconstitutionally sought from and unconstitutionally tendered by the Leader of the Opposition, is not a very reliable source of constitutional wisdom.' See also E. Campbell, 'The prerogative power of dissolution', *Public Law* (1961), pp. 174–6, 178–9.

[4] Forsey, *Dissolution of Parliament*, p. 123; H. V. Evatt, *The King and his Dominion Governors* (1936), p. 101; Laski, *Parliamentary government*, pp. 412ff.; Wilson, *Cases and materials*, p. 28; Keith, *Imperial unity*, p. 88; Morgan, *The Times*, 10 September 1913; Jennings, *Cabinet government*, p. 416. Contra Dicey and Anson in their letters to *The Times*. Professor de Smith (*Constitutional and administrative law* (1971), p. 61), describes Dicey's and Anson's views in 1913 as 'manifestly unacceptable'.

[5] See also Lord Salisbury's similar views, in *Letters of Queen Victoria*, 3rd series, I, 129–30.

Chapter 5

THE RIGHT TO ADVISE A DISSOLUTION

A: WHO ADVISES DISSOLUTION

The first question one usually asks is, who advises dissolution and this inevitably leads to a second question, is the advice binding upon the Monarch? The first question will be answered in section A of this chapter, while the second will be dealt with in section B.

Mr Asquith writes in his *Fifty years of Parliament*,[1] that 'such a question as the Dissolution of Parliament is always submitted to the Cabinet for ultimate decision'. His statement is correct if applied to all dissolutions up to 1910 inclusive: it is strange, however, that Mr Asquith is so categorical. At the time his book was published (1926) two dissolutions at least (1918, 1923) out of a total of four (1918, 1922, 1923, 1924) since 1910 had manifestly been the Prime Minister's decision.

But to return to Mr Asquith's statement, between the years 1841 and 1910 inclusive, the Cabinet was asked for its opinion and ultimately decided on dissolution. But there were colourful, though admittedly rare, exceptions caused by the personality of the Prime Minister in office. And in these cases the final outcome was the decision of one man: the Prime Minister.

Lord Morley, for example, gives a description of the 1886 dissolution that illustrates the point. 'When Ministers went into the cabinet . . . three of them inclined pretty strongly towards resignation . . . Mr. Gladstone, however, . . . at once opened the case with a list of twelve reasons for recommending dissolution . . . His conclusion was accepted without comment.'[2]

In some cases, however, the discussion was more heated and in 1880 it took Lord Beaconsfield's Cabinet two and a half hours to agree on dissolution.[3] Similarly, in 1895 the Cabinet was deeply divided over dissolution and only in the end did Lord Rosebery's and Sir William Harcourt's opinion in favour of resignation prevail.[4] On the other hand Gladstone wrote in the last year of his life that: 'When I proposed the

[1] II, 194.
[2] Morley, *The life of William Ewart Gladstone* (1903), III, 341. See also below, chapter 6.
[3] Monypenny & Buckle, *Disraeli*, VI, 514.
[4] Asquith, *Fifty years of Parliament*, I, 232.

dissolution to the cabinet (in 1874), they acceded to it without opposition, or, I think, even discussion.'[1] But by far the most striking example is Disraeli's 1868 *coup de tête*.

In spring 1868, Gladstone's 'Disestablishment of the Irish Church' Bill was causing Disraeli considerable agitation. Anticipating a Government defeat he wrote to the Queen on 20 April:[2]

Assuming that the first Resolution of Mr. Gladstone, affirming the policy of 'disestablishing' the Church in Ireland, is carried, he would announce that the division has changed the relations which previously existed between the House and the Ministry; that they must consequently consider their position; and then he would move the adjournment of the House ... That, under these circumstances, in the spirit of the Constitution, they were justified in advising your Majesty to appeal to your Majesty's people at the most convenient time, and that your Majesty had been graciously pleased to sanction such a course. Then, it will be, to feel the opinion of the House of Commons, what is that most convenient time, and Mr. Disraeli does not doubt that he can lead the House to adopt the just and truly sensible view of affairs; namely that the appeal to the people should be to the popular voice as represented and registered in the new Constituency. If this view be adopted the rest of the Session will probably be without anxiety. With your Majesty's approbation, Mr. Disraeli would suggest that after the division ... he should communicate the result to your Majesty, and offer the advice (with the previous sanction of the Cabinet) which he has already expressed.

Disraeli seemed to be in a surprisingly democratic mood. He was intending to consult the Cabinet and was even willing to discuss details with the House. However, things did not happen that way.

The Queen disagreed with the recommended procedure. She wrote:[3]

She would, however, press upon Mr. Disraeli the importance of his not feeling as he expresses it, 'for the opinion of the House' as to the proper time for appealing to the country; but that the Government should consider this for themselves, and announce the decision which they may think it right to submit to the Queen, in a manner that shall show no hesitation or doubt as to the policy they mean to pursue.

To this Mr Disraeli answered: 'Your Majesty's wise intimation shall be followed. It is the right course.'[4]

So Disraeli met the Cabinet on 22 April but obtained only a 'general sanction' 'to a policy of dissolution'.[5] He realised that his colleagues were unhappy with the intended course so he wrote another letter to the Queen two days later (24 April).[6] In it he stated: 'Mr. Disraeli would humbly suggest to your Majesty, in the contemplated event of the politi-

[1] Morley, *Gladstone*, II, 483, 486.   [2] *Letters of Queen Victoria*, 2nd series, I, 523ff.
[3] Monypenny & Buckle, *Disraeli*, V, ch. 1.   [4] *Letters of Queen Victoria*, 2nd series, I, 524.
[5] Monypenny & Buckle, *Disraeli*, V, 28.   [6] *Letters of Queen Victoria*, 2nd series, I, 526.

cal crisis which he foresees, that it would, on the whole, be expedient that he should take your Majesty's pleasure personally.' By now, Disraeli was clearly preparing the ground to take his personal initiative and that is precisely what happened. Following the Government's defeat, he visited the Queen at Osborne on 1 May and advised a dissolution without calling a Cabinet and relying on his colleagues' general assent given ten days ago. This is how Monypenny and Buckle described what followed:[1]

This somewhat high-handed departure from precedent was naturally resented. 'Disraeli has communicated with none of us, which is strange', wrote Hardy mildly in his diary. Malmesbury, more roundly, noted: 'The Ministers are very angry with Disraeli for going to the Queen without calling a Cabinet ...'. It is evident from the entries in Hardy's diary, and especially one on 6 May ('A Cabinet before Osborne would have altered everything, but now?'), that Disraeli avoided a preliminary Cabinet because he had good reason to fear that his colleagues would weaken in their resolution now that the moment for action had arrived, but might be trusted to accept a fait accompli.

The real change in procedure came with the First World War. In 1916, after Mr Asquith resigned under pressure from within his Government, the King, in accordance with constitutional precedent, decided to send for the Leader of the Opposition, Mr Bonar Law. Foreseeing that Mr Bonar Law would make his acceptance of office conditional upon the dissolution of Parliament, the King sought the expert advice of Lord Haldane. In his answer, Lord Haldane was the first to depart from the established practice. In it he stated that: 'the only Minister who can properly give advice as to a dissolution of Parliament is the Prime Minister ... the Sovereign cannot entertain any bargain for a dissolution merely with a possible Prime Minister before the latter is fully installed.'[2]

Lord Haldane must undoubtedly have taken into full consideration the increasing importance of the office of the Prime Minister during the War. There was adequate evidence that the Prime Minister's prestige was growing among his colleagues. Asquith's adroit handling of both the Parliament Act and the Home Rule Bill between 1910 and 1914, admittedly with the support of his senior colleagues, provided further evidence of this. When, in the spring of 1915, Mr Bonar Law began to complain of the conduct of the war, Asquith finally agreed to a coalition 'at once and without consulting any of his colleagues'.[3]

The war emphasised the special position of the Prime Minister, which was clearly above the rest of the Cabinet. Prompt and firm action was

[1] Monypenny & Buckle, *Disraeli*, v, 33.
[2] Nicolson, *King George V*, p. 379. For a rather similar case in Greece see below, chapter 9.
[3] Mackintosh, *The British Cabinet*, p. 365; Blake, *The unknown Prime Minister*, p. 246.

required, combined with the ability to exercise plenary authority over a series of policy-making bodies in the Government.[1] By the late summer of 1915, it was abundantly clear – and the inefficiencies of the Gallipoli campaign had strengthened this view – that the Prime Minister was incapable of exercising this plenary authority and effective control. His 'inability to fill the vacuum at the top led to a dispersion of power'[2] and finally to his own downfall.

Lloyd George's dynamic and indefatigable direction of the War – in collaboration with Mr Bonar Law – confirms the above. Hence it is easily understood why the 1918 dissolution openly breached tradition by originating from the Prime Minister himself. According to Professor Mackintosh, in 1918, 'there was no question of consulting the body of the Cabinet',[3] and Mr Bonar Law was clearly inclined to leave it to the Prime Minister to decide. His conciliating and moderate attitude during the Hayes Fisher incident[4] clearly demonstrates that he was willing to acknowledge the Prime Minister's superiority, even if this meant that Mr Lloyd George could dismiss from the Government a Conservative Minister. Yet Mr Bonar Law was only technically speaking subordinate to Mr Lloyd George and his party was the stronger of the two in the coalition.

Jennings states[5] that 'no dissolution since 1918 has been brought before the Cabinet, and all Prime Ministers since Mr Lloyd George have assumed a right to give the advice'. Only the second part of the statement is true. When Sir Ivor wrote the above the Cabinet Papers had not been disclosed, hence the error of statement. A chronological discussion of the dissolutions since 1918 is perhaps necessary.

(a) As far as I know, there is no evidence that the Cabinet discussed that 1922 dissolution. Jennings quotes and disagrees with Lord Blake[6] who mentions that the Cabinet decided on dissolution on 16 September 1922. But the Cabinet meeting which Blake mentions took place while Mr Lloyd George was still in office and was relevant to Mr Lloyd George's possible dissolution and not to Mr Bonar Law's 1922 dissolution.

---

[1] These were: (*a*) The War Council (November 1914–March 1915), (*b*) The Dardanelles Committee (January–October 1915) and (*c*) The War Committee (November 1915–November 1916).   [2] Mackintosh, *The British Cabinet*, p. 361.

[3] Ibid. p. 382. In the Commons Mr Bonar Law stated: 'In my belief there is no custom more clearly defined than that what advice on this matter should be given to the Sovereign is a question not for the Cabinet but for the Prime Minister', *Parliamentary Debates*, 5th series, CX, 2425. This was also Mr Balfour's opinion who stated that: 'the responsibility of a dissolution must rest with the Prime Minister'. Blake, *The unknown Prime Minister*, p. 385.

[4] For further details see Blake, ibid. pp. 381ff.

[5] *Cabinet government*, p. 419. Less categorically, Keith, *The British cabinet system*, p. 304.

[6] *Cabinet government*, p. 419, n. 3; Blake, *The unknown Prime Minister*, p. 450.

Events seem to have taken place as follows. In 1922, Mr Lloyd George faced serious problems with his Coalition Government and the Chanak crisis in September caused the final rupture. On 13 October he warned the King that he might ask for a dissolution, and apparently the Cabinet agreed, though the discussion as far as I know was not officially recorded. In any event Lloyd George, Lord Birkenhead, Austen Chamberlain, Lord Curzon and Lord Balfour had agreed to go to the country 'at the first moment the Turkish crisis would allow'.[1] On 19 October the Conservatives held their famous Carlton Club meeting and decided to stand in the ensuing elections as an independent party. At 5.0 p.m. the same day Mr Lloyd George tendered his resignation, without advising dissolution. Mr Bonar Law was sworn in as his successor and dissolved Parliament.

(b) The 1923 dissolution was clearly constitutional and was based solely on Mr Baldwin's decision to take his protectionist policies to the country. Yet his colleagues were not unanimous on this decision. Volume 35 of Baldwin's private papers, now in the Cambridge University Library, consists to a great extent of colleagues' letters strongly objecting to a possible dissolution. On 8 November 1923 Mr Wood addressed a letter to the Prime Minister embodying the conclusions of Salisbury, Devonshire, Robert Cecil, Lord Novar and Wood himself against December elections. But the Prime Minister, according to one of his biographers, had made up his mind, and his protectionist policies were not the only reason. 'Whether [the Conservatives] won or lost was insignificant. The only thing that could bring together the Conservatives was a general election.'[2]

Though dissolution had been in the air for some time, Baldwin's decision took most of his colleagues somewhat by surprise. For example Robert Cecil wrote to the Prime Minister on 29 October:[4] 'If the dissolution is to be early next year I shall have to let my constituents know as soon as possible where I stand, and so I am anxious to find out. I see great difficulty in going round the Herts. villages advocating a policy [protectionism] in which I have little confidence.' One cannot help but sympathise with Robert Cecil's anxiety, which was shared by many of his colleagues, who still hoped to persuade the Prime Minister in a letter

---

[1] Sir Charles Petrie, *The life and letters of the Right Hon. Sir Austen Chamberlain* (1940), II, 198; Beaverbrook, *The decline and fall of Lloyd George* (1966), p. 184. Dissolution was discussed on and off from late 1921 but Lloyd George could not make up his mind. Beaverbrook, ibid. ch. 7.

[2] Young, *Baldwin*, p. 66. The reasons for the dissolution are discussed more fully in chapter 6 below.

[3] Baldwin Papers, vol. 35.

dated 7 November that 'no one wants a general election'.[1] But Baldwin had made up his mind[2] and on 13 November

the Prime Minister informed his colleagues that the march of events had compelled him to decide to recommend to the King the immediate dissolution of Parliament. Since his statement at Plymouth on the economic policy of the Government, it had become inevitable . . . that the election should take place within the minimum of delay . . . After some discussion it was suggested that . . . the Prime Minister would advise the King to dissolve as soon as possible.[3]

Curzon's reaction was extremely violent but there was nothing he could do. The letter he wrote to his wife on 13 November is extremely illuminating:[4]

I sent you off a telegram by Marconi to tell you that thing you most feared is to happen, and that there is to be an immediate Dissolution of Parlt., with a General Election on December 6 . . .

In an earlier letter[5] I told you how at the Cabinet last week the great majority led by me were entirely opposed to a snap election . . . he [Baldwin] opened the Cabinet this morning by telling us in a sentence that the King had agreed to an immediate dissolution . . . I think the Cabinet was profoundly shocked and incensed at the way in which they have been treated, and at the recklessness with which the govt. and the country, entirely contrary to the will and wish of either, have been plunged into a General Election by the arbitrary fiat of one weak and ignorant man . . . Derby is furious, and says Europe is dominated by madmen . . . Poincaré and Mussolini – and England is ruled by a damned idiot [Baldwin] . . .

Of course if we win by the same or an enhanced majority, he will be justified . . . But if . . . we only get a reduced majority, or possibly no majority at all . . . I think he will then be deposed from the leadership of the Party.

But even Curzon admitted that dissolution was the 'prerogative of the P.M.'. Elections were fixed for 16 November 1923.

(c) In October 1924, the MacDonald Government was obliged to advise a dissolution because of the Campbell case. At the end of September the Conservatives put down a vote of censure. Asquith, in an attempt to keep a balance between Conservatives and Labour and eventually prepare the

---

[1] Baldwin Papers, ibid.
[2] Apparently in this he was encouraged by L. S. Amery who forwarded to him a letter from Garvin quoting Cromwell and encouraging an early dissolution. Baldwin Papers, ibid.; K. Middlemas & J. Barnes, *Baldwin* (1969), p. 239, attribute the letter to Garvin. I was unable to find such a letter in the Baldwin papers and unless it is elsewhere it seems that it was Amery who informed him.
[3] P.R.O. CAB 24/46, 54 (23) 1.
[4] Lady Curzon, *Reminiscences* (1955), pp. 186–7.
[5] On 5 and 9 November. Lady Curzon, ibid. pp. 182, 184.

way for a Liberal Government, tried to compromise by proposing a select committee. On 6 October 1924, the Cabinet agreed 'that, if either the Conservatives vote of censure or the Liberal amendment should be carried, the Prime Minister should advise the King to dissolve Parliament'.[1] On 8 October the Government was defeated in the House and the Cabinet agreed that the Prime Minister should see the King in the morning.[2] On 9 October, the Prime Minister informed his colleagues that the King had granted his request. (The 1924 dissolution is discussed again later.)

(*d*) In 1929 Mr Baldwin was careful to avoid a direct confrontation with his colleagues on the time of dissolution. The Cabinet discussed the forthcoming dissolution as early as October 1928 and particularly the political advantages of having an election at dates falling between May and October 1929. On 1 October 1928 the Cabinet agreed that:

(*a*) the Parliamentary Secretary to the Treasury should circulate to the Cabinet his views on the most advantageous period between May and October 1929, inclusive for holding the general election. (*b*) That the Prime Minister should obtain the views of the Unionist central office on the same question. (*c*) That the Chancellor of the Exchequer should circulate the views of the Treasury on the consequences of delaying the Budget pending the holding of a general election early in the summer.[3]

The next day, 2 October, Sir Samuel Hoare wrote to the Prime Minister maintaining that an early decision on the election date should be taken. He considered the decisions the Cabinet had reached were rather vague and insisted that: 'We ought to decide between May and October, before or in the early days of the session, lay our plans accordingly and give our own people and the world the feeling that we have ourselves decided upon the date and that we have not been driven into a decision by the slow progress of Parliamentary business.'[4] On 10 October 1928, 'the Cabinet agreed that the Prime Minister should circulate to the Cabinet a memorandum giving the political reasons for and against the holding of the general elections in June and in October respectively',[5] and on 12 October 1928 the Conservative and Unionist Central Office sent a secret memorandum to the Prime Minister saying that: 'It would be to the advantage of the Conservative Party that the elections should be held as early as possible'[6] and giving seven reasons for this. In accordance with the above the elections were held on 31 May 1929.

(*e*) The 1931 dissolution (7 October) was proposed to the Cabinet by the Prime Minister, according to A. J. P. Taylor 'perhaps for fear that

---

[1] P.R.O. CAB 23/48 (52 (24) 1*a*).   [2] P.R.O. CAB 23/48 54 (24).
[3] P.R.O. CAB 23/58 (45 (28) 1).   [4] Baldwin Papers, vol. 36.
[5] P.R.O. CAB 23/59 (46 (28) 1).   [6] Baldwin Papers, vol. 36.

the compromise between the parties might break down'.[1] According to Mr MacDonald, three possibilities were offered to the National Government: to break up, to continue without a general election and to take the necessary measures for the stabilisation of sterling or 'to go to the country on the general policy on which the Cabinet were unanimous'. After dismissing the first two possibilities for various reasons the Cabinet agreed 'that the Prime Minister should recommend the King to prorogue and dissolve Parliament on Wednesday October 7th' and concluded by congratulating the Prime Minister 'on the successful issue of his unremitting efforts to obtain unanimity'.[2]

(*f*) In 1935, Mr Baldwin personally took the decision to dissolve Parliament, though there does not seem to have been any serious opposition except for Mr Malcolm MacDonald who objected to a November dissolution because it might give the impression that Baldwin was exploiting the international crisis for party reasons. The Cabinet met frequently during this period and it is likely that it discussed the issue, though, as far as I know, there is no evidence that dissolution was included in the official agenda.

(*g*) In 1945, as far as I know, there is no evidence that Mr Churchill officially consulted his Cabinet on dissolution; it is more probable that he did not. There is little doubt, however, that he had communicated his intention to senior colleagues of his. Thus, he himself writes that at a meeting of the principal Conservative Ministers he actually 'took the unusual course of asking everyone to write his opinion on a slip of paper. All but two were for June'.[3] Churchill could not have felt himself bound in the least by such a decision since he writes that: 'the right to recommend a dissolution to the Crown rests solely with the Prime Minister'.[4] Personally he hoped – and did all he could – to prolong the life of the National Government up to the Japanese surrender. But having failed to obtain Mr Attlee's agreement to carry on, he was finally obliged to resign on 23 May. He was subsequently recommissioned by the King as Leader of the Conservative Party to form a Conservative administration, which he did. He dissolved Parliament – with Mr Eden's encouragement – on 15 June and lost the elections.

(*h*) There is little evidence as to whether Mr Attlee officially consulted his Cabinet in 1949–50. There was, however, some discussion whether the elections should be delayed for a while so as to allow the effects of devaluation to become apparent. But this view was not shared by Cripps, who opposed the idea of having the Budget first. Attlee later denied that

---

[1] *English history 1914–1945* (1965), p. 324.   [2] P.R.O. CAB 23/68 (70 (31) 1).
[3] Churchill, *The Second World War*, VI, 511.   [4] Ibid.

Labour could have won a working majority if he had agreed to postpone the elections. In any event, Parliament was nearing its end and the Prime Minister finally decided to advise a dissolution.[1] Dissolution was granted by the King on 7 January and publicly announced three days later.

(*i*) The 1951 election was more controversial and was finally decided by the Prime Minister. Hugh Dalton notes in his unpublished diary that the 'P.M. announced intention to dissolve, I warmly welcome, and none present oppose'. But Herbert Morrison (and Shinwell) who were in Washington for a meeting of NATO were 'furiously against' the idea.[2] Morrison wished to carry on until the end of the Korean War, which in his view was imminent.[3] This would provide the Labour Government with certain political advantages. But as Dalton, in an earlier entry in his diary commented, 'the P.M. had already made up his mind on the subject'.[4] That it was Attlee's decision to dissolve is also confirmed by Mr Gordon Walker. He writes:

I had some foreknowledge of Attlee's decision to dissolve in 1951. He told me of his intention because I was due to go to a conference at Victoria Falls and he wished me to give prior warning to Sir Godfrey Huggins, Prime Minister of Southern Rhodesia, that the announcement of an election would come in the middle of the conference. I begged Attlee to reconsider his decision to dissolve, but he laconically replied that he had made up his mind.

There is very little information available concerning the more recent dissolutions. Even though it is likely that the Prime Minister of the day would consult some of his senior and closer colleagues, it is very unlikely that any of the recent Prime Ministers would have felt bound to do so. Mr Gordon Walker maintains that the 1966 dissolution was entirely Mr Wilson's decision and he did not even mention it to any of his colleagues.[5] In 1970, however, it seems that the Prime Minister consulted some of his senior colleagues[6] and party officials. On 18 May, Mr Wilson

[1] F. Williams, *A Prime Minister remembers* (1961), pp. 227–9; Gordon Walker, *The Cabinet*, pp. 84, 134; Sir Eric Fletcher, *The Times*, 7 May, and answer from Lord Shawcross, *The Times*, 8 May 1969.

[2] Dalton Papers (Diary), 19 September 1951; Gordon Walker, ibid. p. 85, denies that the Cabinet was consulted. But Dalton's views seem more authoritative.

[3] Hugh Dalton, *High tide and after. Memoirs 1945–1960*, p. 377. The Korean War ended in July 1953 and it is doubtful whether the Labour Government could have lasted that long.

[4] Dalton Papers, 4 September 1951.

[5] Mr Wilson, however, maintains that he informed both Mr (now Lord) George Brown and Mr J. Callaghan of his decision to hold a March election. *The Labour Government, 1964–1970* (1971), p. 201.

[6] Almost all of whom favoured a June election; '. . . after the borough elections the following week, the waverers were to express the same view'. H. Wilson, ibid. p. 780.

was interviewed by the B.B.C. and said that he had consulted a number of his colleagues and particularly the Chancellor of the Exchequer.

(*j*) During Mr Wilson's second Premiership (1966–70) the threat to dissolve was used several times and in accordance with established practice, yet not without discontent. Dissolution was thus reviewed once again, from many angles. Here, we shall focus our attention on one aspect, namely who advises dissolution.

In May 1969 the relations between the Government and the T.U.C. were extremely strained because of the imminence of Labour legislation on industrial relations. Mr Wilson and Mrs Castle seemed to have the bulk of the party and the public on their side, but the unions were determined to resist the Bill and they had the useful support of a minority of left-wing Labour back-benchers. In addition, Mr Callaghan openly encouraged them to resist the Government, thus disagreeing with his Cabinet colleagues and openly violating the principle of collective ministerial responsibility.

By early May the situation had become critical and *The Times* was speaking of an 'imminent attempt to replace Mr. Wilson'.[1] The *Guardian*[2] gave the impression that this was not carried out because of the lack of agreement on a candidate to succeed him. Ministers loyal to Mr Wilson were immediately recruited to give their support to their leader and thus Mr Crossman, Mr Greenwood, Mrs Hart and others were drawn into the battle. At Birmingham Mr Crossman assured his audience that the whole Cabinet shared Mr Wilson's determination to enact the necessary legislation.[3] The Government also had recourse to the 'big stick', dissolution, and Mr Mellish, the Government Chief Whip, told M.P.s in no uncertain terms that if the Government was defeated in the House it would feel compelled to go to the country.

On 6 May, Mr R. T. Paget, Q.C., Labour M.P. for Northampton, wrote to *The Times* and maintained that the Prime Minister must have 'the consent of the Cabinet' in order to dissolve.

In a letter to *The Times* of 7 May, Sir Eric Fletcher, Labour M.P. for Islington North, opposed Mr Paget's views, and insisted that the Prime Minister 'alone – without consultation with the Cabinet – is entitled to ask the Crown for a dissolution'. He was refuted the next day (8 May) by Lord Shawcross, in a letter to *The Times*.

On 9 May Mr Paget returned to the subject and elaborated his views. He maintained that 'nobody disputes that a Prime Minister may ask the

---

[1] 2 May.   [2] 2 May.
[3] *The Times*, 3 May. The Bill was finally dropped after a face-saving compromise was reached in June.

Queen for a dissolution at any time' but concluded that 'the Cabinet, whether or not they all agree with the request, must not take this disagreement to the point of resignation, or if some do resign, that they can be replaced'.[1]

The correspondents of the time seem to confuse two distinct issues. The first is whether the Prime Minister has the right and indeed the obligation to consult the Cabinet and his senior colleagues before dissolving. The second is who finally takes the decision for a dissolution.

That the Prime Minister will usually discuss a possible dissolution with some of his senior and closer colleagues is an historically proven fact, though he is under no constitutional obligation to do this. *A fortiori* he is not obliged to bring this before the Cabinet for an official decision.[2] But it is also equally certain – and the preceding analysis has shown this in some detail – that it is the Prime Minister who finally takes the decision and the responsibility to advise dissolution, even if most prominent members of his administration strongly disagree with him.

Mr Paget derives the Prime Minister's obligation to consult the Cabinet from the fact that the Government has to be continued and if the Cabinet disagrees, resigns and cannot be replaced, the country will remain without an administration. His hypothesis is purely theoretical and without a precedent either in England or, as far as I know, in any other European country. In any event such a contingency would mean that the Prime Minister would be deposed as party leader, in which case the Queen would be faced with a different situation and hence would apply different criteria to reach a decision.

In Mr Paget's view the Queen[3] 'must ... be satisfied that the Prime Minister asking for a dissolution, can govern, until a new Parliament is elected ...'. What Mr Paget does not specify is what criteria the Queen would apply in order to decide whether the Prime Minister was capable of carrying on if the party still acknowledges him as its leader, as it did when Mr Paget wrote the letter. As Professor King writes:[4] 'She could hardly deny him a dissolution on the mere supposition that a majority of his supporters had turned against him.' Nor could the Crown postpone its decision to grant a dissolution until the party reached a formal decision. This would amount to an open intervention in party politics. Under

---

[1] See below, Appendix 4 where these letters are given in full.

[2] 'A decision on election-timing is a lonely one. Whatever the consultations, it is *one man's decision* [italics mine] and if things go wrong he is as likely to be criticised for missing a favourable tide as for plunging in too early.' H. Wilson, *The Labour Government, 1964–1970*, p. 201.   [3] *The Times*, 8 May.

[4] *The Times*, 10 May. See also Q. Hogg's (now Lord Hailsham) views in his article in the *Sunday Express* of 4 May 1969.

such circumstances, Professor Max Beloff's opinion,[1] that 'the old view that the right to a dissolution is automatic may be simple; it is also the only one that meets the case', is the correct one.

However, the idea that a Cabinet should advise a dissolution was not abandoned. On 15 April *The Times* defended this view in a leading article. It suggested that under certain circumstances the Monarch would be justified in departing from the established tradition and refusing a dissolution to his Prime Minister. It added:

if a Prime Minister, defeated in Cabinet, unable to carry his policy in the party meeting, were to ask for a dissolution for the apparent purpose of unnecessarily involving his party in his own downfall, the Queen would have ample grounds for refusing him and dismissing him provided an alternative leader of the majority party was in sight. Perhaps the best solution if a Prime Minister ever asks for a dubious dissolution is for the Queen to follow the nineteenth century practice of granting dissolution to a Cabinet rather than an individual.[2]

Was *The Times* concerned with the future of the Labour Party which was drawn to its doom through the 'follies' of its Leader or was it concerned with an untimely election? If the first is true, with what right can the Monarch intervene in party affairs? If the second supposition is true is it not evident by now that the party – through its leader – determines the time of the elections at the most suitable (to the party) period and regardless of the existence of a major political issue?

Furthermore, the terminology of *The Times* is vague and can lead to misunderstandings. What does 'defeated in Cabinet' mean?[3] That the majority of the Cabinet Ministers is against their Leader? And what if the minority consists of the most prominent members of the party? If on the other hand a few but prominent Cabinet Ministers disagree, but the majority is faithful to their Leader, can one that say the Prime Minister is defeated in the Cabinet? If, lastly, the Cabinet agrees with the Prime Minister, but the rank and file of the party opposes his measures or vice versa, what can the Monarch do? All these are questions that may arise if one attempts to apply the criteria *The Times* suggest. *The Times* also

[1] *The Times*, 13 May.

[2] See also *The Times*, 18 February 1972. This argument (i.e. that the Prime Minister cannot advise dissolution against the wishes of his own Cabinet) was one of the strongest put forward in South Africa in 1939 in support of the Governor's refusal to accept his Prime Minister's advice to dissolve. It must be remembered, however, that in 1939 General Hertzog had been defeated in Parliament (which was not the case in 1969 with Mr Wilson) and that the majority of his party (and indeed of Parliament) was prepared to support an alternative administration.

[3] In 1939 General Hertzog enjoyed the support of less than half the Cabinet and a minority of his party. More important, his chief opponent (General Smuts) was clearly in a position to form an alternative Government.

suggests that the Prime Minister can be dismissed 'provided an alternative leader of the majority party was in sight'. Every party has its own ways and its own procedure to oblige its leaders to resign, but it may be added that the last time this happened was with Mr N. Chamberlain. If the party obliges its leader to resign, the hypothetical question of *The Times* does not exist; if not, the Monarch cannot do so. It is extremely dangerous to transform the Monarch into some sort of party overlord with an initiative in critical situations such as this one. If the Monarch commissioned a member of the majority party, and not its leader, to form a Government, he would be rightly accused of interfering in party politics. King George V was accused of doing so in 1931, yet it can be argued that what he actually did was not so serious and had the consent of the Prime Minister of the time.

Lastly, why, in view of what has been said, should we revert to the nineteenth-century practice of a Cabinet and not the Prime Minister advising dissolution? It is perfectly well established that a Prime Minister may – and indeed usually does – consult his senior colleagues in a possible dissolution. But ultimately the right lies within his powers, and nothing has occurred in recent years that might suggest a departure from this doctrine. The practice cannot be changed unless the whole system of government is reviewed and changed.

B: IS THE ADVICE BINDING FOR THE CROWN?

Having reached the conclusion that advice is necessary for the Crown to dissolve Parliament, it remains to be seen whether the Crown is bound to this advice. In other words can the Crown refuse the Prime Minister's advice to dissolve?

Some authors usually vary their answers according to whether the Government has been defeated in Parliament or not.[1] In my opinion it is perhaps advisable to consider the problem primarily in terms of a majority or a minority Government rather than a defeated or an undefeated one. We shall see later on that it usually makes little difference whether a defeated or undefeated minority Government advises a dissolution; whereas it makes quite a difference whether it is a majority or a minority Government that advises dissolution. Furthermore a Government can always be defeated in a snap vote in Parliament but still remain in majority. This might happen, for example, if a large number of Government backbenchers voted against their party on an important measure – say the

---

[1] Forsey, *Dissolution of Parliament*, p. 106.

Industrial Relations Bill – yet at the same time remained loyal to their party and refused to support any other Government in the existing House. These dissident M.P.s remain on the whole loyal to their party. Indeed it can be argued that it is because they remain loyal to their ideals that they vote against the Government which, in their opinion, has betrayed them. Hence it is most probable that they could react strongly if their opponents obtained a dissolution as a result of their revolt against a particular measure of their party. Thus, it must always be remembered that the ability to defeat a Government does not necessarily imply the ability to command a majority thereafter and it is on this latter point that the Sovereign will have to rely if he is to refuse a dissolution. Lastly, we shall see later on that a Government may decide to advise dissolution before the actual voting takes place, when it still remains in majority. In cases like these the Government is still, technically speaking, undefeated though it may be doubtful whether it still commands the confidence of the House. Admittedly this is a rare situation, though not without a precedent. In any event the above examples amply illustrate the difficulties that may arise from using as a criterion the fact that the Government is defeated or undefeated in the House.

Professor Keith relates the problem to the size of the majority.[1] His views seem to me vague and contradictory. The size of the Government majority has nothing to do with the request for and grant of a dissolution. Twice in the recent past (in the cases of Mr Wilson and Mr Attlee) it has been shown that a small majority can keep a Government in office for quite a long period and in fact is capable of relieving it from backbenchers' pressure. It is in fact interesting to note that a comfortable majority encourages dissatisfied backbenchers to carry their activities to the point of rebellion, since they do not run the risk of jeopardising their party's position in the House.

Thus Keith seems to suggest that the refusal of a dissolution to a Government with a slight majority – in his words a Government 'barely sustained in office' – might under certain circumstances be constitutional. *A fortiori* the King may refuse a dissolution to a minority ministry. Yet, Keith had vigorously attacked Asquith when the latter had stated that the King was not obliged to grant a dissolution coming from a minority Government.[2]

---

[1] A. B. Keith, *Responsible government in the Dominions*, 2nd edn (1928), p. 156. Forsey, *Dissolution of Parliament*, pp. 107, 112, 150, etc. points out Keith's contradictions.

[2] Keith, *Responsible government in the Dominions*, p. 148, describes Asquith's opinion as an 'obvious and regrettable decline in mental powers and sense of political realities' and adds: 'A dictum denounced at the time by all sound constitutional opinion.' Also in *The British cabinet system*, p. 300. Yet eminent contemporaries, as Mr Lloyd George, Sir John Marriott,

Dr Evatt adopts the orthodox view. The King cannot refuse a dissolution to Ministers who are assured of Parliament's support, since automatically this excludes the possibility of an alternative Ministry.[1] This does not just mean that an alternative Ministry must be willing to undertake responsibility for the King's action. It must also be assured that it will be able to carry on with the existing Parliament; otherwise the King will be obliged to grant a dissolution and thus find himself in the awkward position of granting to one political leader what he had previously denied to his opponent.

In 1923 Mr Asquith made it clear that his request for a December dissolution in 1910 had been granted because he had 'a substantial working majority', and continued, 'although our position in the House of Commons was absolutely impregnable, we thought we ought to be fortified by a fresh expression of the judgement of the Nation'.[2]

Had Balfour been commissioned by the King to form a Government he would have found himself confronted with a hostile Parliament and would have been obliged to advise dissolution sooner rather than later. 'The ensuing general election would inevitably have taken the form of a vote of confidence or censure on his [the King's] action. Nothing could have pushed the King more firmly into the centre of the political battle.'[3] Fortunately for the King, Knollys, his Private Secretary, withheld from him Mr Balfour's willingness to attempt to form a government and in fact categorically, 'assured the King that Mr. Balfour would in any event decline to form an administration'. As Roy Jenkins observes, by withholding information from the Crown Knollys 'certainly saved the King from an act of constitutional folly which might well have affected not only his own personal position but the whole future of the British Monarchy'.[4]

Can the Crown refuse a dissolution to a minority Ministry? Opinions differ greatly on this subject. Dicey, for example, maintains that, 'a Ministry placed in a minority by a vote of the Commons have, in accordance with received doctrines, a right to demand a dissolution of Parlia-

Sir John Simon and Professor Ramsay Muir, all endorsed Asquith's views. Keith's opinions are not always completely clear and consistent. Thus in *Imperial unity and the Dominions* pp. 97, 98, 104; *Speeches and documents on British Colonial Policy*, I (1918), pp. ix–x, he seems to imply that the Crown has no right to refuse a dissolution. In later works he is not alway, equally positive. See *Responsible government in the Dominions*, p. xvi; *The King and the Imperial Crown*, p. 140; *The British cabinet system*, pp. 298, 302.

[1] *The King and his Dominion Governors*, p. 260; Forsey, *Dissolution of Parliament*, p. 269, also agrees with Evatt. Wade & Bradley, *Constitutional law*, p. 84, and Lord Simon, *The Times*, 24 April 1950 indirectly accept this.

[2] *The Times*, 19 December 1923.

[3] Jenkins, *Asquith*, p. 245.   [4] Ibid. p. 246.

ment'.[1] He then proceeds to suggest that there are times when a dissolution can be refused to a majority or even imposed against its will, a view which he also held in 1913. Sir William Anson approvingly quotes Lord Aberdeen's saying that 'he had never entertained the slightest doubt that if the minister advised the Queen to dissolve, she would, as a matter of course, do so'.[2] His personal opinion is that 'the prerogative of dissolution is one which the King exercises on the advice and at the request of his Ministers and that a request is not refused' and then proceeds to consider when this request is properly made.

Most constitutional lawyers seem to support the idea that in a divided House, and particularly with a multi-party system, a minority Government – whether defeated or undefeated – is not entitled to a dissolution if an alternative Government is possible and furthermore is capable of carrying on with the existing House.

Asquith's speech to the National Liberal Club on 18 December 1923 made the above quite clear.

Dissolution of Parliament [he said] is in this country one of the prerogatives of the Crown. It is not a mere feudal survival, but it is a part, and I think a useful part, of our constitutional system . . . It does not mean that the Crown should act arbitrarily and without the advice of responsible Ministers, but it does mean that the Crown is not bound to take the advice of a particular minister to put its subjects to the tumult and turmoil of a series of General Elections so long as it can find other Ministers who are prepared to give contrary advice. The notion that a Ministry which cannot command a majority in the House of Commons . . . a Ministry in a minority of 31 per cent . . . in these circumstances is invested with the right to demand a dissolution is as subversive of constitutional usage, as it would, in my opinion, be pernicious to the general and paramount interest of the Nation at large.

Laski's objections to Asquith's doctrine are open to discussion. He insists that Asquith was only preparing the way for a Liberal Government.[3] Laski's arguments clearly apply only to the 1924 situation and presuppose that Asquith, 'being head of a party even smaller than that of Mr. MacDonald, would have been bound, in course of time, to be defeated also, and to have requested a dissolution. To have granted it would have evoked, once more, the accusation that the King was discriminating between parties.'[4]

Laski is too categorical on the subject. Had Mr Asquith been able to

---

[1] Dicey, *The law of the constitution*, pp. 432–3.
[2] Anson, *Law and custom of the constitution*, I, 306.
[3] *Reflections on the constitution* (1962), p. 79. Keith, *The British cabinet system*, p. 300, also took this view. Contra, Lord Simon, *The Times*, 27 April 1950.
[4] *Parliamentary government in England*, p. 410.

take over with the support of the Conservatives, the King could have constitutionally refused Mr MacDonald's request. Thus, Professor de Smith argues that the Queen might be entitled to refuse a dissolution to a minority Government if she has: 'substantial grounds for believing that a stable government can be formed without a General Election'.[1]

Dr Forsey also seems to disagree with Laski, but on different grounds.[2] In his opinion, had Asquith immediately after taking office requested a dissolution which had been denied to Mr MacDonald, the King would have been bound to refuse it. 'But a request for a dissolution by Asquith after defeat would not have been the same thing . . . Refusal of dissolution to MacDonald therefore, would not have been inconsistent with a subsequent grant to Asquith after he had found himself unable to carry on with the existing House.'

Dr Forsey's arguments are, I believe, acceptable only if Asquith advised dissolution after having been able to carry on with the existing House for a reasonable period of time. If on the other hand it was certain – as it was in 1924 – that Mr Asquith was unable to form a viable Government – even for a short period – it would have been dangerous for the Crown to deny Mr MacDonald's advice. In this sense Laski's 'time element' is important.

Sir Alan Lascelles' letter to *The Times* is very near the above.[3] He also believes that the King can refuse a dissolution, but only if an alternative government is feasible, if it can be assured of a working majority and it can be expected to carry on for a reasonable period of time, or in Professor de Smith's words there are 'substantial grounds' for a 'stable government'.

The question of a 'working majority' has been considered above and the dangers it entails have been stressed. It remains to be seen what a 'reasonable' time means, and how the Crown can ever be sure of the existence of an alternative and viable Government.

One cannot but give an abstract answer to the first question. Obviously the Government must be in a position to survive at least the first vote of censure and furthermore be able to carry on. As another correspondent of *The Times* put it, the alternative Government must have 'the ability to command a majority on at least one immediate major issue'.[4] An early defeat will necessarily oblige it to advise dissolution. The shortness of the time that intervenes between the first and second request for a dis-

---

[1] *The Times*, 14 May 1969. See also Sir M. Amos' remarks in *The English Constitution* (1930), p. 108.
[2] *Dissolution of Parliament*, pp. 113ff.
[3] *The Times*, 2 May 1950.   [4] J. Jackson, *The Times*, 27 April 1950.

solution might well cause constitutional grievances, if the requests are treated in a different way.[1]

The second question is equally difficult to answer. In countries where the two-party system prevails, the answer will be obvious in most cases. Dissolution will, as a rule, be granted even if the Prime Minister who advises it has been recently defeated in the House, because, as already stated, an ability to defeat does not necessarily imply an ability to form an effective alternative Government, and consequently the risk of refusing a dissolution is not worth taking. Because if the new Prime Minister is also defeated a dissolution will become inevitable and this would mean that the first Prime Minister's opinion was sound and should have been followed. It would also mean that the Crown 'would be placed in the intolerable and dangerous position' of granting to one Prime Minister what it had recently refused to another.[2] Dr Forsey quoting Dr Evatt approvingly, maintains that, 'where the parliamentary situation embraces three distinct parties and the Ministry had no working majority in the House, the Governor General may refuse dissolution ... The possibility of an alternative Government may be capable of exclusion only by ... a subsequent test vote of the House.'[3] This opinion must have prevailed in the minds of constitutional lawyers who supported the Canadian Governor's decision to commission Mr Meighen to form a Government in 1926.

Lord Byng refused Mr King's advice to dissolve on the 28th of June and immediately sent for Mr Meighen. Mr Meighen had assured the Governor that he could form a viable Government and based his optimism on 'informal promises' of support from a number of Progressives. The Governor did not personally consult the Progressives, until after Mr Meighen was sworn in as Prime Minister.[4] Furthermore the Progressives emphatically maintained that,

Mr. Meighen had no assurance from our group, nor did he seek any assurance ... No promise had been made ... The Progressives requested an interview with Mr. Meighen and secured it at the very time when Mr. Forke was being consulted by his Excellency. In this interview no mention whatever was made of cooperation or assistance, and it was solely for the purpose of ascertaining the procedure Mr. Meighen intended to adopt.[5]

In view of the above it is submitted that the refusal of Mr King's advice is not altogether defensible. An alternative Government was

---

[1] This also seems to be Evatt's opinion, *The King and his Dominion Governors*, p. 64. Forsey seems to disagree, *Dissolution of Parliament*, pp. 238–9.
[2] The argument was pleaded in 1951. See *The Times*, 24–27 April 1951. Its validity is also accepted by Wade & Bradley, *Constitutional law*, p. 85.
[3] *Dissolution of Parliament*, p. 161; Evatt, *18 Canadian Bar Review*, no. 1, pp. 1 and 4.
[4] Forsey, ibid. p. 134.   [5] Ibid. pp. 134–5.

uncertain, and in any event its future was grim. The Progressives, for example, seemed eager to continue the investigation against the administration of Mr King. But this being completed, there was little evidence, if any at all, that they were willing to continue supporting the Conservatives in office. The possibility of an early defeat for Mr Meighen was thus more than probable. One cannot but feel a certain apprehension regarding the speed at which Lord Byng acted.[1] A short delay on his part might have saved him from a great deal of embarrassment. Nevertheless, Lord Byng's decision was granted the benefit of the doubt. The Canadian crisis would have still remained a relatively minor crisis had not Lord Byng subsequently (on 2 July 1926) granted Mr Meighen's request to dissolve, thus giving the impression that he was discriminating.

Despite the above, however, Dr Forsey elaborately and to a certain extent convincingly supports Lord Byng's second decision. Yet, he himself in a different chapter of his book maintains that if a Government came to power as a result of refusing a dissolution to its predecessor and then 'asked for an immediate dissolution, or was at once defeated on a critical division, it would be the duty of the Crown to recall the former government and grant it dissolution'.[2]

One wonders why the above statement does not apply to the Canadian crisis. The words 'at once defeated' are not clear. Is a defeat within five days from assuming office an immediate one? Technically speaking no; in substance yes. In politics one cannot always play with words. Nor can one argue that Mr Meighen advised dissolution in 'new circumstances'[3] which arose as a result of his defeat simply because his defeat was possible, if not probable, from the very beginning. In any event Dr Forsey, in his elaborate and extensive treatment of the Canadian crisis, seems to have overlooked one important point: the Governor's decision, whether right or wrong, created an unprecedented criticism of the Crown and its representative. One wonders whether the granting of Mr King's request on 28 June 1926 would have created as much trouble as its refusal did.[4]

The Canadian crisis clearly illustrates the difficulties the Crown is bound to encounter when faced with requests from minority governments in situations as ambiguous as the above. Prime facie two ways of

---

[1] See, D. J. Heasman, 'The Monarch, the Prime Minister and the dissolution of Parliament', *Parl. Aff.* (1960–1), pp. 94–107 and especially p. 99.
[2] Forsey, *Dissolution of Parliament*, p. 263.   [3] Ibid. p. 236.
[4] The few lines on the Canadian crisis of 1926 claim no deep originality. They merely hope to persuade Dr Forsey to take them into consideration in a future edition of his book. The author feels that little, if anything, can be added to Dr Forsey's scholarly analysis, and in any event the present writer, for one, is not in a position to undertake this task.

solving such problems are likely to exist. First: dissolution becomes automatic and the responsibility is placed on the shoulders of the electorate. Lately this view was taken by Professors Beloff[1] and King[2] and was opposed by Professor de Smith.[3] Thus Professor King argues:

In acceding to a minority Prime Minister's request for a dissolution, the Crown is implicitly acknowledging the superior claim of the electorate to arbitrate among the parties and to try to produce a majority. Were the Crown to refuse a dissolution in such circumstances, the Prime Minister would be forced to resign and the Crown would run the risk that no new Prime Minister could control the House. This actually happened in 1926 in Canada, where the Governor General, having refused a dissolution to a Prime Minister from one party, was forced to grant it to his successor from another party a few days later.

Second, the Crown's discretionary powers are revived in circumstances as critical as the above. This is more likely to happen whenever the two-party system is not functioning properly. It necessarily means that the burden of decision is thrust upon the King and this entails the danger of drawing him into party politics. It seems that the Aristotelian mean must be found; this can happen if the two opposing theories are reconciled, to some extent at least. Lord Simon attempted this reconciliation in 1951.[4] He opposed the 'automatic theory' while making it clear that any initiative on the part of the Sovereign can only be envisaged if an alternative administration is possible.

This 'difficult and intricate question' [of dissolution] cannot be dogmatically answered without considering the circumstances in which it arises ... Is it really suggested that, however recent the last General Election may be and whatever its result, the Prime Minister has the absolute right to require the Crown to put its subjects to the 'tumult and turmoil' of another General Election within a few weeks of the last? And, if the result of the second election does not suit him, can he claim a third? On the contrary I conceive that the Sovereign has the duty, in the case of a freshly elected Parliament at any rate, of considering whether government could be carried on under another head, and that if he thinks that it can, he is acting constitutionally ...

Supposing that, as the result of a General Election, a Prime Minister finds himself left with the support of only a minority in the new House of Commons. He is under no obligation to resign immediately, and his Government may decide to meet the House when it assembles. An amendment to the Address is then carried against them, as happened in 1892. When this happens, can the defeated Prime Minister go

---

[1] *The Times*, 13 May 1969.
[2] *The Times*, 10 May 1969. In 1951 this view was taken by Lord Chorley and Roy Jenkins, both in *The Times* of 26 April 1950.
[3] *The Times*, 14 May 1969, and more extensively in his *Constitutional and administrative law*, pp. 104–7. Also Lord Simon, *The Times*, 24 and 27 April 1950.
   The Times, 27 April 1950. See also, O. Hood Phillips, *Reform of the Constitution* (1970), p. 51.

to the Sovereign and demand another General Election and is the Sovereign bound to grant this request? Of course not. But why not? Because there is an alternative Government available, without sending the electorate again to the polls.

Though the possibility of an alternative Government is a crucial factor, the final outcome in the case of minority Governments will depend on the actual circumstances. Professor de Smith has said that 'in order to define the Queen's conventional obligations in such a situation [as the above], one would have to ask a number of questions'.[1] Thus, no author maintains that the Crown is compelled to refuse a dissolution to a minority Government, even if an alternative administration is possible with the existing House.

Lord Esher, in 1924, correctly advised the Monarch by declaring:[2]

Of course his Majesty could dispense with the advice of Ramsay MacDonald, but only if he could find in Baldwin or Asquith another Prime Minister to take the responsibility. And even then, under present circumstances, with parties balanced as they are in the existing Parliament, and in view of the real issues such as the Russian treaty, I think it would have been unwise to reject Ramsay's advice.

Keith completely agrees with Lord Esher's views.

If a dissolution had been refused, it is certain that the propriety of the King's action would not have been appreciated, and the idea would have been broadcast in the ranks of the electorate that the King had taken the earliest possible moment to rid himself of a Labour ministry, and had refused it the right to appeal to the electors . . . The Crown would have been bitterly assailed . . . and the unique opportunity would have been lost of showing to the Labour party that from the King it could expect absolutely fair and impartial treatment in all essentials.[3]

Thus in MacDonald's case, had the King found an alternative Prime Minister he would have been constitutionally correct in refusing dissolution. Yet he would be giving the impression that he was motivated by party sympathies rather than pure reason; and if there is anything worse than a biased and partial Monarch, it is a Monarch who is believed to be biased and partial.

The frequency of dissolution is of course another aspect to be considered. Obviously this and Asquith's doctrine led Marriott to believe that if MacDonald had advised a dissolution on taking office in January 1924, the King could have constitutionally refused it.[4] Dr Forsey observes

---

[1] *The Times*, 14 May 1969.
[2] Esher *Papers*, IV, 296. See also Professor de Smith's comments, in *Constitutional and administrative law*, p. 106.
[3] *The King and the Imperial Crown*, pp. 171–2.
[4] J. A. R. Marriott, *The mechanism of the modern state* (1927).

that Marriott's view runs contrary to Disraeli's opinions on this matter, according to which a Government can always dissolve a Parliament elected under the auspices of its opponents.[1] The United Kingdom precedents seem to confirm Disraeli's views.[2] Yet, Dr Forsey concludes that: 'in none of these cases had the new ministry taken office almost at the very outset of the first session of the new Parliament ... The arguments in favour of Marriott's views are so obvious and strong as to require no discussion.'[3]

With all due respect the arguments are neither strong nor obvious. Undoubtedly frequent dissolutions are harmful and must be avoided. Dr Forsey has amply shown that the timing of a dissolution may influence its approval. It is obvious that a dissolution at the end of the life of Parliament has a greater chance of being approved than one during the first session. But ultimately it is not the frequency of dissolutions that determines the Crown's final decision but the possibility of an alternative Government.

In his conclusions Dr Forsey seems to agree with the above. He himself states that, 'If a Government secures a dissolution and the new Parliament proves unable even to elect a Speaker, the Government is entitled to another dissolution immediately afterwards.'[4] If this is so, Mr Baldwin could dissolve immediately after his defeat had the Liberals not agreed to support a Labour Government. Why then could Mr Baldwin do it and Mr MacDonald not? Mr MacDonald was likely to – and indeed he did – win the Liberal support, for a time at least, and thus had a constitutional right to be commissioned to form a Government after Mr Baldwin's defeat. In October 1924, when Mr MacDonald was defeated in his turn, all possibilities with the existing Parliament had been tried and the time had come for a dissolution.[5] Had Mr MacDonald been unable to reach an agreement with the Liberals in January 1924, he would have been entitled

---

[1] Disraeli implied this several times. See *Parliamentary Debates*, 3rd series, CL, 1084; CXCI, 1695–1708. Gladstone disagreed with Disraeli's thesis: *Parliamentary Debates*, 3rd series, CXCI, 1710–12. Disraeli also refused to take office in 1873 after Gladstone's defeat because there 'is an idea that this, being my Parliament, cannot be dissolved by me'. Yet, all evidence shows that Disraeli's refusal was purely tactical in aiming to force Gladstone to dissolve. See Ensor, *England*, p. 25.   [2] In 1834, 1852 and 1906.

[3] *Dissolution of Parliament*, pp. 108–9, 263.   [4] Forsey, op. cit. pp. 260–1.

[5] Nicolson, *King George V*, p. 515. In a personal minute the King recorded: 'In granting the Prime Minister's request to dissolve Parliament, I could not help regretting the *necessity* for doing so ...' Ibid. p. 516. Mr MacDonald informed the Cabinet on 9 October, one day after the Government's defeat in the House, that 'the King was willing to grant a dissolution, but that, in view of the desirability of avoiding frequent elections H.M. proposed to send to the Prime Minister for purposes of record a memorandum (which H.M. would show the Prime Minister in advance) to which equally for purposes of record the Prime Minister, with H.M.'s consent, would reply'. P.R.O. CAB 23/48 (55 (24) 1).

to advise and secure a dissolution since no alternative solution was available.

Whether a Government had the previous dissolution is also to be considered; yet it is in itself inadequate to determine a grant or refusal of a dissolution. The time in between two dissolutions is more decisive. Finally, if the Opposition agrees on a new election the Crown must grant a dissolution.

Various other limitations have already been discussed in the first part of the work. It remains to be discussed whether a defeated Prime Minister can advise or ask for a dissolution. The question, by no means an easy one, has been raised at least once in the past. During the 1955 constitutional crisis in Tasmania, the Leader of the Opposition, in a letter to the Governor, insisted that the Prime Minister, having suffered a defeat in the House, 'had forfeited his constitutional authority to advise the Crown'.[1]

In the United Kingdom, it does not seem ever to have been contested that a defeated Prime Minister has the right to advise the Crown. There is no doubt that a Prime Minister does not forfeit the right to advise dissolution, simply by the fact of being defeated. The right is lost after his resignation, and the resignation is completed only when it is accepted by the Monarch. In actual fact the defeated Prime Minister usually carries on till his successor is sworn in.[2] Furthermore, on his resignation, the Prime Minister is entitled to give his views on the political situation and hence advise what he may think is the appropriate course. Whether the Crown is bound by this advice is an entirely different matter and has nothing to do with the validity of the advice.

The Canadian crisis of 1926 was unique in many aspects. One of its most controversial features was that Mr King advised dissolution while a vote of censure was under debate. The pros and cons of Mr King's decision can be found in Dr Forsey's extensive treatment of the crisis, and need not be repeated here.[3] Had Dr Forsey's conclusions been less rigid – he maintains that if a Government asks for a dissolution while a motion of censure is under debate, it is always clearly the Crown's duty

---

[1] Campbell, *Public Law* (1961), pp. 174–6, 178.

[2] Mr King in Canada in 1926 was the only exception. According to Jennings, *Cabinet government*, p. 52, the outgoing Ministers must remain in office until their successors are appointed. Pitt in fact, in 1801, moved the House into Supply and presented the Budget, after his resignation had been accepted. See also Forsey, *Dissolution of Parliament*, pp. 59 and 135, mentioning Mr Prior's dismissal in British Columbia in 1903. A defeated Prime Minister therefore has the right to advise a dissolution; but 'a Prime Minister who has *actually* been repudiated by his own parliamentary party in favour of one of his colleagues can claim no constitutional right at all to demand a dissolution': S. de Smith, *Constitutional and administrative law*, p. 106 (italics mine).

[3] Forsey, ibid. pp. 130–250. See also ibid. p. 269.

to refuse – one would be inclined on the whole to agree with him. Hence the following objections apply to this sentence, and not to his scholarly treatment of the Canadian crisis.

One feels compelled to mention from the very beginning the uncertainty which usually exists on whether a motion of censure, in the parliamentary use of the term, is being debated or not. Broadly speaking, every action the Opposition takes is to embarrass the Government, and in this sense, censure it. The fact that M.P.s from both sides may refer to a specific motion or division as a censure is not in itself sufficient. Furthermore the Whip is usually applied in most cases of serious legislation, thus emphasising the importance the Government attaches to these measures. If eventually these measures are defeated, it is difficult to say whether the Government has been deprived of the confidence of the House, or just prevented from introducing controversial legislation. Even in cases when an individual Minister is censured by the House, the Government is not obliged to resign, unless it decides to share his fate.[1] Admittedly individual ministerial responsibility is rare in our times, but it can still happen.[2]

The main point of disagreement with Dr Forsey lies elsewhere. If a Government decides to advise a dissolution while a motion of censure is under debate, it is obviously violating the rules of fair play and moral obligation. Politics are not the art of amorality, but equally are not always linked with ethics to the extent scholars and academicians would wish. While the motion of censure is under debate the Government is still (in theory at least) in command of the confidence of the House.[3] The Crown cannot deny this simple fact and cannot base its decision on the possible result of the debate. The Crown decides on facts not on possibilities, and unless there is ample, clear and convincing evidence that the Prime Minister does not command a majority in the House, the Crown cannot refuse his advice. A compromise solution could be for the Crown to ask the Prime Minister to ascertain his majority before granting his request. If the Prime Minister agrees, there is no problem. If he does not, then the Crown has serious evidence, but not in itself conclusive, that the Prime Minister has lost the confidence of the House. But the Crown's further

---

[1] This was not the case in Canada. The Stevens amendment described 'the Prime Minister and the Government as wholly indefensible'. The Woodsworth amendment, which would have struck out the condemnation of the Prime Minister, the Government and the Minister of Customs, was defeated on 25 June, by a majority of two. See Forsey, ibid. p. 133.

[2] The resignation of Hoare in 1936 is an outstanding example. Mr Profumo's resignation is yet another example.

[3] If it is a minority Government the Crown has a greater chance of refusing dissolution, but only in accordance with the above.

action must be determined according to the prevailing political situation, and always in accordance with the will of the majority in the House.

By granting a dissolution the Crown does not 'choke off discussion', as Dr Forsey seems to suggest, since the electorate will have the final word, and the Opposition will see that all relevant material is made available. In the words of Professor Dawson, 'The Prime Minister can be left to the people to punish.'[1] Dr Forsey seems to be afraid that a Prime Minister will be able to 'claim immunity of expulsion from office'[2] by threatening dissolution in cases like these, and this could go on *ad infinitum* and result in dictatorship. Dr Forsey is correct only if this procedure is repeated at regular intervals. Had Mr King advised dissolution under exactly the same circumstances, but a year later, would he have been frustrating the electorate's rights? Hence it seems to me that the Crown might be entitled to refuse a dissolution to a Government which is under censure, but it is not always its clear duty to do so.

[1] Quoted by Forsey, *Dissolution of Parliament*, p. 169.
[2] Forsey, ibid. p. 170.

Chapter 6

THE REASONS FOR AND TIMING OF DISSOLUTION

A: THE TIMING OF DISSOLUTION

Having examined who advises dissolution and in what circumstances the Crown may refuse this advice, we shall now discuss the question of the timing of dissolution.

The timing of dissolution is closely associated with the reasons that compel a Government to go to the country and hence this chapter should be read in conjunction with what has been said in chapter 3. For example, an international crisis may develop forcing the Government to seek a new mandate. As we shall see in due course, the Italian invasion of Abyssinia in 1935 hastened Mr Baldwin's plans to seek a new mandate based on re-armament. Or, a Government may be defeated in the House – as Mr MacDonald's was in 1924 – and as a result of its defeat, it might decide to refer the dispute to the country. Finally, to mention a more recent example, the Government may believe that a particular moment is advantageous to the party and thus decide to exploit the favourable mood of the electorate. This last contingency has become frequent nowadays since the parties find a useful ally in the opinion polls.

This, however, has not always been the case. During the nineteenth century party calculations were, of course, taken into serious account in view of a forthcoming dissolution. Nevertheless, as a rule other more important and more general issues determined the timing of dissolution. Thus, eminent statesmen such as Sir Robert Peel and Mr Gladstone have been quoted[1] condemning a dissolution based on purely party reasoning. As a result, in the event of a parliamentary defeat, resignation was, as a rule, preferred to dissolution.

Between 1867 – for most purposes the starting point of these chapters – and 1900, seven dissolutions took place. Their reasons can be discussed briefly.

(a) On 1 May 1868, Mr Disraeli's Government was defeated in the Commons over the Bill for the disestablishment of the Irish Church. He immediately moved the adjournment of the House and in a letter to the Queen stated: 'Under these circumstances the advice they [the Ministers]

---

[1] Above, pp. 35-6, nn. 2 and 3.

would humbly offer your Majesty is to dissolve this Parliament . . . and that an earnest endeavour should be made by the Government that such appeal should be made to the new constituency.'[1] The Queen replied to the Prime Minister that, 'she cannot hesitate, as she has already verbally informed him, to sanction the dissolution of Parliament under the circumstances stated by him, in order that the opinion of the country may be deliberately expressed on the important question [of the Irish Church] . . .'[2] Undoubtedly, Mr Disraeli must have expected to harvest the fruits of his Second Reform Act, and seemed reasonably optimistic as to the outcome.[3] In this, however, he was proved wrong and Mr Gladstone won 384 seats as opposed to 274 Conservatives.

(b) In 1874 Mr Disraeli outfoxed his opponent and as a result won the elections.

In March 1873, Mr Gladstone was defeated in the Commons and tendered his resignation. Mr Disraeli was faced with the choice of an immediate dissolution and a certain defeat at the polls or with the alternative of forming a minority government which would place him at the mercy of a Liberal House. He told the Queen that though he was 'perfectly fit to carry on . . . it would be useless to attempt to carry on the Government with a minority in the House of Commons'. Though the Queen and indeed Mr Gladstone acknowledged his right to dissolve[4] he refused it on the pretext that 'there is an idea that this, being my Parliament, cannot be dissolved by me'.[5] But Disraeli's refusal was a shrewd political move. As Lord Salisbury noted, quoting Hardy, a Conservative leader, 'if we dissolve now, and are beaten, – as we shall be, – we cannot dissolve again for three or four years. If we leave Gladstone to dissolve in July, the chapter of accidents may give us power to turn them out within a year or so; and then we can dissolve again with satisfactory results'.[6]

Mr Gladstone was thus obliged[7] to withdraw his resignation. But practically a year later, faced with internal erosion of the party and steady losses at by-elections, he decided that Parliament had ceased to represent the Nation. He thus dissolved Parliament on 26 January 1874 and lost the subsequent elections. Later on, he gave his reasons for his dissolution. Thus, on 24 April 1874, he declared in the Commons:[8]

[1] Monypenny & Buckle, *Disraeli*, v, 32.
[2] Monypenny & Buckle, *Disraeli*, v, 32; *Letters of Queen Victoria*, 2nd series, i, 524ff.
[3] R. Blake, *Disraeli* (1966), p. 512.
[4] Monypenny & Buckle, *Disraeli*, v, 206ff., 210, etc.; Morley, *Gladstone*, ii, 447–56.
[5] Monypenny & Buckle, *Disraeli*, v, 211.
[6] Lady Gwendolen Cecil, *Life of the Marquess of Salisbury*, ii, 41.
[7] It took the Cabinet three and a half hours to agree. Morley, *Gladstone*, ii, 454. Gladstone, however, suspected Disraeli's trick. Monypenny & Buckle, *Disraeli*, v, 209.
[8] *Parliamentary Debates*, 3rd series, ccxviii, 1122; Morley, *Gladstone*, ii, 485–7.

I have never known a Parliament . . . in which single elections of themselves went so far towards establishing a presumption that the opinion of the country had changed with reference to the politics of those whom it desired to conduct public affairs as that of the last, and the consequence was that from time to time it was a matter of inquiry to us whether our position gave us the strength that was necessary to enable us to conduct with dignity and with credit the affairs of the country.

This, as he indirectly admitted, was the result of him being unable to resign in 1873.

(c) The 1880 dissolution was, of course, advised when the end of the statutory term of Parliament was approaching. Nevertheless, it offers a characteristic example of party politics in the late nineteenth century.

By late 1879 Mr Gladstone was back in active politics, though still not the official leader of the Liberals. He directed his campaign against the Prime Minister's foreign and imperial policies and besides getting himself re-elected for Midlothian his appeal seemed to gain wide acceptance.

Though the Queen had envisaged a dissolution, Mr Disraeli wrote to her on 14 February and informed her that 'the Cabinet today considered the question of dissolution in all its forms and contingencies. They unanimously agreed, that nothing but a very critical state of affairs . . . could authorise such a step.'[1] But as Lord Blake says, 'On that very day news came through which was to produce a complete volte-face.'[2]

In two by-elections at Liverpool and Southwark the Conservatives made unexpected and significant gains. The Queen telegraphed to the Prime Minister, 'I am greatly rejoiced at the great victory at Southwark. It shows what the feeling of the country is.'[3] Following the Conservative victory the Queen saw Disraeli, and wrote in her journal on 5 March 1880,

He [Disraeli] had been against it all the time, and had wished to put it off till the autumn, but now he felt it could no longer be delayed. The reasons were, that there was more agitation, the farmers had had bad times, but were only grumbling, whereas, by delaying, this might take a serious form, and become much more difficult to contend with; foreign affairs were threatening, but nothing at the present moment was stirring. Still they might become critical, if the dissolution were too long delayed . . . A Cabinet was summoned for early tomorrow morning . . . but he did not wish to do so without first consulting me.[4]

On 6 March the Cabinet reconsidered dissolution and came out in favour of an early one,[5] after consulting the Whips and the Central Office.

[1] Monypenny & Buckle, *Disraeli*, VI, 511–12. [2] Blake, *Disraeli*, p. 702.
[3] Quoted by Blake, ibid. p. 703. [4] *Letters of Queen Victoria*, 2nd series, III, 71.
[5] Monypenny & Buckle, *Disraeli*, VI, 514.

Two days later Mr Disraeli announced dissolution, to the great amazement of most members of the House.

The by-elections, however, proved fatally ill-judged and the Conservative Party, hampered by bad organisation, lost the elections. Disraeli bore the blow of defeat 'with an air of dignified imperturbability . . . and refused to allow the Central Office managers who had advised in favour of a dissolution to be made scapegoats'.[1]

(*d*) On 8 June 1885, Mr Gladstone was defeated in the Commons by a vote of 264 against 252.[2] As a result of the recently passed Representation of the People Act (1884), and in view of the final amendments of the Redistribution of Seats Act (1885), dissolution could not be advised at once, so Mr Gladstone resigned. Lord Salisbury, making the mistake Disraeli had carefully avoided in 1874, agreed to form a Government,[3] only to find his administration at the mercy of an unfavourable House. He was obliged to dissolve in 1885 and lost the elections.

(*e*) On 8 June 1886 Mr Gladstone's first Home Rule Bill was defeated in the House[4] by 343 votes to 313 despite the fact that Mr Gladstone had spoken five times in the course of the debate with compelling eloquence and power. He took his case for a dissolution to his Cabinet and as Lord Morley wrote, he 'opened the case with a list of twelve reasons for recommending dissolution, and the reasons were so cogent that his opening of the case was also its closing'.[5] In view of the importance of the Irish question he concluded his speech by saying: 'A dissolution is formidable, but resignation would mean for the present juncture abandonment of the cause.'[6]

In a letter to the Queen he gave his reasons for a dissolution in great detail.[7]

Among the grounds of this advice [i.e. to dissolve] have been the evils of prolonged uncertainty upon an absorbing question, the likelihood of aggravated exasperation between sections and parties, the desirableness of maintaining a continuous action for the purpose of keeping Ireland the better in check and maintaining order there, and the obvious fairness of the argument, which has been and may be used without distinction of party [that] the opinion of the country should be constitutionally taken on a subject which is of vast importance, which was imperfectly before the body of electors at the last Election, and on which the Ministers of the Crown and the present representatives of the people are at variance.

[1] Blake, *Disraeli*, p. 713.   [2] *Parliamentary Debates*, 3rd series, CCXCVIII, 1511, 1528–31.
[3] Lady Cecil, *Marquess of Salisbury*, III, 133–43; *Letters of Queen Victoria*, 2nd series, III, 657–80. For a moment, however, it looked as if Lord Salisbury might have refused the offer and the Queen was anxious to find out whether Mr Gladstone or Lord Hartington would be willing to continue.   [4] *Parliamentary Debates*, 3rd series, CCCVI, 1145–1245, 1304ff.
[5] *Gladstone*, III, 341.   [6] Ibid.   [7] *Letters of Queen Victoria*, 3rd series, I, 143–4.

The Queen hesitated. But even Lord Salisbury, who informed her that she would be entitled to refuse a dissolution, advised her to acquiesce to the Government's request. In a secret memorandum written before the Government's defeat he had told the Queen:

If Mr. Gladstone is refused leave to dissolve, the fact will certainly be known . . . The consequence must be that those who are in favour of Home Rule . . . will think, and say, that the action of the Queen is keeping them from Home Rule. A great deal of resentment will be excited against the Queen; and, if tempestuous times should follow, the responsibility will be thrown on her. This is undesirable, to say the least; especially if no object is to be gained by it. Whether it would diminish her influence seriously or not is difficult to determine; but the risk of such a diminution ought not to be lightly incurred. Her influence is one of the few bonds of cohesion remaining to the Community.

He concluded that if dissolution was advised it should be granted because, 'It is the natural and ordinary course; it will shield the Queen from any accusation of partisanship; it is likely to return a Parliament more opposed to Home Rule than the present.'[1] Thus, the Queen wrote to Mr Gladstone on 9 June saying that:

Though a General Election, barely six months after the last is not usually a desirable thing, under the present circumstances the Queen is strongly of opinion that any delay would tend to keep up and increase excitement and uncertainty, not only in Ireland, but all over the Empire, which would be greatly to be deplored.

Mr Gladstone obtained his dissolution on 27 June and lost the election. The Home Rule controversy had entered its final and critical phase.

(*f*) The 1892 dissolution was advised in view of the approaching end of the life of Parliament. It raises no important questions. As Lord Salisbury's daughter writes,

The sixth year of this Parliament ended in July '92, and, according to the unwritten law which allowed no Parliament to run the risk of dying a natural death under the Septennial Act the session of that year was passed under the shadow of certain dissolution at its close.[2]

(*g*) On 21 June 1895 the Liberal Government was defeated over the Army Estimates.[3] The Cabinet was divided over the question of whether it should resign or advise dissolution. Lord Rosebery told the Queen that the Government was faced with

---

[1] *Letters of Queen Victoria*, 3rd series, I, 129–30. For the Queen's answer see pp. 144–5.
[2] *Marquess of Salisbury*, vol. III; *Letters of Queen Victoria*, 3rd series, II, 118.
[3] *Parliamentary Debates*, 4th series, XXXIV, 1673–1712; *Letters of Queen Victoria*, ibid. p. 522.

two alternatives, resignation or dissolution, and he thought decidedly the former the best. They had had a very bad week with various defeats and very small majorities; and he thought it would be very humiliating to go on with the certainty of being defeated sooner or later; and that it was very bad for the country, as well as for our foreign relations, to have such a small majority.

Lord Rosebery's opinion in favour of resignation finally prevailed.

B: THE TWENTIETH-CENTURY PRECEDENTS

(*a*) On 17 September 1900 the last Victorian Parliament was dissolved. This marked the end as well as the beginning of an era. For the first time party politics were so manifestly the reason for dissolution. Needless to say it caused a deep sensation however much it may now have become a familiar practice.

The 1900 dissolution is also unique in so far as it originated not from the Cabinet nor the Prime Minister but from a Minister of the Crown. In the ensuing elections, Joseph Chamberlain became the central figure, a role perfectly suited to his strong personality.

Chamberlain had been pressing for a dissolution at least from early spring 1900. Parliament was in its fifth year and the Boers had placed their hopes in a change of Government in the United Kingdom. On 11 May 1900 Chamberlain told his audience in Birmingham that the anti-war school had encouraged President Kruger to believe 'that whenever he got into trouble with Her Majesty's Government he could always rely on Her Majesty's Opposition'.[1] He strongly believed that the imminent fall of Pretoria ought to be followed by a snap election that would result in favour of the Government and thus allow it to arrange the forthcoming settlement.

A letter of his to Milner on 23 July 1900 reveals his plans and aims:

I think between ourselves, that a General Election here is quite likely in the early autumn. I wish it could have been taken a month ago. I do not feel inclined to undertake the responsibility of a settlement, which must raise an immense number of difficult questions, without a popular mandate which will strengthen the hands of the Government ... The crisis in Arino, and the possibilities of further trouble in Ashanti and elsewhere in West Africa, complicate the situation and make possible the realisation of what has always been the greatest fear, that public attention should be diverted from what is really the main and simple issue of the South African War and the settlement which is to follow it.[2]

[1] J. L. Garvin, *The life of Joseph Chamberlain* (1933), III, 580.
[2] Ibid. pp. 585–6.

Milner seems to have shared Chamberlain's views on an early election. On 22 August he replied to the above letter:

I was exceedingly grateful for the information you gave me in your letter of July 23rd ... I sincerely hope that a General Election may not be far distant. If it were to result, as I believe it must, in a public vote of confidence in your South African policy, it would do more than anything else to clear the air here and lighten the task of reconstruction. Indeed, I feel the job before us is such a heavy one that without the assured support of the British people nobody can carry it to a successful issue.[1]

Ten days later Paul Kruger fled the country and the Transvaal was annexed. The situation was as Asquith described it 'tempting'.[2] On 17 September Chamberlain obtained his dissolution.

But the political motives of the dissolution were only faintly echoed in Lord Salisbury's memorandum submitted to the Queen a few days earlier. The reasons given were:

1. Parliament is in its sixth year; and precedents are in favour of a dissolution in the sixth year.
2. It would be almost useless to continue the Parliament during another Session; for with the strong expectation which prevails of a dissolution, members spend all their time in canvassing their constituents, and cannot be got together for the work of the House; whereas, if there is a dissolution this autumn, they can devote themselves without reserve to their Parliamentary duties next year.
3. A critical period has been reached in the South African War; and also in the Chinese campaign; and Your Majesty's Government, to whomsoever it may be entrusted, will act with much more confidence and effect if they are fully acquainted with the views of the electors, and are assured of their support. Europe is in an uneasy condition; and, if there should be any disturbance within the next few months, it will be highly inconvenient [if] your Majesty should be compelled, by the efflux of time, to hold a general election in the middle of it.[3]

(*b*) The 1905 dissolution was the direct result of the resignation of Mr Balfour's Government. The Conservatives commanded a majority in the House and Sir Henry Campbell-Bannerman, who succeeded Balfour in the Premiership, had no choice since there was not the faintest chance of an alternative Government with the existing House.[4] That explains why Sir Henry did not even make an attempt to meet the existing House. In any event its legal end was approaching.

(*c*) and (*d*) The two dissolutions in 1910 are well known and need not be discussed here.[5]

---

[1] Ibid.   [2] *Memoirs and reflections, 1852–1927*, I (1928), 151.
[3] *Letters of Queen Victoria*, 3rd series, III, 586.
[4] Sir Sidney Lee, *Life of King Edward VII* (1925–7), II, 189–90.
[5] On the subject consult: J. A. Spender & C. Asquith, *Life of Herbert Henry Asquith, Lord Oxford and Asquith*, I (1932), ch. 20–5; Asquith, *Fifty years of Parliament*, II, 67–114; Nicolson,

The first was caused by the rejection of Mr Lloyd George's Budget by the House of Lords. On 16 November Lord Lansdowne moved an amendment 'That this House is not justified in giving its consent to this Bill until it has been submitted to the judgement of the country'.

Asquith strongly attacked the decision of the House of Lords. He maintained:

This new-fangled Caesarism, which converts the House of Lords into a kind of plebiscitary organ, is one of the quaintest inventions of our time . . . the truth is that all this talk about the duty or the right of the House of Lords to refer measures to the people is, in the light of our political and actual experience, the hollowest outcry of political cant.

With this announcement he tabled a motion which stated 'That the action of the House of Lords in refusing to pass into law the financial provision made by this House for the service of the year is a breach of the Constitution and a usurpation of the rights of the Commons.' The motion was carried by 349 to 134 votes and Parliament was at once dissolved.[1]

In the new House the Liberals introduced the Parliament Act Bill but stagnation followed. By early November the Government, faced with strong opposition from the Lords, decided to advise a new dissolution feeling that it should be 'fortified by a fresh verdict of the Electorate before [it] entered upon the final stages of the struggle'.

However, the advice was given – for the first time in modern constitutional history – on condition that 'in the event of the policy of the Government being approved by an adequate majority in the new House of Commons, His Majesty will be ready to exercise his constitutional powers, which may involve the Prerogative of creating Peers, if needed, to secure that effect shall be given to the decision of the Country'. In Asquith's words, 'The King . . . felt that he had no alternative but to assent to the advice of the Cabinet.'[2] On 18 November the Prime Minister announced in the Commons that the King had accepted his advice to dissolve without disclosing the Sovereign's promise to create new Peers if needed.

(e) Lloyd George's 'second Khaki' or 'coupon' election in 1918 was undoubtedly a successful attempt to exploit a favourably disposed electorate. Nevertheless, Mr Lloyd George had strong arguments[3] that favoured his view. Parliament, in his opinion, had ceased to represent the Nation

---

King George V, pp. 161ff., 174ff., 207ff. Jenkins, *Asquith*, ch. xiv, xv; R. Jenkins, *Mr. Balfour's poodle; an account of the struggle between the House of Lords and the Government of Mr. Asquith* (1963); Evatt, *The King and his Dominion Governors*, ch. 9, pp. 70–89.

[1] Asquith, *Fifty years of Parliament*, ii, 78–9.
[2] Asquith, ibid. pp. 90–1.   [3] Nicolson, *King George V*, p. 429.

and had by far exceeded its statutory term of life. Finally, in view of the forthcoming peace negotiations the Coalition needed a fresh and clear mandate to carry out its tedious task.[1]

The contrary view was held by the King.[2] He convincingly put his points forward on 5 November 1918 when he saw the Prime Minister. His Majesty warned the Prime Minister against the danger of being accused of following Joseph Chamberlain's example in 1900. Lloyd George disagreed with the comparison; in the long run, however, the King was proved right. The King also reminded the Prime Minister that he already had the support of the House as well as that of Mr Asquith. It is submitted, however, that in this respect Mr Lloyd George's arguments are more convincing. Finally, the King was apprehensive of 'the unknown factors of the soldiers' and women's votes', and the danger of disenfranchising a large percentage of soldiers.

Whatever the merit of the King's arguments he finally gave in to his Prime Minister's wishes. Sir Harold Nicolson, praising the King's attitude concludes thus:[3]

The only alternatives open to the King were either to accept Mr. Lloyd George's resignation, which was politically impossible, or to follow his advice. Mr. Lloyd George can scarcely be blamed for insisting upon a dissolution in the winter of 1918. It is not the election itself that is open to criticism but the methods by which, and the manner in which, it was conducted.

(*f*) Mr Bonar Law's 1922 dissolution raises no problems. The Carlton Club coup had aimed at reasserting the Conservatives' independence from the Coalition Government. In any event the feeling was that the Coalition had ceased to represent the Nation, which strongly desired a return to pre-war conditions. With this as a pretext and with a financial policy of strict economy at home and free trade with overseas and Commonwealth countries, the Prime Minister decided to go to the country.[4]

(*g*) The 1923 election is known as the tariff election and there is no reason to doubt that Mr Baldwin strongly believed that protectionism offered a solution to unemployment. Nevertheless it would seem that his desire for a new mandate was not the only – or even perhaps the major – argument that induced him to advise an early dissolution.

Protectionism and even the possibility of a dissolution that would provide the Government with a fresh mandate, had been in the air for some time. But it does not convincingly explain why Mr Baldwin suddenly took the quick decision to dissolve. Newspapers were calling

---

[1] *The Times*, 18 November 1919.   [2] Nicolson, *King George V*, p. 428.
[3] Ibid. p. 430.   [4] See for example *The Times*, 27 October 1922.

for a referendum on the new economic policy and his colleagues favoured a January or February election. He himself said, that the 'march of events' since his Plymouth address had 'compelled' him to an immediate dissolution.[1] The explanation seems only partly convincing.

There is little doubt that in 1923 the Conservative Party was deeply divided. Mr Bonar Law's 1922 Carlton coup had alienated the strong pro-Lloyd George section of the party from their younger colleagues. Mr Baldwin's appointment as Prime Minister in 1923 had done nothing to close the gap. On the contrary it had created new dissatisfactions. Baldwin's attempts to reunite the party had met with little success and with tension increasing in Europe there was a danger of a growing nostalgia for Lloyd George's powerful leadership. Throughout the summer the Prime Minister's 'chief preoccupations were the direct approach of Poincaré, unemployment and Lloyd George'.[2]

By late autumn, Mr Baldwin was informed that Lloyd George – on his way back from America – was likely to adopt protectionism. He was also aware of growing opposition coming from the section of the national press that was favourable to his party!

For the Prime Minister, attack seemed the best form of defence and dissolution was to be the weapon. By going to the country with a new and common policy, his chances of reuniting the party seemed good enough, even if he lost the election. In any event he would consolidate his leadership. Lord Curzon, of course, thought otherwise. He had predicted that in the event of defeat, Baldwin would be deposed from the party leadership.[3] It is true that Baldwin was faced with serious criticism after his defeat. But the short term of office of the Labour Government soon gave him a new chance and the Conservatives rallied once again round their leader; this time with better luck.

Baldwin himself has made the interpretation of his sudden decision no easier. In 1925, he spoke of it as a long-meditated decision to reunite his party, which seems convincing, though it does not fully justify his quick decisions during the last month before dissolution. Twelve years after the event, Baldwin came back to the subject and described to a friend his motives and aims more fully:

Rightly or wrongly I was convinced you could not deal with unemployment without a tariff. After the war, opinion was more fluid and open. On political grounds, the tariff issue had been dead for years and I felt it was the one issue which would pull the party together including the Lloyd George malcontents. The Goat [Lloyd

---

[1] P.R.O. CAB 23/46, 54 (23) 1.
[2] Middlemas & Barnes, *Baldwin*, p. 217.
[3] Lady Curzon, *Reminiscences*, p. 187. See also discussion in chapter 5, p. 77.

George] was in America. He was on the water when I made the speech and the Liberals did not know what to say. No truth that I was pushed by Amery and the cabal. I was loosely in the saddle and got them into line in the Cabinet. Dished the Goat, as otherwise he would have got the Party with Austen and F. E. [Birkenhead] and there would have been an end to the Tory Party as we know it. I shall not forget the surprise and delight of Amery. It was a long calculated and not a sudden dissolution. Bonar had no programme and the only thing was to bring the issue forward.[1]

It is submitted that Baldwin's dissolution had specific party motives:[2] the reunion of the Conservatives under his leadership. The tariff policies, important as they were, were a means of achieving the basic aim. Such an interpretation can only claim to be a personal view and one cannot expect to find written evidence for it. No politician would put such an intention into writing. Baldwin's decision, as all human decisions, was a product of many causes. Yet, his above-quoted statement, if read carefully, reveals how uncertain he felt and to a great extent proves the point. His decision to dissolve against the wishes of most of his senior colleagues was undoubtedly a calculated risk in an attempt to unite the party and, at the same time, consolidate his grip over it. In the long run it proved a step in the right direction.

(*h*) The 1924 dissolution is interesting because it is the first dissolution obtained by a Labour Prime Minister, and because it is the only dissolution in the twentieth century that resulted from a defeat in the House. As already stated the Cabinet had decided in advance, 'that if either the Conservative vote of censure or the Liberal amendment should be carried, the Prime Minister should advise the King to dissolve'.[3] On 8 October, after the defeat, the Cabinet met again and it was agreed that the Prime Minister should see the King the next morning and advise dissolution.

(*i*) The 1929 dissolution, like its predecessor in 1892, was advised towards the end of the life of Parliament and, in this respect, was nothing unusual. Yet, careful preparations had preceded it and the actual moment of dissolution was chosen to meet the interests of the party in office. Thus the Cabinet discussed dissolution twice in October 1928[4] and arrangements were made for the Central Office to give its views on the issue. On 12 October 1928, the Principal Agent of the Conservative and Unionist Central Office sent a detailed memorandum giving seven reasons favouring an early election. His advice was not followed and the elections were finally held in May 1929. Yet, the final two reasons con-

---

[1] Quoted by Middlemas & Barnes, *Baldwin*, p. 212; C. L. Mowat, *Britain between the wars, 1918–1940* (1964), p. 166, is not convinced by the above.
[2] Above, chapter 5, p. 76.   [3] P.R.O. CAB 23/48 (52 (24) 1a).
[4] P.R.O. CAB 23/58 (45 (28) 1) and CAB 23/59 (46 (28) 1) (1 and 10 October).

tained in the memorandum are worth quoting as they illustrate the kind of factors the Central Office usually takes into consideration.

> If there is to be an early election, the Government need not declare its policy until shortly before the dissolution . . . This will be entirely to our advantage. If the election is delayed, some indication of the policy the Government proposes to fight on will be demanded early in the summer, even by members of our own party. This would mean a long summer campaign, and would enable our opponents to attack us at meetings in the open air and place us at a disadvantage, for the technicalities of derating and local Reform can best be dealt with indoors.
>
> The country will anticipate an election shortly after the new register comes into force, and if it is delayed, our opponents are certain to say we are afraid to face the issue.[1]

(*j*) The 1931 dissolution was decided upon by the Coalition partners in order to obtain the famous 'doctor's mandate' in view of the critical economic situation. It raises no special problems.

(*k*) The 1935 dissolution is the only known case in which international affairs played a vital part. Even in 1955 the Suez crisis did not lead to new elections and Mr Macmillan was able to succeed Sir Anthony Eden and in fact stage a remarkable comeback in 1959.

The international tension in Europe and the threatened invasion of Abyssinia had made Mr Baldwin contemplate a dissolution as early as spring 1935. In Neville Chamberlain's words, Baldwin was thinking of asking for a new mandate because 'we were in for a long and anxious period of foreign affairs in which it was essential that we should have a stable Government with the authority of the Nation behind it'.[2]

However, not all members of the National Government felt the same way. On 14 October Mr Malcolm MacDonald sent a three-page letter to the Prime Minister in which he stated:[3]

> I believe that an immediate election will lose the Government the goodwill of very large numbers of its supporters outside the Conservative party, who are keen supporters of the National Government and of its foreign policy in the present crisis, but who are feeling resentful at what they regard as a proposal to exploit the present unity of the Nation on foreign policy to gain a party victory. During the last few days I have listened to the conversation of a variety of people – politicians, civil servants and rank and file friends of the Government – and most of them express the same view. They are fearful in the first place lest by throwing foreign policy at this

---

[1] Baldwin Papers, vol. 36.
[2] Middlemas & Barnes, *Baldwin*, p. 860.
[3] Baldwin Papers, vol. 47; Middlemas & Barnes, *Baldwin*, p. 860, refer to the letter using its phraseology but seem to ascribe it to the Prime Minister (Ramsay) and not his son (Malcolm). This does not seem to be correct, unless they are referring to an earlier letter (9 October) by Ramsay, which, however, is not so strongly phrased. Baldwin Papers, vol. 47.

moment back into party politics the international situation itself is gravely prejudiced and Great Britain's authority impaired, and secondly lest the spirit of willing co-operation between people of the Left and Right in National Government is spoilt.

MacDonald's letter must have impressed the Prime Minister since his secretary noted at the top of the page: 'P.M. has seen and wishes filed.' Yet, with Abyssinia already invaded and with the problem of sanctions hotly debated, the Prime Minister decided to seek a new mandate based on re-armament.[1] On 18 October he wrote to the King:

At the time of my last audience with Your Majesty, it had seemed to me that the election might be held back until the New Year, although in view of the requirements of public finance it could not then have been delayed beyond the first weeks. The ground for this anticipation has, however, been altered by the developments of the international situation and in looking into the possibilities for future policy, the public mind works on the background that the present Government has entered upon the last year of its maximum life. With opinions running so strongly, the alternative of an autumn election seems to me inevitable.[2]

In the Commons, on 23 October he gave the following explanation:

I saw last week that there was, as far as could be seen ahead – and you can see ahead with greater certainty for three weeks than you can for three months – that there was coming a lull in foreign affairs and that, so far as I could see, it would be perfectly safe to have an election in that time. I could not say the same in January.[3]

However, although the re-armament policy was uppermost in his mind, as is obvious from his speeches in the House on 22 October, party politics seemed to have been taken seriously into consideration. As early as August 1935 Baldwin had asked the Central Office for its opinion on an early election. On 1 August 1935 Sir Patrick Gower, Chief Publicity Officer, sent the Prime Minister a personal confidential report which apparently was only partly accepted by Mr Baldwin. Yet, it proves the careful calculations preceding dissolution and hence parts of it are worth quoting:[4]

If Italy were to withdraw from the League and if, as a result, the League appears to be in danger of complete dissolution, I would strongly deprecate the holding of a General Election until some time had elapsed in which to explain the position to the country and counter the misrepresentations in which our opponents would inevitably indulge in order to discredit the Government. However unfair the argument might be it would be said that it was the bungling diplomacy of the National Government

[1] He made this perfectly clear in the House on 22 October.
[2] Quoted by Middlemas & Barnes, *Baldwin*, p. 863.
[3] *The Times*, 24 October 1935.
[4] Baldwin Papers, vol. 47.

which had caused the downfall of the League, and I feel that this would be a very dangerous weapon against us.

. . . If the election were to be held towards the later part of November I cannot help thinking that it would have disastrous effects from the point of view of the Christmas trade . . .

Another factor that influences me is that I do not believe there has been sufficient preparatory work in the constituencies.

. . . Another three or four months intensive effort might make a great deal of difference.

By the end of October Mr Baldwin thought that the time had come to go to the country. He dissolved on 25 October. A year later Keith observed that politically the 'dissolution proved of great advantage, and that this was no doubt fully present to the mind of the Prime Minister'.[1]

(*l*) The 1945 dissolution offers a clear example of how politicians endeavour to combine national and party interests when contemplating a dissolution.

When the war with Germany came to an end, elections had to be held. Churchill had in fact committed himself to this in a speech in the House of Commons. Nevertheless, when the actual moment arrived he changed his mind and wished to prolong the life of the Coalition until the end of the Japanese War. He communicated his views to Attlee who seemed to favour an October election which would have a more complete electoral register. But Churchill – who had been in contact with Eden, then in San Francisco – had reached the conclusion that a June election would suit the Conservatives better. With this in mind he offered Attlee a choice between continuing the Coalition or a June dissolution and even put this proposal into writing. Attlee, however, who 'considered himself the servant as well as the leader of the Labour Party and . . . was going to Blackpool to discover the feeling of the delegates and not merely to tell them what to do',[2] referred the matter to the National Executive of the Labour Party. Its decision favoured an October election and was communicated to Churchill. Two days later the Prime Minister resigned his post and was re-commissioned to form a caretaker Government. He dissolved according to his original plans on 15 June and went to the country.

(*m*) Mr Attlee's dissolution in 1950 took place approximately four months before the legal end of Parliament. It is probable that it was speeded up because of fears of price increases resulting from the recent devaluation. However, political motivation cannot have been significant.

---

[1] *The King and the Imperial Crown*, p. 175.

[2] Churchill, *The Second World War*, IV, 511ff.; R. Jenkins, *Mr. Attlee, an interim biography* (1948), pp. 244–5; Mackenzie, *British political parties*, pp. 328–9.

(*n*) On the contrary the 1951 dissolution was the result of the small majority of seats that Labour had won in the previous elections (315 Labour, 298 Conservatives, 9 Liberal). The Cabinet was divided over the timing of dissolution. Senior ministers such as Morrison strongly opposed the idea of an early election whereas others such as Attlee himself and Hugh Dalton took the opposite view. Considering various losses at by-elections an early dissolution also promised to decrease the size of a possible defeat.

(*o*) Eden dissolved Parliament a month after he took office. The main reason seems to have been the domestic difficulties he was facing, though he himself said on the radio on 7 May 1955, that in view of the international situation the Government should have a clear mandate. Aided by an election Budget[1] he was returned with an increased majority.

(*p*) Announcing the 1959 dissolution Mr Macmillan maintained that in view of important international negotiations the country was called upon to decide by whom it wished to be represented. However, the great improvement of the party's fortunes since 1958 must have prompted him to go to the country and renew his term. The moment was indeed extremely favourable. The economy was booming and while the Labour Party was faced with internal dissension over the issue of the defence policy, Macmillan, enjoying Mr Butler's full loyalty, had a united party behind him. His careful calculations were more than amply rewarded at the elections that followed.[2]

(*q*) Finally, though little is officially known – writing in 1971 – about the last three dissolutions (1964, 1966, 1970) there is no doubt that party considerations played a decisive role in determining the exact date of going to the country.

In 1964 no reasons were given. But Parliament was approaching its statutory end and it had become obvious that the Conservatives could not continue for much longer.

In 1966 Mr Wilson gave his reasons on a B.B.C. interview on 28 February. He said: 'I don't think anyone, certainly anyone in Parliament, thought when we were elected with a majority of five – later three – we could have lasted 500 days and carried through all we have.' The fact that Labour had a small majority which made an early election likely does not exclude the possibility of determining the actual date of dissolution on the basis of party calculations. Though Mr Wilson firmly stated in the same interview that he had 'never been very much pushed around by what the polls say', it is a fact that both opinion polls and a by-election in Hull had shown a clear lead in favour of the Government.

---

[1] Mackenzie, ibid. p. 583. [2] Ibid. pp. 593–4.

Prior to the announcement of the 1970 dissolution the opinion polls showed Labour in the lead for the first time in three years. National Gallup, published in the *Daily Telegraph* on 13 May, showed a lead for Labour of 7.5%. The National Opinion Poll, published in the *Daily Mail* on 14 May, showed a lead of 3.2% and the Marplan Poll, taken before the announcement of dissolution but published a day later in *The Times*, showed a lead of 2.7%. This dramatic change in the fortunes of the Government followed by the immediate announcement of the dissolution led many to believe that party politics had been the determining factor. The Prime Minister denied the accusation in a B.B.C. interview on 18 May. He insisted that he had taken a 'pretty firm' decision to dissolve five to six weeks before the polls and the Budget. Whether the Prime Minister convinced his audience is anybody's guess. But he was certainly right in saying that an election atmosphere had developed which could not have continued for much longer in view of the fact that important decisions were pending. Mr Wilson also told his audience that the Chancellor's opinion was that no economic reasons existed in favour of an early or late election and so 'the decision should be taken on other grounds'. What these other grounds were no one knows – for the time being at least. According to Mr Wilson's B.B.C. interview these were presumably the preceding political decisions, the Common Market negotiations etc. But one can also argue that 'other grounds' could quite legitimately include party calculations which the Prime Minister as the leader of the majority party is bound to take into consideration. And in a recent article written for the *Britannica Book of the Year* and re-published by the *Observer*, Mr Wilson indirectly admitted this by maintaining that even though the improvement in the polls was not the deciding factor in 1970 'the voting in the boroughs was a more decisive test'.

Mr Wilson's article is also interesting because it puts forward a novel theory. He denies that the polls carry – at any rate with him – a decisive weight but maintains that their main relevance is 'in creating a consensus that the date he [the Prime Minister] has pencilled in his diary is the right one'. The view that opinion polls influence the Prime Minister's 'senior colleagues' but not the Prime Minister himself may be correct as far as Mr Wilson's Cabinet was concerned. But, with respect, it seems to lack the logical basis that could make it applicable in all cases. And even in Mr Wilson's case his theory is only partly correct because, as he himself maintains, 'Before I finally announced the date . . . pressure from party and press was such that I should have been thought mad if I had decided to wait until later in the year.'[1]

---

[1] *Observer*, 21 March 1971.

The conclusion seems to be that the timing of and the reason for a dissolution is, at times, extremely difficult to decide. What with by-election results, Christmas trade or summer holidays, the Prime Minister may be faced with serious problems. On 23 October 1935, Mr Baldwin, announcing to the Commons his decision to dissolve, described this semi-farcical situation as follows:

I have long come to the conclusion that you must rule out the spring and summer months because of financial business. You must rule out August and September because of the holidays. You are left with autumn, but in no circumstances must you run into any interference with the Christmas trade . . . You are limited therefore, to a small period in the autumn and early in the year and the early part of the year must depend on the date of Easter in that year.[1]

Exaggerated? Yes. Entirely wrong? No.

[1] *The Times*, 24 October 1935. Harold Wilson, *The Labour Government, 1964–1970*, p. 200, mentions some of the factors that have to be taken into consideration when timing a dissolution. Referring to the 1966 elections, he writes: 'There was a lot to think about. There had not been a March election since 1880 (when the Government lost). There was a risk of bad weather, as in 1963 – or indeed as there was to be in March 1970 – which not only lowers morale and, therefore, Government support, but which also makes many families worse off – building and other outdoor workers are unable to work, an extra bag of coal to buy or, in other cases, more shillings needed in the meter for heating. On the other hand, there is usually a better feeling as the country emerges from winter into spring. These are difficult things to assess in electoral terms.' The above shows how carefully the electorate's probable reaction is studied. Professor Hood Phillips, *Reform of the Constitution*, p. 52, has described 'this squalid practice' (i.e. choosing the dissolution date in accordance with party interests) as 'the least creditable aspect of the British Constitution'.

Chapter 7

DISSOLUTION TODAY

A: CONVENTIONS AND THE CONSTITUTION

Dissolution is one of those peripheral subjects of constitutional law which can be equally interesting to constitutional historians and political scientists alike. The latter, for example, will be eager to know the institutional purpose dissolution is expected to fulfil. In addition its practice can reveal important aspects of the relationship between Government and Parliament and even give a glimpse of the party structure. The constitutional lawyer, on the other hand, will primarily wish to define, as precisely as possible, the limits of the royal prerogative.

Strange as it may seem, the picture a contemporary lawyer would give of dissolution is, prima facie, the same as it was a hundred years ago. In theory, the Sovereign still has the power to dissolve Parliament just as he has the right to appoint or dismiss his Ministers. Theory and practice, however – as so often is the case – are divergent. A chain of precedents has strictly, though not always precisely, defined the Crown's reserve powers. But it is worth noting that this 'legal' evolution of the right to dissolve has been predominantly influenced by broader political arguments. For over a hundred years now dissolution has been exercised in a legally impeccable manner so that the lawyer was never called in to provide a strictly legal solution to an existing problem. On the other hand, the political discussions that surrounded certain of the more controversial decisions to dissolve Parliament – notably in 1910, 1913 and to a lesser extent in 1924 – have greatly contributed towards defining the rights of the Crown on this subject.

To the academic purist, of course, this fusion of political and legal arguments may be reprehensible. For one thing, it might turn a complicated constitutional issue into an arena for party polemics. Some lawyers might also agree with Dicey who plainly stated in his *Introduction to the study of the law of the constitution*[1] that 'the circumstances under which a Minister is entitled to dissolve Parliament [are] ... matters too high for me'. With respect, it seems that few would nowadays accept Dicey's sharp line of division between strict constitutional law and political

[1] pp. 20–1.

science. As Professor E. C. S. Wade writes in his preface to Dicey's *Law of the constitution*, 'constitutional law and political science are divided by a line which it is hard to distinguish'.[1] The former, particularly if it is to be successful in its purpose, is so closely connected to the actual political realities that it is impossible to ignore them. And Dicey was the first to refuse to bind himself to his rules by actively participating in the 1913 controversy and making far-reaching observations on the subject. So the reader must be aware of the fact that the constitutional lawyer is frequently obliged to take into consideration or even rely on views and opinions that one would not term, strictly speaking, legal. Practice and the views of active politicians are thus taken into account when the extent of the reserve powers of the Crown is discussed.

To turn to more concrete conclusions one should, perhaps, make clear from the outset that a royal or forced dissolution is obsolete. The last time a dissolution emanated from the Sovereign's personal initiative was in 1834 and this should speak for itself. Admittedly, in the years that followed and particularly during the reign of Queen Victoria, the Sovereign contemplated exercising the right. This, for example, was the case in 1852, 1859, 1866, 1884, 1893, 1894[2] and, of course, later on in 1913. In all these cases, however, the Prime Minister of the day did not agree and the Sovereign did not press his view further. Of these crises, the most important was that of 1913 which was discussed in an earlier part of this book.[3] Despite views expressed at that time, on the whole politicians and constitutional lawyers rarely encouraged the Sovereign to play an active part in British politics. The exact opposite is, in fact, the truth. Even Lord Salisbury, to quote a statesman who was more than generous when defining the reserve powers of the Crown, expressed his fears that,

a dissolution by the Queen, against the advice of her Ministers, would, of course, involve their resignation. Their party could hardly help going to the country as the opponents of the royal authority; or at least, as the severe critics of the mode in which it had been exerted. No one can foresee what the upshot of such a state of things would be! It might be good; or it might be bad! But there must be *some* hazard that, in the end, such a step would injure the authority of the Queen.[4]

It is suggested that a royal dissolution in our times would not merely be unpolitical; it would also be unconstitutional.

---

[1] p. xxvii.
[2] See *Letters of Queen Victoria*, 2nd series, I, 320; III, 511–13, 515–18, 521; 3rd series, II, 279, 282, 298–9, 431–44. Also J. Bardoux, *La reine Victoria d'après sa correspondance inédite* (1907), II, 553–4.
[3] Above, chapter 4, pp. 63ff.   [4] *Letters of Queen Victoria*, 3rd series, II, 297–9.

The Crown has thus lost the initiative. In England more than in any other European country the power has now shifted to the Prime Minister and the shift might turn out to be as dangerous as undoubtedly it is important. It will have become apparent to the reader that in all the dissolutions discussed in the previous chapters (with the exception of 1913) the question was not whether the King could force a dissolution – for most authors particularly in the twentieth century, the answer would be negative. The question was whether the King could refuse a dissolution to his Prime Minister; this issue is still widely discussed and views differ considerably. No one in particular was or is quite sure whether a convention has emerged that virtually allows the Prime Minister a free hand in the matter.

Flexibility, we are told, has been one of the most important assets of the British Constitution. Usually through conventions it has been able to keep in touch with the rapid change of political, economic and legal ideas of the past two centuries. But conventions have also proved a source of confusion. In our rapidly changing times an extremely flexible constitution can be as dangerous as its rigid counterpart. Quite often, to quote Dr Evatt, 'It is impossible to tell whether the conventions are being obeyed, because no one can say with sufficient certainty what the conventions are.'[1] In the case of dissolution there is the added difficulty that there is considerable doubt whether such a convention exists and in particular what are its limits as regards the Crown's right to refuse the Prime Minister's advice.

Does the fact that no dissolution has been refused in the United Kingdom for well over a century establish a general prescriptive rule or does it merely describe an actual state of affairs and nothing more? In other words, is dissolution regulated by a convention or is it a mere usage? It is submitted that if a usage is to have any relevance to conduct, it must be something more than a mere description of actual behaviour. It must have a prescriptive character and hence resemble a binding rule the exceptions to which cannot always be easily specified. However, if the exceptions could be actually specified (for example, that the Monarch must grant a dissolution except under circumstances X, Y and Z) then the rule would be applicable in this form and would be a convention. 'The difficulties follow from picking out an action such as dissolving and asking about its obligatoriness. But it is the rule about dissolving which is the convention. Correctly stated, it cannot fail to be obligatory.'[2] Does a convention then exist?

---

[1] *The King and his Dominion Governors*, p. xxxvii, and pp. 269–81.
[2] Marshall & Moodie, *Some problems of the constitution*, p. 29.

Jennings suggests[1] three questions to be asked in order to determine the existence of a convention, namely, are there any precedents? did the actors in the precedents believe that they were bound by a rule? and is there a reason for this rule? Jennings' suggestions are not above criticism especially since they provide no clues as to how his various tests are related to each other. But they are widely accepted and for lack of a better method they will be used here.

The existence of precedents is the first test. There have been nineteen requests for a dissolution in the twentieth century (twenty-six since 1868)[2] and not one of them was ever refused. Every one of these dissolutions took place under completely different and occasionally unique circumstances and the fact that they cover a vast number of possible situations and yet never – not even once – were refused, indicates very strongly something more than a chain of precedents.

Jennings, however, argues against the conclusive nature of the above argument. A series of precedents is usually a good indication, yet not conclusive in itself. A number of precedents may not establish a rule; and conversely, a single precedent with a good reason can establish a rule. He goes on to say that all the Sovereigns from Queen Victoria to King George V inclusive 'insisted upon their right to refuse a dissolution, and that the Prime Ministers for the time being ... have approached the Monarch on the same understanding'.[3] This brings us to his second test: the awareness of obligation by the protagonists, a test even more confusing than the first.

This second test is useful only if two things occur: (*i*) all the actors involved agree in their opinions and on their respective obligations (as Jennings suggests in the previous quotation) and (*ii*) they are not mistaken about their obligations. Unfortunately these conditions cannot be easily satisfied.

Conventions are likely to regulate behaviour in delicate and controversial situations and on such occasions it is more probable than not that the protagonists will have conflicting opinions on their respective rights and obligations. Hence, all the dispute and confusion.

Let us first take a general example. Jennings has argued against the conclusive nature of Mr Baldwin's appointment as Prime Minister in 1923. Even if the King felt compelled to select a member of the Lower House to be Prime Minister, he argues, 'it might be that he was mistaken in thinking himself so bound'.[4] Lord Stamfordham's memorandum containing his conversation with Lord Curzon after Baldwin's election

---

[1] *The law and the constitution*, p. 136.
[2] See Appendix 1.1.
[3] Jennings, *The law and the constitution*, p. 135.
[4] Ibid. p. 136.

makes it amply clear that: 'His Majesty . . . felt compelled . . . to base his choice upon what he conceived to be the requirements of the present times: viz. the continuance of the Prime Minister in the House of Commons.'[1] In fact, most historians, politicians and lawyers would agree that Lord Curzon's peerage proved a serious handicap and certainly this was his personal opinion.[2] This is a typical example of the difficulties one faces when deciding what the views of the protagonists really were.

To take an example more relevant to dissolution: Jennings, referring to the 1918 dissolution, comments that: 'The King's decision was, in the circumstances, quite reasonable; but it was not the only possible decision.'[3] Does this suggest that the King could have constitutionally refused his Prime Minister's advice in 1918? Does it also imply that the King retained his right to refuse a dissolution in the future under circumstances similar to those of 1918 even though he did not exercise it then? If it does, then the King's views on his obligations differ considerably from those of Mr Lloyd George and of Mr Bonar Law, since both of them believed that the Prime Minister was entitled to a dissolution. Sir Harold Nicolson also agrees that the King had no real alternative. Jennings, however, insists on his argument and maintains that we do not know what would have happened had the King 'pushed his arguments far enough' and concludes that in any event Mr Lloyd George's resignation would not have been a great national disaster.

Mr Lloyd George's position in history remains to be judged. No controversial personality – and Mr Lloyd George certainly was one – can be praised or condemned in a single phrase. More important, Jennings' judgement is ex post facto. Refusing a dissolution to the Prime Minister of the Government which had won the war and whose personal prestige was at that time very considerable would have been politically unwise and could have given rise to a constitutional crisis of the highest order. It must be remembered that the Prime Minister had advised dissolution on behalf of the National Government, and a refusal would have led to its resignation with no alternative administration possible.

The 1918 dissolution thus reveals two things. First, that under those particular conditions the King had no choice. Second, that there was a

---

[1] Quoted by Nicolson, *King George V*, p. 488.

[2] See for example: Amery, *Thoughts on the constitution*, p. 22; H. Daalder, *Cabinet reform in Britain 1914–1963* (1964), p. 7; Mitchell, *Constitutional law*, p. 30. Churchill's example is further proof. Sir Alec Douglas Home also had to resign his peerage. Lord Curzon's own opinion was expressed with some bitterness in his speech on 28 May 1923 at the Conservative Party meeting when he moved a motion acknowledging Baldwin as leader. He said: 'Lastly, (I breathe this almost sotto voce) Mr. Baldwin possesses the supreme and *indispensable* qualification of not being a peer.' (Quoted by Mackenzie, *British political parties*, p. 41.)   [3] *Cabinet government*, p. 425.

certain amount of disagreement between the protagonists as to their respective rights and duties. As a matter of fact, it is interesting to note that King George V almost invariably objected to the dissolutions of his reign just as his father had had his doubts as regards Sir Henry Campbell-Bannerman's dissolution. And yet they both finally complied with the Prime Minister's wishes.

The third and final test is the 'good reason' criterion. This, like the previous tests, is not free from ambiguities. Does 'good reason' imply 'the making of an appraisal or the mere reporting of one'? Furthermore, who will decide whether the reason is good or bad and what criteria will he apply?

It seems to me that the 'good reason' criterion is exactly the reason for which a convention is obeyed. Not because it will ultimately lead to the violation of a legal rule – as Dicey had originally suggested – but because its violation creates certain political difficulties. More precisely, it tends to destroy the established distribution of authority and weakens the respect due to it. If the Crown played an active role such results would certainly be produced.

It is obvious from the above that Jennings' criteria are not always clear and easily reconcilable. But to the extent that they are, all three can be applied to the general principles which are mentioned below and which emerge from the twenty-six dissolutions of the last hundred years. If this is accepted as correct then it can be argued that a convention exists. However, before the rules are stated a few words should be added in connection with a particularly British attitude.

Most authors who have dealt with the problem tend to take the view that defining the rules which control the exercise of the reserve powers of the Crown is a purposeless if not dangerous enterprise. Sidney Low perhaps epitomised the reasons lying behind this argument when he wrote some fifty years ago that: 'It is of the essence of the English system of Government that it is in a state of constant development.'[1] This is why, so the argument goes, it is preferable to leave the issue in a fluid state. The only concession made to today's political realities is the acknowledgement that the right (to dissolve or refuse a dissolution) will arise only in very exceptional circumstances.

There are two main arguments against the above view. First, that the twenty-six dissolutions of the last hundred years cover a wide variety of possible situations in all of which the Monarch was content to offer his advice – often very wise advice – but ultimately followed the Prime Minister's advice. It is thus difficult to conceive realistic circumstances

---

[1] *The Governance of England* (1914 edn), p. 12.

which will not be covered by the existing precedents and which would lead to the exercise of the right. Second, as Dr D. V. Evatt has convincingly argued,[1] there is no inconsistency between the demand for definition and suitable provision for adaptability and amendment to be contained in such definition. It is therefore submitted that the following rules clearly emerge from the United Kingdom practice and accordingly form the rule about dissolving. It should also be noted that though they do not altogether eliminate the rare possibility of a Crown initiative, they clearly show that the right has shifted to other hands.

(*i*) The Crown cannot force a dissolution upon a Government; this would also imply its dismissal.

(*ii*) The Crown, in the vast majority of cases, must act on the advice of the Prime Minister of the time.

(*iii*) The Crown cannot refuse a dissolution to a majority Prime Minister. The size of his party's majority is irrelevant.

(*iv*) The timing of and reason for the dissolution is left to the Prime Minister's discretion.

(*v*) The Crown may, under certain circumstances, refuse a dissolution to a minority Government (whether defeated or undefeated) provided an alternative Government is possible and able to carry on with the existing House. If the Government is censured it is advisable that the Crown recall its predecessor and grant its request to dissolve.

(*vi*) Though an appeal to the electorate is always proper a series of dissolutions, particularly if they are based on the same reason, might represent a triumph over and not a triumph of the electorate.

(*vii*) A Government which has been granted a dissolution may not proceed to a second dissolution until the new Parliament proves unworkable and no other Government is likely and willing to carry on with the existing House.

(*viii*) The question as to which party was granted the previous dissolution and the timing of dissolution (first or last session of Parliament) are matters which may be taken into account but are not in themselves decisive.

B: THE SHIFT OF POWER

The long procedure of curtailing the royal powers to a minimum has undoubtedly succeeded in its main purpose. But ironically enough it has re-created in a different form the problem political scientists of the past believed had been solved with the introduction of the parliamentary form

[1] *The King and his Dominion Governors*, ch. 1. See also the discussion in ch. XXIX.

of government. The problem essentially is and always has been how to avoid a great concentration of power in the hands of one person or state organ. Admittedly, there is a vast difference between a powerful King and an omnipotent Prime Minister. If anything, the latter is politically responsible to the electorate whereas the mystique of royalty has always relied on exactly the opposite notion. But this having been said, one must point out that, with the passage of time, the Sovereign's actions were increasingly controlled whereas the Prime Minister of the 1970s has such powers that a learned author did not hesitate to find certain similarities with the notorious powers Soviet leaders are generally known to possess.[1]

As far as dissolution is concerned one must observe that though it is relatively easy to find rules regulating the exercise of the right by the Crown, no such rules exist, for the time being at least, limiting the Prime Minister's right to dissolve. It may thus well be that the whole operation of discussing the limits of the reserve powers of the Crown is nowadays for most purposes an idle exercise. The constitutional lawyer of the remaining decades of the twentieth century need not bother himself with such matters but instead should try to formulate new principles regulating the prime-ministerial powers. And the particular danger lies in the fact that the Prime Minister alone is ultimately responsible for the timing and the reason of dissolution and, as previous chapters have shown, is free to use this power against his opponents, whether in the Opposition or his own party. Dissolution has thus been accurately described as a sword 'which while in the scabbard is an instrument of discipline for the Government's own rebels. But it is drawn at the moment least convenient for the Opposition and, as a rule, it is effective.'[2]

For most authors the 'mere existence' of the 'big stick'[3] is sufficient 'psychological influence' to induce M.P.s to remain loyal to their party. This view, however, was recently challenged by an American writer[4] and hence deserves to be reconsidered. It has been suggested that dissolution as a disciplinary tool 'cuts both ways and cuts the Prime Minister most deeply'. To support this argument it is maintained that 'Prime

---

[1] The author is Richard Crossman and his view was that 'the Prime Minister can liquidate the political career of one of his colleagues as effectively as any of the leaders of the Soviet Union can remove rivals'. The sentence was written for the Introduction of Bagehot's *Constitution* but the publishers chose not to print it. Mackintosh, *The British Cabinet*, p. 437. Mr Crossman has further elaborated his thesis in his recent work *Inside view* (1972). Unfortunately, however, his book appeared too late to be considered here.

[2] Q. Hogg (now Lord Hailsham), *New charter*, p. 8.

[3] Jennings, *Cabinet government*, p. 474. B. E. Carter, *The Office of the Prime Minister* (1956), p. 274, describes it as 'this terrifying power'. But see G. Moodie's interesting discussion in *The government of Great Britain* (1967), pp. 96–105.

[4] W. G. Andrews, 'Some thoughts on the power of dissolution', *Parliamentary Affairs* (1959/60), pp. 286ff.

Ministers have dissolved the House of Commons thirty-one times since 1833. Seventeen times they lost office as a result. Six of the seventeen dissolutions since 1900 and six of the eleven since 1918 have produced new Prime Ministers.'[1] For those taking this view the conclusion seems to be that the Prime Minister 'has more to lose' and hence 'dissolution would not seem to be a very attractive weapon'.

It is not necessary to examine here the nineteenth-century experience since we are looking at dissolution as a party weapon and in the nineteenth century parties had not consolidated their grip upon their members to the extent they have today. Since it is precisely this connection of party discipline and dissolution that we are reviewing, it is a mistake to include the nineteenth-century figures. They can confuse but they cannot clarify the situation.[2] Since 1900 there have been nineteen dissolutions, including that of June 1970. Of these the Government won twelve times, that is a Prime Minister has won the ensuing elections. Further, an average of four out of five of the Government's followers who sought re-election were successful. Still, seven defeats out of nineteen might suggest too great a risk for the Prime Minister to take when contemplating dissolution. A closer examination of the seven defeats shows that this is not necessarily so.

To begin with, three of these seven defeats (1923, 1924 and 1929) took place during the anomalous years 1920–30 when the two-party system was not functioning properly. The experience of multi-party countries has shown that dissolution as a political weapon is less effective there. These three dissolutions cannot therefore be taken as conclusive.

A second point that must be made is that the effectiveness of dissolution as a party weapon can be judged only from the cases where the Prime Minister had some freedom in choosing the time to go to the country and not where he was obliged to do so because the statutory term of Parliament had expired. This is the case of the 1945 dissolution. In actual fact we saw[3] that Sir Winston Churchill made several attempts to postpone the elections but met with Mr Attlee's refusal to continue the Coalition Government. Under these circumstances it is difficult to say that dissolution was the Prime Minister's choice.

[1] Since the article was written in 1960 it naturally does not refer to the succeeding three elections. The problem that thus arises is which are the 'six' times Andrews has in mind, since only five such cases actually exist. He could have had two occasions in mind – 1900 and 1922. If this is so he is wrong. In the case of Lord Salisbury his resignation was caused by his failing health and in any event it took place nearly two years after the Khaki elections (11 July 1902). He died thirteen months later. The same applies to Bonar Law in 1922. His resignation was also caused by his failing health and not by dissolution which, after all, had worked in favour of his party.

[2] Andrews seems to accept this, ibid. p. 291.   [3] Above, chapter 6.

Real examples for the view that dissolution can go against the Government are only three, namely 1951, 1964 and 1970. And the closeness of the results, particularly in the first two cases, shows that even then the chances of a defeat of the Government in office are very slim. It is therefore true to say that the 'swing of the pendulum' has certainly not operated at the same rather brief intervals and the pattern nowadays is for governments 'to increase rather than diminish their majorities'.[1] In many cases the Opposition does not win the elections; the Government loses them and in one way or another dissolution is closely connected with the outcome.

It remains to be seen how Prime Ministers have used their right to dissolve. Their practice can, perhaps, be summarised under three headings.

(*a*) If one takes the years 1832 to 1900 one realises that Governments, as a rule, chose to resign rather than dissolve. This happened in 1839, 1846, 1851, 1852, 1855, 1858, 1866, 1879, 1885 and 1895; they dissolved in 1841, 1857, 1859, 1868, 1886 – a ratio of ten to five in favour of resignation. In the twentieth century, on the other hand, with the exception of the MacDonald Government in 1924, no Government has been faced with the alternative of resigning or dissolving. Party discipline and organisation have increased to such an extent that a parliamentary defeat could be envisaged only during the 1920s when the two-party system was not effectively functioning. One can further compare the governmental instability of the years 1832 to 1867 during which it is usually agreed that M.P.s had considerable independence in voting, with the years 1935 (Baldwin) to 1970 (Heath), to realise the contrast. As a result it can be argued that dissolution is no longer a means of referring a case of dispute between Government and Parliament to the electorate simply because no such dispute is likely to occur.

(*b*) Dissolution throughout the last hundred years has frequently been used as a means of appeal to the electorate on a specific issue thus, in a sense, replacing the referendal procedure. It is interesting, in fact, to note that all three party leaders were asked by a 'Television Forum' on the B.B.C. on 26, 27 and 28 May 1970 whether they were willing to hold a referendum on the issue of Britain's entry into the Common Market after the negotiations had been completed. All three answered in the negative and Mr Heath added that if the House was seriously divided a dissolution might follow and the issue referred to the electorate. Even more recently,[2] Mr Wilson speculated on a possible dissolution over the same issue. Thus, twice since 1867, namely in 1868 and 1886, and five

---

[1] Hogg, *New charter*, p. 8.   [2] B.B.C., 'Panorama', 10 May 1971.

times in the twentieth century (1900, 1910 (November), 1923, 1931 and 1935) the Government appealed to the electorate on a specific issue. It should be added, however, that though this has been used as a pretext, notably in 1959, it has not been the operative cause of a dissolution since 1935.

(c) Dissolution is increasingly used as a weapon to be brought into play at the moment least favourable to the Government's opponents. Though party calculations and interests existed in the nineteenth century, only once since 1867 did they decisively influence the timing of dissolution. As previously stated,[1] in 1880 Lord Beaconsfield's Cabinet reversed its previous decision and decided to advise dissolution and new elections on the strength of recent by-election results which were interpreted by the Government to indicate a nationwide swing in favour of the Conservative Party. In the twentieth century the picture is reversed. Out of a total of nineteen dissolutions, twelve were advised or decisively influenced by party politics and calculations, namely the dissolutions of 1900, 1918, 1922, 1923, 1935, 1945, 1951, 1955, 1959, 1964, 1966 and 1970 and in the last two elections opinion polls were widely used to eliminate chances of error. Within certain limits of proven accuracy, these opinion polls have provided party planners with an effective weapon, at any rate sufficiently effective to make many express doubts as to whether they should be allowed to continue in the future.

On the whole, however, one can conclude by stating that dissolution has been used properly. But the comforting thought that there has not been an abuse should not lead to an underestimation of the potential dangers inherent in the right.[2]

[1] Above, chapter 6.
[2] Because of the Common Market enabling legislation there has recently been considerable discussion inside and outside Parliament over the need to hold a referendum or, alternatively, a General Election, in order to allow the electorate the final word. These discussions came too late to be considered in the text but two general comments can be made. So far as the referendum is concerned there is little doubt that it is an institution 'foreign' to English parliamentary practice and to the classical form of parliamentary government. Dissolution, however, has been used by governments at their own discretion, as a means of appealing to the electorate. The whole issue, however, lies beyond the scope of this book and in any event is far too complicated to be discussed here.

PART III

DISSOLUTION OF PARLIAMENT IN GREECE

===

Chapter 8

THE CREATION OF THE NEW STATE AND THE REIGN OF KING OTHO
(1833–1862)

Greece offers convincing support for the view that constitutional law, political science and political history should largely be read in conjunction with one another. This is particularly true as regards the practice of dissolution of Parliament, the understanding of which presupposes a thorough knowledge of Greek, and often international, politics. Consequently, the following six chapters contain a good deal of historical information. However, it must be stressed that even though much of the purely historical material included in the text is new to foreign and Greek readers alike, it should not be regarded as an independent historical survey. It merely purports to provide an outline of the historical and political background and the reader who requires a fuller account should consult some at least of the following more general works: W. Alison-Phillips, *The War of Greek Independence, 1821–1833* (1897); G. K. Aspreas, *The political history of Modern Greece 1821–1921* (in Greek), 3 vols (1930); L. Bower & G. Bolitho, *Otho I, King of Greece* (1939); C. W. Crawley, *The question of Greek Independence. A study of British Foreign policy in the Near East, 1821–1833* (1930); E. Driault, *La Question d'Orient depuis ses origines jusqu'à la paix de Sèvres, 1920* (1921); E. Driault & M. Lhéritier, *Histoire diplomatique de la Grèce de 1821 à nos jours*, 5 vols (1925–6); G. Finlay, *A history of Greece from its conquest by the Romans to the present time, B.C. 146 to A.D. 1864* (1877), vols 6 and 7; G. F. Hertzberg, *Geschichte Griechenlands seit dem Absterben des antiken Lebens bis zur Gegenwart* (1876–9), particularly vol. IV: *Neueste Geschichte Griechenlands von der Erhebung der Neugriechen gegen die Pforte bis zum Berliner Frieden*; N. Iorga, *Histoire des états balkaniques jusqu'à 1924* (1925); P. Karolides, *Contemporary history of the Greeks and of the other peoples of the East from 1821 to 1921* (in Greek), 7 vols (1922–9); D. A. Kokinos, *The Greek Revolution*, 12 vols (in Greek) (1932); E. K. Kyriakides, *The history of contemporary Hellenism from the establishment of the Kingdom of Greece until our own days* (in Greek), 2 vols (1892); M. Lascaris, *The Eastern question 1800–1923*, vol. 1a, b (up to 1878) (in

Greek) (1948); S. Lascaris, *Diplomatic history of Greece, 1821–1914* (in Greek) (1947); Sp. B. Markesinis, *Political history of Modern Greece, 1827–1920*, 4 vols (1966–8) (in Greek); K. Mendelssohn-Bartholdy, *Geschichte Griechenlands von der Eroberung Konstantinopels durch die Türken im Jahre 1453 bis auf unsere Tage*, 2 vols (1870–4), particularly vol. 2: *Von der Verwaltung durch Kapodistrias bis zur Grossjährigkeit des König Otto*; W. Miller, *Greece* (1928); W. Miller, *The Ottoman Empire and its successors, 1801–1927* (rev. edn, 1936); C. Paparrigopoulos, *History of the Greek Nation from the most ancient times until our times*, with a supplement by P. Karolides for the events from 1830 up to 1930 (in Greek), 7 vols (1930); A. Freiherrn von Prokesch-Osten, *Geschichte des Abfalls der Griechen vom Türkischen Reiche im Jahre 1821 und der Gründung des Hellenischen Königreichs, aus diplomatischem Standpuncte*, 6 vols (1867); L. S. Stavrianos, *The Balkans since 1453* (1961); F. Thiersch, *De l'état actuel de la Grèce et des moyens d'arriver à sa restauration*, 2 vols (1833).

A: THE POLITICAL AND SOCIAL BACKGROUND

Seven years of struggle against the Turks led to the recognition of independence for only a small part of the Greek area. This was the result of a compromise between the opposing interests of the Great Powers within their greater conflict on the Eastern Question in its early nineteenth-century phase. It also foreshadowed the immense influence foreign powers were destined to exercise on the future policies of the new kingdom.

This is particularly true for the reign of King Otho. Foreign influence and interventions were frequently open and direct. The Pacifico Affair, the blockade of Piraeus, the events following the Crimean War, and even the enactment of the Constitution illustrates how the Great Powers tried to fashion internal developments according to their own interests. But even after Otho's dethronement many political or, broadly speaking, constitutional crises were directly or indirectly caused by or related to foreign interests and policies. The Cretan question, the Macedonian problem, Greece's position during the First World War and more recently Cyprus, are obvious examples.

To historians of our times this seems fairly easy to explain. Internal events were, as a rule, closely linked to the foreign policies of the Great Powers of the nineteenth and twentieth centuries in the eastern Mediterranean area. The attitude the Great Powers adopted on the problem of the Greek boundaries was also an important contributory factor to internal instability. Wellington in particular feared that the new state would be patronised by Russia and therefore pressed for the creation of a midget state with a dependent status.

But the limited breathing space granted to the newly created state produced made it unviable and produced impossible economic difficulties. Coupled with unfulfilled ideological aims – most of the Greeks were up to 1912 under Turkish domination – they soon led the free Greeks to believe that their survival was vitally linked to a policy of expansion – at the expense, of course, of their Ottoman neighbours.

The new State included only a minority of the Greeks in the Ottoman Empire and its military and economic weakness made it dependent on the goodwill of the protecting powers. Since in every probability its policy would be directed to extending its territory and liberating the unredeemed Greeks, and the generosity of different powers would vary according to the warmth of their attitudes to Turkey, the role of Greece in the development of the Eastern Question was already foreshadowed.[1]

The policy of expansion, however, produced the following inconsistency: its success relied on the support of one or more of the Great Powers and hence Greek politicians had to align themselves with one of them. The assistance, however, of one Power automatically provoked simultaneous counter-action by the others, whose interests never seemed to coincide. Hence, the only course left to Greek statesmen was a series of acrobatic manoeuvres intended to satisfy, if possible, all interested parties.[2] Such policies, however, are usually destined to fail.

Thus, during King Otho's reign there existed three parties – or more correctly three political factions – each of which was attached to one of the Great Powers, i.e. Russia, England and France.[3] They all hoped they could reach power through the assistance and occasional plots of their patron state. Greece was turned into a battlefield of conflicting foreign interests, which in numerous ways hindered, altered or annihilated the political development of the country.

While this seemed to be the attitude of the Great Powers towards Greece, the internal situation and particularly the absence of an organised political and social structure retarded all political change and prevented any rapid development in legal institutions. This state of affairs is reflected in the effective absence of a middle class – traditionally an element of equilibrium – the evolution of which was one of the basic factors of the development of nineteenth-century parliamentarism. Broadly speaking, one can say that up to the middle of the nineteenth century, the Greeks

---

[1] J. Campbell & P. Sherrard, *Modern Greece* (1968), p. 79.

[2] Kapodistrias, for example, sought to obtain financial support from all three Great Powers instead of one lest he become dependent on that one. Codrington, *Memoirs*, II, 165ff. King Otho followed his example with greater success at the beginning of his reign.

[3] These political groups existed from the very beginning of the War of Independence. German influence was not felt until the end of the century.

were divided into two categories or groups of people, both of which claimed to have liberated the country and to be entitled to the spoils of victory. The first and by far the most numerous was that of the tough, native *klefts* and warriors, seamen who had primarily borne the burden of a devastating seven-year War of Independence and were now mostly farmers. The second class comprised rich émigrés and Phanariots who had, indirectly yet greatly, helped the war of liberation both by money and propaganda mainly through the important positions they held in Turkey and elsewhere, and who now formed part of the intellectual élite of the country. Finally, to the above chaotic situation one must add a bankrupt economy.[1]

Under these circumstances it is difficult to expect widespread political maturity and stable legal institutions. The existing society opposed absolute Monarchy in so far as it identified it with maladministration. During the Turkish occupation the Greeks had adopted a particularly democratic system of local administration. When the Revolution broke out, many of the political élite had advocated progressive ideas about the way the Government should be organised. But to the great masses at least, the form of government was a theoretical problem of little concern. Democratic principles of government began to crystallise only at the end of King Otho's reign due to the appearance of a new generation, strongly influenced by growing European liberalism.

The preceding very brief analysis of the social conditions of the first decades of the new kingdom was attempted in order to further the understanding of the actual practice of dissolution. It proves that any discussion on how dissolution was actually practised is of theoretical importance only. Hence the 1844 Constitution will be dealt with very briefly. Parliamentary government had not emerged from the existing political and socio-economic conditions but had been introduced from abroad – as it had been in Belgium – with little initial success. Hence dissolution – as understood today – existed only in the letter of the Constitution. Furthermore, the legal structure of the 1844 Constitution encouraged a monarchical development at a time when the political maturity of the masses was, if not non-existent, certainly unable to oppose autocratic rule.[2] Only when the political training of a nation has reached a high level and

---

[1] The main cause was, of course, the devastating effects of the seven-year War of Independence. When this came to an end many of its fighters were unable to earn a living and a few relied on state pensions, obviously very costly to Greece. Lastly the prospering Greek navy had suffered serious losses during these years and it was not until later that it regained a prominent position in the world.

[2] The various local uprisings during Otho's reign show that the dissatisfaction with his policies remained disorganised and spasmodic up to 1862.

the people have fully understood the purpose and the mechanism of a specific institution, only then can she claim that the specific institution performs its function. And this political ethos did not exist in Greece during the early part of the nineteenth century. Nor could one demand such maturity from a nation that had just thrown off an oppressive foreign yoke and had been deprived of an intellectual renaissance and an industrial revolution. It is thus an undeniable fact that Greece, as a whole, during the early nineteenth century at least, was unable, as a rule, to give proof of a mature political conscience. But then, had the advanced European states ever fully developed their political institutions to a point of perfection?

Whatever may have been the reasons, dissolution remained throughout this period essentially a monarchical device. The absence of an effective check could easily have led to a complete deformation of the institution which would perhaps prejudice future generations against it. If this did not eventually happen it was due to the fact that King Otho rarely had recourse to the extreme method. The institution never became a target for specific attack. It thus survived the Othonian era and was accepted by the new Constitution. In the years to come dissolution was destined to play a more important part in Greek constitutional history.

King Otho was dethroned in 1862. An interregnum followed and finally Prince George of Denmark was elected King of the Hellenes, not of Greece, a difference in terminology that also showed the new attitude towards the Crown.[1] King George's reign lasted for nearly fifty years and coincided with an epoch of important political and socio-economic changes. Perhaps its most characteristic feature and certainly a very important one was the emergence of a middle class, which found its political expression in Charilaos Trikoupis*[2] and later in Eleftherios Venizelos.* As a result, by the end of the century, parliamentarism had emerged as the form of government that satisfied best the existing socio-economic conditions of the country.

During the first period of King George's reign (1864–75), new institutions were introduced yet not fully established. The generation of tough warriors was succeeded by that of Deligeorgis* and Koumoundouros,* a generation of liberal intellectuals and able merchants and craftsmen, who, though numerically still a minority of the population, succeeded in making their influence increasingly felt on both society and institutions as their wealth increased. But the proper functioning of institutions relied on the political maturity of the population which, relatively speaking, was only slowly developing.

[1] See next chapter.
[2] A name followed by an asterisk indicates that a short biography can be found in Appendix 2.

External events, particularly the policy of expansion (the Great Idea) and the Cretan question, continued to play a decisive part in the shaping of internal policies. A change of policy was usually accompanied by a change of Government and more often than not by dissolution. It is interesting to note that in contrast to British practice during this period a defeated Government chose, as a rule, to dissolve rather than resign.

Practically every Government that showed signs of stability was forced through a combination of factors – including court intrigue – to resign. The King's powers, though indirectly curtailed by the new constitution, still remained important. Dissolution, which was one of them, though in theory an institution intended to preserve a balance of powers between the Executive and the Legislative, resulted in practice in the suppression of the vote of Parliament and, ultimately, of the electorate.

Thus, during this period[1] (from the voting of the constitution (1864) to Trikoupis' first Government (1875)) elections were held six times, with an average life for Parliament of approximately twenty-two months. During the same period Greece saw eighteen Governments (including that of Admiral Kanaris★ in 1864) which means that the average life of a Government of that period was approximately five and a half months.

The Crown's approach to politics was to a certain extent incompatible with the new constitution and one of the causes of this instability. The King's attitude was often more authoritarian than Otho's personal rule despite the fact that the latter was a Monarch whereas the former was King in a Crowned Democracy.[2]

Reaction, however, soon came and was personified in Charilaos Trikoupis. The adoption of his theories – though not to the extent that he had wished – was aided by an unexpected fact. By 1880, most of the prominent leaders of the War of Independence and the 1862 Revolution had died. This enabled – for a brief period – the functioning of the two-party system under Trikoupis and Deliyannis,★ and this clash characterises that period of Greek history as the Disraeli–Gladstone clash characterises the 1870s in Britain. By this time, much of the royal power of patronage through which the King had wielded enormous powers was passing over to the Prime Minister and to a lesser extent to the M.P.s. The possession of patronage thus became one of the driving forces in Greek politics and Deliyannis made extensive use of it. But the two-party system was a brief phenomenon in Greek political history and right down to our day parties tend to cohere round personalities rather than principles.

At the close of the century, however, stability was once again inter-

---

[1] Below, chapter 9.   [2] Below, chapter 9.

rupted by economic difficulties and the unfortunate Greek–Turkish war of 1897. The turn of the century left in Greece a disappointed generation obsessed by the idea of a *revanche* that would one day be accomplished. This *revanche* however – unlike the French one following the unsuccessful war of 1870 – did not have as an aim the reacquisition of lost territories. Its ultimate aim was naturally the realisation of the Great Idea. But for the first time the Greeks realised that this could only be brought about after a political, economic and social reorganisation of the state. Thus, the 1909 Revolution is the culmination of a historical process, the firm establishment of the middle class and liberalism – a European phenomenon which took place in Greece with the usual delay.

The second period of King George's reign shows considerable improvement though it is still less than what one would have normally expected. The fact that Trikoupis' doctrines were not fully implemented permitted dissolution to survive as an essential institution. Dissolution was always exercised according to the letter of the constitution. From this point of view King George is legally totally irreproachable. But the political wisdom underlying his decisions to dissolve was, as a rule, always disputed. In several cases as in 1892 it nearly led to an open breach between Parliament and the Crown. The deplorable political instability between 1900 and 1909 eventually resulted in the Revolution. On the whole, however, a certain equilibrium of powers between Legislative and the Government was achieved.

This second period from 1875 saw thirty-eight Governments which means that the average Government remained in power for less than a year. Under these conditions one can see why Greece took such a long time to reach acceptable standards in its political and economic institutions. During this same period Parliament had on an average a twenty-nine month life span – considerably longer than the previous period – yet still not long enough.[1]

B: THE FIRST YEARS

The democratic constitutions enacted during the Greek War of Independence (1821–7)[2] completely ignored the right to dissolve Parliament.

---

[1] During approximately the same period (1874–1909) the United Kingdom saw eleven Governments and eight dissolutions. Thus, the average life of the Government was approximately three years and two months and that of Parliament four years and four months.

[2] Modern Greek constitutional history begins with the Constitution of Epidaurus (1/13 January 1822). It was referred to as 'provisional' in order not to provoke by its liberal clauses the animosity of the Holy Alliance. The 'law of Epidaurus', passed by the Second National Assembly at Astros in April 1823, amended the original text. The new version was

Historically speaking, this can be easily explained by the fact that most of these constitutions had been influenced by the ideas, though not so much by the texts, of the constitutions of the French Revolutionary period which had preceded them. These French prototypes, however, having been drafted – as already stated[1] – under the influence of various absolute theories of popular sovereignty, had ignored the right to dissolve the popular assembly. Besides, contemporary (i.e. eighteenth-century) practice of dissolution in the United Kingdom had further discouraged French constituent legislators who regarded the institution with suspicion as a monarchical instrument. Finally, the American Constitution could not be used as a model because of the system of separation of functions it chose to adopt. Hence the omission of the institution from the texts. In this respect, the Greek legislators faithfully followed the attitude of their French predecessors.

The right to dissolve Parliament was first introduced in Greece by the Constitution of 15/27 March 1832.[2] According to article 243, the Prince had the right to dissolve the Lower House 'after the beginning of the session' and if it was 'violating the constitutional laws or attempting to assail the rights of the Nation or the Prince'. In this event, however, the Prince was obliged to proclaim new elections. The new Parliament had to be summoned within three months of dissolution (art. 157).

However, the text of the Constitution is vague and does not clarify

---

abolished by the Troezene Constitution (1/13 May 1827) which appointed Kapodistrias as Governor of Greece. On 18/30 January 1828 its application was suspended on the Governor's recommendation and this was confirmed by the Fourth National Assembly which also enacted Capodistrias' provisional constitution. After Capodistrias' assassination 'a provisional administrative committee' was appointed but was unable to prevent disorder and political chaos. On 15/27 March 1832 the Fifth National Assembly voted the 1832 Constitution which also remained a dead letter due to the civil war. Finally on 7 May 1832 the Protocol of London appointed Otho as King of Greece. Until his arrival the country was ruled by the Senate.

For the texts of the above constitutions see: A. Mamoukas, *Collection of Greek laws and constitutions* (1837–53); N. N. Saripolos, *The First National Assembly and the regime of Epidauros, 1822* (1907); N. N. Saripolos, *Greek constitutional law* (1915), I, para. 1ff.; A. Svolos, 'The first Greek Constitutions', in *Ephimeris Ellinon Nomikon*, 2 (1935), 737ff.; A. Svolos, *Constitutional law*, I, 41ff.; J. Aravantinos, *Greek constitutional law* (1897), pp. 155ff., 302ff.; Th. Angelopoulos, *The first Greek Parliament* (1926), and *The second Greek Parliament* (1927), all in Greek. See also, A. Manessis, *Deux états nés en 1830; Ressemblances et dissemblances constitutionnelles entre la Belgique et la Grèce* (1959).

[1] Above, Introduction, p. 5.

[2] The first date (15 March) corresponds to the Julian calendar that was in force in Greece until 1923. The second date corresponds to the Gregorian calendar which was introduced in Greece in the twentieth century, but was already in force in the rest of Europe. The difference of days is 12 in the nineteenth century and 13 in the twentieth. The above applies to all double dates in the text. If only one date is mentioned then this corresponds to the new calendar.

whether the Prince could dissolve Parliament for reasons other than those stipulated by article 243. A literal interpretation of both articles 157 and 243 seems to indicate that the enumeration in article 243 was restrictive and not indicative, in the sense that the Prince could dissolve only in the two cases prescribed by article 243 and in no others. Nevertheless, despite this limitation, the introduction of dissolution, coupled with the veto power, which was also given for the first time to the Head of State, demonstrated certain monarchical tendencies which were absent from the previous Constitution. The Constitution of Troezena (1/13 May 1827), closely adhering to the principles of popular sovereignty, had omitted dissolution, thus clearly leading – had it been put into force – to a system resembling that of parliamentary preponderance (*système conventionnel*).

On the other hand, however, the introduction of dissolution by the 1832 Constitution was compatible with the milder form of separation of functions which the new Constitution had attempted to establish.[1] Thus, theoretically at least, dissolution was meant to help the harmonious co-operation between the Legislative and the Executive.

But the 1832 Constitution, drafted in a time of anarchy and social disorder – it followed Kapodistrias'* assassination on 27 September/ 9 October 1831 – was never implemented and remained a dead letter. Hence, any further consideration of its merits and defects seems to be purposeless.

The election of Otho, second son of Ludwig I of Bavaria, as King of Greece (Protocol of London, 7 May 1832), marks the beginning of a new era in Greek constitutional history. Up to 1844, the Greek nation, first under the Regency (25 Jan./6 Feb. 1833 – 20 May/1 June 1835; due to Otho's minority), later under the King himself, was governed autocratically and without a constitution (period of absolute Monarchy). This was brought about by a variety of causes, among which was King Ludwig's personal intervention. On accepting the throne of Greece on behalf of his son, Ludwig asked the 'Great Powers to order their Ministers to resist as far as possible the enactment of a constitution, which would deprive the new Monarch of the necessary means to establish his government'.[2] Thus, on the pretext that it was improper to draft a new constitution before the arrival of the new King, the Greeks were prevented from doing so. Nevertheless, despite the temporary nature of the above arrangement, to which the Greeks reluctantly gave their consent, both the Regency and later Otho himself managed – on various pretexts and with

---

[1] Aravantinos, *Greek constitutional law*, p. 160, n. 142.
[2] Strupp, *La situation internationale de la Grèce, 1821–1917*, pp. 123ff. Also Driault & Lhéritier, *Histoire diplomatique de la Grèce*, II, 84ff.

the assistance of the Great Powers – to postpone the granting of a constitution.

By 1843, however, popular unrest became more apparent. The pressure for government according to a constitution intensified, particularly because of the open encouragement the 'constitutionalists' received from Russia, which was aiming at King Otho's resignation and his replacement by a more Russophile King. The Russians particularly resented the strong influence the British Ministers exercised over the King. Thus, Lyons, the British Minister, had once characteristically told his Austrian colleague Prokesch Osten that, 'A really independent Greece is an absurdity. Greece is either Russian or English and, since she must not be Russian, she must be English.'[1]

The Russians carefully prepared the demand for a constitution hoping that the King would refuse and hence be dethroned. Lyons, however, who had succeeded Dawkins as British Minister to Greece, was quick to realise the Russian plans and when the revolution broke out he sided with the rebels and at the same time convinced the King that he must accept the popular demand in order to save his throne.[2] It would thus be a mistake to attribute the subsequent constitutional changes entirely to specific constitutional or political and ideological demands of the people. As Piscatory, the French Ambassador of the time wrote, Greece was more 'eager for a change in the situation than the establishment of a constitutional régime' and concluded that 'the Greeks want to reduce the Royal initiative so that the nation can advance and prosper',[3] and the Russians, realising this, had tried to exploit this in their favour.

The Constitution of 18/30 March 1844 – a product of the September (3/15 Sept. 1843) Revolution – gave the King the power to dissolve the Lower House on condition that elections followed within two months and the new Parliament met within three months of dissolution (art. 30). The relevant Royal Decree should be countersigned, according to article

---

[1] Lyons (subsequently Minister to Switzerland, Stockholm and finally recalled to act as Admiral, C. in C. in the Crimean War) once wrote: 'I know everything that happens in Court and in the Government. The King does not say a word which does not reach me' and concluded 'our agents can be found everywhere in the Country'. L. Bower & G. Bolitho, *Otho I, King of Greece. A biography* (1939), p. 106; Driault & Lhéritier, *Histoire diplomatique de la Grèce*, II, 172.

[2] See S. Markesinis, *Political history of Modern Greece* (up to 1920), 4 vols (1966–8), I, 190–1; M. Guizot, *Mémoires pour servir a l'histoire de mon temps*, 8 vols (Paris, 1858–67), VII (1867), 276ff., mentioning Piscatory's relevant reports; Ludvig Trost, *König Ludvig I von Bayern*, pp. 54, 106, 133ff., where one can find a detailed account of the events of the September revolution, based on King Otho's private papers. They all prove the active role the Russian Minister Katakazy played in preparing the revolution.

[3] Driault & Lhéritier, *Histoire diplomatique de la Grèce*, II, 236.

23, by the competent minister – usually the Minister of Interior, or the Prime Minister.

The essential elements of the institution were thus provided by the text of the Constitution. The democratic application, however, still remained to be seen; its prospects seemed very poor. The proper functioning of the institution, as we understand it today, depends on the existence of an appropriate political environment within which the institution operates, as well as on the due respect for the letter and spirit of the constitution. The various written guarantees that continental constitutions usually provide, though not unimportant, are, in this respect, of secondary importance.

The 1844 Greek Constitution was essentially monarchic both in letter and in spirit. Based on the French Constitution of 1830 and the Belgian Constitution of 1831, it omitted nevertheless a clause, included in the Belgian prototype (art. 25), stipulating popular sovereignty. It thus further accentuated its monarchic pretensions. Furthermore, the King never forgot that he had been obliged by a military revolution to concede a constitution and had not granted it of his own free will. Both he and his entourage were well-intentioned but obsessed by monarchical ideas, occasionally more appropriate to the seventeenth and eighteenth centuries than to the middle of the nineteenth century. Hence, his interpretations of his powers and duties rarely encouraged democratic development. Instead of reigning he chose to govern in person aided by his Ministers.

The King's views on the role of Parliament are thus quite clear. Parliament should always be favourably disposed towards the Crown. This, if necessary, could be achieved by two means: either the disobedient Parliament would be repeatedly dissolved and eventually replaced by a friendly one, or the elections would be rigged in a manner suitable to the pro-royalist faction. Election results were thus falsified in a preposterous and often naive manner. In certain constituencies for instance, the governmental candidates obtained 99.9% of the vote; in others the votes the Government won were more than the actual number of the electorate. Unfortunately, Parliament – entrusted up to 1911 with the verification of the election results – was in most cases unable to react.[1] By the use of such manoeuvres King Otho was able to avoid frequent dissolutions. During his reign only two Parliaments were prematurely dissolved: the first (1844–7) – the dissolution of which appears to be constitutional since it was advised by the Prime Minister in office – and the sixth (1857–60)

[1] See *Parliamentary Debates* (1868), II, A, α, 17ff., 40, 144, 148ff.; II, A, β, 109. According to a member of the Senate: 'A candidate M.P. in Greece is an appointed M.P. by the Government' (*Senate Debates*, V, Γ, 929).

which, though legally dissolved, was unwisely dissolved. The subsequent events and King Otho's dethronement proved, however, the political dangers inherent in a dubious dissolution.

King Otho's first dissolution took place in 1847 on the advice of his Prime Minister Kolettis* and on account of the 'Moussouros Affair'.

Moussouros, a man of Greek origin, was the first Turkish Minister to Greece, who, evidently to conceal his origin, performed the tasks set by his Government to the detriment of Greece. In this he was encouraged by Lyons, who wanted to cause trouble for Kolettis' pro-French administration. After an incident with the King, Moussouros left Greece blaming Kolettis for the tense situation between the two countries and did not return until after Kolettis' death. Moussouros was later appointed Turkish Ambassador to London. It is characteristic, however, that during the crisis, British foreign policy was encouraging Turkish intransigence and intervened at the last moment to prevent any conciliatory efforts. *The Times* in fact described Kolettis' followers as having no other qualities than: 'intrigue, fraud and baseness in their foreign relations', and, according to Metternich,[1] the crisis was deliberately provoked by Lyons. But the crisis was badly timed. Kolettis, though twice defeated in the House, was still powerful and his popularity was running high at that time because of his firm attitude against Turkey and foreign intervention. Shrewd as he was, he decided to exploit this popular feeling and thus dissolved the House and was returned with an increased majority. However, the abrupt dissolution and the rigged elections caused a series of regional revolts which, nevertheless, were suppressed in time. The incident, once again, illustrates the dependence of internal on external affairs.

During the next thirteen years, King Otho did not use his prerogative to dissolve Parliament. The dissolutions that took place were at the end of the statutory term of Parliament. King Otho did not have to use dissolution. Instead he chose to follow a system of personal government, intervening at elections in order to secure the re-election of his friends and using his immense powers of patronage.[2]

King Otho's second and last dissolution was provoked by the election of the opposition candidate Th. Zaimis,* as Speaker of the Lower House. Zaimis himself later maintained in Parliament[3] that, on the eve of his election, the King summoned approximately sixty M.P.s and strongly

[1] *Mémoires, documents et écrits divers*, 8 vols (Paris, 1881–6), VII, 390.
[2] He also reverted to his previous tactics and appointed all major political personalities to embassies abroad thus ridding himself of their presence. S. Trikoupis, J. Kolettis, A. Mavrocordatos and others all served abroad at times.
[3] *Parliamentary Debates* (1868), II, A, 269.

advised them to vote for the Government's candidate, Kaliphronas, who ironically enough was later involved in the 1862 Revolution that dethroned his benefactor. He also threatened possible rebels with dissolution in the event of Kaliphronas losing the election. The House, however, defied the King's wishes and duly elected Th. Zaimis as Speaker by a vote of 63 to 46. At a time when governments remained in office thanks to the support of bayonets and not because of the confidence of the House, (as a Cabinet Minister observed),[1] the result of the vote – coming from a rigged Parliament – demonstrated political maturity of the highest order. King Otho, furious with the result, dissolved Parliament and excluded from the subsequent elections all except one of the rebel M.P.s who had voted for Zaimis.[2]

Otho and his strong-minded Queen passionately loved Greece, but both were unable to deal with the critical events of their reign. Otho, who was slow, pedantic and childless – an issue which created serious problems of succession – confused the role of a constitutional King with that of a Prime Minister. At the beginning of his reign his subjects were not fully aware of the meaning of a constitution. By the end of his reign however they were fully aware of the meaning of government according to a constitution. The Crown was identified with the governing party and was opposed by a new generation of liberal politicians. Furthermore, though a devoted follower of the Great Idea, Otho was held responsible for the delay in its realisation. Italy's rapid unification was in this respect a painful contrast to the Greek. Thus, the Crown's policy of interference with party politics soon bore its fruits and the Bavarian dynasty paid the price. Growing national discontent led first to the abortive Nauplion Revolt (February 1862) and then to the successful October 1862 Revolution which dethroned the King and deposed the Wittelsbach Dynasty.

[1] Markesinis, *Political history*, I, 254. Ministers retained their office as long as they possessed the confidence of the Crown. See *Parliamentary Debates* (*Senate*, II, B, 392ff.). Two Cabinet Ministers in fact informed the House that though defeated they had decided to remain in office because the King had ordered them to do so (*Senate*, V, A, 187ff.). A. Mavrokordatos was the only Prime Minister to resign after being defeated at the elections. Markesinis, ibid. I, 204. Kolettis was exactly the opposite. He was once informed that Parliament was about to withdraw its confidence from his government. His answer was: 'Very well. But I shall still retain my confidence towards it.' M. Thouvenel, *La Grèce du Roi Othon* (1896), p. 2. The naiveté of this answer must be compared with a similar sentence by M. de Fourtu, Minister of Interior of the de Broglie Government in France in the late 1870s. Fourtu, supporting President MacMahon's constitutional right to dissolve the House on the advice of a defeated Government, addressed the House and said: 'Messieurs, nous n'avons pas votre confiance. Vous n'avez pas la nôtre.' Matter, *Dissolution*, p. 123.

[2] Among the Government M.P.s who voted for Zaimis was the author's great-grandfather, S. Markesinis, after quarrelling with the King over this issue. The King, however, decided to make a personal exception and allowed Markesinis to stand for re-election. The incident was reported in the Athens newspaper, *Estia*, on 7 October 1895.

Chapter 9

THE CONSTITUTION OF
16/28 NOVEMBER 1864[1]

A: THE YEARS OF TRANSITION (1864–1875)

The 1862 Revolution dethroned King Otho but never envisaged changing the form of government into a Republic. It had wished to put an end to the King's personal rule and once this was accomplished it was still willing to grant him important rights which only conventions and practice eventually curtailed. There is no difficulty in explaining this attitude. With the exception of France, Europe was ruled by royal families all of which were entrusted with extensive legal and political rights and so Greece could have hardly escaped this trend. Besides, even if the Greeks had been willing to switch to a Republic, it is doubtful whether the Great Powers would have allowed such a drastic change.[2] Hence, quite naturally, the blame was primarily put on the way the 1844 Constitution had been operated rather than on the actual deficiencies of the provisions of

---

[1] The text is published in the *Official Gazette* (1864, pp. 301ff.). For the preparatory works see the official minutes of the Second Constituent Assembly (vols I–VI, of the Official Journal). To the general bibliography set out in chapter 8, pp. 125–6, add the following specialised works: N. N. Saripolos, *Das Staatsrecht des Königreichs Griechenlands* (Tübingen, 1909) and the following works in Greek: N. I. Saripolos, *Treatise on constitutional law*, 5 vols, 2nd edn (1874); Diomides-Kyriakos, *Interpretation of the Greek Constitution*, 2 vols (Athens, 1904); J. Aravantinos, *Greek constitutional law*; H. Zeggelis, *Parliamentary law*; A. Manessis, *The democratic principle in the 1864 Constitution* (Thessaloniki, 1966); H. Kyriakopoulos, *The influence of the principles of the French Revolution on the 1864 Constitution* (Thessaloniki, 1956); J. Krestenitis, *The royal prerogative and more specifically dissolution of Parliament* (Athens, 1873). On the functioning of parliamentary government see N. N. Saripolos, *The parliamentary system of Government in its latest form* (Athens, 1921), A. Svolos, *Problems of parliamentary democracy* (Athens, 1931) and D. Petrakakos, *Parliamentary history of Greece*, 3 vols (1935–46).

[2] At the plebiscite that took place 230,016 voted for Prince Alfred, second son of Queen Victoria; 2,400 for Prince Eugene of Leuchtenberg and 6 for Prince George who subsequently became King. Twenty-three votes were cast in favour of a Republic. It is also interesting to note that at various stages Gladstone, Stanley, (later) Earl of Derby were offered the crown of Greece. Disraeli, commenting on Lord Stanley's candidacy, wrote that had he been offered it and been younger he would have seriously considered accepting it; Monypenny & Buckle, *Disraeli*, IV, 331–2. In an official report on 25 October/6 November 1862, Ch. Trikoupis, then Chargé d'Affaires in London, states that he informed Lord Palmerston that Greece would never become a Republic and mentions the former's satisfaction and approval. *Charilaos Trikoupis, Analecta*, A, vol. 14 (Athens, 1912), p. 5. See also, E. Prevelakis, *British policy towards the change of dynasty in Greece, 1862–1863* (1953).

the text, and, as a result, the section of the Constitution concerning the powers of the Crown was scarcely amended.

The right to dissolve Parliament was no exception. King Otho had hardly used the right and hence there was little ground for serious complaint. Apart from a minor change – the provision that the decree of dissolution should be signed by the whole Cabinet and not merely by the competent Minister – the letter of article 37 of the 1864 Constitution was identical to article 30 of the 1844 Constitution. Professor N. I. Saripolos had even suggested that dissolution ought not to be subjected to the general rule that the Sovereign's acts must be countersigned by his Ministers, but his recommendation was not accepted. Article 37 was interpreted both by Professor N. I. Saripolos and Professor Diomides-Kyriakos very broadly and in a manner that allowed the King to even force a dissolution against his Government.[1] But in phrasing and interpreting the article in such a wide manner they seem to have neglected one important change.

Whatever the feeling towards monarchy however, the new Constitution was substantially a product of a revolution which had sought and achieved the establishment of the principle of popular sovereignty. The fact that the new Constitution had established a 'Crowned Democracy' and not a 'Constitutional Monarchy' – a difference in terminology that is, perhaps, more familiar to continental lawyers – is of the utmost importance. In the former the importance of the popular element is increased at the expense of the Crown. In 1864 the Constitution was no longer a pact between the King and his people, but a product of the exclusive will of the latter, in accordance with the French doctrines of popular sovereignty. Thus, the Assembly and later on Parliament, reserved all constituent authority to itself.[2] And the King's proclamation to the Greeks on 18/31 October 1863, began, in accordance with the above, as follows: 'Ascending the Throne to which your vote has called me....'[3]

The above antithesis between the extensive royal rights on the one hand and the profoundly democratic principles on the other inevitably created serious difficulties of interpretation. Where the royal right atrophied, as in the case of the Veto, no problem arose. But in the cases

---

[1] *Treatise on constitutional law*, I, 322–8; Diomides-Kyriakos, *Interpretation of the Greek Constitution*, I, 346–8. Also C. Paparrigopoulos, *History of the Greek Nation* (1935), VI, 215.

[2] Art. 107, in accordance with articles 21 and 44, excluded the King from a future revision of the Constitution, thus establishing the so-called pure form of 'Crowned Democracy'. Art. 131 of the Belgian prototype is, in this respect, more conservative since it considers the King a constituent factor.

[3] Markesinis, *Political history*, II, 16. See also the Resolution of 10/22 October 1863, published in the Government *Gazette* of the same year, p. 26.

where a right was exercised, as with dissolution, then serious controversy was not avoided.

During the first ten years of his reign, King George I proved unable to grasp these important constitutional changes. His youth and his politically unwise entourage led him into grave political blunders similar to, if not worse than, those that King Otho had committed and had in fact paid for so dearly. Authoritarian rule led to an open breach of the new Constitution and nearly resulted in King George's dethronement. But the Monarchy was saved at the eleventh hour thanks to the intervention of Charilaos Trikoupis, an eminent nineteenth-century Greek statesman. Though in subsequent years the rules of parliamentary government that he sponsored were not closely followed, the new political ethos that he introduced in Greek politics proved of immense importance. Thus, owing to his political innovations, his first Premiership marks the beginning of a new period in modern Greek constitutional history. The form of government remained that of a Crowned Democracy; but rules of parliamentary government were also introduced.

King George's reign can be thus subdivided into two distinct periods. The first starts with his accession to the Greek Throne and ends in 1875 with his famous speech from the Throne, while the second covers the years 1875 to the 1909 Revolution. The remaining three years of his reign blend with the next era, inaugurated by the 1911 Constitution. Political and constitutional events during these three transitional years are determined by three factors: the success and subsequently conciliatory policies of the Revolution, the King's attempts to avoid drastic political changes and the appearance on the political scene of a new powerful personality – Eleftherios Venizelos.*

King George I had arrived in Greece on 17/29 October 1863 and for nearly a year waited for the National Assembly to complete its task. The Assembly, unlike its predecessor, was unjustifiably delaying its work. Finally the King, in a proclamation on 6/18 October 1864, demanded that the Assembly complete its work within ten days; otherwise he threatened to leave Greece. The King's action, though legally ineffective – since it was directed against a sovereign body – and at the same time politically dangerous, created a profound sensation. Public opinion reacted favourably and the Assembly was obliged to conform to the King's wishes. On 17/29 October 1864, the constitutional text was voted and on 16/28 November 1864, the King, in the presence of the Assembly, took the oath to abide by the Constitution.

But the King's passion for politics, coupled with the inability to form a viable Government, mainly due to the existence of numerous political groups and parties, eventually brought the Crown to an impasse. One Government rapidly succeeded another in office. The application of orthodox parliamentary rules – and in this sense the proper use of dissolution – could have provided a solution to the problem. This, however, did not happen. From 1868 onwards, the King repeatedly intervened to secure the re-election of his friends and participated in more ways than one in party politics.[1] Dissolution was yet another useful device in the Sovereign's hands. It eventually became a source of constitutional embarrassment.

The first dissolution under the new constitution was granted to Alexander Koumoundouros, who had succeeded Admiral Kanaris as Premier on 2/14 May 1865. Koumoundouros immediately dissolved Parliament and held elections with a relative degree of order and without too much governmental intervention. This, however, was to his disadvantage since rigging elections was the usual way of remaining in power. He therefore lost but remained in office until the autumn of 1865 when he was defeated in the House over his budget and was obliged to withdraw.

Parliament – which included for the first time deputies from the Ionian Islands[2] – was divided into numerous political groups that prevented the formation of a stable Government. Five Governments followed[3] within approximately a year until finally on 18/30 December 1866 Koumoundouros was sworn in for a third time as Prime Minister, with Charilaos Trikoupis as Minister for Foreign Affairs. Trikoupis' presence in political life, together with Koumoundouros' strong personality, gave, for the first time since 1862, a feeling of security and confidence in the country's future.

It was during this Ministry that the treaty of Voeslau between Greece and Serbia was concluded; a treaty particularly notable because it represented the first alliance of Balkan States for the promotion of their

---

[1] See, *Minutes of the Second Constituent Assembly* (1864), VI, 23ff., 995ff. See also speech by the M.P. Milissis in *Parliamentary Debates* (1869), III, A, β, 75.

[2] The Greek islands of the Ionian Archipelago were under Venetian domination until the treaty of Campoformio (1797) when they were transferred to France. In 1800, due to Russian, Turkish and Greek efforts, they became semi-autonomous only to be returned to France by the treaty of Tilsit (1807). They were gradually taken over by the British and the treaty of Paris (5 November 1815) officially placed them under British protection – a solution which had been actively encouraged by John Kapodistrias, then Russia's Joint Secretary for Foreign Affairs. During the last years of Otho's reign the islands were offered to Greece provided the King ceased all disputes with Turkey, a condition which was finally rejected. The Protocol of London of 25 May/6 June 1863 and the treaties of London of 1/13 July 1863 and 12/29 March 1864 acknowledged the Greek sovereignty and guaranteed the neutrality of Corfu.

[3] Headed by Deligeorgis, Voulgaris, Koumoundouros, Benizelos-Roufos, and Voulgaris again.

national interests.[1] Efforts had been made in the past to bring about a Greco-Serbian alliance, but the final treaty was signed in 1867. On Trikoupis' initiative and under his guidance the treaty was negotiated in Voeslau, a suburb of Vienna, by the Greek diplomat and special envoy Peter Zanos,[2] was signed on 14/26 August 1867 and ratified by the two states. Bulgaria, still not a recognised state, was explicitly excluded from all the arrangements. The treaty, however, was never implemented because of Koumoundouros' subsequent dismissal and the mysterious murder of the Serbian Prince Michael Obrenovits.

But it was a different issue of foreign policy that brought the Government down and led to a new dissolution. By the end of 1868, Koumoundouros and Trikoupis were already in a quandary about the deadlock which the Cretan question had reached. Crete had witnessed various insurrections in 1841 and 1856, but when in 1866 the island unilaterally proclaimed its union with Greece, the limit was reached. Bitter fighting broke out in the island and the Greek Government made various attempts to oppose Turkish misrule and even sent an expeditionary force to help the rebels. International opinion was against the movement and the revolt was finally suppressed. In 1869, at a conference in Paris, the Greeks were strongly advised not to provoke the Turks further.

In the meantime, however, the King, who had just returned from a long tour in Europe, was pressing for a more pacifist policy towards Turkey. Thus, while the Government, leading and occasionally being led by a bellicose public opinion, was preparing for war, the King, who always 'listened attentively to British advice',[3] openly adopted a different policy. His talks with European rulers had convinced him of the folly of fighting against Turkey. The Greeks were once again asked to be patient. Nevertheless, the adoption of a different policy by the Crown led to the resignation of the Government despite the fact that it had an overwhelming majority in the House (120 to 80). Koumoundouros, however, abstained from any strong criticism of the Crown, despite the fact that the King's action had caused a profound sensation. The legal side of the problem was not extensively discussed at the time, since the emphasis was placed on the political aspects of the crisis. Approximately twenty-five years later the King repeated this decision by dismissing Theodore Deliyannis.* Deliyannis, however, unlike Koumoundouros, refused to resign and was thus formally dismissed by the King.

---

[1] S. Markesinis, *Political history*, II, 57ff., provides the only available account of events based on Zanos' unpublished papers. See also, S. Laskaris, *La première alliance entre la Grèce et la Serbie. La traité d'alliance de Voeslau du 14/26 août 1867* (1953).

[2] Laskaris, ibid. pp. 22ff.

[3] Campbell & Sherrard, *Modern Greece*, p. 103.

However good the intentions of the King – and there is every reason to believe that they were – it is doubtful whether his method of imposing his opinion was the most appropriate one. There is little doubt – considering the military strength of the two nations and the ambiguous position of the Great Powers – that a war between Greece and Turkey would have led, except for a miracle, to a Greek military defeat. But it is also dangerous for a Sovereign to attempt to impose his will in a manner leading to direct confrontation with his people. The fact that no such confrontation followed can only be attributed to Koumoundouros' restraint.

The new Government was a caretaker Government formed on 20 December/1 January 1868 by A. Moraitinis, President of the Supreme Court. Parliament was prorogued for forty days and when it next met Moraitinis was no longer in power. The critical situation demanded a political Government. King George was obliged to commission Voulgaris* to form a Government after having failed to persuade Koumoundouros to return to office. D. Voulgaris immediately dissolved Parliament and held elections so scandalously corrupt as to be proverbial even after their post-electoral connection with the arbitrary dismissal of Koumoundouros, which had caused a great hubbub.[1]

The second Parliament of the 1864 Constitution (1868–9) had a brief life span. At the beginning of January 1869, the Cretan question had reached its acutest form between those advocating war, and those favouring the European policy of appeasement, while the Government wavered between one policy and the other. It finally resigned and was succeeded by Theodore Zaimis,* a pro-European pacifist. In fact, the Cretan revolt ended during this Government's rule. Zaimis eventually dissolved Parliament and new elections without terrorisation and unfair intervention were held in the summer of 1869. He obtained a majority in the House enabling him to attract a large number of right-thinking people who opposed the electioneering methods of the others. This Government actually managed to celebrate an anniversary of power in January 1870, a rare example during the first years of King George's reign. But this state of affairs was too good to last for a long time.

In April 1870, bandits captured a party of English tourists near Marathon, and would not release them unless a heavy ransom was paid and an amnesty granted. Some of the prisoners were finally murdered, an act which provoked hostile reaction abroad and led to the resignation of the Government. The subsequent Franco-Prussian War of 1870 distracted attention from Greece. But the pressure from abroad was such that in

[1] *Parliamentary Debates* (1868), II, A, α, 12ff., 41ff.; II, A, γ, 114ff., 207ff., 270ff.

July 1870 the Government was forced to resign.[1] E. Deligeorgis succeeded Zaimis on 9/21 July 1870 for a period of about three months during which Parliament was not sitting.[2] Deligeorgis, anticipating defeat in the House, advised dissolution but the King refused. When Parliament next met Koumoundouros took over the Government (3/15 December 1870) and with the support of Zaimis and the tolerance of Voulgaris managed to remain in office for nearly a year. In November 1871, the Koumoundouros Government lost the confidence of Zaimis and was obliged to resign office. Zaimis was summoned (28 October/9 November 1871) but he, too, failed to secure the confidence of the House and resigned. Finally a Coalition Government was formed with Voulgaris and Koumoundouros. In mid-July, however, the Government, although maintaining a majority in Parliament, resigned on the King's intervention owing to the acuteness of the 'Laurion affair',[3] and was replaced by a minority Ministry headed by E. Deligeorgis (8/20 July 1872), which remained in office up to the beginning of 1873.

The 'Laurion Affair' developed into a kind of scandal with a particular international flavour (and with certain similarities to the Panama Affair during the Third French Republic). Its roots went back to the early 1860s when a French and Italian firm had obtained the right to excavate the ancient mines of Laurion. In due course various problems arose among which the most important was whether the concession included the right to exploit the slag and dross. The opposition soon turned the issue into a scandal and members of the Government were accused of having interests in the affair. In 1871, Koumoundouros legally settled the case in favour of the Greek state, only to provoke stormy resentment on the part of the French and Italian Governments. The Deligeorgis administration, which succeeded Koumoundouros, protested against this foreign intervention and refused the mediation of Russia, England, Austria and Germany. Finally a Greek firm bought out the foreigners, and was given the right to exploit the slag as well. With the 'Laurion affair' over, Deligeorgis decided to go to the country. His calculations nevertheless were wrong and he lost the elections. His electoral defeat, however, did not lead to his resignation. On the contrary, not only did he remain in office, but he also directed the business of the House dur-

---

[1] The official reports are contained in the following two publications: *Correspondence respecting the capture and murder by brigands of British and Italian subjects in Greece* (London, 1870), and *Documents concerning the robbery on the Marathon road* (Athens, 1870).

[2] Deligeorgis' Government was the only one – with the exception of that of the U.S.A. – to recognise immediately the newly created Third French Republic (23 August/4 September 1870).

[3] For which see A. Syngros, *Memoirs* (1908) (in Greek), III, 51ff.

ing the verification of the election results – a decision which was criticised at the time.[1]

The Deligeorgis administration was finally succeeded by a Voulgaris Government which dissolved Parliament on 25 April 1874 and held new elections. These proved the apotheosis of violence, corruption and governmental intervention. Voulgaris naturally won. But this unfairly elected Parliament was destined to become the starting point of a new constitutional era.

It was ten years since the Constitution had been put into force and it was now possible to revise it as Voulgaris intended doing with the purpose of placing it on a more monarchical basis. The King had long held the same view, which he had confessed in strict confidence to Sir Henry Elliott, the British Ambassador in Constantinople,[2] in a talk just after the Dilessi murders on 4 May 1870. But neither Sir Henry, neither the Earl of Clarendon, the Minister of Foreign Affairs, nor Gladstone, then Prime Minister, was ready to assist the King in this. Without British support, the King avoided committing himself.[3] But public opinion, becoming aware of the situation, began to feel uneasy. The time had come for the needful and salutary change. Only the leader was lacking: a leader who dared to act. Charilaos Trikoupis (son of Spyridon Trikoupis, Capodistrias' Prime Minister) was the statesman who took the initiative in buttressing the regular functioning of the Government within the democratic framework of parliamentary government instead of trying to make the Constitution more monarchic. The importance of Trikoupis' innovations therefore deserves further consideration.

B: TRIKOUPIS AND THE THEORY OF 'PROCLAIMED MAJORITY'

Voulgaris' inordinate electoral intervention and his intention to revise the constitution in an undemocratic manner have already been mentioned. Mass reaction to this state of affairs found its champion in Ch. Trikoupis. His political career had already begun brilliantly with his handling of the

[1] See Lomvardos' speech in *Parliamentary Debates* (1874), V, B, 19ff. and 173ff. His speech, *Parliamentary Debates* (1874), V, B, 20, is highly critical of the use of the right to dissolve Parliament as a means of imposing minority Governments against the will of Parliament. But see also E. Deligeorgis' views, ibid. p. 21.

[2] It is characteristic of the attitude of the Great Powers that at critical moments throughout the nineteenth century the British Ambassador at the Port exercised a kind of supervisory function over Greek affairs. Two Ambassadors in particular, Sir Stratford Canning and Elliot himself were greatly involved in Greek problems and their role in future developments proved decisive.   [3] Markesinis, *Political history*, II, 72.

union of the Ionian islands and in the course of his Ministry in the Koumoundouros Government of 1867 during which he concluded the treaty of Voeslau. He was already the leader of a small party and almost regularly failed in the elections owing to open intervention against him. His great moment, however, had arrived. Demonstrating the qualities of true leadership, appreciation of the situation, foresight and timing, but also familiar with the weaknesses and failures of the Government, he had a solution at hand and dared to take the initiative. He published anonymously his well-known article on the situation in the newspaper 'Kairoi' (Times) of 29 June 1874 entitled, 'Who's to blame'. It contained an extremely strong attack on Court intrigue. It exposed the fact that all evils, especially after 1867, were due to Court intervention in a continuing attempt to form minority Governments. He emphasised that none of these governments was 'appointed to office on the recommendation of the representatives of the people' and described these tactics of the Crown as an 'abuse of the constitutional privilege of choosing and dismissing Ministers, leading to the multiplication of parties and the disruption of the system of Government'. He further added that Voulgaris, Deligeorgis and Zaimis had all been summoned to form a government though their parties respectively numbered 12, 7, and 27 M.P.s. His conclusion was that Greece was governed as an absolute monarchy and in his second article he emphasised that the 'disregard of parliamentary rules of government by the dethroned dynasty had led the Nation to the 1862 Revolution'.

The article was considered as derogatory to the Crown and resulted in the prosecution of the editor of *Kairoi*, G. Kanellides, who was eventually imprisoned. But Trikoupis then appeared before the prosecution and disclosed that he was the author of the offending article, whereupon he was imprisoned instead of Kanellides, but after twenty-four hours he was released by a court decree.

Both the article and the imprisonment of its author made a great impression. Voulgaris, however, was not brought to his senses and his increased recklessness led him in an openly unconstitutional manner (because of the lack of a quorum) to pass his Budget in the House (30 November/12 December 1874). All this infuriated public opinion which was now definitely directed against the King. The Crown's dire position lent wide credence to the rumours repeated in the European press, that the King meant to abdicate. But at the beginning of the next year the situation was saved in an unexpected manner. The King, adopting his favourite method and apparently with British encouragement,[1] called on Trikoupis to form a Government with the right to dissolve the rigged Parliament and hold new elections.

[1] Markesinis, *Political history*, II, 86.

On 9 May 1875 Trikoupis formed his new Government.[1] He dissolved Parliament and held what may well be described as the first exemplary elections.

At the opening session of the new Parliament (the seventh since the voting of the new Constitution in 1864) the King personally delivered the Speech from the Throne, written by Trikoupis. He stated in no uncertain terms that it was 'an indispensable condition for those called to govern the country to possess the "proclaimed confidence" of the representatives of the people'.[2]

It must be made clear that on several occasions it was advocated in Parliament that the rules of parliamentary government should be introduced in Greece.[3] Thus, it was the explicit intention of many liberal politicians to apply – even to a limited extent – the principles of parliamentary government. Unfortunately it was never achieved in practice and thus until 1875 the appointment of minority governments tended to lead to an anti-parliamentary and undemocratic application of the articles of the Constitution.

Trikoupis' pure doctrine presupposed that a Government about to be sworn in should possess the proclaimed or demonstrated confidence of the House. And if this was not obvious from the election results, then the King should wait to see which party would elect the Speaker and that party's leader would then be commissioned to form a Government. Deliyannis however – a leading parliamentarian and Trikoupis' greatest opponent – considered that the Government need not have the House's confidence at the time of its appointment but should eventually get it in order to remain in power. If it failed to secure the confidence of the House then it would have to resign or advise dissolution. In other words, Deliyannis maintained that the King could appoint a minority Government, but in this case the House's subsequent approval was a sine qua non if the Government were to remain in office. If it were defeated then it could advise dissolution. Trikoupis' doctrine in this respect was quite the opposite since, in practice, it restricted dissolution only to the majority party. His rejection of minority Governments was based on the doctrine of relative parliamentary supremacy.[4] Deliyannis, however, rejected this

---

[1] After only a short period of proper government he managed to introduce – to some extent at least – a respectable political ethos, very different from that of the corrupt Voulgaris era, but was unable to win the elections. Trikoupis' movement also coincides with a growing attempt by the political world to obtain increasing powers of patronage: towards the end of the century and onwards the powers of the Prime Minister increase at a steady pace.

[2] *Parliamentary Debates* (1875), VII, A, α, 1ff.

[3] *Parliamentary Debates* (1871), III, B, α, 4, 6; (1874), V, A, β, 162ff.; V, B, 19ff., 173ff.

[4] Trikoupis' doctrine was elaborately expounded in 1902 by his follower and subsequently Prime Minister, Stefanos Dragoumis. See *Parliamentary Debates*, IE (23 January 1902), particularly p. 81.

through fear of what he called a 'parliamentary dictatorship'. He thus stated in Parliament in 1903 that: 'personally I reject the absolute doctrines of the Speech from the Throne of 1875. If the Crown is tied to the absolute doctrine of "proclaimed majority", then it is likely that we shall reach tyranny through the functioning of parliamentary institutions.'[1] He concluded the speech by saying that personally he did not oppose the formation of minority Governments provided they resigned or dissolved if they failed to secure the confidence of the House.

Subsequent parliamentary practice in Greece adopted Deliyannis' views[2] and hence dissolution played an important role in Greek constitutional history. It was repeatedly decided that it was the King's prerogative to give a mandate to a minority Government on condition that it should appear before Parliament and seek a vote of confidence. When later, in 1927, the principles of parliamentary government were laid down by the Greeks in a definite constitutional form they were ordained in accordance with the prevailing system, that is with Deliyannis' views.

But even if parliamentary government, as understood by Trikoupis was never put into practice, at any rate it aided the smoother working of the governmental system, if anything by obliging defeated minority Governments to resign, and because of the new political ethos it introduced. Later on, the establishment of broad electoral areas further clipped the wings of the local party agents who always played an important role in Greek politics. But it did not succeed in creating party principles on account of other more general economic and social reasons which will be discussed later on. In any case, the personality of Charilaos Trikoupis, whether in Government or in Opposition, dominated Greek politics for the next twenty years. It was he who first tried to set Greece on the proper path of constitutional development as in Western Europe. His influence was such that the next twenty years may be regarded as the Trikoupis era.

After the speech from the Throne, Parliament was prorogued until the autumn. When it met again, Trikoupis, foreseeing that the House was unfavourable towards his party, resigned on 12 October 1875, in conformity with his doctrines, without waiting for a motion of censure. Thus, A. Koumoundouros and Th. Zaimis formed a Coalition Government on 27 October/9 November 1875.

[1] *Parliamentary Debates*, ΙΣΤ, α (26 February 1903), 402–3.
[2] In accordance with his views: G. Theotokis, *Parliamentary Debates*, ΙΣΤ, α (26 February 1903), 409; L. Petimezas, ibid. (25 February 1903) (in appendix), 1648; K. Konstandopoulos, ibid. (26 February 1903), 388ff.

C: THE NEW DOCTRINE IN PRACTICE (1875–1909)

During the subsequent years of King George's reign dissolution was frequently exercised, yet it ceased being the invariable rule. Thus, the seventh Parliament of the 1864 Constitution (July 1875 – November 1879) was dissolved normally at the end of its legal term.[1] Dissolution was granted to the Prime Minister of the day, A. Koumoundouros, who held elections which his party won. He remained in office until 6/18 March 1880, when he resigned having suffered defeat on the question of the Budget. Ch. Trikoupis was returned to power on 10/22 March 1880 and remained in office until 13/25 October 1880 when in his turn he resigned, after his party failed to elect the Speaker of the House. A. Koumoundouros was sworn in on 13/25 October 1880 and remained in power until 1882, when he advised dissolution in order to include in the future House members from the newly annexed territories of Thessaly. Paradoxically the electorate of the newly annexed provinces refused him its support, and thus effectively contributed to his electoral defeat. The Trikoupis administration that followed on 3/15 March 1882 proved one of the most successful Governments of the nineteenth century and in fact managed to remain in office until 11/23 February 1885. But Trikoupis' constructive economic policies proved unpopular and resulted in his defeat at the irreproachable elections that followed.

Th. Deliyannis won the elections and, on 1/13 May 1885, formed his first Ministry, which remained in power only for a year. Deliyannis resigned on 26 April/8 May 1886 as a result of the tense situation in the Balkans. The immediate cause was Bulgaria's unilateral annexation on 20 September 1885 of Eastern Romelia which had been decreed by the Congress of Berlin as an autonomous and self-governing province, as opposed to the treaty of San Stefano, which had made it part of Greater Bulgaria.[2] Public opinion was highly agitated and the King was hostile towards his Government's complacent attitude. But on this occasion the Crown followed a policy of restraint and allowed events to take their course. By April 1886 the Government was forced by events to resign. The King then summoned Trikoupis but the latter declined the offer

---

[1] This Parliament witnessed considerable governmental instability mainly due to the critical phase of the Eastern Question due to the Russian–Turkish confrontation, for which inter alia consult R. W. Seton-Watson, *Disraeli, Gladstone and the Eastern Question* (1962), R. T. Shannon, *Gladstone and the Bulgarian agitation 1876* (1963); and for the Greek side Markesinis, *Political history*, II, 94–122.

[2] For historical events see Markesinis, *Political history*, II, 107ff., 139ff., 180ff. The geographical boundaries of Bulgaria were of great importance to the British because of the fear of Russian imperialism in the Balkans. Hence their varying attitudes towards Greece. For details see Seton-Watson, *Disraeli, Gladstone and the Eastern Question*.

because his party was in a minority in the House. The King was thus obliged to form a caretaker Government headed by the President of the Supreme Court, Demetrios Valvis (May 1886).

This Government was soon succeeded by one led by Ch. Trikoupis, who had in the meantime managed to elect a member of his party as Speaker of the House, thanks to Government M.P.s who crossed the floor[1] (9/21 May 1886). Both the Crown and Trikoupis had eventually reached their objectives, through a series of skilful parliamentary manoeuvres that had in fact enhanced the public image of the Crown. There are many similarities between the 1886 crisis and the events of the summer of 1965 that provide yet another proof that Greek constitutional history occasionally repeats itself. The 1965 crisis naturally will be treated more extensively in due course,[2] but perhaps the most striking difference between the two crises is that the 1886 crisis was adroitly handled according to accepted parliamentary rules, whereas the 1965 crisis, after a series of controversial decisions, led to the 1967 military coup d'état.

Trikoupis was able to pursue a pacifist policy and in fact exploited his new-found majority by swiftly carrying through important legislation. One of the most important measures was the establishment of large electoral areas and the reduction of the number of deputies from 245 to 150.

But once the crisis was over, the majority began to show signs of indiscipline, inclining once again towards Deliyannis. By late 1886 the House was unmanageable and Trikoupis had to ask for a dissolution.[3] New elections were held on 16 January 1887 in which he gained a substantial majority. D. Rallis*, however, attributed the dissolution to so-called reasons of 'constitutional ethics' because of the change of the electoral law. This opinion, however, can be easily rejected both by consulting Trikoupis' speech in Parliament when introducing the electoral Bill, as well as by subsequent constitutional history. Thus, in 1906 and 1907, despite substantial alterations in the electoral system, no dissolution was advised. There seems little doubt that the 1886 dissolution was advised after Trikoupis realised that the House was unable to conduct its business properly.

By 1890, Trikoupis had been in office – with an interval of one year (1885–6) – for nearly eight years, a record number that few Greek Prime Ministers can claim. In the subsequent elections, however (14/26 October 1890), he was defeated and resigned immediately the results became

---

[1] Deliyannis described in Parliament this mass revolt (69 M.P.s deserted in one night) as a 'black event' in the history of Greek Parliamentarism.

[2] Below, chapter 13.

[3] N. Stratos confirmed this in a speech in Parliament in 1917 when he reviewed all dissolutions since 1882 – see *Parliamentary Debates*, Κ, β, 154.

known. Th. Deliyannis was summoned to form his second Ministry on the same day and remained in power for two years.

Deliyannis' term in office was abruptly ended in 1892 by his dismissal by the Crown. The 1892 crisis is one of the most important constitutional and political crises during King George's reign and it deserves detailed consideration. Furthermore, it seems to be unique in contemporary European constitutional practice.

By the beginning of 1892, the economic situation in Greece was very disquieting. The Greek State was unable to pay its foreign loans, contracted with various foreign countries. New loans were unavailable and raising the necessary exchange at home was leading to grave inflation. The electorate seemed quite aware of the forthcoming danger of bankruptcy and was disturbed by the Government's apparent inability to prevent it. The King naturally shared the same feeling and was contemplating a personal intervention. Prince Nicholas, third son of King George I, provides a first-hand reliable account of the events. His unpublished diary[1] clearly demonstrates his father's anxieties and reveals his thoughts. He thus wrote on 14/26 February 1892: 'Papa [*sic*] spoke to me today for the first time about this subject [the financial situation]. He told me a great deal and informed me of his intention to dismiss his Ministers and appoint a new Government in an attempt to prevent bankruptcy.' Three days later, on 17/29 February 1892, the King seemed more determined to proceed with his plans. Here is what his son had to say:

Today Papa decided to put an end to the Deliyannis Government. He had been contemplating this for a long time and had decided to do it on the first Monday in Lent. Thus, at 3 p.m. he sent Mr. Kalinsky[2] to Mr. Deliyannis' home to inform him that the King wishes him to resign ... In half an hour Mr. Kalinsky had returned with the information that Mr. Deliyannis had immediately agreed and that he would invite his Ministers to inform them accordingly. This took place at 4 p.m. ... but by 11 p.m. there was still no reply. He [the King] then sent Mr. Papadiamandopoulos to Mr. Deligeorgis[3] [a minister at that time] to find out what was happening. This was what was happening. Deliyannis, after Kalinsky had left, summoned his Ministers and several backbenchers and told them what had occurred. A heated discussion followed which ended with the Cabinet's decision not to resign. Furthermore it immediately wrote an impertinent letter to the King which stated that 'article 31 of the Constitution has given the King the right to appoint and dismiss Ministers. Hence,

---

[1] It is taken from Markesinis, *Political history*, II, 222ff., who first published extensive extracts from the Prince's diary.

[2] The King's Private Secretary.

[3] Not to be confused with Epaminondas Deligeorgis, the former Prime Minister who had died on 14/26 May 1879.

it is for His Majesty to exercise against us the right of dismissal, as the Ministry has no right to resign because it commands the absolute confidence of Parliament.'

The next day Deliyannis convened the House and presented a slightly altered picture of the events. He maintained in a speech in Parliament that he had informed the King's (first) emissary that he would tell his friends and decide accordingly, but that he had not committed himself to anything at all. It seems probable that Deliyannis' version is not the correct one; that he had agreed to resign and that he subsequently changed his mind under the influence of his friends. In any event, at the end of his speech, Deliyannis refused to resign and asked for a vote of confidence which he promptly got to the accompaniment of applause and cries of victory.

The King in the meantime (on the eve of 17 February and before the meeting of Parliament) having received the news that Deliyannis refused to resign, had asked Trikoupis to form a Government. Trikoupis declined the offer, because he was in a minority in the House. Instead he advised the King to form a caretaker (or as they were called then a colourless) Government, and proceed immediately to new elections thus referring the disputed issue to the electorate. This, too, is mentioned in the Prince's diary. The King chose instead to appoint a political Government and sent for Konstantopoulos, a member of the third small party, as Prime Minister. Konstantopoulos accepted the offer and left the Royal Palace at 1 p.m. of the 18th intending to return with a list of future Ministers for the King's approval. By 2.30 p.m. of the 18th he returned, having failed to find candidates for ministerial posts even among his own party.

Thus, the following paradox occurred. On 18 February, at 3 p.m., while Parliament was giving its overwhelming support to Deliyannis, Konstantopoulos had already been appointed his successor (though not sworn in) and was busily seeking Ministers to replace the Deliyannis administration.[1] Konstantopoulos eventually succeeded in his efforts and was sworn in while the Deliyannis Ministry was dismissed by a Royal Decree, countersigned by the new Prime Minister.[2] Parliament was eventually dissolved on 12/24 March 1892 and lively elections followed on 3/15 May 1892. The election campaign was fierce and several newspapers hinted at the King's dethronement if Deliyannis won. Happily for the Crown he did not.

The King's daring initiative was admittedly in line with the letter of the Constitution, but none the less politically dangerous for the Crown.

---

[1] *The Times* of 6/18 March 1892 gave a full account of the story.
[2] Government *Gazette* of 1892.

The smooth operation of the contemporary form of a Crowned Democracy is based more or less on the automatic functioning of the State mechanism. A decisive role for the King is incompatible with the doctrine of Royal immunity, which no metaphysical interpretation can shield from criticism in our times when it comes into collision with crude reality. The King's exceptional intervention must be rare and restricted to moral grounds.

Trikoupis then justified the King's action, saying that there was no disagreement between King and people, since what the King had done was to appeal to the electorate to solve an existing dispute between himself and his Government. Trikoupis' justification of the royal decision was obviously based on arguments of political expediency, destined to shield the Crown from political attack. In this respect his motivation can be compared with Pitt's and Peel's similar reactions in 1782 and 1835, when they both shielded the Crown though they disagreed with the Sovereign's actions.

It was the political arguments underlying his dismissal that Deliyannis openly challenged and not the legality of his dismissal which nobody – Deliyannis himself included – ever contested.[1] He severely criticised the Crown's actions, both during the election period that followed his dismissal as well as in Parliament in 1893, and later on in 23 January/5 February 1902,[2] and again in 26 February/11 March 1903.[3] In this last speech, addressing Konstantopoulos he said: 'You must thank God that the 1892 elections were not favourable to my party, because had I been in a majority I would have taught you what ministerial responsibility means when you countersign a decree dismissing a Ministry in office.' Thus, there was a further question at issue and Deliyannis was eager to point it out, i.e. what would happen if the people had disapproved of the King's initiative?

According to Karolides,[4] a contemporary Greek historian of the turn of the century, Trikoupis himself unreservedly held that Deliyannis was right in 1892 and admitted that because of political necessity he stood by the side of the King, when he was in danger in that year. Thus, strangely enough, Trikoupis, who disagreed with the constitutionality of Deliyannis' dismissal, supported the King on grounds of political expediency, whereas Deliyannis, who acknowledged the Crown's legal right to dismiss a Government and appoint a minority administration, openly opposed the Crown on purely political grounds.

[1] See Deliyannis in one of his most interesting speeches in the House on 26 February 1903 in *Parliamentary Debates*, ΙΣΤ, α, 390, 400ff. and 403.

[2] *Parliamentary Debates*, ΙΕ, γ, 23 January 1902, 77.

[3] *Parliamentary Debates*, ΙΣΤ, α, 390 and 403.

[4] *Contemporary history of the Greeks*, VII, 308, n. 1.

Trikoupis' views, as expressed to Karolides, are in strict conformity with his doctrine of 'proclaimed majority'. But as previously stated, his pure doctrine was never strictly followed in Greece. The Deliyannis version was finally adopted according to which a minority Government could be appointed provided it immediately obtained the confidence of the House or dissolved if it were censured. Had Trikoupis' doctrine been fully implemented, dissolution would have been rarely used since it would only be possible for a majority party to advise it. In practice this would have produced similar results to those in the United Kingdom, where dissolution, as a rule, though not without exceptions, is advised by the majority party. The fact that Trikoupis' doctrine was applied in its mild form was accepted by the leading Greek constitutional lawyers, N. N. Saripolos and A. Svolos.[1] The latter in fact maintained that the 1927 Constitution legally established the prevailing practice, determined up to 1927 by usages and conventions.

Obviously [Svolos continued] the explicit formulation of the principles of parliamentary government by the new Constitution (1927) is, from the point of view of constitutional orthodoxy, a retreat from Trikoupis' pure doctrine of parliamentary majority rule, because the new constitution does not require that the newly appointed Ministry possess the 'proclaimed confidence' of the House. On the contrary it allows the formation of a minority government, provided it immediately obtains a vote of confidence or dissolves Parliament in the event that it is defeated in the House.

And the 1952 Constitution followed, in this respect, its 1927 predecessor, and hence all relevant argumentation can be applied for the period 1952–68 as well. Despite this however, during the summer of 1965, when King Constantine II 'dismissed' Mr Papandreou's Government, several constitutional lawyers and politicians supported the opposite view and referred to the Trikoupis doctrine in condemning the King's actions. It may be suggested that this interpretation was influenced by political arguments rather than by authentic legal reasoning.

Thus, there is little doubt that the Crown's action in 1892 was in conformity with the letter and practice of the Constitution. But it is also equally true to say that it was politically dangerous, and in fact – as far as I know – a unique precedent in contemporary European practice for a Ministry to be dismissed in this way. Furthermore, despite what leading constitutional lawyers have occasionally maintained, it would seem that legal and political considerations go hand in hand in matters like this. A strictly legal interpretation of any constitution, ignoring the

[1] Svolos, *The New Constitution*, p. 389. See also Saripolos, *The parliamentary system of government*, p. 42 and n. 4 mentioning relevant bibliography.

political and economic background, is bound to be purely academic and of little interest to lawyer and political scientist alike. It is in this context that one cannot justify the events of 1892 and in fact one has serious doubts on the way the crisis was handled. Needless to say, a similar action under the 1968 Greek Constitution would be totally unimaginable – but this, of course, will be discussed later on.

Trikoupis won the 1892 elections and remained in office until 27 April/ 9 May 1893. He was temporarily succeeded by Sotiropoulos on 29 April/ 11 May 1893 only to return to power on 30 October/11 November 1893 and resign again at the beginning of 1895 after failing to save the Greek economy from bankruptcy. A 'colourless' administration was appointed headed by the Greek Ambassador in Paris N. Deliyannis (12/24 January 1895) which dissolved Parliament on 20 February 1895 and held elections on 16/28 April 1895. This Parliament was the thirteenth of the new Constitution and was dissolved after having demonstrated that it was totally unable to produce a viable administration. But the N. Deliyannis caretaker Government met with feelings of suspicion and was referred to by the daily newspapers as the 'Court Government'.[1] Trikoupis' party lost the elections and Trikoupis himself failed to get re-elected. He died soon after. With his death the ephemeral two-party system collapsed. Once again it was proved that the departure of a strong personality from the political scene tends to have disruptive effects. The disappearance of the acknowledged leader always leads to a revival of personal ambitions. Trikoupis' party did not escape this rule.

The Parliament that followed lasted for two years (1895–7) during which three Governments were formed. These were headed by Th. Deliyannis (April 1895 – April 1897), D. Rallis (19 April/1 May 1897) and A. Zaimis (21 September/3 October 1897) who dissolved the House and held elections on 7/19 February 1899. The remote, yet decisive cause of this dissolution was the unfortunate Greek–Turkish War of 1897.[2]

The next Parliament (the fourteenth of the new Constitution) survived for a longer period and saw two governments. The first was headed by G. Theotokis* who resigned quite unexpectedly in 1901. The crisis that led to the Government's resignation was caused by a translation of the Gospel (*Evangelion* – hence the crisis was called the *Evangelika*) into

---

[1] The Athens daily newspaper *Asty* (13/25 January 1895) maintained that: 'The Prime Minister and most of the ministers have direct or indirect connections with the Court . . . This is quite a serious case . . . because Ministers are the advisers of the Crown and hence have the right under certain circumstances to disagree with it. But when aides or court officials are appointed Ministers then the situation is reversed and they do not advise the Crown but the Crown advises them.' It further predicted that the elections would be rigged.

[2] See Markesinis, *Political history*, II, 274ff.

vulgar Greek (*demotiki*). The translation was undertaken under the Queen's auspices and published despite the contrary opinion of the Holy Synod and the Minister of Education. It stirred up passions and resulted in clashes in the streets between students and the police with 11 dead and nearly 100 wounded. The Government was accused of brutality in dispersing the crowds and eventually resigned. It was succeeded by the minority government of A. Zaimis with the support of G. Theotokis who would not accept Th. Deliyannis (12/25 November 1901). The Government met with great opposition in the House, was finally obliged to dissolve Parliament,[1] and held elections on 17/30 November 1902, the results of which, however, were uncertain since neither of the two big parties (Theotokis' or Deliyannis') had an overall majority. Deliyannis, however, was eventually commissioned. During the sixteenth Parliament (November 1902 – March 1905) five Governments exercised authority. The governmental instability was caused both by the fluid composition of the House and the increasing tension over Macedonia. The Governments of this Parliament were led by: Th. Deliyannis (10/23 December 1902), G. Theotokis (27 June/10 July 1903), D. Rallis (August 1903), G. Theotokis again (15/27 December 1903) and Th. Deliyannis again (17/30 December 1904) who finally dissolved the House on 22 December 1904/4 January 1905. Dissolution was advised because no stable Government could be formed.[2] The Government won the elections (20 February/ 5 March 1905) and remained in office until Deliyannis' assassination in 1905.

The seventeenth Parliament had an extremely short term. Deliyannis' assassination led to the formation of a new Government by his two chief supporters – Mavromichalis and Rallis, 9/22 June 1905) – who were unable, however, to hold the party together for long. They finally gave way to an administration led by G. Theotokis who on 8/21 December 1905 dissolved Parliament and held elections on 26 March/8 April 1906. Theotokis won the elections and remained in office for nearly three years. He resigned for no apparent reason just before the 1909 military Revolution, and was succeeded by D. Rallis.[3]

---

[1] According to N. Stratos dissolution was caused because Parliament was in disaccord with public opinion. *Parliamentary Debates* (1917), Κ, β, 155.

[2] Stratos, ibid.

[3] According to Prince Nicholas' *Diary*, 'Theotokis, seeing that matters were getting out of hand, looked for an excuse to quit the leadership.' Quoted by Markesinis, *Political history*, III, 80.

D: THE 1909 REVOLUTION AND THE
NEW CONSTITUTION (1911)

Aristotle's statement that: 'Though sedition springs from small occasions, it does not turn on small issues'[1] may be applied to the 1909 military Revolution. Its causes, of course, cannot be discussed here, though one might suggest that they stemmed from the 1897 war and the subsequent political and economic instability.

The 1909 military Revolution is undoubtedly a turning point in Greek constitutional history, despite the fact that its constitutional innovations were in no way comparable to the radical constitutional changes brought about by the 1862 Revolution. This does not mean that the revised text is devoid of important new clauses. However, it does imply that the real influence of the revolution will be found primarily in the successful reorganisation of the State which it stimulated.

The success of the Revolution on the night of 27 August 1909 immediately resulted in the resignation of the Rallis Government. The Army's primary target was the convocation of a Revisionary Parliament, which would modernise the text of the 1864 Constitution, and the granting of an amnesty to all who had taken part in the revolt. Despite the fact that the 'Military League' had never demonstrated any anti-monarchic feelings[2] and was in fact pressing for the revision of the non-fundamental articles of the Constitution, the King could not conceal his fears for the Crown. Public opinion on the other hand was pressing for a Constituent Assembly that would be in a position to reconsider the form of government.

Mavromichalis, who had succeeded Rallis in the Premiership, disagreed with the above and resigned. He was succeeded on 18/31 January 1910 by S. Dragoumis whose main task was to prepare elections for a Revisional Assembly on the basis of what Parliament had agreed on in previous debates. Thus, on 30 June/13 July 1910 Parliament was dissolved and elections for a Revisional Assembly (composed according to the Greek Constitution of double the usual number of M.P.s) were held on 8/21 August 1910.

The composition of the new Parliament was a real mosaic. The old parties held the majority between them. In all they held 205 seats (Theotokis 94, Rallis 64, Mavromichalis 34 and Zaimis 13), against 150 independents. These were divided into groups of which the largest was the Thessalian group numbering 45. The Socialists came next with a smaller

---

[1] *Politics*, 1303b, trans. by E. Parker (Oxford, 1948).
[2] See the revolutionary declaration first published in the *Memoirs* (1925) of the leader of the Revolution N. Zorbas (pp. 15–22); also, Markesinis, *Political history*, III, 358.

group and approximately 15 were favourably disposed towards E. Venizelos. Furthermore there was no agreement on the legal nature of the Parliament and on the powers of the assembly.

The main new feature, however, was the election of E. Venizelos as Member of Parliament for Attica and Boetia, which at that time formed one constituency, despite the fact that he had not been an official candidate. Venizelos' star had been for some time continuously in the ascendant, mainly because of his record in Crete. He was increasingly looked upon as the only person who could help Greece overcome its present complicated problems.

Venizelos was in Lucerne when he heard of his personal success. He came to Athens via Crete and immediately delivered an important political speech describing briefly but clearly the situation and the possible remedies. Despite the vociferous objections of his audience, he insisted that the new Assembly be of a revisional nature and restrict its work to the non-fundamental articles of the 1864 Constitution.[1] Venizelos' firm stand, coming at a moment of confusion both in and outside Parliament, established him as a statesman who leads and is not led by the people and furthermore, earned him the Crown's favour. Thus, the King fearing nothing from Venizelos' conciliatory policies,[2] eventually commissioned him on 6/19 September 1910 to form his first Government, despite the small number of M.P.s that followed him.

The first Revisional Parliament was obsessed from the very beginning by the fear of dissolution. The Athens newspapers daily predicted dissolution if Venizelos was defeated in the House. The patchwork composition of Parliament – indicating that Venizelos' possible defeat would result in governmental instability and political chaos – gave credibility to the above rumours. All this was at a time when both the electorate and the Army favoured a speedy return to normality. Thus, an extremely important, though rarely occurring, constitutional problem arose and was debated in detail in the House. The problem had two aspects. First, could the King – who was not considered a constituent factor and was deprived of any initiative in the revisional sphere – dissolve a Revisional Assembly, and thus obstruct its revisional task? Second, was it true that Venizelos had ensured beforehand (and in fact made it a condition of his acceptance of office) the King's promise to dissolve if defeated in the House? Furthermore was this constitutionally possible?

[1] The full text of the speech is reprinted in Markesinis, *Political history*, III, 361.
[2] Venizelos had in the past come into direct conflict with the King's son, Prince George, High Commissioner in Crete, over the future of the island. He was thus disliked by the Royal Family. E. Howard's *Theatre of life* (1936), II, 18, is revealing as regards the English attitude to the question.

The very interesting debate that followed on 8/21 and 9/22 October 1910, was opened by A. Eftaxias who in a well-argued speech gave a negative answer to the above questions. 'Dissolution', Eftaxias maintained, 'cannot be ensured in advance by a future Prime Minister, but can be practised only at a given moment of crisis and when no other course is left.'[1] Referring to the royal prerogative, Eftaxias insisted that the 'present Parliament is indissoluble as being a sui generis Revisional Assembly'. He based his opinion on the argument that 'since the present revision was undertaken contrary to the specific provisions of the 1864 Constitution, Parliament could not be legally considered as revisional but as a sui generis Revisional or Constituent Assembly, exercising a restricted but self-emanating constituent authority'.[2]

A. Papanastasiou* succeeded Eftaxias on the floor and agreed that Parliament was indissoluble. But referring to Eftaxias' first argument he maintained that it concerned 'a family affair between the Crown and its Government'.[3]

G. Theotokis, who spoke next, took exactly the opposite view. In his opinion Parliament could be dissolved but he thought that the Government could not obtain in advance permission to dissolve if defeated in the House.[4]

The Prime Minister was persuasive in his answer to the legal problem. In his speech he maintained that,

It is the government's opinion that if this body were to be proclaimed a Constituent Assembly, it would be a sovereign body, and hence indissoluble and that the Royal Prerogative would be ineffective in this case. Yet, if this body is not a Constituent Assembly, but is merely a Parliament composed of double the usual number of M.P.s, then this body is not sovereign, it does not abolish any other power nor does it attract – in the name of the people – total sovereignty. It is a Parliament entrusted with the revision of the non-fundamental articles of the Constitution. Hence, the Crown has the right to exercise its prerogative, if the necessary circumstances arise.[5]

Venizelos, as already stated, considered the House a Revisional Assembly and thus did not oppose the possibility of dissolution. Venizelos' views were accepted furthermore by such eminent Greek constitutional lawyers as Professors Saripolos and Svolos. It is obvious however – and in fact it is indicated in his speech – that Venizelos' stand was based on political motives taking into account the fluid situation in the House.

Venizelos left Eftaxias's second question unanswered, i.e. whether he had made his acceptance of office conditional upon an immediate dissolu-

[1] *Parliamentary Debates, 1st Revisional Parliament,* 9 October 1910, p. 208.
[2] Ibid. p. 208.   [3] *Parliamentary Debates,* ibid. p. 211.
[4] *Parliamentary Debates,* ibid. p. 211.   [5] Ibid. p. 213.

*

tion if he were defeated in Parliament. There is no specific evidence on this matter, but what is said in the following paragraph indicates that it is most unlikely that this had in fact happened. What seems most likely is that Venizelos accepted the mandate predicting dissolution if it were needed, but without having ensured it beforehand.

The appropriate legal answer however seems to lie in a document that Lord Haldane gave to Lord Stamfordham on 5 December 1916 referring to a very similar situation:

The Sovereign cannot entertain any bargain for a dissolution merely with a possible Prime Minister before the latter is fully installed. The Sovereign cannot, before the ɜvent, properly weigh the general situation and the Parliamentary position of the Ministry as formed.[1]

At the subsequent vote of confidence there was no quorum,[2] and Venizelos, interpreting it as a lack of confidence, tendered his resignation. The King, however, refused to accept it on the grounds that 'The lack of a quorum was not a clear and undoubted sign that it was impossible for the present assembly to work with the government', and asked Venizelos to put the matter to the vote 'so as to make the assembly's disposition clearer to the Government'. Venizelos agreed with the King that Parliament should be consulted once more, but there is still no indication that the King had decided upon dissolution. Though the King rightly refused dissolution up to the last moment, Venizelos managed with great skill to reach what he had obviously envisaged from the beginning. In the conversation that followed between King and Prime Minister, the King 'admitted the possibility of the prerogative being used in the case of his being persuaded that the House, as constituted, was unable to work systematically and effectively'.[3] But he never gave a promise. Venizelos then asked the King if he would make a statement to the Press to this effect but the King refused this too. Finally, however, the two men, aided by S. Dragoumis, drafted a brief and vague statement. But unexpectedly this statement was published by an Athens daily and caused a great sensation. Whether Venizelos had leaked the information or not is unclear. Despite his efforts to renounce the validity of the publication he did not manage to avoid an uproar. He did manage, however, to obtain dissolution and the fact remains that the King, willingly or not, was forced to agree to it.

The result of the vote was 208 for the Government out of 266 present.

---

[1] Quoted by H. Nicolson in *King George V*, p. 380.
[2] *Parliamentary Debates*, ibid.
[3] Markesinis, *Political history*, III, 113.

The same night the Prime Minister declared that 'it was necessary for the government to study the result of the vote'. Next day, 12 October 1910, Parliament was dissolved and elections for a second Revisionary Parliament were announced for 28 November/11 December 1910. The old political parties abstained from the elections (the first abstention in the parliamentary history of modern Greece) on the argument that Parliament was illegally dissolved. But apart from the serious doubts that there may be about the validity of this claim this abstention proved politically erroneous and was seriously detrimental to the parties. Greek history has frequently shown that when abstention is not followed up by revolt, it leads to the dispersal of those who abstained and only time and the opportune moment can help them to reorganise themselves.

The Second Revisionary Parliament met on 21 January 1911 and quickly completed its work – the prevailing line of the revision was the need to strengthen the rule of law but without any decisive alterations. The revision was finally kept fundamentally within the bounds of the 1864 Constitution. All the same progress was achieved in the protection of personal liberties by the provision of further guarantees for subjects' personal freedom, the freedom of the press and of property.[1] Compulsory expropriation was considered[2] on behalf of the landless peasants and measures were taken against the possibility of the Army becoming involved in politics.[3] The Courts of Justice instead of Parliament became competent to solve any dispute over election results,[4] and lastly the permanency of civil servants was secured.[5] The revisional procedure was also simplified.[6]

The voting of the Constitution was followed by a new dissolution (20 December 1911) and elections on 12 March 1912. E. Venizelos won them and for the next three years remained the undisputed master. This was the last dissolution of the reign of King George I.

---

[1] Articles 5, 6, 12, 14.   [2] Article 17.   [3] Article 71.
[4] Article 73.   [5] Article 102.   [6] Article 108.

Chapter 10

THE 1911 CONSTITUTION AND THE
TWO DISSOLUTIONS OF 1915

A: THE PROTAGONISTS OF THE CRISIS

Venizelos' triumph in the 1912 elections – and this time the Opposition
parties took part – was followed by approximately three years of governmental stability and unimpaired material progress, a rather rare phenomenon in modern Greek history. Thanks to unity within the nation, the
ability of the King and the General Staff in military matters, and Venizelos'
undoubted statesmanship, the country nearly doubled its boundaries.[1]
Furthermore, it achieved a satisfactory standard of economic stability
and at the same time acquired important progressive social and labour
legislation.

Internal stability, however, still depended heavily – as future events
were clearly to demonstrate – on external affairs. Despite the long-lasting
effects of the treaty of Bucharest (10 August 1913) – a compromise which
successfully ended the Balkan Wars – vital problems still remained to be
solved. For Greece in particular, the Archipelago Islands (Chios, Samos,
Mytilene etc.) and Northern Epirus still remained an unsolved problem.
History seems to indicate that a tense situation has been the rule rather
than the exception in the Balkans.

The First World War brought the Balkan peninsula into the fore-
ground. After all, the War had started in Sarajevo. As military operations
progressed, the attitude of the various Balkan states became a problem of
considerable interest to the belligerents. The question of alliances became
acute, and Greece found herself obliged to take sides in the European
conflict. Unfortunately for the country, its leaders were deeply divided
over this issue. The political differences were reflected in a serious controversy over the royal prerogative to dissolve Parliament – exercised
twice in 1915. It led to open rebellion, scission and finally to the exile of
the King. It resulted, as Venizelos himself observed, in a repeated violation
of the rules of parliamentary government[2] during the years 1915–20.

---

[1] Bulgarian greed is also an important factor since it led to the Second Balkan War from
which Greece emerged victorious.
[2] *Parliamentary Debates*, K, α (28 September 1915), 184 and K, α (21 October 1915), 535.

It therefore seems extremely important to examine the crisis in detail, and its understanding presupposes a considerable knowledge of the historical events.

During 1915 two policies were mainly advocated. The first was expressed by the Prime Minister, while the second was identified with the King. This in itself was extremely unfortunate since it was and is incompatible with the Crown's position in the parliamentary form of government. C. Zavitsianos, a prominent Liberal M.P. and Speaker of the House in 1915, once said Greece's problems stemmed from the fact that Constantine was a King who also wanted to be Prime Minister.

However, it would be totally wrong to believe – as political fanaticism did not hesitate to advance – that the King's motives were 'to further his personal interests and those of his dynasty'.[1] The King – to the very end – was motivated by what he truly believed to be the good of his country and on several occasions, particularly during the first period of the crisis, his fears and anxieties were proved absolutely correct. Venizelos himself in 1915 explicitly stated that 'it is inconceivable that a King could desire the destruction of his country'.[2] What Venizelos and his party contested was the Crown's right to have a policy and furthermore to attempt to impose it on a reluctant Government. In this context it is clear that Venizelos was absolutely correct in maintaining that 'in the parliamentary form of government the Crown never has a personal policy'.[3] Political fanaticism, however, blurred the issues only to confuse further the constitutional aspects of the crisis.

King Constantine I was not a Germanophile in the sense his adversaries have suggested – nor was his family as a whole inclined in favour of Germany. With the exception of his wife – sister of Kaiser Wilhelm II – and certain members of his entourage, the other members of his family were definitely pro-Entente.[4] What seemed to influence the King was Germany's military superiority and organisation, a fact more or less universally accepted. Furthermore – and in this respect the King was absolutely in tune with the majority of his subjects – the Kaiser's anti-panslav theories presented a considerable attraction. These calculations however did not prevent the King from realising the importance of the Entente Powers. He was particularly aware of the possibility of a naval blockade by the British and French fleets in the event of Greece joining

[1] Kafandaris, *Parliamentary Debates*, K, β (11 August 1917), 196.
[2] *Parliamentary Debates*, K, α (21 October 1915), 533.
[3] Ibid. See also N. Stratos, *Parliamentary Debates*, K, β (11 August 1917), 151ff. and 154, and Kafandaris, *Parliamentary Debates*, K, β (11 August 1917), 196ff.
[4] G. Streit, *Diary*, II, *a*, 75 (26 March/8 April 1915).

Germany. He had therefore reached the conclusion that a policy of neutrality was the most advisable course.

E. Venizelos on the other hand was definitely pro-Entente. As early as the turn of the century and while still in Crete he had actively demonstrated his pro-British tendencies. Venizelos' confidence in the United Kingdom was in fact so great that in a memorandum to the King on 17 February 1915 he maintained that 'England, even if left alone will finally be in a position to dictate the terms of peace'[1] – a belief that few, if in fact any, shared in the United Kingdom itself.

B: THE HISTORICAL BACKGROUND

Before examining the legal aspects of the crisis a brief summary of the events is essential.

Venizelos' wish to retain good relations with the United Kingdom, in particular had led him to propose as early as January 1914 a Greek–British alliance in order to preserve the status quo in the eastern Mediterranean. This early overture of Venizelos is usually ignored or underestimated by historians, yet it is characteristic of Venizelos' attitude and anxiety to align Greece with the United Kingdom, even before the beginning of the War. His efforts, however, produced no results.

In August, the First World War broke out. Venizelos, particularly in the beginning, believed that it would be soon over and hence was in a hurry to bring Greece out on the side of the Entente – which in his opinion would win the War. Within this in mind, he made two proposals with the King's more or less reluctant approval, offering to place the Greek armed forces at the disposal of the Entente, but he was rebuffed in both his attempts (1/14 August 1914 and 5/18 August 1914). It is important furthermore to add that Venizelos did the above without asking for anything in exchange for Greece.[2]

Venizelos' proposals were turned down on Sir Edward Grey's insistence – which in fact attracted serious criticism from both Lloyd George and Churchill. In Sir Edward's opinion the acceptance of the Greek offer would provide hostile reaction from Turkey – which still remained

---

[1] Quoted by Markesinis, *Political history*, III, 274.

[2] Venizelos' offers were deliberately made before the outcome of the first battle of the Marne was known so as to demonstrate Greece's sincerity and Lord Grey notes the fact that 'Venizelos...no matter how bad the fortunes of the Allies sometimes appeared to be, remained...a staunch friend'. Grey of Falloden, *Twenty-five years* (1925), II, 173. The King, however, more cautious in his approach, had asked Venizelos to await the outcome of the battle. *Parliamentary Debates*, K, α (28 September 1915), 184 and K, α (21 October 1915), 535.

uncommitted. In his memoirs Lord Grey is willing to accept responsibility for turning down Venizelos' offers. He maintains that:

The Cabinet appreciated it [Venizelos' offer of 18 August 1914] but after considera-tion, decided that it would be impolitic to accept it. This was in accord with the advice I gave to the Cabinet and for this I have never disclaimed and have always been ready to accept full responsibility. The wisdom of that advice has been severely impugned. I still think it was right, and that had we accepted this or a subsequent Greek offer in the early days of the war, the consequences might have been very serious, perhaps fatal to the cause of the Allies. The consequences, in my opinion, would have been the immediate entry of Turkey into war on the side of Germany; the immediate or early entry of Bulgaria into the war against Serbia probably; the unsettlement of Russia's whole-heartedness in the war.[1]

Grey's reasoning was of course in accordance with the traditional, one could even term it bureaucratic, method of the Foreign Office which as a matter of principle viewed Greek problems in relation to Turkish affairs.[2] However, one cannot but wonder how the Foreign Office was unable to realise by the end of August that Turkey had already sided with the Central Powers and was just playing for time.[3] It is therefore possible to maintain that Lloyd George was right when he said that if the Greek offers had been accepted

... the whole story of the Dardanelles would have been different. The story of the whole war would also have differed fundamentally from that which was told by events. But for some inscrutable reason Sir Edward Grey rejected Greek overtures of help. His tiresome hesitancies helped us into war but they hindered us when we were well in it. A more virile and understanding treatment of the Balkan situation would have brought Greece and also Bulgaria into the war.[4]

And Sir Winston Churchill concluded that 'This magnanimous offer [Venizelos'] made as it was while all was so uncertain and even before the main battle in France [the first battle of the Marne] had been joined,

---

[1] *Twenty-five years*, II, 173–4.
[2] See above, chapter 9, footnote 2.
[3] Apart from the German interests in the Baghdad railway a number of events clearly revealed Turkey's orientation. By the end of 1913 the German General Liman von Sanders was appointed Field-Marshal – Inspector-General of the Turkish army and was later entrusted with the defence of the capital in the event of war. He subsequently successfully undertook the task of fortifying the Gallipoli peninsula. In August 1914 two German warships joined the Turkish fleet and the British naval mission was requested to leave Turkey. Furthermore, the Sultan, in an unprecedented gesture towards a Christian state, ordered special prayers to be offered throughout the Ottoman Empire for Germany's victory. On 28 September 1914, Turkey closed the Dardanelles to commercial ships, thus seriously affecting Russian trade; yet the Foreign Office was still undecided and hoped for Turkish neutrality. The bombard-ment of Sevastopol by the Turkish fleet on 16/29 October 1914 proved the last straw to British tolerance. [4] *War memoirs*, I (1933), 390.

greatly attracted me.'[1] Be that as it may, the conclusion was that Venizelos was rebuffed and during the next month or so was anxiously contemplating a way to achieve his aims. Then the following incident occurred.

Churchill conceived his idea of the Gallipoli campaign as early as autumn 1914 and his plans – still in a vague form – required Greek assistance. The Admiralty therefore instructed Admiral Kerr – Chief of the British Naval Expedition in Greece[2] – to find out if the Greeks would be willing to participate in the project. The King, in a private conversation with Admiral Kerr, made it plain that Greece would not participate in what seemed to him a superficially planned and risky operation. When Venizelos found out about the conversation, he interpreted it as a change of policy on the King's part and tendered his resignation. The King, however, did not accept it and Venizelos was finally persuaded to withdraw it. The crisis seemed temporarily to have been averted.

By the beginning of 1915 the situation had been drastically altered. Turkey had already joined the German camp (5 November 1914) and the Dardanelles plans were well advanced. Furthermore the situation in Serbia was extremely disquieting. Greece had signed a treaty of mutual defence with Serbia, but its terms did not specify whether it was applicable even in the event of a European war as Venizelos claimed – or was limited to Balkan wars and conflicts as the anti-war parties maintained. At the beginning of the War, however, Venizelos was unwilling to send troops to help Serbia against Austria. He feared a possible Bulgarian attack which would cut off their troops from the Greek mainland. He therefore considered it preferable for the Greek army to remain within the country's frontiers, ready to assist Serbia in the event of a Bulgarian attack. At this early stage, Pasits, the Serbian Prime Minister, refrained from pressing Greece through fear of provoking the uncommitted Bulgaria.[3]

During the winter of 1916, however, the ineffectiveness of the Russian army indicated that Germany would soon be able to withdraw troops from the Eastern front and come to the aid of Austria. A Serbian débâcle seemed imminent and the allies, wanting to avert it but at the same time unable themselves to help, were pressing Greece. The Entente was

---

[1] *The World Crisis, 1911–1914* (1923), p. 485. He concludes (p. 486) that he had to conform with the Cabinet's decision on 'increasing misgivings'.

[2] Rear-Admiral Mark Kerr (1864–1943) was appointed head of the British Naval Mission in Greece between 1913 and 1915. For a time he simultaneously served as C. in C. of the Greek fleet and it was during this period that he was asked by the Admiralty to find out about Greece's possible help in a future Gallipoli campaign. Churchill, in his *World Crisis*, p. 488, publishes part of his correspondence with the admiral.

[3] Markesinis, *Political history*, III, 291–2.

willing to grant Greece important territorial concessions on the coast of Asia Minor in exchange for her help to Serbia. But Greece was also asked to cede Greek provinces to Bulgaria in order to attract her support or at least her neutrality. Venizelos was willing to give Kavalla – a decision severely criticised at that time – in exchange for the Smyrna area, but also insisted that Bulgaria should proclaim at least a benevolent neutrality and Rumania take an active part on the side of the Entente. Greece's position depended more or less on the attitude of her neighbours, but no agreement was reached and, once again, the question was dropped altogether.

Meanwhile the Gallipoli campaign began in February 1915, and efforts to attract Greek support intensified despite Russian objections to Greek involvement in the Straits area. The Admiralty badly needed Greek troops to assist naval operations and it would have exercised even greater pressure had it not been hindered by the secret treaty of March 1915 between the United Kingdom and Russia. This treaty had dramatically reversed nineteenth-century British foreign policy by granting Constantinople and the Straits to the Russians. The latter were therefore quite unwilling to see Greek troops in the Gallipoli area.[1] Whatever British intentions might have been, the Greek Army Staff strongly opposed Greek involvement, stressing the military dangers of what subsequently proved to be an inefficiently organised and unco-ordinated enterprise.[2] Venizelos on the other hand was more interested in the political consequences of Greece's participation than concerned with the military aspects of the issue. In a Crown Council that followed on 18 February/3 March and 20 February/5 March 1915 he forcefully argued in favour of his views.[3] The opposition leaders present agreed with him and even George Theotokis – an openly pro-German political leader – thought that the Crown – for purely constitutional reasons – should follow the advice of the Prime Minister. The Crown Council reached no decision and it was left to the King to decide. He finally decided against Venizelos and the latter tendered his resignation.

D. Gounaris* was appointed his successor with the support of the anti-Venizelist parties, despite the fact that he had only one follower in the House. He was obliged to dissolve Parliament and held elections on 31 May/13 June 1915, which Venizelos won. Though defeated, Gounaris remained in office on the pretext of the King's recent illness. The real

---

[1] Russia's objections were again the main reason for turning down Venizelos' offers (22 March 1915) to participate in the Dardanelles campaign. Grey, *Twenty-five years*.

[2] Metaxas' memorandum published in his *Diary*, II, 407ff., was submitted to the Prime Minister on 17 February/2 March 1915.

[3] His post facto speech, however, in Parliament on 13/26 August 1917 concerning the Dardanelles operation appears ill-prepared and unconvincing.

cause, however, was the King's hesitation to recall Venizelos to power, a hesitation both politically and constitutionally condemnable since – as Streit suggested – 'Most Greeks were still in favour of Venizelos'.[1] For a moment the King considered an immediate second dissolution but was finally persuaded not to attempt it. Instead, and in order to gain time, the King had recourse to his exceptional right to postpone the meeting of Parliament for a month. Again the pretext was the King's illness but the real cause was political intrigue – Venizelos had to be kept out of office. It must be noted, however, that the King's main advisers at the time – Streit and Gounaris – strongly objected to the Sovereign's attitude but the latter remained adamant. During these months, the King, perhaps owing to his illness, was particularly abrupt and intransigent in his views of his rights and duties towards his country – an attitude entirely incompatible with the prevailing form of government.[2] Venizelos was finally recommissioned to form a Government on 10/23 August 1915, after having agreed to a policy of neutrality 'if the present conditions remain unchanged'.[3]

On 8/21 September 1915 Bulgaria ended her opportunist policy and mobilised in favour of the Central Powers. Greece answered with a general mobilisation and the treaty with Serbia was again brought into play. This time the Allies pressed Greece even harder to help Serbia, and England temporarily considered ceding Cyprus in exchange for this help. Venizelos had hoped to avoid this situation and in fact had opposed the idea of sending Greek troops to Serbia in order not to provoke Bulgaria. But it was also clear that he would support Serbia if Bulgaria attacked her. The General Staff, on the other hand, favoured mobilisation as a purely defensive measure. It argued, to a certain extent correctly, that Serbia would be unable to fulfil her treaty obligation by providing a force of 150,000 men on the Bulgarian front in the event of war. So, the argument went on, if Serbia cannot fulfil her obligations, Greece is not bound by hers.

Venizelos then suddenly decided to ask the Entente to provide this force. Whether he actually did (as seems possible) or did not, is controversial. The fact is that the first Allied troops landed in Thessaloniki in October 1915, thus openly violating Greek neutrality. The Allies' decision

---

[1] Streit, *Diary*, II, *a*, 117.

[2] The King's absolutist and monarchical tendencies had been revealed during the First Balkan War in his correspondence with Venizelos, for which consult Markesinis, *Political history*, III, 186. His views on his rights and duties, in 1914–15, were more akin to theories of divine monarchy than to principles of a Crowned Democracy. See again Markesinis, ibid. IV, 20ff.

[3] Markesinis, *Political history*, IV, 39.

to land troops in Greece created a sensation and caused discontent. The issue was debated in Parliament[1] but Venizelos was lukewarm in his condemnation of the Allies. The King, angered by Venizelos' attitude and fearing that the situation would provoke a hostile German reaction, obliged him to resign. A. Zaimis was sworn in and formed a neutral Government with the tolerance of the Liberals. In October, however, after an unfortunate incident in the House, the Liberals withdrew their tolerance and the Government resigned. The House was dissolved and elections followed. The Liberals abstained in protest against the 'repeated violation of the Constitution'. The crisis was now entering a new phase that would end with the exile of the King.

The one-sided elections of 6/19 December 1915 were followed by successive governments led by Skouloudis, Zaimis, Kalogeropoulos, Lambros and Zaimis again, during which Greek neutrality was repeatedly violated by the belligerent states. The internal scission spread to all aspects of public and private life.[2] Never was the nation more divided. Needless to say, in the middle of the controversy stood the Crown, increasingly identified with one section of the community, i.e. the anti-Venizelist parties. But when the Crown ceases to be the Head of State and becomes the leader of a political party – even if this party represents the majority – the form of government is seriously altered. The King as party leader suffers from the dangers inherent in the position: i.e. criticism. And the Crown is *ex definitione* above parties and criticism. In August 1916 a military revolution broke out in Thessaloniki, aided by General Sarail. Venizelos eventually became its leader and a separate state was created in Macedonia. The country was now virtually divided in two.

The series of events that led to the King's exile[3] on 29 May 1917 cannot be discussed here, though one could raise a familiar point in these chapters, i.e. that yet again the moving force was a foreign power – France on this occasion. Constantine's second son Alexander was declared King on 30 May 1916 and Venizelos recalled to Athens and appointed Prime Minister. In an unprecedented decision, the Parliament of 31 May/13 June 1915, characteristically referred to as the 'Lazarus Parliament', was restored to life, since it was considered as more representative of the will of the people – a highly contestable theory.

These, briefly, were the internal events up to 1917. One must, I believe,

---

[1] *Parliamentary Debates*, K, α (21 September/4 October 1915). The King actually encouraged the Government to support Sir E. Grey's proposal and offer Cyprus to Greece. Jenkins, *Asquith*, p. 422 (n. 1).

[2] Details of events in Markesinis, *Political history*, vol. IV.

[3] The King did not formally resign or abdicate. Venizelos wrongly maintained the opposite in Parliament in 1917.

at this point, pause to examine the numerous legal questions arising, among which one may mention the following:

(*i*) Was the postponement of the meeting of Parliament in May 1915 constitutional and according to orthodox parliamentary rules? Furthermore was the delay in recalling Venizelos to power politically justifiable?

(*ii*) Was the dissolution of 18/30 April 1915 constitutional?

(*iii*) Was the second dissolution (December 1915) constitutional and what arguments did the opposing parties put forward?

(*iv*) Had the Entente any legal right to land forces on Greek territory thus violating Greek neutrality? (The problem is particularly interesting from an international law point of view, since the United Kingdom had, after all, entered the War because of the violation of Belgian neutrality.[1])

(*v*) Was the revival of the May Parliament legal and how was it justified?

Obviously all these problems cannot and will not be examined here. Attention will primarily be concentrated on questions (*ii*), (*iii*) and (*v*), since they seem to be directly related to the problem of dissolution.

C: THE TWO DISSOLUTIONS

In the speech in Parliament in 1917, G. Kafandaris treated extensively the legal aspects of the 1915 crisis.[2] The discussion and the arguments that were then put forward must be viewed with great caution not only because of the prevailing political fanaticism but also because the Liberals monopolised the House. With the exception of Stratos and Rallis, most of their opponents were in exile or in prison and a state of martial law existed. Despite these deficiencies, however, Kafandaris' arguments do provide some information on the 1915 events.

Kafandaris strongly condemned the two dissolutions and described the first as more 'contemptible' than the second. His speech was well argued, though he did not manage to escape the current political emotionalism and indulged in a great deal of rhetorical flourish. Hence his interpretation of the Constitution is often controversial and must be viewed with caution.

Kafandaris' reasoning emanated from the principle that 'in a Crowned Democracy the King is nothing but a passive State Organ in the administration of public business – a mere channel of the popular will. All political authority is concentrated in the hands of the people and their representatives: Parliament and Government.' Kafandaris concluded:

[1] Or, at least, this was the legal pretext because, as Asquith wrote to the King, Britain's attitude in the event of a German violation of the Belgian neutrality was a matter of 'policy [rather] than of legal obligation...' Jenkins, *Asquith*, p. 363.

[2] *Parliamentary Debates*, K, β (11 August 1917), 196ff.

A Crowned Democracy, though in form not an authentic Republic because of the existence of a non-elective and irrevocable factor in the functioning of Government, is nevertheless in effect a true and pure Republic. We derive this from the explicit provisions of the constitution, which provide that all authority stems from the Nation [Art. 21], that only Parliament is competent to revise the constitution [Art. 108] – [a clause accentuating this passive role of the Irresponsible Authority] – that Parliament can be self-convened [Art. 54] and is free to regulate the progress of its business [Art. 38]. Furthermore the Constitution furnishes definite proof that the royal prerogatives, theoretically available to the King, belong in practice to the Executive, the Government ... since we observe that no action of the King, is valid unless countersigned by the competent minister.[1]

Referring to the April dissolution, Kafandaris had nothing but strong criticism for the Crown. He maintained that

The first dissolution[2] was more contemptible [than the second[3]] because the King not only opposed the majority of the House and the Government, not only did he ignore the opinion of the majority of the Greek people who supported the Liberals, but he also set himself against the whole of the Greek people. You remember [he said, addressing the House], that on February 18th [1915] the King held a Crown Council in the Royal Palace in which both the majority and the minority leaders took part. They unanimously approved the policy that the Prime Minister proposed and some of the leaders present went further in that direction. Thus, the responsible Government, the leaders of the other political parties, the majority and the minority of Parliament, the majority and the minority of the country ... accepted one national policy. Only one person did not approve and in fact disagreed: the King. And his arbitrary opinion prevailed over the united will of the Greek nation. Tell me if this befits a Crowned Democracy or an impudent authoritarian regime?

It is submitted that Kafandaris' description of the position of the monarchy in a Crowned Democracy is more or less convincing. But, it must be added, it is a closer approximation to the theoretical ideal than an accurate description of the actual Greek practice in the late nineteenth and early twentieth centuries. Despite the articles of the Constitution that he mentioned – and even those that he omitted[4] – which, as he correctly maintained, emphasised the rights of Parliament, the King was still – in theory and practice – entrusted with important powers. For example one cannot ignore how very real and effective was the royal power to appoint Ministers[5] – and it remained so up to the 1968 Constitution. This power was unaffected by the fact that it was more or less limited to persons that

---

[1] *Parliamentary Debates*, ibid. pp. 197–8.   [2] Of 18/1 May 1915.

[3] Of 29 October/11 November 1915.

[4] As for example article 44 which stated that the King has only those rights expressly granted to him by the Constitution.

[5] Article 31 stated: 'The King appoints and dismisses his Ministers.'

would eventually have to obtain the confidence of the House or else advise the dissolution.

Venizelos himself did not contest the legality of the April 1915 dissolution. Speaking in Parliament on 21 October 1915, he said: 'I accept the Crown's right to disagree – in accordance with the Constitution – with the responsible government',[1] and in the previous chapter it has been shown that this was the accepted practice in Greece. With the exception of Ch. Trikoupis and his faithful follower S. Dragoumis, nobody ever contested the Crown's right to appoint a minority Government and dissolve the House. After all, Venizelos himself twice came to power and dissolved though technically in a minority in the House.

It would therefore seem that Kafandaris erred in condemning the first dissolution, though he was right in indicating that the dangers lay elsewhere, namely in the Crown's decision to oppose the unanimous opinion of the political world as expressed in the Crown Council. The fact, of course, that the anti-Venizelist parties subsequently changed opinion and supported the King's appointment of D. Gounaris as Prime Minister offers some justification of the Crown's decision. A political Government took the responsibility for the King's action. But it is nevertheless true that the decision to oppose the majority of the House came from the King himself and with it came all the political dangers inherent in such decisions.

The dissolution of 18 April/1 May 1915 need not be discussed further since the second dissolution of 29 October/11 November 1915 soon became the focus of attention and acute controversy. As already stated, the Liberals abstained from the December 1915 elections maintaining that the Crown had repeatedly violated the Constitution. The constitutional issue had two aspects. The first was that the electorate had made its decision on foreign policy[2] in the May–June elections and hence the Crown could not dissolve again within such a brief period of time. The second aspect was that a second dissolution based on the same reasons was unconstitutional. As early as September 1915 Venizelos had carefully prepared the ground for a battle on the constitutional issue. After Zaimis' appointment as Prime Minister in September 1915, Venizelos delivered in Parliament one of the most telling and most interesting speeches of his career. After explaining the reasons for his resignation he expressed fears regarding the conduct of Greek foreign policy by the Zaimis Government. He insisted that 'our parliamentary system of government is no longer on its proper basis', and

---

[1] *Parliamentary Debates* (1915), Κ, α, 533.

[2] Venizelos explained his foreign policy at least twice in Parliament. See *Parliamentary Debates* (1915), Κ, α, 184ff. and (1917), Κ, β, 266ff.

that 'Parliament has been transformed from a representative body into a society of notables'.[1]

Zaimis' resignation followed soon after and Venizelos delivered another speech, this time clearly indicating the constitutional issue that would be at stake in the ensuing elections. Venizelos, as already stated, acknowledged the Crown's right to disagree with the Government but concluded that repeated dissolutions were undoubtedly unconstitutional.

It was in this sense that a disagreement between Crown and Government occurred in February 1915 but it was solved by the popular vote [in May]. If you believe that the Crown may ... ignore the freely expressed opinion of the people ... if you believe that it can proceed to a second dissolution – after having appealed to the electorate and received its verdict – supposedly in order to obtain a new verdict and then yet another, then this means that you grant that the liberal Greek Constitution ... is nothing but a scrap of paper.[2]

Venizelos' conclusion was that since the 'Crown has assumed control of the administration of public affairs ... Parliamentary Democracy has ceased to exist'[3] in Greece. He was clearly emphasising the violation of the Constitution and preparing for the future battle.

It is clear from the above that the proximity of the two dissolutions, though in itself not desirable, was not the primary cause of grievance since the Crown's right to disagree with the Government and appoint a minority Ministry was not seriously contested. From Venizelos' speech it seems clear that the real objection was that the second dissolution was based on the same reason as the previous one. This in fact is the second aspect of the constitutional issue, theoretical and practical at the same time. Theoretically, of course, there seems to be little doubt that repeated dissolutions, particularly if based on the same reason, represent a triumph over the electorate and not of the electorate, or, according to French doctrine: 'dissolution sur dissolution ne vaut pas'. Hence all the vigorous efforts by subsequent constituent legislation in Greece and elsewhere to control the frequent exercise of the prerogative. But the dispute lay elsewhere – namely if the dissolution of 29 October/11 November 1915 was in fact based on the same reasons as its predecessor.

D. Gounaris in his answer to E. Venizelos' speech laid the basis of what was to become the essential argument of the pro-royalist parties: namely that the second dissolution was justified by the change in the situation.

It is impossible to maintain that the same question was disputed because the disagreement in February was over an issue [Gallipoli] which soon after disappeared

[1] *Parliamentary Debates* (1915), K, α, 184.
[2] *Parliamentary Debates* (1915), K, α, 533–4.
[3] *Parliamentary Debates*, ibid. p. 534.

and the new Government [after the May–June elections] would not and in fact could not pursue the policies it had advocated in February and which had led to its resignation. It cannot be argued that public opinion has changed its attitude over a policy that was to be followed in recent months, a policy decided after the elections and over which the new dispute arose, since this policy was never submitted to the Greek people ... Hence nothing prevented the Crown from believing that, due to the change in the situation, the Greek Nation had reached a different decision from the one previously expressed in the [May] elections.[1]

Gounaris' speech was delivered in October 1915. When the issue was again discussed in 1917 the King was in exile and Venizelos' position in the House unassailable. It is impossible to relate in detail what was said in the House in 1917 and therefore one can only choose more or less arbitrarily a few extracts from the various speeches, reminding the reader that the debate took place virtually in the presence of a one-sided House and in an atmosphere of extreme political fanaticism.

N. Stratos devoted a substantial part of his long and moderate speech to the legal side of the crisis.[2] He examined in detail the Greek dissolutions since 1880 and maintained that the Crown had the right to appoint a minority Ministry and dissolve the House. Summarising the precedents he concluded that dissolution could be advised for one of the following reasons:[3] termination of the legal term of Parliament; impossibility to form a Government in the House; dissolution in order to increase the Government's majority (based on party reasons); disaccord between Parliament and People; and disagreement between Crown and Government. Under the last heading Stratos placed the 1892 and 1895 dissolutions.

Kafandaris disagreed with Stratos. In his opinion[4] there were basically three reasons for dissolving Parliament: the impossibility of providing for a stable Government; the fact that Parliament does not reflect public opinion; and disagreement between Crown and Parliament. In his view the third case constituted the purely monarchical dissolution and had not been practised until 1915. His opinion was that the 1892 and 1895 dissolutions were caused by the fact that the Government was not truly representative of public opinion,[5] and not because of the Crown's interference. We have seen, however, that Stratos' opinion is closer to the truth.[6]

The section of Stratos' speech concerned with the justification of the second dissolution is, I think, original in its approach and interesting though not always entirely convincing.

[1] *Parliamentary Debates* (1915), Κ, α, 536.   [2] *Parliamentary Debates* (1917), Κ, β, 149ff.
[3] *Parliamentary Debates* (1917), Κ, β, 152–3.   [4] *Parliamentary Debates* (1917), Κ, β, 199.
[5] Ibid. See also *Parliamentary Debates* (1917), Κ, β, 154–5.
[6] See above, chapter 9.

Stratos examined the problem in theory and in practice. He admitted that foreign theorists condemned repeated dissolutions but maintained that Greek law did not provide for such contingencies. No precedent existed and furthermore the Constitution was silent on the matter. Stratos at this point attempted a rather unfortunate comparison with the two dissolutions of 1910 in the United Kingdom.[1] Confusing at a certain point the 1910 crisis with the 1913 Ulster crisis, Stratos maintained that the clash between Commons and Lords was finally resolved by law. He insisted that English constitutional law did not provide an answer to what should be done if the Lords continuously rejected – as, in his opinion, they legally had the right to do – legislation of the Commons. A second dissolution became necessary within less than a year and the conflict was finally solved by the Parliament Act 1911. Why could Greece not solve similar problems in more or less the same, so to speak, civilised way? He then proceeded to establish that the situation had changed since the dissolution of May 1915. By autumn 1915, he said, the Greek–Serbian treaty had become the main issue.

Stratos' conclusion is carefully drawn but debatable. Between February and December 1915 new events had changed the situation. Furthermore the Liberal majority had been considerably reduced in the 1915 elections compared with the 1912 results.[2] The weight of all these arguments sufficiently justified an appeal to the electorate to decide on Greece's future. The above views are open to discussion. The comparison with the 1910 crisis in the United Kingdom is undoubtedly unfortunate. Stratos was wrong in maintaining that the Lords could repeatedly reject the Commons' legislation. A convention required that the Commons had the last word in money bills[3] and the 1910 controversy had started with Mr Lloyd George's Budget. Furthermore, a great constitutional crisis did take place, though it did not reach the point of open rebellion. Lastly it is extremely difficult to compare the written Greek constitution with its unwritten British counterpart, particularly on delicate questions of lacunae in the law.

Stratos must have realised the dangers and difficulties of such comparisons and thus chose to elaborate the practical side of his argument, mainly that different circumstances justified a new dissolution. In this respect, he elaborated Gounaris' position but his efforts failed, mainly because each camp had already made up its mind on the events and their interpretation and was merely trying *a posteriori* to defend their actions. The *Parliamentary*

---

[1] *Parliamentary Debates* (1917), Κ, β, 157ff.
[2] *Parliamentary Debates* (1917), Κ, β, 164.
[3] Marshall & Moodie, *Some problems of the constitution*, p. 25.

Debates clearly demonstrate that the arguments were basically political, deeply influenced by party loyalties. Thus, the constitutional issue was more than once confused or obscured in their debates. But, to use a Victorian phrase, the voice of impartial posterity cannot adhere to narrow-minded arguments nor can it be influenced by party thinking. It is wrong to ask whether the Nation had decided in May about Gallipoli and in December about Serbia – which in actual fact had ceased to exist. Nor is the applicability of a treaty a subject for the electorate to decide in the form of a referendum. 'In a well-governed country,' Kafandaris rightly maintained, 'the question of war and peace cannot be decided at elections . . . it is the Government, emanating from the people, which decides, if it considers it necessary or advantageous for the State to embark upon the adventures of war.'[1] It is safe to conclude that the Nation votes for a political programme known to it only in its very broad outlines and can only subsequently approve or disapprove of how the Government carried out this programme. In this sense one must agree with Venizelos when he said that in the May elections the Nation did not decide on Gallipoli.

Knowing my policies with regard to both home and foreign affairs in their general outlines, orientated not towards your camp [the Central Powers] but towards the opposite one, and with due respect for the existing treaties [with Serbia], the Nation decided to answer the question that the Crown had raised in a way that showed that it placed its fate in the event of war, in the hands of the Liberals.[2]

One thing, however, that the electorate had not realised was the ever-widening rift between its equally popular leaders. It would perhaps have been preferable if the issue had been openly presented to the Nation to decide between the Crown or the Prime Minister. But then of course the whole form of government would have been seriously modified and altered, and this everyone wanted to avert. The best proof that the above arguments were more or less invented in the years that followed the 1915 crisis is provided by the fact that the King's entourage was contemplating a second immediate dissolution in June 1915. The most important reason that this threat never materialised was because there was a danger it would appear as a minor coup d'état.[3] A few months would have to elapse so that the wished-for dissolution would not seem an act directed personally against Venizelos. Thus the royal entourage was aware that dissolution, though unrestricted in theory, is subject to certain limitations in practice. There is always a limit one must not exceed; in 1915 this limit was exceeded and the Nation pays for it to this very day.

[1] Kafandaris, *Parliamentary Debates* (1917), Κ, β, 202.
[2] *Parliamentary Debates*, ibid.   [3] Streit, *Diary*, II, 17–18.

The December 1915 dissolution has been discussed in some detail since it is considered the main cause of the controversy that followed. A peculiar outcome of that crisis remains to be briefly discussed in the next few pages. In their proclamation to the Greek people on 9/22 November 1915 the Liberals had stated their reasons for abstaining from the elections. Among other reasons they include the following statement:

We are confronted with an open violation of our form of Government which is daily infringed. Repeated dissolutions and attempts to impose personal policies inaugurate a system of government that can be found only in absolute monarchies such as Prussia ... Holding elections at a time when a great number of Liberal M.P.'s of the last Parliament are serving in the Forces and hence unable to campaign actively ... when the combatant section of the population is in the army ... and when the government is prepared to allow its friends to vote but retains its enemies under strict military discipline ... is only part of the scenery of a political farce unworthy of free nations.

The statement thus clearly emphasised that the future Parliament would not reflect the opinion of the electorate. In the years to come many of these arguments were further expounded by Greeks and foreigners alike. Thus on 8 July 1916 the Great Powers insisted that they had a right and in fact a duty to intervene since

the Greek Constitution had been ignored, the free exercise of vote restricted, Parliament dissolved twice within less than a year ... and elections held amidst general mobilisation in a manner proving that the present Parliament did not reflect public opinion.

And on 10 June 1917, the High Commissioner of the Powers in Greece, Jonnart, maintained that 'The Great Powers considered the second dissolution contrary to the spirit of the constitution and the basic principles of a parliamentary form of government'.[1] The result of all this was the totally unprecedented and undoubtedly unconstitutional restoration to life of the May 1915 Parliament ironically referred to as the 'Lazarus Parliament'.

There is little doubt that the violations of the Constitution were only a pretext for foreign intervention. A strong Greek Government was needed to bring Greece into the War on the side of the Entente. The best way to do

---

[1] However, in a letter to Prime Minister Ribot (22 July 1917), Jonnart describes the intervention as 'une page peu glorieuse pour la France, je la ferme bien vite'. Quoted from the Quai d'Orsay Archives by A. F. Frangoulis, *La Grèce, son statut international, son histoire diplomatique* (2nd edn of his previous *La Grèce et la crise mondiale*, 1926), 2 vols (1934), I, 499. Also quoted by S. P. Cosmetatos, *The tragedy of Greece* (1928), p. 296 (Eng. transl. of the original French edition, *L'entente et la Grèce pendant la Grande Guerre (1914–1915)* (1926)). See also S. P. Cosmin, *Dossiers secrets de la Triple Entente: Grèce 1914–1922* (1969). Raymond Recouly, *Jonnart en Grèce et l'abdication de Constantin* (1918), omits to mention the letter.

this was to revive the May Parliament where the Liberals commanded a working majority. New elections would of course have been the orthodox measure to take but the Allies considered this dangerous in view of the chaotic internal situation.[1]

Deposing the Royal Dynasty was another alternative which, however, was soon abandoned because of British and Italian reaction. The last possibility was a dictatorship but this again was rejected because it would only mean that the Entente would be violating the Constitution it was apparently striving to preserve intact. So the May Parliament was revived[2] and three years of disguised authoritarian rule followed during which numerous unconstitutional measures were taken by the Government, including the decision to suspend the constitutional provision guaranteeing the permanency of the judiciary, a measure that even the Metaxas dictatorship in 1936 had hesitated to take.

It was during this Parliament that the events of 1915 were discussed. Liberal leaders vigorously tried to justify the revival of the old Parliament. Kafandaris compared it with the prolongation of the French and British Parliaments.[3] This comparison was unfortunate to say the least. Clearly there is a great difference between prolonging the life of an existing Parliament and reviving a Parliament whose term has legally expired. Furthermore in England and France, Parliament itself decided on the prolongation and by a normal procedure while this was not the case in Greece.

This Parliament also discussed the position of the monarchy and decided that its successor would be a Revisional Parliament that would ratify the decisions of its predecessor and define in a more suitable way the rights and duties of the Crown.[4] Elections were to be held on 25 October 1920 but King Alexander's sudden death altered the situation. Parliament was immediately reconvened, Admiral Koundouriotis was appointed Regent and the elections were postponed until 1/14 November 1920.

At the elections the Liberals were defeated and Venizelos failed to return to Parliament, a result that led Professor Svolos to suggest that the elector-

---

[1] On 14 June 1917 M. Ribot telegraphed to Jonnart that: 'If the state of opinion in Greece was favourable to Venizelos, he might proceed to elections; otherwise he should recall the Venizelist Chamber which was dissolved by the King two years before.' Quoted by Cosmetatos, *The tragedy of Greece*, p. 288.

[2] Jonnart clearly wished to avoid a general election, so naturally the revival of the 1915 Parliament was the only feasible alternative that preserved appearances. Yet, he too doubted whether this was legal. Even though E. Repoulis had assured him that it could be done Jonnart felt obliged to obtain a second opinion, that of Andreas Michalakopoulos. As his advice was similar to that of Repoulis, Jonnart agreed to the revival of the dissolved Parliament. (Unpublished documents from the S. Markesinis Papers.)

[3] *Parliamentary Debates* (1917), K, β, 205.

[4] Venizelos in *Parliamentary Debates* (1917), K, β, 205.

ate had subsequently approved the King's policies.[1] Whether this is true or not the fact remains that the Liberals were defeated and their opponents got their way. A plebiscite was immediately held[2] and King Constantine I returned. The new Assembly was to be a Constituent Assembly and it set out to complete its task.

In the autumn of 1922 the Asia Minor disaster occurred and was followed by a military coup d'état. Its leaders gained control and forcibly dissolved the House. King Constantine was obliged to abdicate, formally this time, in favour of his son George II. A new Assembly was to be convened in Athens when suddenly a pro-Royalist military coup took place but was suppressed. The King was considered an accomplice and was obliged to leave Greece on an 'indefinite holiday'. Koundouriotis was re-appointed Regent and the new Assembly was to decide on the form of government. The 1864/1911 Constitution was in fact dead.

Venizelos became Prime Minister for a few days but resigned, unable to pursue his policies. The Fourth Constituent Assembly convened in Athens in 1924,[3] on the recommendation of A. Papanastasiou, abolished the Monarchy and proclaimed Greece a Republic. A referendum was held – the integrity of which was as usual doubted – and the Nation apparently justified the Assembly's decision. The 1864/1911 Constitution was now legally abolished. Greece entered a new era of republicanism which was destined to last just over ten years.

[1] Svolos, *Constitutional law*, p. 67.
[2] The plebiscite was held on 22 November/5 December 1920. The King returned on 6/19 December 1920.
[3] This, too, was forcibly dissolved by General Th. Pangalos on 30 September 1925 without having completed the new constitution. Pangalos remained in power until General Kondylis' successful coup overthrew him and appointed once again Admiral Koundouriotis as President of the Republic.

Chapter 11

THE REPUBLIC (1927–1935)

A: YEARS OF INTERNAL STRIFE AND THE NEW CONSTITUTION (1927)

The constitutionally anomalous years of the early twenties came to an end with the enactment of the 1927 Constitution. The years that had preceded it were ones of internal strife and ephemeral constitutional changes, brought about usually by force or threat of violence and various army interventions that had stemmed from the 1922 Asia Minor disaster. These years, rich in socio-economic changes and innovations, are perhaps interesting to an historian or a modern sociologist. But to a constitutional lawyer, who is interested primarily if not solely in the normal function and the actual working of a constitution, they have little to offer.

The most notable characteristic of the early and middle twenties – apart from the usually irregular legislative process – was the existence of a strong republican movement, particularly in the refugee areas. This republicanist trend, common to most European countries after the First World War, had, of course, its ups and downs. But, a coincidence of factors opened the way for an active minority to transform Greece into a Republic. To many, of course, the idea of a Republic remained repulsive, just as the Monarchy never offered any attractions to the new and younger sections of the population. But as time passed the Republic was increasingly accepted and it seems doubtful whether the Monarchy would have been restored in 1935 had it not been for Venizelos' abortive coup in the spring of the same year. And the best proof comes from the 1936 elections in which the Republican parties still held a majority over the Royalists.

The main feature of the 'Republican Constitution' of 3 June 1927 was that it did not recognise a hereditary Head of State.[1] It explicitly described

---

[1] There exists no comprehensive study of the period. For the events see: Paparrigopoulos, *History of the Greek Nation*, VI, ch. 8 and 9; Stavrianos, *The Balkans*, pp. 661–88; E. S. Forster, *A short history of Modern Greece 1821–1956*, 3rd edn (1960), pp. 148–98; Campbell & Sherrard, *Modern Greece*, pp. 127–57; and G. Daphnis, *Greece between the wars*, 2 vols (1955) (in Greek). The best available analysis of the Constitution is found in Professor Svolos' books: *Constitutional law, The revision of the Constitution* (1933), and *The new Constitution* (1928), this last book, however, being politically biased. On the powers of the President see S. Markesinis, *The Head of State*. The preparatory works can be found in the *Minutes of the Fourth Constituent Assembly*, vols I–V; *Ephimeris Sizitiseon of the Fourth Constituent Assembly*,

Greece as a Republic and added in article 2 that 'all powers emanate from the Nation, exist for its sake and are exercised according to the Constitution'.

Faithful to the post-war trend, it incorporated rules of parliamentary government in its text in an attempt to provide them with greater sanctity and precision. Article 88 stipulated that: 'All Ministers are collectively responsible for the general policies of the Government and each of them individually is responsible for the acts of his competency' and Article 89 provided that: 'The Government must possess the confidence of Parliament. After being formed. . .it is obliged to seek a vote of confidence. If, on the formation of the Government, Parliament is in recess, it is convened within fifteen days so as to express its opinion on the [new] Government. . .' Likewise, dissolution was also strictly controlled by the Constitution.

According to article 79 the President could dissolve only the Lower House – but not the Senate. The composition of the latter changed according to a specifically provided procedure.[1] Of its 120 members, 90 were elected by the people for nine years. Every three years 30 of them stood down for re-election, 10 were elected by the Senate and the Lower House and held office during the term of the Lower House. Finally the remaining 20 were drawn from various professions and served for a period of three years.

The dissolution of the Lower House was subject to two limitations. The study of the minutes of the Constituent Assembly reveals that it was predominantly historical rather than legal reasoning that imposed these limitations. The recent crisis of 1915 had haunted the minds of the legislators since 1920 and hence they adopted these two limitations: the first was borrowed from article 5 of the Constitution of the Third French Republic while the second was taken from article 25 of the Constitution of Weimar (1919).

The first limitation stipulated that the concurrent opinion of the Senate was necessary for the President to dissolve the Lower House. The idea was again MacMahon's concept of an 'Assemblée modératrice' that would keep a watchful eye over the President's activities. In this respect the Senate was a conservative element of the new Constitution and was always regarded as such by Venizelos, conscious of preserving the new order of affairs. Thus, Article 79 provided that:

vols I–V(1924–5); and the *Ephimeris* of 1926–7, vols I–II. Information (often biased) about the events can also be found in a number of published diaries and private papers of Generals and politicians of the period.

[1] Art. 59.

The President of the Republic may dissolve Parliament before the end of its term with the concurring opinion of the Senate which can be obtained on his recommendation and after being agreed to by the absolute majority of the members of the Senate. Discussion on the President's proposal must be concluded and decision reached within three days at most from the time of submitting the proposal. If time elapses without an answer the proposal is considered to be rejected.

This last sentence was added so as to avoid a direct confrontation between the President and the Senate.

But the Greek constituent legislators apparently did not consider this guarantee sufficient. A similar limitation had failed to produce the expected results in France in 1877 and this had to be taken into account. Furthermore, it offered no solution if the 1915 crisis was repeated in the future. On the other hand, there was little doubt that dissolution should be maintained to avoid parliamentary chaos similar to that in France during the Third Republic. What remained to be discovered was a further limitation and this time the Weimar Constitution served as a model. Thus, article 79 para. 2 stipulated that: 'Dissolution of two consecutive Parliaments on the same grounds was forbidden.' However, what would happen, if, despite this constitutional provision, a second dissolution was in fact exercised? As is usually the case the constitutional text was a *lex imperfecta*. No possible sanction was suggested and hence one cannot conclude that the second dissolution was invalid. It seems fair to maintain that political difficulties would follow but in no event any legal sanctions. Furthermore, article 79 para. 4 provided that the relevant Decree should be signed by the Cabinet and elections should follow within forty-five days of dissolution. Finally the Constitution recognised the so-called self-dissolution if it were decided by a majority of the House.

The Constitution made no provision about dissolving the National Assembly. The critical problem was left to be solved in practice. The National Assembly, which consisted of the two Houses (Parliament and the Senate) met on exceptional occasions – such as the election of a President or a revision of the Constitution – and hence its life span was never determined in advance. It ceased to exist only when it had fulfilled, in one way or another, its specific purpose. In this sense, the National Assembly was undoubtedly indissoluble.

But the whole problem is more complicated than it appears at first sight. Could the President dissolve the Lower House (since he could not dissolve the Senate) and thus indirectly put an end to the Assembly and obstruct its task?

The constitutional text did not specify whether the Lower House could be dissolved while the National Assembly was in session. Nor did it say whether the Lower House could be dissolved once the revision of the Constitution had been decided. The minutes of the preparatory committees gave no indication of the legislator's wishes. As Professor Svolos suggests,[1] the only guiding line was the 1910 dissolution of the First Revisional Parliament. The 1910 precedent was quite clear; a revisional House can be dissolved. If this principle is applied, one conclusion can be drawn: If the right to dissolve Parliament can be exercised in the case of a House which has been elected *ad hoc* to revise the Constitution, it is only logical to conclude that it can be equally exercised against an ordinary House whose members are participating in a revisional procedure. Furthermore, Professor Svolos maintained that article 79 of the 1927 Constitution was of a general nature and made no exceptions whatsoever. 'Dissolution', Svolos maintained, 'is a basic institution of the form of government and in this respect it is of general applicability. Hence, in cases where an exception should be made it ought to be explicitly mentioned.'[2]

One may of course argue that the President cannot dissolve the National Assembly since this right is not explicitly granted to him by the Constitution. Article 86 repeated article 44 of the 1864 Constitution and maintained that the 'President had only those rights expressly attributed by the Constitution'. Furthermore, one could also mention the more general argument according to which the President does not participate in the revision of the Constitution and hence he cannot dissolve the House, thus indirectly interfering with the work of the Assembly.

Neither of these arguments, however, is entirely convincing. As far as the first is concerned one must observe that the President does not violate the Constitution since he does not dissolve the Assembly – which he has no right to do – but the Lower House, which is clearly within his rights. The second point can be refuted by two arguments: first, that such an initiative of the President's would postpone but not prevent the revisional work; second, the dissolution can be exercised only with the concurrent opinion of the Senate which is part of the Assembly. The Senate can therefore decide whether it will grant its consent to dissolution, thus putting an end to the life of the National Assembly, or withhold it, in order to allow the completion of the revision of the Constitution.

Despite its theoretical interest, it is unnecessary to discuss the matter further, since the right to dissolve the National Assembly never arose in practice.

[1] *The revision of the constitution*, p. 57. See above, chapter 9.
[2] *The revision of the constitution*, p. 58. For further details see ibid. pp. 55–64.

B: DISSOLUTION IN PRACTICE

Up to now we have seen that dissolution during the Republic was subjected to various, rather complicated, limitations. Whether in fact these limitations did produce the expected results is contested and will be discussed later on. At this stage we shall review the events related to the various dissolutions.

The Republic lasted just over eleven years (25 March 1924 – 3 November 1935). The first elections were held on 7 November 1926 and the first Parliament was dissolved on 6 July 1928. The second Parliament lasted nearly four years and was dissolved on 19 August 1932. It was followed by the third brief Parliament which was dissolved on 24 January 1933. From the ensuing elections (5 March 1933) the fourth Parliament emerged which was dissolved on 1 April 1935, to be replaced by the Fifth Constituent Assembly (elections of 9 June 1935). This too was soon dissolved by the King who in the meantime had returned to Greece. Thus, within a period of nine years (1926–35) there were four dissolutions (1928, 1932, 1933, 1935, not counting the dissolution of the Fifth Constituent Assembly), the life of the average Parliament being just over two years – by no standards a satisfactory length of time.

The elections of 7 November 1926 were carried out impeccably. General Kondylis, who had overthrown the Pangalos dictatorship in August of the same year, was clever enough not to take part in the elections that followed so as not to arouse suspicions as to their integrity. The electorate's vote was split among a number of political parties because of the system of proportional representation adopted for the elections. On the whole the Venizelists obtained a majority of the votes of the refugees in the suburbs of Athens and the northern provinces, while the Royalist parties remained predominant in the southern part of Greece.

The result of the elections compelled a coalition Government, which was worthy of its name, 'Oecomenical', since it included under Zaimis' Premiership all the important political leaders, namely, Kafandaris, Michalakopoulos, P. Tsaldaris, Metaxas and A. Papanastasiou. This Government was successful, both in the field of foreign affairs and especially in its effort to correct the chaotic economic situation it had inherited from the previous unstable governments. Finally, it was during this Government's term that the 1927 Constitution was put into force. But one of the Government's main objects, national reconciliation, was scarcely achieved. For various reasons, the parties that formed the coalition soon fell apart and the Government became a prey to internal corrosion.

By the end of 1927, Tsaldaris and Papanastasiou had left the Government, seriously affecting its future.

Furthermore – and in a sense more important – Venizelos (in Paris since his resignation from the Government in 1924), though asserting that he did not intend to return to active politics, came back to Greece and was in fact seriously undermining Kafandaris' leadership of the Liberal Party. Kafandaris was eventually obliged to resign the party leadership on 19 May 1928 and Venizelos announced his return to politics on 23 May of the same year in order to preserve the status quo from dictatorship or anarchy. With the Government seriously split, doubt and confusion prevailed until Zaimis was finally forced to resign. Admiral Koundouriotis – the President of the Republic – recalled Venizelos to office and the latter formed his sixth Government on 4 July 1928.

The way Venizelos returned to power was unusual to say the least.[1] The fact that he himself was not in Parliament and that his party was in a minority in the House, cannot be considered an irregularity, though of course it is not commendable. It was obvious, however, that Venizelos would be unable to govern with the parliamentary set-up which he inherited. Whether this justified a dissolution or not can be contested. The split of the party forces and the exhaustion of the various forms of coalition government seemed nevertheless to provide a plausible excuse for Venizelos' insistence on going to the country. But there is little doubt that his own equivocal attitude had greatly contributed to undermining the position of the previous Government – the record of which was in many respects quite praiseworthy – and in creating the rather fluid situation in which he found himself in 1928. This aspect, however, of the 1928 dissolution seems to have political rather than legal overtones and hence will not be discussed further.

In any case, Venizelos' request to dissolve Parliament was granted and at the same time the President was persuaded to alter the electoral law to a system of simple majorities. Venizelos' experience at the 1920 elections had taught him not to take any risks with a volatile electorate. The alteration of the electoral system, however, brought about by a decree of questionable constitutional validity, was naturally meant to suit Venizelos' party. The subsequent years in fact provide sufficient proof of how Venizelos changed the electoral law so as to suit his own party.

What, however, was mostly disputed was the President's right to dissolve the House without the opinion of the Senate – which had still not been created. The anti-Venizelist camp argued with vigour and indeed with some persuasiveness, that the organisation and functioning of the

[1] Svolos, *The new Constitution*, p. 389 and n. 1.

various State organs had not at that stage been completed. Hence, dissolution could not be exercised because of the non-existence of the Senate, the State organ entrusted with the control of the proper exercise of the prerogative. In this respect there is little doubt that the constituent legislators had meant to subject the President's right to dissolve Parliament to the Senate's control. Venizelos' arguments, though not entirely convincing, may be closer to the correct answer. He emphasised that the legislative had been functioning properly since 1926 – and in fact continued to do so until 1929 – without the Senate's existence, which, nevertheless, was essential according to the Constitutional text. No one had ever contested the legality of the legislation thus passed, though in fact it had been passed by only one of the two competent bodies according to the Constitution. And the explanation for all this was naturally the fact that the Senate still remained to be created by an organic law. The same should be applied – according to Venizelos – to dissolution, particularly since it was neither the President's nor his own responsibility that the Senate had not been created up to that point.

With this in mind, Venizelos proceeded to a dissolution without even appearing before the House for a vote of confidence according to article 89, a decision criticised by Professor Svolos as being opposed to orthodox parliamentary procedures.[1] The latter in fact maintained that the Government was obliged, both by the spirit of the Constitution and by parliamentary convention, to appear before the House and seek a vote of confidence regardless of whether it had decided to proceed to a dissolution. It was obvious nevertheless that since Venizelos had made his comeback to active politics, expediency was foremost in his mind.[2] He dissolved the House without appearing before it, creating a precedent which he himself followed in 1933, and conducted a carefully planned electoral campaign. Aided by the electoral system he won an overwhelming majority of 223 seats out of the total 250 and embarked on four years of uncontrolled personal rule.

Venizelos' four years of office are extremely interesting, particularly since they inaugurate a policy of *rapprochement* towards Turkey and especially towards Italy. It is not, however, the purpose of this work to discuss such matters. What characterises these years most is perhaps the tremendous de facto concentration of power in the hands of the Prime Minister, who was increasingly alienated from his old friends and lieutenants, such as Kafandaris, Papanastasiou, Zavitsianos and others.

---

[1] *The new Constitution*, p. 392.
[2] The political overtones of the dissolution are confirmed by a discussion Karolides had with Admiral Koundouriotis, then President of the Republic, which Karolides mentions in his sixth edition of Paparigopoulos' *History of the Greek Nation*, VI, 386 (footnote).

Furthermore, the Prime Minister had demonstrated particularly strong conservative feelings by introducing legislation severely curbing press freedom and the activities of the emerging Communist Party which had disappointed his most liberal and/or radical followers.[1] By 1931 the disarray in the Republican ranks could not be concealed any longer. Combined with strong attacks from the press and the Populists, it began to shake the Government. In 1931, Great Britain abandoned the gold standard, to which the drachma was closely linked through holdings of sterling. The last blow had been dealt. By May 1932, Venizelos decided to give way to a Papanastasiou administration, only to return to office within a week or so. He eventually advised dissolution, which coincided with the end of the statutory term of Parliament, reverting once again to the system of proportional representation and thus demonstrating his belief in expediency alone. For it was he himself who, four years previously in 1928, in a constitutionally debatable manner had introduced the majority system, only to change when he decided that it no longer suited his purposes. Passions were now thoroughly roused, especially when Papanastasiou revealed that a military league existed – with the knowledge of Venizelos – sworn not to allow the formation of any government that would not expressly recognise the régime. It was further alleged that Venizelos was even considering amending the Constitution so as to introduce a clause similar to the famous article 48 of the Weimar Constitution, giving extraordinary powers to the Government in the event of internal disturbances.[2]

In this kind of atmosphere elections were held in September in which the Liberals were defeated (the Populists obtained 33.42% of the vote and 95 seats, whereas the Liberals retained a slight majority with 33.80% and 98 seats). Tsaldaris was asked to form a minority Government with Kondylis and Metaxas on condition that he waived his hesitations about the régime, which he did. Eight years previously, recognition of the régime by Metaxas had cost him his followers. Now that Tsaldaris had gathered the pro-royalists on his side, he was asked to do the same thing if he were to become Prime Minister.

The Liberals, however, were unable to tolerate a Populist government for long. They defeated Tsaldaris in the House on 13 January 1933 and obliged him to resign. Venizelos once again found himself in office and dissolved the House once more without appearing before it to seek a vote

[1] In reality his 'conservative' opponent D. Gounaris proved to be (especially by some of his speeches in the 1920–2 Parliament) in many respects more liberal and progressive.

[2] The Prime Minister had in person proposed the law in his speech in Parliament. His views, however, were opposed by Professor Svolos in the Introduction of his *Revision of the Constitution*.

of confidence. Reverting again to a system of majority representation, he held elections on 5 March 1933 but despite his alignment with all the Liberal political leaders he was defeated. Within less than six years Venizelos had altered the electoral system three times, had three times obtained the President's consent to dissolve Parliament, and twice had done so without even appearing before the House.

Dissolution, as expected, was criticised on these grounds, but then one wonders whether Zaimis could have acted otherwise. Perhaps the President would have been better advised to appoint a caretaker Government to conduct the elections. But this alternative appears purely hypothetical, given Venizelos' majority in both Houses and his still very high prestige and influence in the country.

There is little doubt that this dissolution was an open provocation to the anti-Venizelist camp. Venizelos himself had agreed – undoubtedly for tactical reasons – to give P. Tsaldaris a chance. Nevertheless he was too quick in changing his mind. Had he been more patient, Tsaldaris would have undoubtedly succumbed to the grave problems his Government was facing. Dissolution is a safety valve, and a way of solving a crisis, not creating a new one. For a number of reasons the rift between the two political camps had been widening for the previous three or four years and dissolution did nothing to bridge this gap. Furthermore it became apparent that the existing constitutional limitations were powerless to prevent what seemed to be (and actually was) an abuse of the right by one party.

There exist of course a number of explanations for the final collapse of the Republic. It seems to me that the 1928 and 1933 dissolutions contributed to that effect. They had unhappy side effects, they widened the gap between the two political factions and undoubtedly hastened the collapse of the Republic.

When the election results were known Plastiras staged a coup d'état to prevent Tsaldaris from coming to power. His attempt never really got off the ground and he soon fled the country and Venizelos was accused of having inspired the coup. The bitterness the abortive coup provoked only increased the factional passions. Metaxas, abandoning his conciliatory efforts, personally accused Venizelos of the coup while the latter only miraculously escaped from an assassination plot. Venizelos defended Plastiras in the House[1] only to provoke fresh reaction from the Populist Party, the leader of which (Gounaris) had been executed by a firing squad on Plastiras' orders in 1922. He never completed his defence and suddenly left Athens, never to return again. His adventurous and outstanding career had thus come to an inglorious end.

[1] *Parliamentary Debates* (15 May 1933), pp. 136ff.

The end of the Fourth Parliament was no less adventurous. On 1 March 1935 a military coup – this time staged by the Navy – took place and it was later revealed that Venizelos was behind it. It was easily suppressed and only speeded the process which the Republicans were most anxious to avoid.

The suppression of the revolt was followed by a series of arbitrary and constitutionally dubious acts. On 1 April 1935, the Senate was abolished, Parliament was dissolved and elections for a Constituent Assembly were to be held on 19 May. In a stream of constitutional decrees that followed, the security of judicial tenure was undermined, and many Venizelist officers were retired.

On 2 May 1935 the elections were postponed until 2 June 1935[1] because the emergency measures had to be prolonged owing to the fact that the trials of the rebels had not been completed. An Act of 14 May 1935 gave the Government the power to suspend further articles of the Constitution. Elections were postponed once again for the same reason and were finally held on 9 June 1935 with the abstention of all the Venizelist parties.

Tsaldaris won the elections and now firmly – as he thought – in the saddle was unwilling to speed the restoration of the Monarchy. The right wing of his party and Metaxas did not remain inactive. In June 1935 Kondylis openly proclaimed his support for the King and on 10 October Tsaldaris was forced to resign. Events moved swiftly. Kondylis became Prime Minister and, aided by the Rump Parliament, on 10 October 1935 proclaimed the restoration of the Monarchy and 'provisionally' put into force the 1911 Constitution 'until a new one should be voted'.[2] The same Act appointed Kondylis as Regent and stipulated that a confirmatory plebiscite would be held on 25 November 1935. The result of plebiscite – the fairness of which was seriously contested – was favourable to the King who returned to Greece on 25 November 1935. Five days later, on 30 November a caretaker Government headed by C. Demertzis, professor of the Law Faculty of the University of Athens, was formed, on 17 December 1935 the Constituent Assembly was dissolved and on 26 January 1936 elections were held. The dissolution, totally unprecedented as it is, deserves further consideration.

The appointment of Demertzis was undoubtedly an impartial act intended to satisfy, if possible, all political parties. However, for many it came as a surprise. Kondylis in particular had hoped that he would be asked to continue as Prime Minister,[3] while Tsaldaris believed that he

[1] Government *Gazette*, A, no. 171, 759.　　[2] Government *Gazette*, A, no. 436, 2295.
[3] Memorandum of General Kondylis to the King as reported by the Athens daily *Ellinismos*, 23 November 1935.

should have been commissioned to form the new Government since his party held a majority in the Rump Parliament of 1935. In the event Demertzis was appointed and speculation that elections were imminent was considerable. The daily newspaper *Kathimerini* strongly opposed the idea of elections and took the view that the Assembly was indissoluble.[1] However, it did admit that the House was one-sided and did not represent the Nation.[2]

Political leaders were soon summoned to the Royal Palace to give their advice. Kondylis, Metaxas and Michalakopoulos advised an immediate dissolution but were unable to agree on the electoral law.[3] Tsaldaris opposed dissolution and insisted that he should be asked to form a Government.[4] Finally, Sophoulis favoured dissolution but informed the King that the Liberals accepted him as de facto King and would reconsider their attitude towards the Crown depending on its future impartiality![5] The pro-Tsaldaris press, of course, strongly opposed the idea of a dissolution on the grounds that the Assembly was a sovereign body and was thus indissoluble.

C: THE 1935 DISSOLUTION

There is certainly little doubt that dissolutions cannot be legally exercised against the will of a sovereign body – as a Constituent Assembly is by definition. It is either self-dissolved, as in the case of the 1864 Greek Constituent Assembly, once it has completed its work, or it is brought to a violent end because of a revolution or coup d'état, as in 1922. But there is no constitutionally recognised way in which the Executive can abruptly terminate the business of such a body. In this respect King George's decision to dissolve the Fifth Constituent Assembly seems prima facie to offer a notable exception and as such to justify the criticisms against his decision. In actual fact it does not.

It is easy, of course, to suggest that the King actually demonstrated his 'strength' by dissolving the Assembly. Apart from the fact that this does not legally explain or justify the dissolution, it does not correspond to reality. It seems to me that the King's position by the end of 1935 was neither impregnable nor in any sense strong enough to allow him to take

---

[1] 2, 13, 14, 15 November etc.
[2] *Kathimerini*, 17 November 1935.
[3] Kondylis proposed a system of simple majorities, while Michalakopoulos and Metaxas favoured a system of proportional representation.
[4] *Ellinismos*, 28 November 1935.
[5] This was related to me by Professor Th. Angelopoulos, former member of the Conseil d'Etat and at that time Head of the King's political bureau.

such daring decisions without being sure that they were legally correct and politically acceptable in one way or another to the majority of his people. The following paragraphs explain why the 1935 dissolution was entirely constitutional, in accordance with accepted parliamentary rules, and even politically wise.

Anyone who studies the legal arguments advanced mainly in newspapers (in the form of articles or letters) will be struck by their inadequacy. Despite its legal and political importance the crisis was not – on the whole – treated in the legally befitting manner. The Populists opposed the decision, whereas the Venizelists remained silent, mainly because dissolution did not affect them, since they were not represented, as we have seen, in the dissolved House.[1]

The real constitutional issue lies not in the question whether the King can or cannot dissolve a sovereign body (to which all give a negative answer) but whether in fact the dissolved House was still at the time of its dissolution a Constituent Assembly and hence sovereign in its powers. There is adequate evidence in my opinion to suggest that the dissolved House was not at the time of dissolution a Constituent but merely a Revisional Parliament with a limited authority and by no means above all other powers of the State.

It is true of course that the elections of June 1935 were to provide a Constituent Assembly. But one must never forget that the 1935 elections followed the abortive Venizelist coup which had thrown the country into immense confusion and disorder. The origin of the Assembly was therefore undoubtedly of a revolutionary (or in any event a constitutionally abnormal) character. Its primary object was – as it was subsequently proved – to ratify the constitutionally dubious measures, taken after the abortive coup and restore the Monarchy, rather than to create an entirely new constitution. This is also evident from the phrasing of the Constituent Act of 10 October 1935. Having ratified these acts and restored the Monarchy, it had in substance completed its task – as the forcible dismissal of P. Tsaldaris in fact revealed. And the fact that the Assembly did not even make an attempt to continue its task but on the contrary sought to obtain a confirmatory plebiscite, adequately demonstrates that the restoration of the Monarchy was its basic aim. That the Assembly – supposedly expressing the supreme will of the Nation – felt it had to ask the electorate yet again if it approved the change of régime, is more than indicative of the basic aims it pursued.

Furthermore, the Assembly itself had publicly – though admittedly

[1] The pro-Liberal newspaper *Eleutheron Vima* favoured dissolution on 8, 9 and 11 November 1935, on the grounds that the present Assembly did not represent the Nation.

indirectly – acknowledged a change of character in its resolution of 10 October 1935, in which it abolished the 1927 Constitution and 'provisionally' put into force the 1911 Constitution, until it could be adapted to meet the new circumstances. The word 'provisionally' could have no other meaning than that the 1911 Constitution would be temporarily used until adapted to meet the new realities. But adapting a constitution does not mean creating an entirely new one. In other words – and this was more or less universally accepted – the 1911 Constitution would provide the essential basis of the future organisation of the State functions. But an Assembly that imposes on itself limitations to all basic issues of the future constitution is in effect preventing itself from creating a new one. By accepting to work within a given framework it clearly resigns all sovereign authority. Whether it could be the same House that would undertake this revisional task or not is, in this case, of little importance. What is important is that the Assembly, by restoring the Monarchy and re-adopting the 1911 Constitution, terminated its creative and original task. Further improvements could be made and would be made by a provisional House and the source of authority of this House could be found nowhere else but in this very decision of the Constituent Assembly and therefore the 1911 constitutional procedure need not be adhered to. Finally, the fact that the Assembly had resigned its sovereign powers is evident from the following argument. The Assembly, by asking the Nation to decide by referendum the form of government, acknowledged the Nation's supreme right to decide on such issues. It goes without saying that once the Nation has decided the Assembly cannot alter this decision. In which case it can only revise the constitution along the lines of the referendum. The Assembly is thus transformed into a Revisional Parliament and deprived of its sovereign authority.

But the dissolution was not only legally correct but also in accordance with parliamentary rules as applied in Greece since 1875, as it was exercised by a caretaker Government which proceeded to elections. And though it is true that the Government was late in dissolving the House (it was appointed on 30 November 1935 and dissolved on 17 December 1935) a plausible explanation exists for this too. Elections could not be proclaimed until the process of amnesty was completed in an attempt to reconcile the two political camps. Furthermore, the Government cannot be criticised for not appearing before the House – as Venizelos was in 1928 and in 1933 – since no similar provision existed in the 1911 Constitution. Thus again the King's action was in every respect absolutely correct.

Lastly, one may add that the dissolution was politically wise and in fact did not expose the Crown to any serious danger. The dissolved House had emanated from one-sided elections – the integrity of which was seriously contested – and ignored what was subsequently proved to be the views of half of the population. It merely represented the political faction which opposed the abortive 1935 coup, while ignoring a whole political world which had not disappeared from the political scene merely because it had abstained from the elections. With the arrival of the King, a fresh start was needed if the King were to reign over all his subjects and not just over a section of the population. Neglecting the Liberals would only have undermined the new régime and diminished the changes of the future constitution. Dissolution was thus essential and in fact not dangerous since the one section of the population (the Liberals) was not affected by it and in fact favoured it, while the other section, being pro-royalist, could not openly oppose the newly returned King. Furthermore, as we have seen the majority of political leaders had recommended this course to the King.[1]

How, then, can one summarise the practice of dissolution during these years? The problem must be seen in its historical context. The 1920s and 1930s were in every respect anomalous and transitional years. They were difficult years for Europe, and even more difficult for Greece which was forced to accept refugees equalling one-fourth of its original population. As the years passed, the magnitude of the 1922 disaster became more apparent. Social problems, problems of welfare and of the distribution of wealth, were all acute and worsened during the slump years. It was a frustrated society which in one way or another had been caught up in war for ten years (1912–22). The same generation had met those 'two imposters, triumph and disaster' and was courageously fighting for a better future. But these conditions did nothing to bridge the gap between Royalists and Venizelists which had been opened in 1915. The two factions remained alive in the form of numerous political parties which, aided by the electoral law, increased the general instability. Furthermore, in due course the emergence of Socialist and later Communist parties destroyed the equilibrium that existed between the two political worlds, and this was strongly felt in the 1950s and 1960s. It was only during the last years of the Metaxas dictatorship that the Nation found itself united and was able to resist and defeat the Italian aggression.

Greece between the Wars can provide ideal examples for élitist theories. Out of a total of eighteen years (1922–40), Parliament existed for only nine (1926–35) and of these five (1928–33) were in fact years of Venizelist autocracy. Throughout these years dissolution came either from the

---

[1] The dissolution was supported in an article by S. Markesinis in *Ellinismos*, 19 November 1935. It was later opposed as unconstitutional by E. Kyriakopoulos, *A history of the new Constitution* (1952), p. 23.

Army or the party. Despite the numerous referenda the Nation rarely if ever had an effective say in its future. Dissolution became more a weapon in the hands of the governing party than an appeal to the people. Coupled with frequent changes in the electoral system it became monarchical in its nature, though the Monarch was replaced by the Party Leader. The constitutional guarantees were quite unable to prevent an abuse of the right. Once again it was proved that the working of a constitution depends on the stability of its environment. There is little doubt that the 1928, and 1933 dissolutions stemmed from Venizelos' powerful personality. Had it not been for Venizelos, dissolution might well have fallen into disuse as it did in France, though this of course is a mere hypothesis. One conclusion, however, seems fairly established: Dissolution, improperly practised in 1928 and 1933 hastened the collapse of the Republic through the turmoil it aroused.

Chapter 12

THE DICTATORSHIP, THE WAR AND
THE NEW CONSTITUTION

A: THE METAXAS DICTATORSHIP AND THE
SUSPENSION OF THE CONSTITUTION

The Fifth Constituent Assembly was dissolved on 17 December 1935. Elections for the Third Revisional Parliament followed on 26 January 1936 and were conducted under a system of proportional representation. The Royalists and the Republicans won 143 and 141 seats respectively, while the Communists with 16 seats held the balance.[1]

The outcome was definitely disquieting. The emergence of the Communist Party had led to the erosion of the previously established voting habits of the electorate. The traditional equilibrium between Royalists and Republicans had been shattered. Instead, the new concepts of Right, Left and Centre were to be adopted in the future. Approximately fourteen years earlier, the Labour Party in the United Kingdom had, by its performance at the 1922 elections, virtually signed the death warrant of the Liberals; the old scheme of Tories and Liberals had come to an end.[2]

The Liberals and Communists were quick to reach a secret agreement. The Sophoulis–Sclavainas pact, named after the Liberal and Communist leaders respectively, enabled them to elect Sophoulis as Speaker of the House in a secret ballot.[3] But the same procedure could not be followed in the event of a vote of confidence where the ballot is open.[4] Sophoulis was thus unable to form a Government and the King was obliged – with the compliance of the parties – to retain Demertzis' caretaker Government in

---

[1] On the whole eleven parties were represented in Parliament. The four pro-royalist parties obtained 47.33%, an increase of 1.14%, compared with the results of the 1933 elections. The Republicans obtained 43.86% of the vote and the Communists 4.76%. (*Official statistics of the elections of 26 January 1936.*)

[2] This analogy, however, should not be taken too far, for in England Labour virtually replaced the Liberals whereas in Greece the Communists did not acquire such strength but became instead a balancing force destroying previously established voting patterns.

[3] At the first ballot, Sophoulis obtained 142 votes, the Royalist candidate 139 and the Communist 13. A second ballot became necessary and this time Sophoulis was elected by 158 votes against 137. (*Parliamentary Debates of the Third Revisional Parliament* (6 March 1936), pp. 5–6.)

[4] There is some analogy in this respect with Papandreou's Government in 1963. See below, chapter 13.

office, while the politicians sought a way out of the impasse. But the secret agreement soon became known[1] and created a considerable uproar. Its significance with regard to future developments should not be underestimated. The Nation, for the first time perhaps, came to realise the possible threat Communism represented to the established order.

On 13 April 1936, Demertzis died of a sudden heart attack. John Metaxas, his deputy Prime Minister and Minister of Defence since March 1936, was requested to carry on. The reasons for Metaxas' appointment are not quite clear. In view of the political dissensions and communist unrest the Army was pressing the King to play a more active role. The Sovereign, however, was unwilling to do so and appointed Metaxas, who was respected in military circles, to bring the Army under closer control.[2] He appeared before the House and obtained a vote of confidence.[3] The political parties had been given an extended time limit in which to provide a solution; but the dissensions between them were clearly discouraging. In Parliament, Metaxas made it clear that one of the prime objects of the Government was to complete the impending revision of the 1911 Constitution.[4] But the House showed little interest and it finally adjourned on 1 May for the summer recess having scarcely accomplished anything. It was to meet again only after the Second World War.

On the night of the 3rd/4th August 1936, Metaxas, taking advantage of an imminent general strike, the increasing Communist menace to public security, and the mounting tension in foreign affairs took the initiative. A Royal Decree, signed by a reluctant King,[5] suspended articles 5, 6, 10, 11, 12, 14, 20 and 95 of the Constitution. A second Decree, issued the same day, dissolved Parliament without provision for new elections,[6] the official explanation maintaining that the 'declaration of Martial Law made dissolution compulsory'. Yet, according to article 91 para. 3 of the 1911 Constitution then in force, the exact opposite was true.[7]

---

[1] The agreement was concluded on 19 February and it is very likely that E. Venizelos was aware of this. Its contents were made known by the Communists on 2 April because of Sophoulis' continuing support of the Demertzis Government.

[2] From Professor Th. Angelopoulos' Unpublished Papers.

[3] Out of 261 votes cast only 16 opposed Metaxas (among which, G. Papandreou, A. Papanastasiou, A. Mylonas, the two latter with some reservations, and the Communists) despite the fact that Metaxas was known to favour an open dictatorship. The legality of Metaxas' rise to power is thus quite remarkable and, perhaps, bears some resemblance to Hitler's. (See *Parliamentary Debates* (1936), p. 79.)

[4] 25 April 1936. See also the Speech from the Throne, 2 March. (*Parliamentary Debates*, ibid. pp. 4 and 46.)

[5] From Professor Th. Angelopoulos' Unpublished Papers.

[6] Government *Gazette*, A, 324.

[7] Art. 91, 2: 'In the event of war or general mobilisation due to external dangers, a special law shall provide for the temporary, partial or complete, suspension of articles 5, 6, 10, 11, 12, 14,

This article explicitly provided that Parliament should be immediately convened – even if dissolved – within five days of the publication of the Decree imposing Martial Law. If this did not happen, the Decree was automatically annulled. This view nevertheless was not officially accepted. On the contrary, it was argued that article 91 para. 3 was not applicable, since the declaration of Martial Law was based on the 24th Constituent Act of 14 May 1935 (of a revolutionary nature),[1] ratified by the Fifth Constituent Assembly during the summer of 1935.[2]

These arguments can be seriously questioned. Apart from the fact that the validity of the said Constituent Act remains questionable after the coup d'état of 10 October 1935, the supplementary nature of the Act must always be borne in mind.[3] Article 91 para. 3 was never formally abolished and even if one accepts that the 24th Constituent Act was still in force one must remember that it was of a supplementary nature. If this is so – and since the 24th Constituent Act remained silent on the issue – article 91 para. 3 was applicable and the convocation of Parliament should have followed the declaration of Martial Law. The 1936 dissolution, however, need not be discussed further, because of its arbitrary and unconstitutional nature.

20 and 95 of the Constitution. . . This law is implemented. . . by a Royal Decree with the permission of the House.'

Art. 91, 3: 'If the House is not in session, the [above] law can be implemented by a Royal Decree, without the permission of the House. The same Decree, at the risk of being automatically annulled, must convene the House within five days, even if the session is over or Parliament has been dissolved, so that it can decide whether it will retain or cancel the said Royal Decree.' This article basically differs from article 48 of the Constitution of Weimar (1919) in one respect, namely, that the emergency powers cannot be invoked in the event of internal disorder. Article 91 of the 1952 Constitution, however, was enlarged to include this possibility too.

[1] 'In the event of public disorder, or threat of public disorder, Decrees, published on the recommendation of the Cabinet, may suspend, in all or part of the State, articles 10, 11, 12, 13, 14, 15, 16, 18 and 100 of the Constitution.' (Government *Gazette*, A, 195.) The 24th Constituent Act followed article 48 of the Weimar Constitution, and allowed the suspension of certain articles of the Constitution in the event of internal disorder. The imitation, however, was only partial since it omitted the obligation to consult Parliament. Thus the Act offered Metaxas two advantages. First, that he could invoke the emergency powers because of internal disorder. Second, he did not have to rely on Parliament. The question, however, is, was the 24th Constituent Act still in force? (see discussion in the text).

[2] 5 July 1935. (*Parliamentary Debates*, ibid. p. 44 and Government *Gazette*, A, 319.)

[3] This is acknowledged by the introductory report to the said Royal Decree. Besides, articles 5, 6 and 95 could not have been suspended by the 24th Constituent Act. (See Government *Gazette*, A, 324.)

B: THE WAR

The German invasion and subsequent occupation of Greece obliged the King and the Government to leave the country and finally seek refuge in London. The Government, roaming in exile, did not return to Greece until 18 October 1944. In the meantime, Governments of questionable legality – occasionally referred to at that time as 'Quisling' Governments[1] – were formed in Greece, but many of their acts were subsequently annulled.

During the foreign occupation, the Crown's position was widely reviewed. The majority of political parties held the King personally responsible for Metaxas' dictatorship.[2] Thus, on 30 March 1942, on the initiative of the Liberals, and despite the objections of certain Royalists, an agreement was signed between the various political leaders still in Athens; this stated that when Greece was liberated the Crown's position would be definitely settled by means of a referendum.[3] Under this pressure, the Greek Government in exile yielded and agreed that the King would return to Athens after the liberation and elections for a Constituent Assembly would be held. It would then be up to the Assembly to decide in a sovereign manner the future of the monarchy. On 4 July 1943, the King broadcast a public statement in accordance with the above. But the party representatives and particularly the Communists – now in Cairo – were not satisfied. They insisted that the King declare that he would not return to Greece until a referendum had been held resulting in his favour. On 19 August 1943, the Government, under E. Tsouderos, was once again obliged to give in to their demands. The King, however, after consulting Churchill and Roosevelt, did not change his previous position, as defined in his broadcast of 4 July. On 8 November of the same year, however, he

---

[1] In contrast to the legal Government abroad, the occupation administrations were referred to as 'Quisling Governments', regardless of any agreements with the invaders. The fact, however, remains that they were illegal governments, deriving their de facto authority from the occupation forces. On the subject: M. A. Pesmazoglou, *The legal nature of the Greek Government during the enemy occupation* (1942) (in Greek).

[2] Sir Llewellyn Woodward, *British foreign policy in the Second World War* (1962), pp. 350–63; Tsouderos, *Greek anomalies in the Middle East* (1945), p. 16.

[3] Woodward's account of the British attitude (*British foreign policy*, pp. 350ff.) is very interesting and it is unfortunate that the new and enlarged version of his book, which does not cover these years, was prematurely interrupted by his death. See also Tsouderos, *Greek anomalies in the Middle East*, pp. 47ff. Most of the more general events discussed in this section are dealt with more extensively in the following books which should therefore be consulted: Sir Reginald Leeper, *When Greek meets Greek* (1950); Field-Marshal Earl Alexander of Tunis, *The Alexander memoirs 1940–45*, ed. by J. North (1962); the Earl of Avon, *The Eden memoirs*, I, *The reckoning* (1965); Harold Macmillan, 2nd vol. of his autobiography, *The blast of war 1939–1945* (1967).

addressed a letter to his Prime Minister stating that he would consider the problem of his return 'in due time' taking into consideration the 'National interest' of his country.[1]

The King's letter, though deliberately ambiguous and non-committal, was nevertheless accepted by the political leaders. His reservations were considered 'purely formal', lacking 'substantial meaning' (19 January 1944). The 'Lebanon Charter'[2] (20 May 1944) and the subsequent announcement of the new Prime Minister, George Papandreou, on 12 July 1944, referred to this letter (of 8 November 1943) and went a step further by declaring that the King would only return after a referendum resulting in his favour had been held. The Royalists, as might be expected, strongly protested against this arbitrary interpretation of the royal letter and the King refused to appoint a Regent. Eventually, and after protracted negotiations, a compromise solution was reached according to which the King would remain acting Sovereign but would prolong his stay abroad.

C: DRAFTING A NEW CONSTITUTION

The return of the Greek Government was soon after followed by a Communist uprising, in December 1944. It was only suppressed at the eleventh hour thanks to the despatch of British troops, for which Churchill, Macmillan and Field-Marshal Alexander must be credited. In order to further efforts of reconciliation, the King finally gave in to foreign pressures and signed the Regency Law (31 December 1944).[3] Archbishop Damaskinos was appointed Regent. Soon after it was agreed that the referendum should precede the elections for the Constituent Assembly (Agreement of Varkiza, 12 February 1945).[4] This timetable, however, was

---

[1] Tsouderos, ibid. pp. 72–4.

[2] In 1943 the Communists, anticipating an imminent liberation of Greece, launched a series of attacks against other resistance groups and successfully infiltrated the Greek Army and Navy in Cairo. The result was mutiny and rebellion which was eventually suppressed. After protracted negotiations the Lebanon Charter was signed which provided the basis of a government of National Unity. The conclusion of the agreement, however, became possible only after the United Kingdom and Russia settled their post-war spheres of influence in May–June 1944. A few months later the Communists violated the agreement and renewed their violent activities. See G. Papandreou, *The liberation of Greece* (1945), pp. 54ff. For the period see also Tsouderos, ibid., and P. Kanellopoulos, *The years of the Great War* (1964), each giving his personal account of the events.

[3] *Foreign Relations of the U.S., Diplomatic Papers*, IV (1944), 178.

[4] The blood-bath into which the Communists plunged Greece in December 1944 was ended with the agreement of Varkiza of 12 February 1945 which was achieved thanks to the intervention of the British Army. The British, however, were pressing for an agreement before Yalta and thus serious concessions were made to the Communists among which was the right to operate a legitimate party for their 'entirely illegal purposes'. (Campbell & Sherrard,

reversed once again with the agreement of the Attlee Labour Government; the referendum would follow the elections but no definite date was fixed. The indefinite postponement of the referendum satisfied the Republicans who believed that the King would be forgotten. In this aim of theirs, they found in the Regent a willing ally, as he was equally eager to delay the King's return and thus prolong his Regency.

The fact, however, that the elections preceded the referendum had an adverse effect on the Republican and Communist interests. The return of the King became the main electoral issue which, furthermore, united the Royalist parties. The Republicans on the other hand, disunited among themselves, contested the elections placing all their hopes on the proportional representation system which was conveniently adopted. But the collaboration of the Royalist parties minimised the effects of the electoral law and indeed transformed it into a system of simple majorities. Furthermore, the Communists abstained from the elections and when they subsequently realised their mistake and decided to participate, they were not given the chance. The result of all these mistakes was an overwhelming victory for the Royalists (31 March 1946). After a long struggle they succeeded in convincing the British Government that the referendum should be held at the earliest possible date and 1 September 1946 was finally chosen. The result was in favour of King George II, who returned to Greece (1946) and retained Constantine Tsaldaris as Prime Minister.

One of the first subjects discussed by the new Parliament was its legal nature. Those who favoured a thorough revision of the Constitution regarded it as a Constituent Assembly, whereas their opponents, favouring a revision on a smaller scale, considered it as a Revisional Parliament.[1] The issue was not clear. True enough, the elections of 31 March 1946 were for a Revisional Parliament and the Regent addressed it as such in the Speech from the Throne.[2] But the Republicans, referring to the various documents including the King's speeches, etc., insisted that the House was a Constituent Assembly with sovereign powers.[3] The House never pronounced a formal decision despite the fact that the issue was debated during the answer to the Speech from the Throne and while discussing the phrasing of the referendum question.[4] The question put to the electorate gave an indirect answer to the above problem. The electorate was asked whether

Modern Greece, p. 181.) The Communists took advantage of this and made a final attempt between the years 1946 and 1949. The activities of the Communist Party throughout this period are well covered by Professor D. Kousoulas' book, *Revolution and defeat* (London, 1965).

[1] *Parliamentary Debates of the Fourth Revisional Parliament* (1946), pp. 12ff., 155–67, 295ff. etc.
[2] *Parliamentary Debates*, ibid. p. 3.   [3] Papandreou, *Parliamentary Debates*, ibid. pp. 26–8.
[4] See S. Markesinis, *Parliamentary Debates*, ibid. pp. 295ff.

it wanted King George II to return to Greece or not. It was not asked about the form of government (Monarchy or Republic). The referendum was, in effect, turned into a plebiscite and this change was obviously meant to satisfy the Royalist M.P.s who had fought and won the elections on the royal issue.[1] The House was thus indirectly acknowledging important limits to its authority.

The revisional work, however, progressed very slowly, mainly due to the communist guerilla warfare. By December 1949, a draft of the proposed amendments was submitted to the House. It was never put to the vote. On 8 January 1950, with the revisional work about to be completed, the House was suddenly dissolved. According to the Royal Decree, elections for an ordinary Parliament would be held on 5 March 1950.

The dissolution of the 1946 Parliament raises mainly political questions. It was legally advised and granted, with the end of the legal term only three months away. Only those who considered the House a Constituent Assembly could be expected to challenge the legality of the dissolution. But they did not; a further proof that they too doubted the sovereign nature of the House.

Legally correct as the dissolution was, politically it fell little short of being a mystery. It remains inexplicable why the House was unexpectedly and hurriedly dissolved on the eve of the actual voting of the new constitution and why, furthermore, did none of the political leaders – many of whom were adversely affected by dissolution – protest against it? Moreover, how was a Revisional (and *a fortiori* a Constituent) Parliament dissolved without provisions simultaneously being made for elections for a new Revisional Parliament?

As far as the political aspect of the problem is concerned, the available material provides few and indefinite answers, all of which naturally belong to the field of politics rather than law. It is most probable that the 1950 dissolution was acceptable to all. Political parties in and outside the House had different, but cogent, reasons to welcome immediate dissolution. For the parties already represented in the House, immediate elections were necessary in order to check Field-Marshal Papagos' growing prestige, particularly after he had successfully terminated the guerilla war. A newly elected House would prove rumours of his future involvement in politics unfounded and would check his ambitions before it was too late. These rumours had been reinforced when Papagos publicly announced that he had decided to resign from the Army.[2] Subsequently, however, he was

---

[1] A certain analogy exists with the 1935 Referendum. See above, chapter 11.
[2] Throughout December 1949, these rumours were persistent and caused political anxieties to leaders such as C. Tsaldaris and S. Venizelos. See the Athens daily, *Estia*, 29 and 30 December.

more or less reluctantly obliged to withdraw his resignation which had caused considerable reaction in political circles. For those not represented in the House, elections offered new opportunities. They were now fully aware how foolish had been their decision to abstain from the 1946 elections and were determined not to repeat their mistake.

The legal aspect of the dissolution is more complicated, though it did not arise until after the elections, and again for purely political reasons. Dissolution of the Revisional Parliament is a recurrent theme in Greek constitutional history. What is said here must be read in conjunction with what was said in chapter 9 in relation to the 1910 dissolution. From a purely legal angle the dissolution of a Revisional Parliament is not prohibited. The 1910 and 1935 precedents confirm this, despite the traditional suspicion with regard to the binding force of precedents. In practice, Greek politicians, in contrast to theorists, seem to place considerable emphasis on precedence which they value more 'than interpretation and in fact make them equal to legal rules'.[1]

Yet the 1950 dissolution differed basically in one respect from both its predecessors. Parliament was dissolved without provision being made for a new Revisional House to continue its unfinished work. We have maintained,[2] that a dissolution exercised against a Revisional House necessarily leads to a new Revisional Parliament. The contrary would infer that the King (or President) could prevent the revisional work by forcing a dissolution. Thus, even if it were not specifically provided, the new House is automatically a Revisional one and this principle is known in Greece as the theory of 'automatic continuation'.

The above opinion, however, is correct only under certain conditions and it is doubtful whether it can be applied to the 1950 dissolution. One must always bear in mind that all European constitutions of the nineteenth and twentieth centuries prescribed a certain (short) period of time – usually the first session – within which the revisional task should be completed. The ultimate reason for such provisions is extremely wide. The task of revision is undertaken only when it is absolutely necessary and public opinion is ripe enough for a change. If this is so, endless discussions

On 31 December, Papagos stated that he would not get involved in politics, unless 'unexpected factors arose'. On 6 January 1950, he resigned his Army post, only to withdraw his resignation the next day. On 11 January, four out of the seven morning dailies openly favoured Papagos and asked him to review the situation and change his decision. He refused to do so, though he did not commit himself for the future. (It is characteristic of the anxiety felt by some political leaders that they signed a document – which the Prime Minister (Diomides) handed to the King – in which they explained why, in their opinion, Papagos should be kept out of politics. From the S. Markesinis Papers.)

[1] S. Markesinis, in the Athens daily, *Estia*, 10 May 1950.
[2] Above, chapter 1.

and protracted procedures are not necessary. If the driving force is strong enough, the revision can be completed within the first session. If, however, such conditions are lacking, then it is perhaps preferable for the whole revision to be postponed or even cancelled. This leads to one conclusion: if the Crown intervenes during the first session – or, in any event, at a very early stage – then dissolution might be regarded as provocative, irrational and even unconstitutional. But if Parliament is inexcusably delaying its revisional work in a manner revealing unwillingness or even total inability to complete the revision, the previously stated rule cannot apply. Evidently new factors, definitely more important and cogent, have made their appearance and are setting aside the revision originally decided upon.

This, it seems to me, was the case in 1950. The 1946 Parliament had been debating revision for three years and nine months, but was unable to approve the final draft. One has only to compare this record delay with the accomplishments of the 1911 Parliament which concluded its task in less than forty meetings and within the first session, to realise that the situation was not sufficiently developed in the years 1946–50. The need for a new Constitution was not so pressing. The 1946 Parliament decided to revise the 1911 Constitution, without adhering to its prescribed procedures – yet another example of an illegal constitution. Its main purpose was to decide on the return of the King and this, as we saw, had been the campaign issue. Once this had been accomplished, no other pressing reason for a revision seemed to exist. The 1911 Constitution was in force and could certainly survive, for an interim period at least. On the other hand, between 1946 and 1950, important problems had emerged and had to be dealt with. The suppression of the communist guerilla war, the establishment of internal order, the tackling of grave economic difficulties were more urgent than a revision of the constitutional text. This could – and should – have been left for a new and more representative body.

But, as previously noted, the 1950 dissolution was not discussed until later that year and particularly during the summer of 1951. The theory of 'automatic continuity' was devised later to justify the legality of the 1952 Constitution.[1] Its theoretical foundations were unsound and to understand the dangers it entails one must perhaps envisage the following case. Suppose, for example, that the 1946 Parliament was not dissolved but

---

[1] It was elaborated in the House by Mr D. Papaspyrou, then Minister of Justice. *Parliamentary Debates* (18 December 1951), B, α, 239–44. It was also adopted by a controversial decision of the Conseil d'Etat, no. 1899/1952, published in the *Efimeris Ellinon Nomicon*, 1952, pp. 743ff., which emphasised the need to put an end to the constitutional uncertainty. This argument, however, is clearly one of political expediency rather than a result of legal reasoning.

reached the end of its term without having completed its work. According to the theory of 'automatic continuation', the succeeding Parliament would automatically assume a revisional nature to complete its predecessor's task. Suppose that this Parliament, too, failed to complete its task, then the next one would continue it and so on *ad infinitum*. A situation of continuous constitutional uncertainty would thus be created, clearly dangerous and legally unacceptable.[1]

The controversy over the legality of the 1950 dissolution and the fate of the revision began in May 1950, after a relevant resolution was tabled but failed to pass in the House.[2] In the issue, King Paul had particular interests at stake. He was eager to put an end to the constitutional uncertainty not least out of fear that it might eventually be solved by a less favourable House. Furthermore, the King was anxious that the second draft, prepared by a special committee of the 1946 Parliament, be approved and accepted. It contained extremely favourable clauses relating to the succession to the Throne (at the expense of Prince Peter of Greece whom the Royal Family positively disliked) as well as to the question of the Regency, which was drafted in a way favouring the Queen.[3] Accordingly the political leaders held a conference in the Royal Palace under the chairmanship of the King. It was decided that the Constitution would be approved or rejected in one session. The proposal, however, failed to obtain the minimum number of signatures and the issue was temporarily set aside.[4]

Meanwhile, however, it had become obvious that new elections were unavoidable if the country were ever to obtain a stable Government. Since the last elections, minority Governments had held office and few could conceal their concern for the continuing ministerial instability that had existed in Greece since the Liberation. In July 1951, owing to the imminence of new elections and under considerable pressure from the King, the constitutional issue was brought up again for consideration. In a new Crown Council, the political leaders – with Markesinis absent and Papandreou retaining certain reservations – signed a protocol binding the new Parliament. The protocol called for elections for an ordinary Parliament, which nevertheless would have limited revisional competence and would, within a given period of time, decide to accept or reject en bloc the

[1] S. Markesinis, *Parliamentary Debates*, ibid. pp. 244–52.

[2] *Parliamentary Debates* (2 May 1950), A, α, 97–9.

[3] In contrast to the 1911 Constitution, arts. 50 and 53 of the 1952 Constitution appointed the Queen as Regent in the event of death or grave illness of the King. The innovation was extremely important since the Crown Prince Constantine was at that time a young boy unable to succeed his father.

[4] The meeting took place on 15 May with the participation of S. Venizelos, C. Tsaldaris, G. Papandreou, E. Tsouderos and P. Kanellopoulos. See Sgouritsas, *Constitutional law*, p. 172 and C. Georgopoulos, *Elements of constitutional law* (in Greek), 1 (1968), 389.

existing constitutional draft.[1] The elections were to be held on 9 November 1951.

The electoral law adopted was a carefully drafted, modified system of proportional representation, designed to favour the larger parties at the expense of Papandreou, Markesinis and the parties of the Left. At the same time, it was evident that no single party could obtain a working majority. To all this, however, the Crown gave its full support, firmly believing that weak parties and parliamentary majorities increased its powers of arbitration.

The day Parliament was dissolved, Papagos publicly declared his decision to contest the elections (30 July 1951). Papagos' decision had remained a secret that few knew, hence its announcement came as a shock to all who wished to keep him out of politics. His prestige was great and though he personally lacked any experience in politics, his chances of victory were clearly good – a prospect that annoyed many, including the Crown. It was only recently revealed and confirmed in the press, that Queen Frederica was so annoyed and at the same time so determined to stop Papagos, that she persuaded the King to summon immediately to the Royal Palace General Tsakalotos, then Chief of the Joint Military Staff, and in a quite unconstitutional manner ordered him to place Papagos under arrest. Happily Tsakalotos refused and an open crisis was averted.[2]

At the elections Papagos obtained 37% of the popular vote. The percentage was inadequate for him to form a Government yet it had the negative result of making it impossible for any other party to form a Government. With Papagos unwilling to accept the premiership in a coalition Government,[3] General Plastiras managed to form a narrow coalition and immediately proceeded to vote the Constitution[4] according to the above-mentioned protocol of the political leaders. Relying on the theory of 'automatic continuity' the Government succeeded in voting what came to be known as the '1952 Constitution',[5] despite strong objections expressed by the Opposition spokesman S. Markesinis, on

---

[1] For the text see Sgouritsas, *Constitutional law*, p. 174. The new Parliament could vote or reject the constitutional text only during the period of the first session.

[2] This was first published by the Athens weekly newspaper *Embros* on 17 January 1970 and was confirmed by General Tsakalotos himself on 24 January 1970; more important nobody denied or doubted the facts contained in it.

[3] S. Markesinis in particular was opposed to the idea. On the other hand Kanellopoulos and Karamanlis favoured the idea of a coalition (*Parliamentary Debates* (12 March 1958), Δ, γ, 447). The refusal to join the coalition was proved tactically correct. The inherent weaknesses of the Plastiras Government soon led to new elections from which the Right emerged so strong that it remained in power for twelve years.

[4] *Parliamentary Debates* (21 December 1951), B, α, 332.

[5] The most thorough, though at times politically biased, general work is Professor A. Manessis' *Guarantees of the observance of the Constitution*, 2 vols (Thessaloniki, 1956–65).

behalf of Papagos' Greek Rally Party, which had obtained over a third of the popular vote.

The theory of 'automatic continuity' has already been discussed and rejected as dangerous. Four points, however, remain to be made to show that the 1952 Constitution was unconstitutionally voted. On 25 July 1951,[1] four Ministers – all of them M.P.s – signed a motion calling for the observance of the constitutional procedure of article 108 of the 1911 Constitution, then in force. They thus seemed to realise that the 1950 Parliament had no revisional authority to proceed and revise the Constitution. Yet, the same M.P.s, one of whom was the then Prime Minister Mr S. Venizelos, three days later accepted or signed the July 1951 protocol which was based on the opposite concept and according to which the 1950 Parliament agreed to transmit its revisional authority to its successor, which was thus allowed to approve or reject the existing draft. If, despite the above, the political leaders considered the 1950 Parliament as a revisional chamber, why did they not proceed to approve the draft – particularly since they held between them the necessary majority to accomplish this – and instead decided to let the succeeding (1951) Parliament do this for them? There was definitely no hurry, as far as the voting of the Constitution was concerned, since the House had scarcely existed for one year. If the new (1951) House were to be allowed to revise the Constitution, why did not they call for elections for a Revisional House, as Mr G. Papandreou had asked for?[2] Lastly, why and how did the 1951 Parliament consider itself bound by the July 1951 protocol? That a protocol signed by ex-leaders of the old House can bind its successor is legally completely inexplicable. Particularly if one bears in mind that the protocol was not unanimously approved, many of the leaders who had signed it were no longer present in the House and Papagos, who had now obtained 37% of the vote had never signed it.[3]

But the Plastiras Government had many problems to face besides the constitutional one and its slender majority made its task practically impossible.

---

[1] *Parliamentary Debates*, Α, β, 1475.
[2] Last clause of the above-mentioned protocol.
[3] Stephanopoulos and Kanellopoulos, who had signed the protocol, had in the meantime dissolved their own parties and had joined Papagos (31 July 1951). See *Estia* of the same date.

Chapter 13

THE LAST PHASE

A: THE RISE AND THE FALL OF THE RIGHT
(1952–1963)

Plastiras' Government soon proved itself unable to pursue an effective programme, yet Greece desperately needed a strong Government to face the critical problems confronting the country.

Fully aware of these difficulties, Papagos launched a nationwide pre-electoral campaign during the early summer of 1952, and succeeded in creating an electoral atmosphere. Faced with Papagos' serious challenge, and with the Americans openly stating that the proportional system prevented effective use of their aid, Plastiras was finally forced to give in and accept an electoral confrontation with a system of simple majorities. Papagos had thus won the first round by forcing a polarisation of political forces which resulted in his favour. Parliament was thus dissolved and elections were held in November 1952.

Papagos outlined his political programme in a speech in Thessaloniki which became known as the 'Thessaloniki pact', since it took the form of a contract between the future Prime Minister and the People. The Greek Rally's main aims were: Economic development by means of attracting foreign investment, the overall objective being the increase and fairer distribution of the national income; a fresh start after the recent internal strife; improvement of relations with Turkey and establishment of relations with Yugoslavia in an attempt to provide the latter with a link with the Western world – a daring new step in international relations in the Balkans; further development of Greek–English relations – Papagos was always eager to find a solution to the Cyprus problem which he regarded as the only cloud in Greek–English relations;[1] and strengthening of the democratic form of government which necessarily implied curtailing the activities of the Crown.

The electorate gave the Greek Rally a clear mandate to carry through its programme. With 49% of the electoral vote and 247 seats in Parliament

---

[1] The British military liaison officer and subsequently military attaché, Brigadier Godfrey Hobbs, was informed about this by Papagos himself while the latter was still in the Army as Field-Marshal. At this stage, however, the British Government, which was accordingly informed, apparently took the whole problem rather light-heartedly.

out of a total of 300, Papagos was firmly in the saddle and the Party embarked on its ambitious programme. Papagos was to remain in office for nearly four years.

The economic recovery of the country was the number one priority for the next two years and the responsibility of Markesinis who was appointed Minister of Economic Coordination.[1] Exports soon soared, foreign capital in the form of industrial credits was attracted mainly from France, Germany and Italy, and commercial relations with the Soviet Union were established for the first time. A planned economy, aided by freedom of imports and a radical and successful devaluation of the drachma soon put Greece firmly on the road to economic recovery and the year 1953 witnessed the first post-War budget which balanced and which, further-more, had also achieved a considerable surplus.

On the other issues, however, the Papagos Government was only partially successful. A Greek–Turkish–Yugoslav pact was signed; the question of Cyprus was officially reopened in the early summer of 1954 and came to a critical point by the end of the same year when a Greek resolution demanding the right of self-determination for the island was turned down in the United Nations on the grounds that it concerned an internal problem of the United Kingdom. By 1955, with the Turks drawn into the dispute on the insistence of the United Kingdom, relations between the latter and Greece rapidly deteriorated and had reached a critical stage by the time of Papagos' death in October 1955.

Curtailing the royal powers likewise met with great resistance. From the moment Papagos had decided to play an active political role he had become unpopular with the Court and Markesinis was held responsible for his involvement in politics. Furthermore, as previously stated, a strong Government implied less interference by the Crown, and this could not be easily tolerated. Consequently, Markesinis disagreed with Papagos and finally resigned in April 1954. At the same time, although the Crown viewed Papagos with suspicion owing to his firm policy over the Cyprus question,[2] his popularity still remained considerable despite various set-backs; hence his opponents were obliged to wait. By 1955, however, with Markesinis out of the way and Papagos seriously ill, the problem of his succession became acute. In a speech in the House, Markesinis maintained[3]

---

[1] By order of the Prime Minister, the Ministries of Finance, Commerce, Industry, Labour, Transport, Public Works, Agriculture, Merchant Marine and the Banks were also placed under the supervision of the Minister of Economic Coordination.

[2] The King viewed with great anxiety Papagos' firm handling of the Cyprus question as he was afraid of the possible repercussions this might have on his *personal* position. Stephano-poulos, Private Papers.

[3] *Parliamentary Debates* (extraordinary session), 11 October 1955, Γ, 9.

that at least three months before Papagos' death the King had taken the first initiative to find a successor to the Field-Marshal. It is now believed that the move to replace him began at a much earlier stage, but had not been put into effect because of the difficulty Papagos' dismissal would create. The King's wish was to find someone to succeed the Prime Minister from within his own party and to avoid commissioning a leader of the Opposition. Whether the King would have appointed Stephanopoulos as Papagos' successor is doubtful. It was only due to Papagos' insistence[1] that Stephanopoulos became acting Prime Minister a day before Papagos' death and the King gave in to the wish of the parliamentary majority. It is likely, however, that Karamanlis was already considered at this point as a preferable alternative to Stephanopoulos and that the British Ambassador in Athens was aware of this. In any event, it seems that both British and Americans were pressing for a person who would be willing to negotiate some kind of compromise settlement over Cyprus.[2]

On Papagos' death, the head of the King's Political Bureau, Ambassador Koutsalexis, visited Mr Stephanopoulos and asked him to tender his resignation.[3] According to Mr Stephanopoulos, Koutsalexis, speaking on behalf of the King, said that this was a pure formality, so as to give the King the opportunity to exercise his prerogative and appoint a Prime Minister. Stephanopoulos had been assured by the King himself at Papagos' deathbed that he would be re-commissioned the next day. However, to his amazement and disappointment, the following day, Mr Karamanlis was asked to form a Government, and on 6 October he addressed the Greek Rally M.P.s – the majority of whom were known to favour Stephanopoulos[4] – and asked them for their support. The daily newspapers reported that Karamanlis, replying to a journalist's question, maintained that the King had commissioned him to form a Government with the right to dissolve Parliament if he were defeated.[5] Papandreou, commenting on this in Parliament on the 11 October, rightly maintained that the object of Karamanlis' statement was to oblige the Greek Rally M.P.s to give him a vote of confidence and added that: 'the fate of this House [1955] depends on whether Mr. Karamanlis obtains a vote of con-

---

[1] S. Stephanopoulos' unpublished Private Papers.

[2] Campbell & Sherrard, *Modern Greece*, p. 257; K. Young, *The Greek passion*, p. 276.

[3] The text is based on Mr Stephanopoulos' personal and unpublished account, as well as on his papers of the time.

[4] The Stephanopoulos unpublished papers contain a document signed by approximately 100 M.P.s pledging him their support. Furthermore, the Greek Rally M.P.s had unanimously expressed their confidence in him on 1 October (*Kathimerini* of 2 October) in respect of his handling of foreign affairs. Despite the above, the King's unconditional support for Karamanlis swayed his followers in one night.

[5] *Kathimerini*, 6 October 1955.

fidence'.[1] Stephanopoulos also insisted that the pressure from the King and the threat of dissolution definitely helped Karamanlis obtain the necessary number of votes.[2]

Whether or not dissolution played the important role Papandreou and Stephanopoulos maintained it did, the fact remains that with Markesinis in opposition and Stephanopoulos inactive, the choice of Karamanlis as Prime Minister met with little real opposition from the parliamentary group of the Greek Rally. Therefore, with the Royal blessing and with the threat of dissolution, Karamanlis was able to persuade the majority to withdraw their support from Stephanopoulos. On the night of 12 October Karamanlis finally obtained a vote of confidence in the House. Except for brief intervals, he remained in office until 1963.

Karamanlis' appointment became, as expected, a subject of controversy and the royal initiative was severely criticised.[3] Apart from the King's unethical behaviour towards his Prime Minister, what most of the people concerned at the time failed to emphasise adequately was that the irregularity of his action lay not in the appointment of Karamanlis as Prime Minister – which, according to prevailing opinion, was legal and constitutional – but in his appointment as party leader against the expressed will of the late Prime Minister and the parliamentary majority. The fact that Karamanlis subsequently managed to obtain the party's confidence only slightly alters the problem, since it still leaves the King open to criticism, i.e. that he used his influence to impose Karamanlis as party leader. What equally deserves further consideration is that those who supported Karamanlis' appointment justified it on various grounds and not least on the basis of British precedents.

When one draws parallels between the constitutional practice of different countries, one must be careful. As far as this particular case is concerned, the truth is that the British Monarch had, until recently, the right to appoint the Prime Minister, but never the right to appoint a party leader. One of the guiding principles of English constitutional law is that the Crown is above parties, and what would bring the Crown into party politics more than interference in the process of electing their leader? But even when it comes to electing a Prime Minister the role of the Crown

---

[1] *Parliamentary Debates* (extraordinary session), 11 October 1955, Γ, 14.

[2] The King's pressure was the reason given to Stephanopoulos by his followers when they informed him that they could no longer support him. (From the Stephanopoulos Papers.)

[3] Karamanlis' appointment was supported by *Kathimerini*. It was severely criticised by Papandreou, Markesinis, and S. Venizelos. See also *Estia* of that period. Karamanlis' appointment was also criticised amongst academic circles. See for example, A. Wamvetsos, *Deviations from the parliamentary form of government* (1960) (in Greek), p. 267; P. Dagtoglou, 'Constitutional developments from the introduction of the Constitution to the death of King Paul', *Ephimeris Ellinon Nomikon*, January 1966.

has seriously diminished in the twentieth century. It would be necessary to go back to the nineteenth century to find an example of the exercise of the prerogative, and surely Greek politicians or theorists of the 1950s were not well advised to do this, particularly if one considers that the British form of government is that of a Constitutional Monarchy, whereas that of its Greek counterpart is a Crowned Democracy. As far as the twentieth century is concerned, we have seen that in the United Kingdom at least twice the King, when given the chance to choose a Prime Minister, chose the person the party or the particular circumstances asked for, rather than the person he himself favoured. Both in 1923 and in 1940 Baldwin and Churchill were elected each on different grounds instead of Lord Curzon or Lord Halifax, whom the King would have personally preferred. Lately too, in the case of Mr Macmillan and Sir Alec Douglas Home, the Queen relied on the advice of a senior statesman of the calibre of Sir Winston Churchill or that of the outgoing Prime Minister who was backed by party soundings – and even so, the hubbub that followed obliged the Conservatives to alter their selection process of a leader, so as to avoid embarrassing the Crown.

Karamanlis, however, obtained a vote of confidence and with the Cyprus question getting out of hand, he decided to go to the country and obtain a fresh mandate. Parliament was by now approaching its end, so Karamanlis passed an exceptionally complicated electoral law which was a combination of proportional representation and simple majorities. The law clearly aimed at furthering the chances of the National Radical Union Party, which Karamanlis had founded in the meantime. Confronted with such a hybrid electoral system, the opposition parties were forced to form a popular electoral front, including the M.P.s of the extreme Left (E.D.A.). Markesinis' Progressive Party, however, did not join this so-called electoral Popular Front.

The elections resulted in favour of Karamanlis who obtained 47% of the vote with a slight majority in seats (165 out of a total of 300). Markesinis' non-participation in the popular front deprived it of a vital three per cent that would have given it a majority of the seats as well as of the popular vote. It is fair to note that despite the criticism the electorate had undoubtedly returned the National Radical Union (E.R.E.) as the major single party and seemed to approve Karamanlis' appointment as the successor of Papagos.

Karamanlis' years of office are controversial. Taking advantage of the economic and political stability that he had inherited from the Greek Rally Party, and with the open support of the Crown and the Americans, he preserved internal stability and proved a capable administrator. But it was in the field of foreign affairs that his first Government met its greatest difficulties. The situation in Cyprus was chaotic. General Grivas was waging a guerilla war against the British and, in 1956, talks in London had broken down between Archbishop Makarios and the Colonial Secretary, Lennox-Boyd. A fortnight later, the Archbishop was exiled to the Seychelles, only to be made a hero to his people. 'It was fortunate for E.R.E. that this occurred just after and not before the elections.'[1]

The details of the evolution of a problem as complicated as that of Cyprus cannot be traced here. Suffice it to say that by 1958 it had weakened the Government, members of which began to show signs of rebellion. At the same time the Crown, whose position had been considerably strengthened by the appointment of Karamanlis, was now disquieted by the deterioration in Greek–British relations and was in a quandary regarding its future actions. Karamanlis, realising that he was losing control of the situation, attempted to introduce a Bill establishing a system of reinforced proportional representation, which penalised coalitions and at the same time gave him greater control over his own party. He was too late, however. L. Eftaxias resigned from the party on the grounds that the Government was not conducting the foreign policy properly. Others soon followed, though this time the pretext was the electoral law. Karamanlis was thus finally obliged to resign.[2]

What followed Karamanlis' resignation is extremely complicated to relate here in detail. The small parties decided to open talks for an electoral coalition with the Left and Markesinis undertook the negotiations.[3] These, however, broke down over the issue of Greece's alliance with NATO. When the Communists later decided to give in on this subject, it was too late and the negotiations were not renewed. The impact, however, was tremendous and led the Liberals and E.R.E. to set their differences temporarily aside and agree on a modified system of proportional representation that would hinder the coalition which everybody considered imminent.[4] The system was so devised as to favour in a scandalous way the first and second parties, as was expected: E.R.E. and the Liberals.[5] The Bill was finally passed by a caretaker Government.

In the meantime Karamanlis had the opportunity to return to power

---

[1] Campbell & Sherrard, *Modern Greece*, p. 259.

[2] 5 March 1958 (*Parliamentary Debates* (12 March 1958), Δ, γ, 429).

[3] The first negotiation took place between Markesinis and the Communist leaders Eliou and Brillakis, the second with Passalides and Glezos.

[4] Karamanlis publicly acknowledged the existence of an agreement in Parliament. *Parliamentary Debates* (12 March 1958), Δ, γ, 430; so did Papandreou, ibid. p. 432.

[5] *Parliamentary Debates* (Alamanis, leader of E.P.E.K., Plastiras' party), ibid. pp. 433, 435 and Passalides (the leader of E.D.A.), ibid. p. 438.

since some of the M.P.s who had deserted him had returned to his party. Technically speaking, dissolution was not necessary since Karamanlis had reasonable hopes of obtaining a slight majority and could form a new Government. Karamanlis, however, though criticised by Kanellopoulos in the House, cunningly refused to accept this compromise solution and chose to go to the country instead.

The exchanges between Karamanlis and Kanellopoulos in the House on 12 March 1958 are extremely revealing both for the 1958 and the 1952 dissolutions. Kanellopoulos maintained that 'It is improper...to submit the country to the turmoil of election each time a number of M.P.s disagree with their leader.'[1] He further reminded Karamanlis that he too had taken the same view in 1951, when Papagos had refused to enter into a coalition with Plastiras and was pressing for new elections.

From a theoretical point of view Kanellopoulos' view is correct. Under the particular political circumstances, however, Karamanlis was right – especially as far as his own interests were concerned. He was thus quick to point out that all the important parties were pressing for elections and also to show that there was no similarity between 1951–2 and 1958.[2] The 1956 Parliament was unable to provide a strong Government at a time when the country badly needed one. As stated he was subsequently proved right since he renewed his mandate and thus finally obtained full control over his party. But the political motivations of the dissolution can hardly be denied.

In the meantime the Progressives and the other opposition parties formed a smaller coalition which did not include the Left.[3] Parliament was dissolved on 29 March 1958 and elections followed on 11 May 1958. These elections were in certain respects a landmark in post-war Greece. The intrigue over the electoral law apparently backfired. The Communists emerged as the second strongest party and gained all the electoral advantages. Venizelos came in third and P.A.D.E., the smaller coalition under Markesinis' leadership, fourth with 10% of the vote. The electorate seemed to have penalised the Liberals for their ineffective opposition during the two preceding years, as well as for their co-operation with the Right in passing the electoral law.

Karamanlis, with a diminished but nevertheless renewed mandate soon reached an agreement over Cyprus. The London–Athens–Zurich agreements were ratified after a fierce debate in the House. Cyprus became an

[1] *Parliamentary Debates*, ibid. pp. 446 and 447.
[2] *Parliamentary Debates*, ibid. p. 447. S. Markesinis later agreed with Karamanlis' handling of the affair. See *Parliamentary Debates*, 11 June 1958, pp. 41–2.
[3] For details see Markesinis, *Parliamentary Debates*, 11 June 1958, pp. 41ff.

independent state and special provisions were made to safeguard the rights of the Turkish minority in the island. Time, however, proved that the agreements provided a temporary solution and nothing more.[1]

The Liberal defeat had its impact on the party. After having been reduced to a third-rank power, the party split into a number of smaller ones. Papandreou survived with a mere handful of followers while Venizelos finally handed his party over to General Grivas, who in the meantime had apparently decided to follow Papagos' example and play an active part in politics. Lastly, the 'Group of Ten' was formed by a number of prominent politicians of the Centre as well as of Karamanlis' rebels, who were disillusioned with their respective leaders.[2] With the Centre disunited and weak the Opposition was monopolised by the Communists to the great annoyance of all, not least the Army, which began to show signs of unrest. The seeds of the 1967 coup d'état had been definitely sown.

The complete disarray in the ranks of the non-Communist Opposition was a matter of great concern to all interested in Greek politics. The Crown once again decided to play an active part. This time it attempted to reunite the Centre and it is likely that Karamanlis more or less gave his blessing, thus hoping to rid himself of the Communist threat. Long negotiations followed and the political leaders of the Centre, finally realising that their political death was imminent if they continued to compete individually for adherents, decided to acknowledge Papandreou's leadership and create the Centre Union party.[3]

By October 1961 Karamanlis felt that the time had come for new elections. With his mass campaign against the Communists producing results and with international tension over Berlin, the moment seemed favourable for a sudden dissolution. Furthermore, the Cypriot problem was in a calm phase. Last but not least, party reasons favoured an immediate dissolution before the united Centre gained impetus and became a serious threat to E.R.E. However, during the electoral campaign, the Centre Union announced its electoral co-operation with the Progressive Party. The electoral coalition was on equal terms and it was agreed that, in the event of victory, Papandreou would become Prime Minister, and Markesinis deputy Prime Minister, once again responsible for the economic ministries.

The electoral campaign took place with a non-political Government in

---

[1] The constitutional text has correctly been described by Professor S. de Smith, *The new Commonwealth and its constitution* (1964), p. 282, as a 'tragic and occasionally an almost ludicrous document'.

[2] From Athanasiades-Novas' and J. Toumbas' private Unpublished Papers.

[3] According to Mr Novas the plan was to reunite the parties of the Centre and then seek co-operation with Markesinis.

power, composed of ex-members of the Royal Court and personal friends of the King. Its composition was suspect, but Papandreou and Venizelos did not openly criticise it at this point. Their first reaction came towards the end of the electoral campaign but it was already too late.[1]

At first, Karamanlis' timing of the dissolution proved to be correct as far as his party's interests were concerned. The odds were in his favour that he would be returned to office. But as the election date approached the Centre–Progressive coalition gained momentum and, for the first time since five years of E.R.E. rule, an alternative Government seemed probable.

To this, E.R.E. decided to react and here it found a useful ally in the so-called non-political Government of General Dovas. As Campbell and Sherrard observed, 'E.R.E. was ruthlessly determined to remain in office'.[2] Orders went out to the gendarmerie and the police constabulary to campaign against the Communists. The order was ingenious. A direct and indirect terrorisation of the Left vote would result both in the decrease of its strength as well as the increase of the vote of the Right. Strange as this may seem, it was based on a very simple concept. It was expected that the non-fanatic voters of the Left would abandon their party allegiances as a result of this campaign. These voters would then vote for E.R.E. and not for the Centre – even though it was ideologically closer to their beliefs – mainly because E.R.E. was the party that could guarantee that they would not be prosecuted after the elections. Besides, E.R.E. could influence the popular vote in many ways, not least through the various functions of the State apparatus which it completely controlled after nine years of power.

Despite all this the Centre and the Progressive parties gained ground to such an extent that on the eve of the elections General Kardamakis, then Chief of the Joint Military Staff, visited Markesinis and informed him that if the coalition won the elections next day the Army would like to see Markesinis in the Ministry of Defence. Otherwise it would be difficult to conceal the impression that the victory of the Centre did not represent a slide towards the Left, something the Army definitely disliked.[3] The Army was clearly restless and showed signs of returning to its previous tactics of intervening in party politics. The question, however, was dropped when it became apparent that the elections had resulted in favour of E.R.E., which obtained 50% of the vote and 178 seats in the House and Karamanlis formed his last Government.

[1] From S. Markesinis' private Unpublished Papers.
[2] *Modern Greece*, p. 265.
[3] From S. Markesinis' Unpublished Papers. Markesinis reserved his answer until he had consulted Papandreou and Venizelos.

The electoral campaign has been described in some detail because the events that took place were the main cause of the next dissolution, approximately two years later. The defeat of the coalition resulted in its partial split. Markesinis favoured the idea of opposing Karamanlis in the House and conducting a new campaign, as Papagos had done nine years earlier. This would eventually lead to a new dissolution and a new confrontation and the coalition would then be able to challenge the Right in a straight fight with a system of simple majorities. Following the elections Markesinis visited Papandreou who agreed with him but was later swayed by Venizelos.[1] Instead Papandreou launched a fierce attack against Karamanlis, the Army and eventually the Crown for unconstitutionally retaining Karamanlis in power. Papandreou's 'relentless struggle', as he himself called his cause, helped him keep the Centre united but reached great extremes and created an atmosphere of deep political divisions within the Nation which reached its peak during the summer of 1965. Nevertheless it was ruthlessly conducted and met with little or practically no resistance from Karamanlis.

The reasons why Karamanlis pursued such an ineffective policy against Papandreou's mounting pressure are not clear. It is clear, however, that he was opposed to the idea of a new dissolution, which would give the impression of giving in to the demands of the opposition. It can be argued, however, that had he gone to the country at that stage and before Papandreou's campaign had gained impetus he would have won. But Karamanlis' luck was rapidly deserting him. As his power waned the Crown started undermining its old *protégé*, while trying at the same time to split the Centre by encouraging Venizelos to pursue his own ambitions.

By 1963, political fanaticism was intensified and was further aggravated by an incident in Thessaloniki which resulted in the death of Lambrakis, an M.P. of the Left. Papandreou openly accused Karamanlis of being morally responsible for Lambrakis' death and passions were once more aroused. All of a sudden, Karamanlis appeared tired, unimaginative and vulnerable. His objections against a royal visit to London proved the last straw. Karamanlis opposed the idea of the King going to London and recommended a postponement. The immediate cause seemed to be growing fears of demonstrations in London against the royal visit. There were serious reasons to anticipate that this would happen and in fact the Greek Queen, while in London a few months earlier, had been attacked by demonstrators. Karamanlis was undoubtedly correct in maintaining that

---

[1] S. Markesinis' Papers. (In a telegram to Roosevelt in 1944 Churchill had said of Papandreou that the latter 'changed his mind about three times a day'. *Foreign Relations of the U.S., Diplomatic Papers*, v (1944), 174.)

the King should follow his Prime Minister's advice, but the King insisted on going to London, particularly since he had prearranged the invitation. With all political parties – except the Progressives – opposing the royal visit, a new crisis was looming.

For Karamanlis, the options were limited. He was obliged to resign without even being able to protest against his more or less forced resignation. He left Greece after having recommended as Prime Minister P. Pipinelis,[1] until then Minister of Commerce, who paradoxically had equally opposed the idea of the royal visit to London, but who was now willing to conform with the royal wish. In the event the royal visit took place in the summer of 1963 without any disturbances.

During the summer, Pipinelis proceeded to vote a new electoral law. Papandreou, who in the meantime was in a dilemma because his 'relentless struggle' had come to an apparent impasse, found in Pipinelis' appointment new grounds for complaints and therefore renewed his efforts; this time, he insisted on the resignation of the Court Government and called for a dissolution of Parliament. At a Crown Council that followed, the King finally gave in to Papandreou's demands. Dissolution had been Papandreou's objective and he had reached it. In one night he had become the strong man who dictated his views to the King; thus Karamanlis was obliged to contest the elections with a grave psychological handicap.

B: THE CENTRE UNION IN POWER (1963–1965)

The result of the elections was indecisive. The Centre Union gained a slight majority over the E.R.E. party while the Communists and the Progressives held the remainder of the seats. A new Government crisis loomed ahead. Confronted with such a situation, Markesinis offered his 3.5% of the vote to Karamanlis, who would thus gain a slight majority over Papandreou and could claim the mandate to form a Government, according to the theory of a proclaimed majority. Karamanlis, however, was slow in taking a decision. He seemed confident that the King would not commission Papandreou until after the election of the Speaker.[2] In contrast, Papandreou showed astonishing activity. He succeeded in

[1] Before commissioning Pipinelis, the King had tried to persuade the President of the Conseil d'Etat Mr Ch. Mitrelias to form a caretaker Government. He replied that he was willing to do so provided Messrs S. Markesinis and Venizelos were willing to co-operate. Markesinis categorically refused and Mitrelias turned down the King's offer – a rare example in Greek history. (Mitrelias, Unpublished Papers.)

[2] S. Markesinis' Unpublished Papers. After the elections Karamanlis and Markesinis had a long private meeting about which very little is known.

persuading the King – who was seriously ill – to commission him to form a Government, a decision favoured by the royal entourage which wished to end the conflict with the Centre Union. Furthermore, and in order to obtain the King's permission, he did not hesitate to adopt unorthodox parliamentary tactics assuring the King that he was willing to retain as Ministers of Interior, Defence, and Public Security, persons enjoying the absolute confidence of the Crown, in exchange for the Premiership. He also promised not to change the Chief of the Joint Military Staff without the King's permission.[1] The King naively accepted the proposition and what seemed to be Papandreou's capitulation proved, in effect, a shrewd move. He was in a position to bargain for a whole month before Parliament met to elect a Speaker and eventually give a vote of confidence. Papandreou was further assisted by a fortunate event. In the course of his eight years of office Karamanlis had produced a surplus in the budget but was unwilling to use it lest it might create inflationary effects. Apart from the rather doubtful wisdom of the economic policy the fact is that this surplus offered Papandreou a unique opportunity, which he was quick to realise. By initiating considerable public spending, he was able to sway the electorate in his favour. Thus, with his chances of political bargaining considerably reduced, deprived of political initiative, and faced with his opponent's immense power of patronage, Karamanlis decided not to fight, gave up and left Greece after appointing Kanellopoulos as his successor.

The King's decision to ask Papandreou to form a Government, despite the fact that he had only a slight majority which in any event was not in a position to give him a vote of confidence, was not according to the prevailing opinion unconstitutional. However, it was not in absolute conformity with parliamentary rules as applied in Greece. In such cases the Crown is usually advised to wait and see which party elects the Speaker and then appoint its leader as Prime Minister. Otherwise, it can be accused of favouring one party at the expense of the other, and this is precisely what happened.

Papandreou finally resigned and with no alternative Government possible new elections became necessary. These political manoeuvres met with complete success whereas the Crown's plans suffered a grave setback with the sudden death of Venizelos.[2] At the elections the Centre Union obtained a large majority and Papandreou formed his new Government. But Venizelos' death did not save Papandreou from internal strife. He was soon faced with problems within his own party over the question of

[1] The compromise went even further. Papandreou was unable to rely on Communist support in an open ballot when he formed his Government. But he accepted the Communist vote (in a secret ballot) in order to elect the Speaker and gain time.

[2] It must be remembered that the Crown always encouraged Venizelos' ambitions thus undermining Papandreou.

patronage and internal discipline. Once in power the Centre Union devoted considerable time to attacking E.R.E. and its former leader for alleged scandals, accusations which were finally rejected by Parliament. To this E.R.E. reacted by insisting that Papandreou's Government was allowing Communist infiltration in the State mechanism, and also by a series of attacks against the Prime Minister's son for alleged scandals.

In the foreign field Papandreou was confronted with the Cyprus question. The previous agreements had by the end of 1963 broken down and there was serious inter-community trouble which very nearly brought about a Greek–Turkish war in the summer of 1964. The war was finally avoided but Papandreou lost the chance to negotiate a permanent solution on the basis of the so-called Dean Atcheson plan which was never fully published but is believed to have provided a sound basis.

Andreas Papandreou's ambitions proved the final straw to his father's Government. This time he was accused of instigating a revolt in the Army, which became known as the 'Aspida affair'. When his father decided to replace the Minister of Defence who was conducting the inquiries against the 'Aspida' the crisis came to a head.

G. Papandreou's right to dismiss his Minister was legally unquestionable. In our times, a Minister that does not share his chiefs' views can only resign from his post. Otherwise he has to conform with the Prime Minister's opinion. The Minister of Defence thought otherwise and was clearly encouraged in this by the King. Papandreou, on the other hand, remained adamant. He insisted that the Minister of Defence be dismissed and intended to take over this Ministry himself.

Suddenly, and in an unprecedented way, the King addressed three letters in a rather rude tone to his Prime Minister,[1] informing him that he would not give in to his demands until the 'Aspida' inquiries were concluded. It might be inferred that this was because Andreas Papandreou, the Prime Minister's son, was alleged to be involved in the conspiracy and that consequently, if placed at the Ministry of Defence, his father might be eager and furthermore in a position to conceal his son's involvement. Despite the subsequent trial of a small number of rather low-ranking officers, it is practically impossible to pronounce judgement on this very complicated affair which the present Greek Government has officially closed with the granting of amnesty to all those involved.

In any event Papandreou decided to resign despite the fact that a few

[1] There is little doubt that the King exceeded his duties by addressing such letters to his Prime Minister and it is remarkable that Papandreou remained silent in the beginning. Only later, and after Markesinis had criticised the letters in Parliament (*Parliamentary Debates*, 3 August 1965, p. 37), did he react strongly. The exchange of letters between the King and Papandreou was published in the daily press on 16 July 1965.

weeks earlier (25 June 1965) he had asked for and obtained a vote of confidence in the House. Possibly he believed that by resigning he would gain tactical advantages. But his passive attitude would have cost him dearly had it not been for the subsequent mistakes of the Crown. Within a matter of hours, three of his senior Ministers, i.e. the Speaker of the House Mr Novas, retired Rear Admiral J. Toumbas and Mr Costopoulos, formed a new Government, only to arouse suspicions that the whole crisis was prearranged so as to rid the King of Papandreou.[1]

C: THE ROAD TO THE COUP (1965–1967)

The royal initiative can be justified only by the letter of the Constitution and, perhaps, by the seriousness of the situation. What followed, however, soon became a serious deviation from orthodox parliamentary rules.[2]

Theoretically, of course, the King can appoint and dismiss his Ministers. In practice, however, this can happen only under certain circumstances. The right to appoint a minority Ministry is acknowledged by Greek practice regardless of whether this Government can obtain a viable majority in the House. A majority of one is sufficient and indeed practice has shown that Governments with slight majorities can survive for a long time and, furthermore, pass important legislation. But if this Government fails to obtain a vote of confidence, then it must resign or advise a dissolution. Repeated attempts on the part of the Crown to form a Government against the wishes of the parliamentary majority is clearly an abuse of the royal prerogative and here lies the central point of the controversy and the main weakness of all the theories that were devised to support the royal initiative. Papandreou was, no doubt, obliged to resign but, technically speaking, he was not dismissed. Had he refused to resign and obliged the Crown to dismiss him he would have undoubtedly put the King in a very grave position. But he did not and thus gave the King a chance to form another Government. Up to this point the Crown's action was in accord-

---

[1] Both Mr Novas and Mr Toumbas deny that they were involved in any conspiracy against their ex-leader. Nevertheless the speed with which the new Government was sworn in to succeed Papandreou did nothing to displace these suspicions.

[2] Papandreou's best exposition of his arguments can be found in the official edition of the *Crown Council Minutes* (1 and 2 September 1965). A partisan but interesting analysis of events (which, in addition, has been approved by G. Papandreou) can be found in E. Kotsaridas, *The story of the crisis* (1966). The Athens dailies *Vima* and *Avgi* (extreme Left) should also be consulted. For the opposite views one should also consult the *Parliamentary Debates* (especially Kanellopoulos' and Markesinis' speeches), the *Crown Council Minutes* (Kanellopoulos Markesinis, Pipinelis, Athanasiades-Novas and Tsirimokos) and the dailies, *Estia* and *Kathimerini*.

ance with the letter at least of article 31 of the 1952 Constitution. But the fact that the Constitution (according to some)[1] allows the Sovereign complete freedom in appointing a new Government does not mean that he can exercise this power *ad infinitum*. If one took the letter of article 31 to its logical extremes it would suggest that if Stephanopoulos' second attempt to form a Government had failed, the King would have been free to continue appointing minority Prime Ministers for two more years. The irrationality of this proposition is so obvious that it needs no discussion. The conclusion thus seems to be that even if the King is free to appoint whomsoever he wishes as Prime Minister he is not free to exercise these rights over and over again if his nominees fail to obtain the support of the House. But from the moment one admits, as one should, that the Crown cannot persistently defy the wishes of Parliament, a new – this time predominantly political – argument comes into play namely, at what point does the use of the right become an abuse? Whether the King reached this point when appointing Novas, Stephanopoulos, Tsirimokos and Stephanopoulos again, is a matter on which opinions may differ. The fact remains that the right was repeatedly used within a very short period of time and in this respect the royal initiatives were not merely unpolitical – as the events that followed clearly showed – but also unconstitutional.

But the King committed a further mistake by commissioning a senior member of Papandreou's party to form the next Government, clearly a flagrant violation of the principle that the King is above party politics.[2] The Karamanlis precedent could not be repeated for two reasons: first, in 1965 the Monarchy did not have the power it had in 1955 to impose a Prime Minister; and second in Karamanlis' case Papagos was dead, whereas in Mr Novas' case the leader of the party was alive. The King, so to speak, deposed the leader and appointed a member of the party to succeed him. And to complicate matters still further the Papandreou rebels maintained that they represented the Centre Union and that it was Papandreou himself who had violated the party principles.

The critical circumstances, however, and the necessity not to leave the Crown exposed to criticism, obliged the parties of the Right (E.R.E.) to give a vote of confidence and the Progressives to give a simple vote of tolerance[3] for Mr Novas' Government, which nevertheless was defeated in the House. The political crisis entered a new phase.

---

[1] But not all. Professor Manessis for example (*Guarantees of the observance of the Constitution*, II, 417ff.) maintains that the King's rights are severely restricted by article 78 of the Constitution.

[2] Admiral Toumbas accepts this (Toumbas' Unpublished Papers). See also Markesinis, *Parliamentary Debates*, 3 August 1965, p. 39.

[3] Markesinis made it clear that his party gave a vote of tolerance to Mr Novas' Government only in order to assist a quick return to normal life.

By this time Papandreou had become active and was pressing for an immediate dissolution and new elections. Despite desperate efforts to shatter the unity of his party, the great mass of his followers remained loyal to their leader.

There is little doubt that the proper solution would have been a coalition Government or a caretaker Government that would eventually conduct elections and would refer the dispute to the electorate. In either case a dissolution would soon be advised since Parliament had clearly ceased to represent the electorate. Nevertheless, neither of these things happened and Greek political life reached its lowest ebb. Mass efforts were made to break up the Centre Union and attract Markesinis' votes for the new Government formed by Mr Tsirimokos who, only a fortnight earlier, had bitterly attacked Mr Novas for betraying Papandreou and who was now prepared to follow his example. The confusion was further increased by the fact that Tsirimokos, an outspoken opponent of Karamanlis, who had even moved the impeachment procedure against the former leader of E.R.E., now found himself depending on the party that he had accused of fraudulent conduct and which (wrongly) even suspected him of being a communist. His extremely left-wing ideas had always shocked the voters of the Right and yet they were now called upon by the King to support his Government. In addition to all this, the Crown was openly fighting Papandreou and clearly abusing its constitutional rights.[1]

Eventually, and after Tsirimokos' defeat in the House, a Crown Council followed (1, 2 September) during which Markesinis proposed a broad coalition Government under Papandreou. On his refusal, however, to accept the compromise,[2] a narrow coalition Government was formed headed by Mr Stephanopoulos. It survived for nearly sixteen months during which it re-established law and order and kept the growing inflation under some control. But it was too late. The Nation was deeply divided and it was evident that the Centre, already more to the Left than it had been originally, had a good chance of winning the election.

In a sudden but secretly prepared movement, however, Kanellopoulos, Karamanlis' successor to the E.R.E. leadership since 1963, withdrew his support from Stephanopoulos.[3] Once again (since 1955) the Crown had played an active role, intriguing against its own Prime Minister. Only recently did General Taskolotos, whom the King wanted to appoint Prime

---

[1] Later, the Queen Mother told Mr Mitrelias, former President of the Council of State, that the only way to fight a ruthless person (Papandreou) was through an equally ruthless man (implying Tsirimokos). (Mitrelias, Unpublished Papers.)

[2] It is believed that he was pressed by the extremist elements of his party headed by his son, not to accept participation in any form of coalition.

[3] Stephanopoulos, Unpublished Papers.

Minister at that time, reveal the above[1] and confirm Mr Stephanopoulos' allegations. In any event Stephanopoulos was suddenly obliged to resign and a caretaker Government headed by John Paraskeuopoulos was formed which, in turn, soon resigned and Kanellopoulos was sworn in and dissolved the House without appearing before the House. Dissolution was the only and the obvious thing to do. The House had ceased to represent the Nation and it was unable to produce a viable Government. Yet, in the eyes of the people the process that had started in July 1965 with Papandreou's dismissal had now been completed with the ascendancy of E.R.E. to power.[2]

Papandreou's campaign, however, had nothing to fear. His vindication at the polls was expected and Markesinis in a public speech predicted that the elections would never take place. Rumours also predicted a coup by the Generals who would never allow Papandreou to regain power. The King believed that he could always rely on his Generals. What he had not foreseen was that the Colonels would act more swiftly. In the early hours of 21 April, army tanks slipped into Athens and the rule of Parliament, already shaken and outraged, had come to an inglorious end. The Army had once again intervened in Greek politics.

[1] Published in the Athens daily, *Eleftheros Kosmos*, on 17 May 1970.
[2] On this both Mr Stephanopoulos and Mr Toumbas entirely agree.

Chapter 14

A SUMMARY OF THE GREEK
EXPERIENCE

A: GREEK THEORY AND PRACTICE

In the preceding chapters the emphasis was laid on the practice rather than the theory of dissolution in Greece. The more theoretical opinions on dissolution were introduced in the text only when this became necessary in order to understand the actual practice.

As already stated, the relevant article of the constitutional text has scarcely – if at all – changed in the past one hundred and twenty-five years. Indeed, most of the articles defining the constitutional position of the Crown have remained practically unaltered up to the 1968 Constitution.[1] And one must always bear in mind that the 1844 Constitution was drafted as a monarchical document.

True enough, important new clauses[2] were introduced in subsequent Constitutions which provided a sounder democratic basis for the Greek form of government. But these general clauses only indirectly influenced the position of the Crown. It took the remaining part of the nineteenth century and the early twentieth century to shape more clearly the powers and duties of the Crown and this again occurred through conventions and usages rather than legal rules. Thus, for example, no one since 1892 has seriously suggested that the King can dismiss his Prime Minister despite the fact that the letter of the Constitution remained unchanged up to 1968. And this is confirmed by the recent cases of Stephanopoulos (1955) and Papandreou (1965), in both of which the Crown was extremely anxious to obtain, by various means, their resignations, rather than openly dismiss them.[3]

But as far as dissolution is concerned these new and general provisions not only proved insufficient to prevent constitutional crises, but, furthermore, were unable to keep pace with the changing political and social realities of Greek public life.

[1] Above, chapter 9.
[2] As for example arts. 44 and 21 of the 1864 Constitution, repeated by all subsequent texts.
[3] Stephanopoulos, Unpublished Papers. Following Papandreou's resignation the King expressed his delight that the Prime Minister had resigned and that his dismissal was not necessary (Markesinis, Unpublished Papers). This is also confirmed by Admiral Toumbas' Unpublished Papers.

On the whole, Greek constitutional legislators have been proved conservative. This at least seems to be a reasonable conclusion if one judges them from their unwillingness to alter drastically the Constitutions they inherited – an amazing conservatism considering their revolutionary origins. The above, coupled with the rigidity of the constitutional texts, invited, so to speak, new revolutions and offers one explanation why all the constitutions came to a violent end.

A purely theoretical interpretation of the constitutional texts has therefore been deliberately omitted. Such an analysis, apart from being monotonous since the changes relevant to dissolution have not been significant, would also run the risk of being defective mainly by ignoring how the law actually operated in practice. On the other hand, examining the practice of dissolution through the various phases of contemporary Greek constitutional history not only makes the narrative more interesting: it also demonstrates the ineffectiveness of constitutional provisions alone to secure the proper functioning of parliamentary government.

B: THE RIGHTS OF THE CROWN

The letter of the Greek Constitutions has always acknowledged the Crown's right to dissolve Parliament. With the exception, however, of the 1927 Republican Constitution which laid down two serious limitations,[1] the other texts subjected the exercise of the right to a very limited number of basic rules. The restrictions emanating, directly or indirectly, from the texts can be summarised as follows:

(*a*) The Crown has the right to dissolve. The right also belongs to the Regent but not to the Cabinet acting in the absence of the King, according to article 50 of the 1952 Constitution.[2] This contingency, however, never arose in practice.

(*b*) The Crown's right does not constitute a prerogative, in the sense that dissolution is only valid if another State organ countersigns the relevant Decree. Since 1864, it has been the Cabinet that must countersign the Decree. The Royal Decree is nevertheless valid even if only one Minister – usually the Prime Minister – countersigns it, as a result of the doctrine of ministerial responsibility. A Minister who wishes to avoid responsibility can do so only by resigning his post.

(*c*) Dissolution takes the form of a Royal Decree and must be published in the Government Gazette.

---

[1] Above, chapter 11.
[2] Also art. 52 of the 1911 Constitution, art. 52 of the 1864 Constitution.

(*d*) Elections must follow and the new Parliament must meet within a given (short) period of time.

(*e*) No reason for dissolution need be given. Hence the Government can exercise wide discretion on deciding dissolution.

(*f*) The Crown and the Government cannot give dissolution a retroactive effect.

(*g*) The King may dissolve only after being sworn in and after formally undertaking his duties. Similarly, the King cannot dissolve after having abdicated or if, for any reason, he is not performing his functions and a Regent replaces him.

(*h*) Ministers can only participate in the act of dissolution while in office.

Apart from the above principles, the constitutions gave no clues to a number of vital questions. Interpretation and practice filled the gap. It must be added, nevertheless, that Greek constitutional lawyers – unlike their British counterparts – do not place such emphasis on precedents and rarely consider them as binding. Hence the following rules are of relevant value:

(*a*) The Crown must act on the advice of the Prime Minister of the time. The Prime Minister is the only official adviser of the King. Important as this rule is, it is not legally enforceable. Greek kings ignored it as a rule, or underestimated its significance and were thus dragged into frequent political crises of the highest order.

(*b*) If the Government resigns, the Crown has the right to appoint its successor and grant dissolution. In this case, however, the new Ministry must undertake responsibility for the above.

(*c*) The Crown may appoint a minority Government, but in this event the newly sworn-in administration is obliged to seek a vote of confidence and must, if defeated, resign or dissolve. This, however, cannot happen *ad infinitum*, and if it does, as for example in the summer of 1965, it is clearly an abuse of the royal rights and therefore contradicts the spirit of the Constitution and is furthermore politically unwise.

(*d*) It is widely maintained that a series of dissolutions, especially if they are based on the same reasons, are particularly to be condemned. The only time this happened was in 1915.

(*e*) It is generally, though not unanimously accepted that in extreme cases the Crown has the right to refuse a dissolution to a majority Prime Minister. In this event, however, the minority Government that is bound to follow must conform to rule. In practice this does not seem to have occurred.

(*f*) Parliament can be dissolved only after having been properly constituted. In Greece this happens after the election of a Speaker.

If one compares the above general rules with the conclusions drawn at the end of the British chapters,[1] one will immediately realise that the Crown in Greece clung to its nineteenth-century prerogatives far longer than it did in Great Britain and, indeed, in any other European Monarchy. In this sense the Greek Monarchy is the only one in Europe that prolonged well into the twentieth century, as the 1965 crisis demonstrates, its clash with the more democratic elements of society. Similar confrontations took place in the rest of Europe in the nineteenth century.

The outcome of the confrontations of the Crown and its People was, as a rule, unfortunate for the country. Despite its good intentions the Crown was dragged into numerous political crises, as the preceding chapters showed, and never managed to conceal its political sympathies towards various parties and people. The result was that in a period of 137 years one dynasty was deposed; five times (1862, 1917, 1922, 1923, 1967), the Greek kings were obliged to leave their country; ten successful revolutions or coups d'état were staged (1843, 1862, 1909, 1917, 1922, 1925, 1926, 1935, 1936, 1967). Once the King was obliged to stay abroad though remaining technically acting King (1944) and later was obliged to appoint a Regent. Dissolution was exercised forty-eight times.

No simple explanation for the above is valid. Great crises are always caused by more than one factor. But one cannot fail to observe that in all these cases dissolution played, in one way or another, directly or indirectly, an important part.

The main reason seems to be that the King was not merely a figurehead, but an active political factor in Greek public life. With the exception of Denmark, no other European Monarchy offers, in the twentieth century, an example of a dissolution caused by a conflict between Monarch and Parliamentary majority. The last recorded conflict between Crown and Parliament that resulted in a forced dissolution occurred in the United Kingdom in 1834, in Holland in 1853, in Belgium in 1857 and in Denmark in 1920.

A few examples will suffice to prove the accuracy of the above. Three times in Greece since 1864 a strong Government was openly obliged to resign, namely in 1868, 1873 and 1892, and the minority Government that succeeded it had to dissolve as it was unable to form a viable Government.[2] During the twentieth century, twice in 1915, a confrontation between Crown and Government led to a dissolution[3] – and that does not include

---

[1] Above, chapter 7.   [2] Above, chapter 9.   [3] Above, chapter 10.

the numerous post-war interventions of the Crown nor the 1965 crisis which eventually led to the 1967 dissolution and the military coup d'état.[1] What was the result of all these crises and to what extent did Greece suffer? That is for historians to assess; here one can only note that they took place.

C: GREECE AND OTHER EUROPEAN MONARCHIES

How do the reasons for dissolution in Greece compare with those in other European monarchies? Since 1864, for most purposes the starting point of this work, 41 dissolutions took place and were based on the following reasons (on several occasions a dissolution was based on more than one reason)[2]:

Conflict between House and Government	18
Conflict between Crown and Parliament	7
Party politics	10
End of term approaching	7
Dissolution by force (revolution etc.)	4
The House not representing the Nation	3
Other reasons	3
Dissolution *de plein droit*	0
Appeal to the electorate on a special issue	0
Conflict between the two Houses	0

The following general conclusions can be drawn from this analysis:

(*a*) Greece offers examples of forced dissolutions. However, these took place in the twentieth century and during a particularly unstable and transitory period (1922, 1925, 1935, 1936).

(*b*) As we shall see in the final conclusions,[3] dissolution in Europe in the twentieth century has hardly ever been caused by a defeat of the Government in the House. In the United Kingdom for example, the last time this occurred was with the Labour Government in 1924. In Greece this is not so and one can attribute it, among other reasons, to the lack of an organised party system and party discipline. Since 1862, dissolution was caused 18 times by a defeat in the House and the subsequent impossibility of forming a viable Government. These eighteen dissolutions represent nearly half of the total number – clearly a high percentage. Furthermore, of those eighteen, ten dissolutions, practically two-thirds of the total, took place in the twentieth century. Dissolution therefore in this sense seems to represent an element of equilibrium between Executive and Legis-

---

[1] Above, chapter 13.   [2] See Appendix 1.2.   [3] See below, chapter 15.

lative. Furthermore, its threat can be expected to produce results on a disorderly or undecided House. Karamanlis' threat to dissolve Parliament in 1955 seems to offer a good example of the effectiveness of the threat to dissolve.

(c) Can it be argued that dissolution backfires on the government that advises it?

During the nineteenth century (i.e. 1864–1900), out of fifteen dissolutions, the Government won on six occasions and lost on eight (excluding the 1892 dissolution). In the twentieth century, the picture is reversed nine-to-five in favour of the Government. But conclusions cannot be drawn from the above without the risk of being defective. There are various reasons for this. Dissolution was in several cases granted to a very small party and was in itself unable to guarantee electoral victory (i.e. Constantopoulos in 1892, Zaimis in 1899, 1902 etc.). Furthermore, during the last twenty years (1950–70) out of a total of eight elections, six were conducted by a caretaker Government, an element that confuses the issue.[1] However, if one takes the twentieth-century practice as a basis, one conclusion seems reasonably well founded: that dissolution granted to a big, organised party, clearly increases its chances of an electoral victory. Papandreou's 1963 dissolution is a characteristic example.

(d) Dissolution has been caused by party politics ten times – eight times in the twentieth century. In this respect Greece follows the pattern of modern European developments.

One more observation remains to be made. It is obvious that despite the existence of dissolution – and indeed its frequent use – it was impossible to avoid ministerial instability. This statement is, I believe, particularly interesting since the French ministerial instability of the Third and Fourth Republics is frequently attributed to the fact that since 1877 dissolution had fallen into disuse. Does this mean that dissolution after all does not contribute to governmental stability? I do not think so. Though this issue is discussed in the final conclusions a few words can be added here.

France and Greece make difficult subjects of comparison, not least because the former has an elected Head of State, whereas the latter has a hereditary King. It is true of course that neither country was spared

---

[1] Caretaker Governments have been common since the Second World War in an attempt to secure impartial elections and minimise royal interventions. In practice, however, they extended the royal powers by allowing the King complete freedom in choosing the Government. Nor have they always been above suspicion, as the 1961 elections clearly proved. The usefulness of caretaker Governments was discussed by the Special Committee of the Third Constituent Assembly and strongly denied by one of its members, B. Markesinis. *Minutes* (1921), pp. 192ff.

frequent crises. But it would seem that the reasons were different, though in both cases linked with the right to dissolve Parliament.

In the case of France, dissolution fell into disuse after 1877. In the Fourth Republic, it was restricted to such an extent that the conditions under which it could be exercised arose only once (1955) within a period of twelve years. Despite the firm impression of the French legislators that dissolution could effectively contribute to ministerial stability, in practice politicians hesitated to use it. Taking into consideration the French electoral law, which favoured the existence of numerous political parties, one can of course have doubts whether dissolution alone could have solved the French problem. It is difficult, however, to maintain that a number of these crises would not have been avoided if the threat of dissolution had been more effective.

Greece's case is distinctly different. The right to dissolve was clearly abused. Furthermore, in most controversial cases it was used unpolitically.

Dissolution, given to a minority Government (as for example in 1868, 1869, 1872, 1874, 1892, 1915 twice, 1928 etc.), perhaps against the wishes of the majority, can hardly be expected to have beneficial effects. Similarly, dissolution that openly favours a party – as for example in 1915, 1933, 1956, 1963, 1967, etc. – can have equally bad results. Finally, a dissolution that, rightly or wrongly, is interpreted as a means of imposing the Crown's policy on a certain issue – as for example in 1915 or 1967 – is bound to have constitutionally embarrassing effects. All this emphasises what has repeatedly been stated in these chapters: that it is not enough to make sure that dissolution is legally correct; it must also be in accordance with orthodox parliamentary rules and furthermore it must be politically wise.

D: GENERAL COMMENTS

Perhaps two more general conclusions can be drawn from the above. First, irregularity seems to have been the rule rather than the exception in Greek constitutional history. The best proof comes from the history of the constitutions themselves. Not one of them came into force according to the pre-established legal order. They were all products – in one way or another – of power in the broadest sense of the term. They all stemmed from revolutions or coups d'état. It is an undeniable fact that, with the exception of Trikoupis' rules of parliamentary government, all other major constitutional innovations have their ultimate source in revolutions. At this point, however, one is compelled, I believe, to note a basic difference between past and present as expressed in the 1967 military coup and this is that the Government has over-extended its stay in office beyond any precedent.

As far as dissolution is concerned it was exercised in accordance with the letter of the texts, but usually contrary to orthodox parliamentary rules and established procedures. Legal interpretations were influenced by and even at times subordinated to political motives and arguments. This of course is not a uniquely Greek characteristic. In all countries, political motivation or even intrigue was at times involved in constitutional issues. Roy Jenkins, in his biography of Asquith[1] – to quote an example connected with dissolution – tells us how Lord Knollys, the King's Private Secretary, withheld, in what was to be proved the best interest of the state, Mr Balfour's willingness to form a Government in 1910 and thus helped Mr Asquith obtain his dissolution. But this political and even Court intrigue happened in Greece much too often or, to put it in a slightly different way, it happened openly.

It is a fact that no important constitutional crisis can be examined apart from its political background. It seems to me that no lawyer will ever fully understand the crises and their solutions if he overlooks the driving political forces of the times, and this is as true for Greece as it is for the United Kingdom. For perhaps in public law – more so than in the domain of private law – the ultimate solutions to important questions are based on the power of certain political groups to enforce them, rather than on their righteousness, based on abstract political values. There is a limit of course which must be observed – even in politics. There comes a moment when solutions in order to survive must be something more than a mere expression of power. Where this limit lies is not easy to discover and varies from country to country and epoch to epoch. This is why the functioning of parliamentary government depends on the prevailing general conditions and not merely on legal rules. In terms of dissolution this means that an unconstitutional or unpolitical dissolution does not always cause unfortunate and immediate results. But, it sets off a chain of events which usually culminate in an open crisis. In Greece's case, the statement is undoubtedly true.

The second conclusion is connected with the position of the Greek monarchy, vis-à-vis its people. Its attitude towards dissolution was not, as a whole, satisfactory, to say the least. Excluding dissolution arising from the approaching end of the term of Parliament, only a small minority of the remaining dissolutions were truly above criticism. The unfortunate results the dissolution crises provoked demonstrate that it is not enough for a dissolution to conform with the letter of the text alone.

[1] *Asquith*, p. 245.

Greek kings had far too often a personal policy which they wished to impose on a reluctant majority. Of course, no one would wish to deny Otho's integrity and romantic ideals; George I's shrewdness and realism; Constantine I's courage, or George II's quiet and wise character. Nor does anyone blame the Crown alone for all the crises. Undoubtedly the absence of an organised social and political structure, particularly in the nineteenth century, favoured an unstable development. But the Crown rarely used its powers to forestall crises. Its numerous interventions – at least as far as dissolution is concerned – and its continuous attempts to govern and not to reign, only aggravated and complicated the situation. As a Greek historian observed:

The letter of the Greek Constitutions gives the Crown a series of rights which, if actually practised, would transform the government from a crowned democracy to a constitutional monarchy. It is amazing that the Greek dynasty though of Danish origin never understood the way royalty functions in northern Europe and . . instead chose to adopt a Balkan version.[1]

From the above it seems logical to assume that dissolution has failed to fulfil its institutional purposes. Its misuse or abuse was the rule rather than the exception. It remains to be seen whether the unfortunate past will impair the future of the institution.

[1] S. Markesinis, *Political history*, IV, 109.

PART IV

Chapter 15

THE TRANSFORMATION OF THE
INSTITUTION (CONCLUSIONS)

The exercise of the right to dissolve Parliament still makes the headlines. In 1958 M. Debré, then Minister of Justice and responsible for the drafting of the new French Constitution, described it as 'l'arme capitale de tout régime parlementaire';[1] in 1968 it was included in the new Greek Constitution and in 1969 the circumstances under which dissolution should be exercised were widely debated by the correspondents of *The Times*,[2] a debate which revealed a wide difference of opinion. Dissolution may still be in theory the 'idée maîtresse'[3] of parliamentarism; in reality it has lost much of its original justification.

For classical parliamentary government, dissolution was an essential device since it secured in the constitutional field the balance of power which had been achieved in the social and political arena between Crown, aristocracy and the middle class. Thus, an unworkable Parliament always ran the risk of being dissolved, and in order to avoid the exercise of the right by a vindictive Government, the consent of the Sovereign (or another State organ such as the Senate in France in 1875 or in Greece in 1927) was required. But as we saw earlier in this book,[4] this rather precarious balance was destroyed by the introduction of universal suffrage. In actual fact it is worth remembering that parliamentarism was introduced in most European countries between 1831 and 1917 and, more precisely: 1830 in France; 1831 in Belgium; 1848 in Holland; 1868 in Luxembourg; 1875 in Greece; 1884 in Norway; 1901 in Denmark and 1917 in Sweden. On the other hand, democracy based on universal (male) suffrage came later and indeed in certain countries much later: 1848 for France; 1919 for Belgium; 1917 for Holland; 1919 for Luxembourg; 1898 for Norway; 1901 for Denmark. It is only in the case of Greece (1864) and Sweden (1909) that universal suffrage was introduced before parliamentary government began to operate.

---

[1] 'La nouvelle constitution', *Revue française de science politique* (1958), p. 22.
[2] See Appendix 4.
[3] Duguit, *Traité de droit constitutionnel*, II, 824.   [4] Above, chapter 2.

Universal suffrage resulted in the radical transformation of parliamentary government and completely altered the justification for many of its institutions. Yet, paradoxically, these changes were not reflected in the various constitutional texts until much later. (In theory the 1946 French Constitution corresponds best to this new type of democratic parliamentarism; in practice it developed serious defects.) The institutional framework thus survived these great political and social changes practically untouched and consequently dissolution remained intact in the various constitutional texts and even acquired greater prominence in several post-World War One constitutions; in France it was even looked upon as a panacea that would solve the country's political difficulties. But dissolution had to be reconciled with the novel concept of a Parliament deriving its strength directly from the electorate. Challenging a popularly elected Parliament was indirectly defying the electorate. So an ingenious but impracticable formula was found. Whenever the two functions of the State (Government and Parliament) were at a deadlock the electorate was asked to arbitrate. In the words of the French Prime Minister Waldeck-Rousseau, 'la faculté de dissolution, inscrite dans la constitution, n'est point pour le suffrage universel une menace, mais une sauvegarde. Elle est le contrepoids essentiel aux excès du parlementarisme, et c'est par elle que s'affirme le caractère démocratique de nos institutions.'[1]

The solution sounded attractive and even convincing on paper but in practice reconciliation was not as easy as that. For example, it was not clear what exactly arbitration was to produce. Presumably, the electorate was to decide between the appellant (King or Government) and the respondent (Parliament). However, no matter what the verdict was the (theoretical) balance between Executive and Legislative was destroyed. The Executive that dissolved Parliament frequently saw its opponents returned with greater strength and, as a result, saw its own power diminish further. Similarly, the Parliament which by defeating the Government of the day had forced an election often saw the defeated Government returned to power with a larger number of supporters. And finally there were times (as for example in the United Kingdom in 1910) when the electorate refused (or was unable) to arbitrate in a constructive manner and returned the political parties with substantially the same number of supporters in Parliament, and the political situation was back to square one. Arbitration was thus consciously or subconsciously linked with the concept of balance of powers, and dissolution regarded as a re-equilibrating device.

But this equilibrium had ceased to exist and could not be artificially

[1] Quoted by Duguit, *Traité de droit constitutionnel*, II, 811.

created. Two examples from Greek practice illustrate the difficulties involved.[1] In 1915 two dissolutions strengthened rather than weakened Parliament, and the King, who had dissolved in an attempt to obtain a more docile House, was eventually obliged to leave the country. Fifty years later a Greek King found himself once again in conflict with the parliamentary majority. This time, however, dissolution was persistently avoided and instead a series of acrobatic and constitutionally doubtful manoeuvres followed in an attempt to resolve the crisis. Dissolution in the first case did not, and in the second case was not expected, to produce a differently constituted Parliament. These cases prove that the electorate's arbitration which follows a dissolution does not necessarily lead to a re-equilibration of the forces in Parliament. Countries which thus believed in or enjoyed some degree of balance of powers could no longer expect dissolution to guarantee this equilibrium.

Then, there was another group of countries, notably France during the Third Republic, in which universal suffrage enhanced the position of Parliament to such an extent that as a result dissolution atrophied and the House was left free to make and unmake ministries with complete impunity. At this stage one may suggest that whatever the purpose of dissolution (arbitration or re-equilibration or both) the one thing the right to dissolve Parliament could provide is an effective threat against Parliament's excessive use of ministerial responsibility. This view was certainly held by many French authors and politicians of the Third Republic who believed that, if dissolution had been practised, it could have prevented the political chaos that prevailed. The remedy is hypothetical and hence its effectiveness cannot be judged. But if one draws a parallel with the Greek practice the argument is only partially convincing. Both countries suffered from notorious ministerial instability and both countries had more than two parties competing for office. But though Greek Governments frequently used dissolution, in most cases they met with little success. Belgium too has a long history as regards dissolution but there also ministerial instability was not avoided. It is indeed difficult to see what dissolution alone could have done to combat this instability at a time when the electoral system encouraged deep divisions and the existence of numerous parties. It was the inevitable price these countries paid for attempting to secure a fairer representation of the electorate in Parliament.

Finally, in countries such as the United Kingdom, where the Government was politically no longer on a level with Parliament, dissolution could not re-establish an equilibrium that had ceased to exist. From the end of the nineteenth century a defeat of the Government in the United

[1] Above, chapters 10 and 13.

Kingdom became extremely unlikely and consequently: 'while the doctrine of collective ministerial responsibility remains unchanged, its practical importance has been greatly reduced'.[1] Dissolution thus ceased to be the counter-weapon to Parliament's right to demand the resignation of the Government, simply because in the course of time Parliament was deprived of this right. Similarly, dissolution was no longer expected to provide the means of solving a dispute between Government and Parliament since the political party mechanism ensured that no such disputes arose between parliamentary majority and Government. The result of this transformation is obvious. Rather than counterbalancing ministerial responsibility, dissolution provides the party in office with a weapon which can be used both in order to foster internal unity and as a means of solving a dispute with the Opposition (not Parliament as a whole) at a time most convenient to the governing party. Even in Belgium, where parliamentary defeats have been far more frequent than they have been in the United Kingdom, for over a century dissolution has not been pronounced immediately after a defeat of the Government in Parliament.

The outcome of the changes described in outline in the previous paragraphs is that in countries such as the United Kingdom, Belgium and Greece, dissolution has played an active and frequently controversial part but not as the balancing device which nineteenth-century parliamentarism had known.[2] On the contrary it has assumed a variety of roles and purposes, four of which deserve special mention mainly because they illustrate the flexibility of the institution: (*i*) Dissolution is advised in view of the approaching end of the statutory term of Parliament. (*ii*) An appeal to the electorate is made on the grounds that Parliament has ceased to represent the electorate. (*iii*) Dissolution is advised in lieu of a referendum.

This last topic has been the subject of frequent discussions during the recent Common Market negotiations in the United Kingdom. The Labour Opposition in particular, eager no doubt to force an early election, argued strongly in favour of a dissolution in order to give the electorate a chance to decide on British membership of the E.E.C.; it was rebutted by the Conservative Government which relied on the old and more or less generally accepted argument that a referendum (or a referendal procedure) is inconsistent with the traditional form of parliamentarism. Whatever the pros and cons of the respective views, one has to be aware of the fact that a dissolution in lieu of a referendum presents a number of problems. For one thing, the elections which will follow will almost certainly be

---

[1] A. H. Birch, *Representative and responsible government* (1969), p. 137. Birch adds: 'It is clear that the doctrine...does not occupy the place in the present political system that is commonly claimed for it.'   [2] See Appendices 1.4, 1.5.

fought over a variety of issues and consequently the verdict as to the particular issue that caused the dissolution will be vague and probably unsatisfactory.

(*iv*) Finally, and probably most important, dissolution became a party weapon and entered upon a new and vigorous phase of its history. Its threat kept the party in office united, and its exercise was meant to strike a blow at the Opposition and make its position even worse. If the electorate did exercise a re-equilibration it was no longer between Government and Parliament as a whole, but between government majority and parliamentary opposition. Liberated from its past to varying degrees in different countries, dissolution was transformed into an effective party weapon subject to little or no control.

To conclude, it is also interesting to note that in most European countries, not only have the above four developments almost completely replaced the original purpose of dissolution, but their relative importance has also varied from time to time. In Belgium, for example, most of the dissolutions of the second half of the nineteenth century and up to the First World War were advised because it was believed that Parliament had ceased to represent the electorate. Even more striking and significant is the fact that while during the early and middle half of the nineteenth century parliamentary defeat was the main reason for dissolution, dissolution is nowadays almost invariably caused by party politics of one kind or another.

If the above brief survey is, as it is submitted to be, correct it is difficult to ascribe to dissolution any specific institutional purpose. Nor can it be described as an essential institution to the twentieth-century concept of parliamentarism. Norway, to give one example, has undoubtedly enjoyed a parliamentary form of government and yet never had any use for dissolution. Dissolution may well be an important party weapon, but as it is currently exercised it can hardly be argued that it performs an institutional function. For those who refer to parliamentarism with the nineteenth-century concept in mind this is bound to come as a shock. But the evolution of parliamentarism can be better understood through a political and sociological (rather than strictly legal) approach.[1] And if this method is followed it is easy to understand how its various mechanisms and institutions became atrophied or had their purposes re-adapted in accordance with the changes of society.

In countries then such as the above, the question is not – as is often argued – whether the King can refuse his Prime Minister's advice or,

[1] For a brief but excellent analysis, see G. Burdeau, *Droit constitutionnel et institutions politiques* (1969), pp. 142–54.

which is even more doubtful, dissolve against the wishes of his own Prime Minister. For all practical purposes he cannot. Experience has shown that in the few remaining European monarchies the Sovereign has been stripped of most, if not all, of his previous powers. And where the King defied this change – as he did in Greece – the monarchy and the country ended up in serious trouble. In a sense, it is therefore strange that the debate in the national press in England in 1969 was restricted to that particular question. The various correspondents (including some well-known authorities), when giving their opinions, were undoubtedly aware of the recent increase of prime-ministerial power. Yet, they had very little to say about the need to control these powers. Broadly speaking, they seemed satisfied with the existing controls and safeguards.[1] The first and the most widely accepted safeguard is the Crown's legal right to refuse a dissolution.[2] But this is historically out-dated and, as the previous chapters have shown, dangerous, in so far as it drags the Crown into the centre of political strife. The second safeguard (indirectly suggested by only a few writers) was that the decision to dissolve is effectively taken by the Cabinet and hence there is little danger of uncontrolled personal power. But this argument is misleading as well as unconvincing. It is misleading because it creates the false impression that dissolution is a prerogative exercised on the advice of the Cabinet and not the Prime Minister and this has not been the case for over fifty years now. It is unconvincing because it seems to rely on the rather peculiar assumption that while the Prime Minister appears personally unscrupulous (to the extent of advising a dissolution against his own party), his Cabinet colleagues are the vigilant protectors of minority rights and will consequently prevent him from advising an unfair dissolution. But even if this were so, the safeguard disappears whenever the Cabinet (or a majority within it) backs its leader (as it most frequently does) in his decision to dissolve in order to surprise and harass the Opposition. This is the case *par excellence* where dissolution is being used as a party weapon and for party reasons, and consequently requires the closest scrutiny as it is under these circumstances that dissolution can be used to prolong the party's term in office. It can thus be argued that the real problem nowadays is whether or not the Prime Minister (or the Cabinet) should be allowed to use such a weapon with little or no control, and, for the time being, no satisfactory solution seems to have been suggested.

Summarising the experience of most European countries one would probably be able to place them into one of two main categories. In the

---

[1] See Appendix 4.

[2] Thus, see Jennings, *The British Constitution* (1966), p. 118.

first, which includes, among other countries, France and the Scandinavian states, dissolution has atrophied. As a rule it takes place towards the end of the statutory term of Parliament and under these circumstances constitutional problems can rarely if ever arise. One could, perhaps, proceed a step further and praise this state of affairs but this, in effect, would mean arguing the case for fixed Parliaments. In any event, in these countries dissolution seems to have no 'present', let alone a 'future'. In the second category of European countries, in which the United Kingdom, Greece and Belgium must be placed, dissolution is frequently exercised, often under controversial circumstances. Naturally, of course, important differences exist between these countries. For example, the exercise of the right to dissolve Parliament has been criticised in the United Kingdom but no one can claim that it has been abused. The position in Greece is the reverse, and it has been shown that some of the dissolutions left very deep scars. But despite these differences there exist certain common features. Apart from the frequency of the use of the right, which has already been mentioned, all three countries show one common trend, namely, that political motives are increasingly determining the use and timing of the right to dissolve Parliament. However useful or even necessary a politically motivated dissolution may appear to political parties, it can hardly be argued that under these circumstances it performs an institutionally essential task. To put it in another way: if one were drafting a constitution for a new State in which conditions such as the above prevailed, one would not feel compelled to include dissolution in the constitutional text. One wonders, however, whether the right to dissolve Parliament could be provided with a constitutionally more essential part to play.

The possible answer may become more obvious if, once again, the problem is examined against its proper background: the present state of the parliamentary form of government. Opinions may, of course, differ as to the extent of the present crisis of parliamentary government, but few, in fact, would deny that it is currently going through a critical transitional phase. The extension of the franchise inevitably contributed to the increase of State activity as the Government of the day tried to satisfy the needs of ever-increasing sections of the community. The conception of the true sphere of governmental activity was thus radically transformed and the modern State now regulates much of the daily activities of mankind. The judicial control of the administrative action grew as the Courts, with varying degrees of success,[1] addressed themselves to this task. But the

---

[1] See, for example, Professor C. J. Hamson's comments on the efficacy of the British system of administrative justice compared with the work of the French Conseil d'Etat (*Executive discretion and judicial control*, p. 16); and B. Chapman's *British government observed* (1963).

general political control of the Government, traditionally entrusted to Parliament, did not keep pace with this change and at times was even weakened. Parliament became increasingly subordinate to the Government, at least in so far as matters of general policy were concerned. In most countries the legislative initiative has, for some time now, passed almost exclusively into the hands of the Government and the possibility of a governmental defeat becomes more and more unlikely as the modern political parties consolidate their grip over their members. In 1966 the Leader of the House of Commons told his colleagues that the House had 'surrendered most of its effective powers to the Executive',[1] and not a single member was willing to contradict him. Paradoxically, perhaps, the quest for greater social and economic equality has resulted in the curtailment of some of the older liberties. To many lawyers and political scientists Parliament is little more than a forum of publicity for political discussion.[2] Under these circumstances there seems to be little room for dissolution.

The crisis of modern parliamentary democracy cannot be discussed here. A number of changes, such as an increase in decentralisation and local government, a combination of political and specialist Ministers in the Cabinet and even a directly elected Prime Minister, have been suggested as possible remedies. As far as dissolution is concerned, one could envisage the institution as a means of providing protection for the parliamentary minority and not as a weapon against it.

One of the great problems of modern democracy is that the rights of the electorate are exercised only every four or five years, thus giving the Government a free hand for the interim period. And an intelligent Government can usually find political ways of extending its period in office even further.[3] Thus the Government can pass legislation at the end of its term relying on what one could call 'stale popular support'. In days gone by the Crown could dissolve Parliament if it believed that it had ceased to represent the Nation. The system failed because the power was exercised in an arbitrary manner and because the exercise of the right always endangered the position of the Crown by bringing it into the centre of political controversy. But the idea behind it could prove useful if

---

' We do not have a developed system of administrative law – perhaps because until fairly recently we did not need it. . .' per Lord Reid in *Ridge* v. *Baldwin* [1964] A.C. 40.

[1] *Parliamentary Debates*, 5th series, DCCXXXVIII, 479.

[2] Crick, *The reform of parliament*, p. 27. For a general survey of the functions of the House of Commons see also R. Butt, *The power of parliament* (1967); and *Parliament: a survey* (a volume including contributions from various authors) (1952).

[3] 'Parliament need not prolong its own life. We have nearly reached the stage when the polls plus the prerogative in the hands of the Premier can do it for them': Q. Hogg, *New charter*.

it were adapted to modern conditions and realities. For instance dissolution could be demanded by a large number of M.P.s, say 45%, who could thus challenge the Government's right to continue to govern. To avoid abuses one could add numerous limitations. For example, one could demand that such a decision could be taken only by two consecutive votes at a month's interval, or only if a series of by-election results showed a significant change in public opinion; or that it could not be taken during the first two years of Parliament; or finally that M.P.s who signed such a petition should also simultaneously agree who the next Prime Minister should be if the recommendation was adopted in the ensuing elections. This last proposal, however, is of little value to two-party countries. But then it must be remembered that, with the exception of the United Kingdom and possibly West Germany, the other European countries have more than one, and often five or six parties fighting for office and, as a result, though it is relatively easy to defeat the Government, it is frequently impossible to agree on its successor.

As stated, however, the purpose of this book is not to examine or criticise the whole system of government. The above general ideas were included merely to illustrate the varying and always important role dissolution has played in the evolution of the parliamentary form of government, and the English and Greek theory and practice confirm this. Whether it will continue to do so in the future still remains to be seen.

APPENDICES

APPENDIX 1

List of dissolutions and Prime Ministers

Reasons for dissolution

1. Dissolution *de plein droit*
2. Conflicts between the two Houses
3. End of term approaching
4. Conflict between House and Government (governmental instability, impossibility to form a viable government for any reason etc.)
5. Conflict between King and parliamentary majority
6. The House does not represent the electorate
   (*a*) Change of public opinion (by-elections), electoral law, etc.
   (*b*) New territories not represented
7. Party politics
8. Appeal to the electorate on a special issue
9. Dissolution by force (revolution, coup d'état etc.)
10. Other reasons, including foreign policy, end of revisional or constituent task etc.)

1.1 *Dissolution in the United Kingdom (1867–1970)*

No.	Dissolution date	Election date	Prime Minister	Result	Reason
1	31 July 1868	11 Nov. 1868	B. Disraeli	lost	4, 8
2	26 Jan. 1874	Feb. 1874	W. E. Gladstone	lost	6*a*
3	24 Mar. 1880	3 Apr. 1880	B. Disraeli	lost	7, 3
4	11 Nov. 1885	23 Nov. 1885	Lord Salisbury	lost	6
5	27 June 1886	July 1886	W. E. Gladstone	lost	4, 8
6	28 June 1892	July 1892	Lord Salisbury	won	3
7	8 July 1895	July 1895	Lord Salisbury	won	4
8	17 Sept. 1900	28 Sept.–20 Oct. 1900	Lord Salisbury	won	7, 8
9	8 Jan. 1906	12 Jan.–9 Feb. 1906	H. Campbell-Bannerman	won	3, 4
10	10 Jan. 1910	14 Jan–9 Feb. 1910	H. Asquith	won	2
11	28 Nov. 1910	2 Dec.–19 Dec. 1910	H. Asquith	won	2, 8
12	25 Nov. 1918	14 Dec. 1918	D. Lloyd George	won	7
13	24 Oct. 1922	15 Nov. 1922	A. Bonar Law	won	6, 7
14	26 Oct. 1923	6 Dec. 1923	S. Baldwin	lost	7, 8
15	9 Oct. 1924	29 Oct. 1924	R. MacDonald	lost	4
16	10 May 1929	30 May 1929	S. Baldwin	lost	3

1.1 *(cont.)*

No.	Dissolution date	Election date	Prime Minister	Result	Reason
17	7 Oct. 1931	27 Oct. 1931	R. MacDonald (Nat. Gov.)	won	8
18	25 Oct. 1935	14 Nov. 1935	S. Baldwin	won	10, 8, 7
19	15 June 1945	5 July 1945	Sir W. Churchill	lost	7, 3, 6a
20	7 Jan. 1950	23 Feb. 1950	C. Attlee	won	3
21	5 Oct. 1951	25 Oct. 1951	C. Attlee	lost	7
22	6 May 1955	26 May 1955	Sir A. Eden	won	7
23	18 Sept. 1959	8 Oct. 1959	H. Macmillan	won	7
24	25 Sept. 1964	15 Oct. 1964	Sir A. Douglas Home	lost	3, 7
25	10 Mar. 1966	31 Mar. 1966	H. Wilson	won	7
26	29 May 1970	18 June 1970	H. Wilson	lost	7

1.2 *Dissolution in Greece (1844–1970)*

No.	Dissolution date	Election date	Prime Minister	Result	Reason
		October 1843 (Elections for 1st National Assembly)	A. Metaxas	—	—
1		1844	A. Mavrokordatos	lost	10
2	14 Apr./26 Apr. 1847	14 June/26 June 1847	J. Kolettis	won	4, 7, 3
3	9 Sept./21 Sept. 1850	30 Oct./11 Nov. 1850*	A. Kriezis	won	3
4	23 Sept./5 Oct. 1853	30 Oct./11 Nov. 1853*	A. Kriezis	won	3
5	5 Oct/17 Oct. 1856	30 Oct./11 Nov. 1856*	D. Voulgaris	won	3
6	24 May/5 June 1859	July 1859	Ath. Miaoulis	won	3
7	16 Nov./28 Nov. 1860	16 Jan./28 Jan. 1861	Ath. Miaoulis	won	5
8		24 Nov./6 Dec. 1862 (Elections for 2nd Nat. Assembly)			
		May 1865	A. Koumoundouros	lost	10
9	26 Jan./7 Feb. 1868	21 Mar./2 Apr. 1868	D. Voulgaris	won	5, 4
10	17 Mar./29 Mar. 1869	16 May/28 May 1869	Th. Zaimis	won	5, 4
11	27 Dec. 1871/ 8 Jan. 1872	26 Feb./10 Mar. 1872	D. Voulgaris	won	4
12	28 Nov./10 Dec. 1872	27 Jan./8 Feb. 1873	E. Deligeorgis	lost	5, 4
13	25 Apr./7 May 1874	23 June/5 July 1874	D. Voulgaris	won	4
14	19 May/31 May 1875	18 July/30 July 1875	Ch. Trikoupis	lost	4

* Date of convocation of Parliament. For the first two elections it is often impossible to quote precise election dates due to the peculiarities of the electoral system.

1.2 (cont.)

No.	Dissolution date	Election date	Prime Minister	Result	Reason
15	25 July/6 Aug. 1879	23 Sept./5 Oct. 1879	A. Koumoundouros	won	3
16	22 Oct./3 Nov. 1881	20 Dec. 1881/ 1 Jan. 1882	A. Koumoundouros	lost	6b
17	11 Feb./23 Feb. 1885	7 Apr./19 Apr. 1885	Ch. Trikoupis	lost	7
18	6 Dec./18 Dec. 1886	4 Jan./16 Jan. 1887	Ch. Trikoupis	won	4
19	17 Aug./29 Aug. 1890	14 Oct./26 Oct. 1890	Ch. Trikoupis	lost	7
20	12 Mar./24 Mar. 1892	3 May/15 May 1892	C. Konstantopoulos	lost	5
21	20 Feb./4 Mar. 1895	16 Apr./28 Apr. 1895	N. Deliyannis	—	4
22	9 Dec./21 Dec. 1898	7 Feb./19 Feb. 1899	A. Zaimis	lost	3
23	19 Sept./2 Oct. 1902	17 Nov./30 Nov. 1902	A. Zaimis	lost	4
24	22 Dec. 1904/ 4 Jan. 1905	20 Feb./5 Mar. 1905	Th. Deliyannis	won	4
25	1 Feb./14 Feb. 1906	26 Mar./8 Apr. 1906	G. Theotokis	won	4
26	30 June/13 July 1910	8 Aug./21 Aug. 1910	S. Dragoumis	—	10, 3
27	12 Oct./25 Oct. 1910	28 Nov./11 Dec. 1910 (Opposition abstained)	E. Venizelos	won	4
28	20 Dec. 1911/ 1 Jan. 1912	11 Mar./24 Mar. 1912	E. Venizelos	won	10
29	18 Apr./1 May 1915	31 May/13 June 1915	D. Gounaris	lost	5, 4
30	29 Oct./11 Nov. 1915	6 Dec./19 Dec. 1915 (Liberals abstained)	S. Skouloudes	lost	4
31	10 Sept./23 Sept. 1920	1 Nov./14 Nov. 1920	E. Venizelos	lost	3
32	11 Sept./24 Sept. 1922, Revolution: Parliament dissolved 16 Dec. 1923		S. Gonatas	—	9
33	30 September 1925, General Pangalos dissolves by force 7 Nov. 1926		G. Kondylis	—	—
34	6 July 1928	19 Aug. 1928	E. Venizelos	won	7
35	19 Aug. 1932	25 Sept. 1932	E. Venizelos	won	3
36	24 Jan. 1933	5 Mar. 1933	E. Venizelos	lost	7
37	1 Apr. 1935	2 June 1935 (Liberals abstained)	P. Tsaldaris	won	(resulted from the 1935 coup)
38	17 Dec. 1935	26 Jan. 1936	C. Demertzis	—	6a
39	4 August 1936, Metaxas' coup d'état: Parliament dissolved 31 Mar. 1946 (Communists abstained)		Th. Sophoulis	lost	9 —
40	8 Jan. 1950	5 Mar. 1950	J. Theotokis	—	3, 7
41	30 July 1951	9 Sept. 1951	S. Venizelos	lost	7
42	10 Oct. 1952	16 Nov. 1952	D. Kioussopoulos	—	7

No.	Dissolution date	Election date	Prime Minister	Result	Reason
43	11 Jan. 1956	19 Feb. 1956	C. Karamanlis	won	3, 7
44	29 Mar. 1958	11 May 1958	C. Georga-kopoulos	—	4
45	20 Sept. 1961	29 Oct. 1961	C. Dovas	—	7
46	26 Sept. 1963	3 Nov. 1963	S. Mauromi-chalis	—	5, 4, 6a
47	8 Jan. 1964	16 Feb. 1964	J. Paraskevo-poulos	—	4
48	14 Apr. 1967	(19 May 1967)	P. Kanello-poulos	—	5, 4, 7

21 April 1967, Military Revolution
(Elections postponed indefinitely)

1.3 *Dissolution in Belgium (1850–1970)*

No.	Dissolution date	Election date	Prime Minister	Reason
1	4 Sept. 1851	27 Sept. 1851	C. Rogier	4
2	12 Nov. 1857	10 Dec. 1857	C. Rogier	5
3	16 July 1864	11 Aug. 1864	C. Rogier	4
4	8 July 1870	2 Aug. 1870	J. d'Anethan	6a
5	17 June 1884	8 July 1884	J. Malou	6a
6	23 May 1892	14 June 1892	A. Beernaert	1
7	19 Sept. 1894	14 Oct. 1894	J. de Burlet	6a
8	7 May 1900	27 May 1900	P. de Smet Maeyer	6a
9	13 May 1912	2 June 1912	C. de Broqueville	6a, 7
10	22 Oct. 1919	16 Nov. 1919	G. Cooreman	1
11	1921	20 Nov. 1921	H. Carton de Wiart	6a, 7
12	6 Mar. 1925	5 Apr. 1925	G. Thennis	7
13	1929	26 May 1929	H. Jasper	3
14	28 Oct. 1932	27 Nov. 1932	C. de Broqueville	7
15	16 Apr. 1936	24 May 1936	P. van Zeeland	3, 7
16	6 Mar. 1939	2 Apr. 1939	Pierlot	4, 7
17	9 Jan. 1946	17 Feb. 1946	Van Acker Charbon	4, 7
18	19 May 1949	26 June 1949	P. H. Spaak	4, 7
19	29 Apr. 1950	4 June 1950	G. Eyskens	4, 7
20	12 Mar. 1954	11 Apr. 1954	Van Houtte	3, 1
21	1958	1 June 1958	Van Acker Charbon	3, 1
22	20 Feb. 1961	26 Mar. 1961	G. Eyskens	8, 7
23	1965	23 May 1965	Th. Lefevre	3, 1
24	1 May 1968	31 Mar. 1968	P. van de Boeynants	3

1.4 *Reasons of dissolution in the United Kingdom, Greece and Belgium*

No.	Reasons	U.K. 1868–1970	Greece 1844–1970	Belgium 1850–1970	Total 19th cent.	20th cent.	Grand total
1	Dissolution *de plein droit*	—	—	5	1	4	5
2	Conflict between the two Houses	2	—	—	—	—	2
3	End of term approaching	7	12	6	9	16	25
4	Conflict between House and Government (governmental instability etc.)	5	19	6	14	16	30
5	Conflict between Crown and Parliament	—	8	1	5	4	9
6	The House does not represent the electorate	4	3	6	7	6	13
7	Party politics	13	11	10	4	30	34
8	Appeal to the electorate on a special issue	7	—	1	—	8	8
9	Dissolution by force	—	3	—	—	3	3
10	Other reasons	—	4	—	2	2	4

1.5 *The changing purposes of dissolution in the nineteenth and twentieth centuries*

No.	Reason of dissolution	U.K. 19th cent.	U.K. 20th cent.	Greece 19th cent.	Greece 20th cent.	Belgium 19th cent.	Belgium 20th cent.
1	Dissolution *de plein droit*	—	—	—	—	1	4
2	Conflict between the two Houses	—	2	—	—	—	—
3	End of term approaching	2	5	7	5	—	6
4	Conflict between House and Government (governmental instability etc.)	3	2	9	10	2	4
5	Conflict between Crown and Parliament	—	—	5	3	1	—
6	The House does not represent the electorate	2	2	1	2	2	3
7	Party politics	1	12	3	8	—	10
8	Appeal to the electorate on a special issue	2	7	—	—	—	1
9	Dissolution by force	—	—	—	3	—	—
10	Other reasons	—	—	2	2	—	—

1.6   *Prime Ministers and number of dissolutions obtained*

United Kingdom 1868–1970	Greece 1844–1970	Belgium 1846–1970
Lord Salisbury 4	E. Venizelos 6	C. Rogier 3
S. Baldwin 3	Ch. Trikoupis 4	G. Eyskens 2
B. Disraeli 2	D. Voulgaris..........4	C. de Broqueville 2
W. E. Gladstone 2	A. Koumoundouros ...3	Van Acker Charbon ..2
H. Asquith...........2	A. Kriezis 2	J. d'Anethan..........1
R. MacDonald 2	A. Zaimis 1	J. Malou 1
C. Attlee.............2	A. Metaxas 1	A. Beernaert..........1
H. Campbell-	A. Mavrokordatos 1	J. de Burlet 1
Bannerman 1	J. Kolettis 1	P. de Smet Maeyer....1
D. Lloyd George 1	Ath. Miaoulis 2	G. Cooreman 1
A. Bonar Law 1	Th. Zaimis 1	H. Carton de Wiart ...1
Sir W. Churchill 1	E. Deligeorgis 1	G. Thennis 1
Sir A. Eden 1	C. Konstantopoulos ...1	H. Jasper 1
H. Macmillan 1	Th. Deliyannis........1	P. van Zeeland........1
Sir Alec Douglas	S. Dragoumis 1	P. H. Spaak 1
Home.............1	D. Gounaris 1	Van Houtte 1
H. Wilson 2	S. Skouloudis 1	T. Lefevre............1
	N. Plastiras 1	P. van den
Total 26	Th. Pangalos 1	Boyenants..........1
	P. Tsaldaris 1	
	J. Metaxas 1	Total 24
	J. Theotokis 1	
	S. Venizelos 1	
	C. Karamanlis 1	
	P. Kanellopoulos......1	
	Total 41	

1.7   *British Prime Ministers (1900–1970)*

Marquess of Salisbury	– 1900 – 11 July 1902	C
A. Balfour	12 July 1902 – 4 Dec. 1905	C
Sir Henry Campbell-		
Bannerman	5 Dec. 1905 – 5 Apr. 1908	L
H. Asquith	5 Apr. 1908 – 25 May 1915	L
H. Asquith	25 May 1915 – 5 Dec. 1915	Coal. Gov.
D. Lloyd George..............	6 Dec. 1915 – 19 Oct. 1922	Coal. Gov.
A. Bonar Law	23 Oct. 1922 – 20 May 1923	C
S. Baldwin	22 May 1923 – 22 Jan. 1924	C
J. R. MacDonald..............	22 Jan. 1924 – 3 Nov. 1924	Lab.
S. Baldwin	4 Nov. 1924 – 4 June 1929	C

1.7 (cont.)

J. R. MacDonald	5 June 1929 – 24 Aug. 1931	Lab.
J. R. MacDonald	24 Aug. 1931 – 7 June 1935	Nat. Gov.
S. Baldwin	7 June 1935 – 28 May 1937	Nat. Gov.
N. Chamberlain	28 May 1937 – 10 May 1940	Nat. Gov.
Sir Winston Churchill	10 May 1940 – 23 May 1945	Coal. Gov.
Sir Winston Churchill	23 May 1945 – 26 July 1945	Caretaker
C. Attlee	26 July 1945 – 26 Oct. 1951	Lab.
Sir Winston Churchill	26 Oct. 1951 – 5 Apr. 1955	C
Sir A. Eden	6 Apr. 1955 – 9 Jan. 1957	C
H. Macmillan	18 Jan. 1957 – 13 Oct. 1963	C
Sir Alec Douglas Home........	18 Oct. 1963 – 16 Oct. 1964	C
H. Wilson	16 Oct. 1964 – 18 June 1970	Lab.
E. Heath	18 June 1970 –	C

1.8 Greek Prime Ministers (1844–1967)

1a	Andreas Metaxas	3/15 Sept. 1843 – Feb. 1844
1	Constantine Kanaris	Feb. 1844 – 30 Mar./11 Apr. 1844
2	Alexander Mavrokordatos..	30 Mar./11 Apr. 1844 – 4/16 Aug. 1844
3	John Kolettis	6/18 Aug. 1844 – Aug. 1847
4	Kitsos Tzavellas	5/17 Sept. 1947 – 8/20 Mar. 1848
5	George Koundouriotis	8/20 Mar. 1848 – 15/27 Oct. 1848
6	Constantine Kanaris	15/27 Oct. 1848 – 12/24 Dec. 1849
7	Anthony Kriezis	12/24 Dec. 1849 – 16/28 May 1854
8	Constantine Kanaris	16/28 May 1854 – (temporarily appointed until the arrival of Mavrokordatos)
9	Alexander Mavrokordatos..	17/29 July 1854 – 22 Sept./4 Oct. 1855
10	Dimitrios Voulgaris	22 Sept./4 Oct. 1855 – 13/25 Nov. 1857
11	Athanasios Miaoulis	13/25 Nov. 1857 – 26 May/7 June 1862
12	John Kolokotronis	26 May/7 June 1862 – 10/22 Oct. 1862
13	Dimitrios Voulgaris	10/22 Oct. 1862 – 12/22 Nov. 1863
14	Aristides Moraitinis	9/21 Feb. 1863 – 11/23 Feb. 1863
15	Con. Zenovios Valvis	11/23 Feb. 1863 – 26 Mar./7 Apr. 1863
16	Diomides Kyriakos........	27 Mar./8 Apr. 1863 – 29 Apr./11 May 1863
17	Benizelos Rouphos	29 Apr./11 May 1863 – 25 Oct./6 Nov. 1863
18	Dimitrios Voulgaris	25 Oct./6 Nov. 1863 – 5/17 Mar. 1864
19	Constantine Kanaris	5/17 Mar. 1864 – 16/28 Apr. 1864
20	Con. Zenovios Valvis	16/28 Apr. 1864 – 26 July/7 Aug. 1864
21	Constantine Kanaris	26 July/7 Aug. 1864 – 2/14 May 1865
22	Alexander Koumoundouros	2/14 May 1865 – 20 Oct./1 Nov. 1865
23	Epaminondas Deligeorgis ..	20 Oct./1 Nov. 1865–2/14 Nov. 1865
24	Dimitrios Voulgaris	3/15 Nov. 1865 – 6/18 Nov. 1865
25	Alexander Koumoundouros	6/18 Nov. 1865 – 13/35 Nov. 1865
26	Epaminondas Deligeorgis ..	13/25 Nov. 1865 – 28 Nov./10 Dec. 1865
27	Benizelos Roufos	28 Nov./10 Dec. 1865 – 9/21 June 1866

1.8 *(cont.)*

28	Dimitrios Voulgaris	9/21 June 1866 – 18/30 Dec. 1866
29	Alexander Koumoundouros	18/30 Dec. 1866 – 20 Dec. 1867/1 Jan. 1868
30	Aristedes Moraitinis	20 Dec. 1867/1 Jan. 1868 – 25 Jan./6 Feb. 1868
31	Dimitrios Voulgaris	25 Jan./6 Feb. 1868 – 25 Jan./6 Feb. 1869
32	Thrasyvoulos Zaimis	25 Jan./6 Feb. 1869 – 9/21 July 1970
33	Epaminondas Deligeorgis ..	9/21 July 1870 – 3/15 Dec. 1870
34	Alexander Koumoundouros	3/15 Dec. 1870 – 28 Oct./9 Nov. 1871
35	Thrasyvoulos Zaimis	28 Oct./9 Nov. 1871 – 20 Dec. 1871/1 Jan. 1872
36	Dimitrios Voulgaris	25 Dec. 1871/1 Jan. 1872 – 8/20 July 1872
37	Epaminondas Deligeorgis ..	8/20 July 1872 – 9/21 Feb. 1874
38	Dimitrios Voulgaris	9/21 Feb. 1874 – 27 Apr./9 May 1875
39	Charilaos Trikoupis	27 Apr./9 May 1875 – 15/27 Oct. 1875
40	Alexander Koumoundouros	15/27 Oct. 1875 – 26 Nov./8 Dec. 1876
41	Epaminondas Deligeorgis ..	26 Nov./8 Dec. 1876 – 1/13 Dec. 1876
42	Alexander Koumoundouros	1/13 Dec. 1876 – 26 Feb./10 Mar. 1877
43	Epaminondas Deligeorgis ..	26 Feb./10 Mar. 1877 – 19/31 May 1877
44	Alexander Koumoundouros	19/31 May 1877 – 26 May/7 June 1877
45	Constantine Kanaris	26 May/7 June 1877 – 14/30 Sept. 1877
46	Alexander Koumoundouros	11/23 Jan. 1878 – 21 Oct./2 Nov. 1878
47	Charilaos Trikoupis	21 Oct. /2 Nov. 1878 – 26 Oct./7 Nov. 1878
48	Alexander Koumoundouros	26 Oct./7 Nov. 1878 – 10/22 Mar. 1880
49	Charilaos Trikoupis	10/22 Mar. 1880 – 13/25 Oct. 1880
50	Alexander Koumoundouros	13/25 Oct. 1880 – 3/15 Mar. 1882
51	Charilaos Trikoupis	3/15 Mar. 1882 – 19 Apr./1 May 1885
52	Theodore Deliyannis	19 Apr./1 May 1885 – 27 Apr./9 May 1886
53	Dimitrios Valvis	30 Apr./12 May 1886 – 9/21 May 1886
54	Charilaos Trikoupis	9/21 May 1866 – 24 Oct./5 Nov. 1890
55	Theodore Deliyannis	24 Oct./5 Nov. 1890 – 18 Feb./2 Mar. 1892
56	Constantine Konstantopoulos	18 Feb./2 Mar. 1892 – 10/22 June 1892
57	Charilaos Trikoupis	10/22 June 1892 – 3/15 May 1893
58	Sotirios Sotiropoulos	3/15 May 1893 – 30 Oct./11 Nov. 1893
59	Charilaos Trikoupis	30 Oct./11 Nov. 1893 – 12/24 Jan. 1895
60	Nicholaos Deliyannis	12/24 Jan. 1895 – 31 May/12 June 1895
61	Theodore Deliyannis	31 May/12 June 1895 – 18/30 Apr. 1897
62	Dimitrios Rallis	18/30 Apr. 1897 – 21 Sept./3 Oct. 1897
63	Alexander Zaimis	21 Sept./3 Oct. 1897 – 2/14 Apr. 1899
64	George Theotokis	2/14 Apr. 1899 – 8/20 Nov. 1901 – 12/25 Nov. 1901
65	Alexander Zaimis	12/25 Nov. 1901 – 24 Nov./7 Dec. 1902
66	Theodore Deliyannis	24 Nov./7 Dec. 1902 – 14/27 June 1903
67	George Theotokis	14/27 June 1903 – 28 June/11 July 1903
68	Dimitrios Rallis	28 June/11 July 1903 – 6/19 Dec. 1903
69	George Theotokis	6/19 Dec. 1903 – 16/29 Dec. 1904
70	Theodore Deliyannis	16/29 Dec. 1904 – 31 May/13 June 1905
71	Dimitrios Rallis – Kyriakoulis Mavromichalis	9/23 June 1905 – 30 Nov./13 Dec. 1905

1.8 *(cont.)*

72	George Theotokis	8/22 Dec. 1905 – 7/20 July 1909
73	Dimitrios Rallis	7/20 July 1909 – 15/28 Aug. 1909
74	Kyriakoulis Mavromichalis	15/28 Aug. 1909 – 18/31 Jan. 1910
75	Stephanos Dragoumis	18/31 Jan. 1910 – 6/19 Oct. 1910
76	Eleftherios Venizelos	6/19 Oct. 1910 – 25 Feb./10 Mar. 1915
77	Dimitrios Gounaris	25 Feb./10 Mar. 1915 – 10/23 Aug. 1915
78	Eleftherios Venizelos	10/23 Aug. 1915 – 24 Sept./7 Oct. 1915
79	Alexander Zaimis	24 Sept./7 Oct. 1915 – 25 Oct./7 Nov. 1915
80	Stephanos Skouloudes	25 Oct./7 Nov. 1915 – 9/22 June 1916
81	Alexander Zaimis	9/22 June 1916 – 3/16 Sept. 1916
82	Nicholaos Kalogeropoulos	3/16 Sept. 1916 – 27 Sept./10 Oct. 1916
83	Spyros Lambros	27 Sept./10 Oct. 1916 – 21 Apr./4 May 1917
84	Alexander Zaimis	21 Apr./4 May 1917 – 14/27 June 1917
85	Eleftherios Venizelos	14/27 June 1917 – 4/17 Nov. 1920
86	Dimitrios Rallis	4/17 Nov. 1920 – 24 Jan./6 Feb. 1921
87	Nicholaos Kalogeropoulos	24 Jan./16 Feb. 1921 – 26 Mar./8 Apr. 1921
88	Dimitrios Gounaris	26 Mar./8 Apr. 1921 – 3/16 May 1922
89	Nicholaos Stratos	3/16 May 1922 – 9/24 May 1922
90	Peter Protopapadakis	9/24 May 1922 – 28 Aug./11 Sept. 1922
91	Nicholaos Triantaphylakos	28 Aug./11 Sept. 1922 – 16/29 Sept. 1922
92	Anastasios Charalambis	16/29 Sept. 1922
93	Sotirios Krokidas	17/30 Sept. 1922 – 14/27 Nov. 1922
94	Stylianos Gonatas	14/27 Nov. 1922 – 11 Jan. 1924
95	Eleftherios Venizelos	11 Jan. 1924 – 6 Feb. 1924
96	George Kafandaris	6 Feb. 1924 – 12 Mar. 1924
97	Alexander Papanastasiou	12 Mar. 1924 – 24 July 1924
98	Themistokles Sophoulis	24 July 1924 – 7 Oct. 1924
99	Andras Michalakopoulos	7 Oct. 1924 – 26 June 1925
100	Theodoros Pangalos	26 June 1925 – 16 Aug. 1926
101	George Kondylis	16 Aug. 1926 – 4 Dec. 1926
102	Alexander Zaimis	4 Dec. 1926 – 4 July 1928
103	Eleftherios Venizelos	7 July 1928 – 26 May 1932
104	Alexander Papanastasiou	25 May 1932 – 5 June 1932
105	Eleftherios Venizelos	5 June 1932 – 4 Nov. 1932
106	Panagis Tsadaris	4 Nov. 1932 – 16 Jan. 1933
107	Eleftherios Venizelos	16 Jan. 1933 – 6 Mar. 1933
108	Alexander Othonaios	6 Mar. 1933 – 10 Mar. 1933
109	Panagis Tsaldaris	10 Mar. 1933 – 10 Oct. 1935
110	George Kondylis	10 Oct. 1935 – 30 Nov. 1935
111	Constantine Demertzis	30 Nov. 1935 – 13 Apr. 1936
112	John Metaxas	13 Apr. 1936 – 4 Aug. 1936
113	John Metaxas	4 Aug. 1936 – 29 Jan. 1941
114	Alexander Korizis	29 Jan. 1941 – 18 Apr. 1941
115	Emmanuel Tsouderos	21 Apr. 1941 – 14 Apr. 1944
116	Sophokles Venizelos	14 Apr. 1944 – 26 Apr. 1944
117	George Papandreou	26 Apr. 1944 – 3 Jan. 1945

1.8 (*cont.*)

118	Nicholaos Plastiras	3 Jan. 1945 – 8 Apr. 1945
119	Peter Voulgaris	11 Aug. 1945 – 17 Oct. 1945
120	Archbishop, Regent, Damaskinos	17 Oct. 1945 – 1 Nov. 1945
121	Panayotis Kanellopoulos ..	1 Nov. 1945 – 22 Nov. 1945
122	Themistokles Sophoulis ..	22 Nov. 1945 – 4 Apr. 1946
123	Panayotis Poulitsas	4 Apr. 1946 – 18 Apr. 1946
124	Constantine Tsaldaris	18 Apr. 1946 – 24 Jan. 1947
125	Dimitrios Maximos	24 Jan. 1947 – 29 Aug. 1947
126	Constantine Tsaldaris	29 Aug. 1947 – 7 Sept. 1947
127	Themistokles Sophoulis ..	7 Sept. 1947 – 30 June 1949
128	Alexander Diomides	30 June 1949 – 6 Jan. 1950
129	John Theotokis	6 Jan. 1950 – 15 Apr. 1950
130	Sophokles Venizelos	23 Mar. 1950 – 15 Apr. 1950
131	Nicolaos Plastiras	15 Apr. 1950 – 21 Aug. 1950
132	Sophokles Venizelos	21 Aug. 1950 – 27 Oct. 1951
133	Nicolaos Plastiras	27 Oct. 1951 – 11 Oct. 1952
134	Demitrios Kioussopoulos ..	11 Oct. 1952 – 19 Nov. 1952
135	Alexander Papagos	19 Nov. 1952 – 4 Oct. 1955
136	Constantine Karamanlis ..	6 Oct. 1955 – 5 Mar. 1958
137	Constantine Georgakopoulos	5 Mar. 1958 – 17 May 1958
138	Constantine Karamanlis ..	17 May 1958 – 20 Sept. 1961
139	Constantine Dovas	20 Sept. 1961 – 4 Nov. 1961
140	Constantine Karamanlis....	4 Nov. 1961 – 19 June 1963
141	Constantine Pipinelis	19 June 1963 – 28 Sept. 1963
142	Constantine Mauromichalis	28 Sept. 1963 – 8 Nov. 1963
143	George Papandreou	8 Nov. 1963 – 31 Dec. 1963
144	John Paraskevopoulos	31 Dec. 1963 – 19 Feb. 1964
145	George Papandreou	19 Feb. 1964 – 15 July 1965
146	George Athanasiades-Novas	15 July 1965 – 20 Aug. 1965
147	Elias Tsirimokos	20 Aug. 1965 – 17 Sept. 1965
148	Stephanos Stephanopoulos	17 Sept. 1965 – 21 Dec. 1966
149	John Paraskevopoulos	22 Dec. 1966 – 31 Mar. 1967
150	Panayotis Kanellopoulos ..	3 Apr. 1967 – 21 Apr. 1967

APPENDIX 2

Short biographies of Greek politicians

1. *Athanasiades-Novas, George* (1893-) Author, poet, politician, Member of the Greek Academy. Held various ministerial posts. Speaker of the House. Succeeded George Papandreou in the Premiership in 1965 but was defeated in Parliament.

2. *Deligeorgis, Epaminondas* (1829-79) Lawyer and politician, leader of a political party. M.P. Held various ministerial posts. Prime Minister (1865, 1865, 1870, 1872-4, 1877). Deligeorgis, an outstanding orator, was among the leaders of the young intellectuals who led the Revolution against King Otho in 1862.

3. *Deliyannis, Theodore* (1826-1905) Greek statesman and political party leader. M.P. from 1862 to his assassination. Held numerous ministerial posts. Greece's envoy at the Congress of Berlin. Prime Minister (1885-6, 1890-2, 1895-7, 1902-3, 1904-5). Deliyannis, a leading parliamentarian of his time, in contrast to his opponent Trikoupis, was very sensitive to public opinion and remained to his death popular with the masses. The two-party system functioned in Greece during his first two terms in office.

4. *Demertzis, Constantine* (1876-1936) Professor at the University of Athens. M.P. Held various ministerial posts and on the return of King George II became Prime Minister, an office which he held until his death (April 1936).

5. *Dragoumis, Stefanos* (1842-1923) Politician, member of an old political family. M.P. Held various ministerial posts. Prime Minister 1910. During his Premiership the national finances were considerably improved. Dragoumis, a devoted follower of Trikoupis, was a firm believer in the principle of 'proclaimed majority'.

6. *Gounaris, Dimitrios* (1866-1922) Greek politician. M.P. Held various ministerial posts. Prime Minister (1915, 1921-2). Gounaris, a most progressive and liberal politician, was Venizelos' principal opponent in the 1915 crises, and a fervent believer in Greek neutrality. He was executed in 1922 by a firing squad after a farcical trial by a military court which found him guilty of high treason in connection with the Asia Minor disaster. Undoubtedly, however, the atrocious act was politically motivated, and deprived Greece of an excellent orator and one of its most progressive politicians.

7. *Kafandaris, George* (1873-1946) Liberal and republican politician. M.P. Held various ministerial posts. As Minister of Finance in 1927 he successfully re-organised the Greek economy. Prime Minister 1924. Though originally a close associate of Venizelos at one stage he became one of his most bitter critics.

8. *Kanaris, Constantine* (1790-1877) Admiral, hero of the War of Independence. Minister of the Navy. Prime Minister (1844, 1848-9, 1864, 1864-5, 1877).

9. *Kanellopoulos, Panayotis* (1902-) Author, Professor at the University of Athens, member of the Academy of Athens. M.P., political leader. Held various ministerial posts. Deputy Prime Minister and temporary Prime Minister 1945, 1967 (until the coup d'état). Exiled during the Metaxas' dictatorship, when the War broke out

he joined the resistance groups. Succeeded Karamanlis in the leadership of
E.R.E. in 1963 when the latter left Greece on his self-imposed exile in Paris.

10. *Kapodistrias, John* (1776–1831) Greek diplomat and statesman. Joined the
Russian Foreign Office and eventually became with Nesselrode, Minister for
Foreign Affairs of Russia. As a diplomat he worked hard for Swiss neutrality and
for the adoption of the federal system of government. He distinguished himself
at the Congress of Vienna and the Second Treaty of Paris (1815) and Aix-La-
Chappelle (1818). In 1827 he was elected Governor of Greece, a post he retained
until his assassination in 1831. His diplomatic genius and his creative work in
Greece is now generally acknowledged.

11. *Karamanlis, Constantine* (1907–) Leader of E.R.E., M.P. Held various ministerial
posts. Prime Minister (1955–8, 1958–61, 1961–3). Following his defeat in 1963
he left Greece and has lived in Paris ever since in self-imposed exile. During
his Premiership the London–Zurich–Athens agreement over Cyprus was
signed.

12. *Kolettis, John* (1773–1847) Veteran of the Independence War. M.P. Minister of
Interior, Defence. Minister in Paris (1835–43). Prime Minister (1844–7). Kolettis,
creator and ardent supporter of the Great Idea, was considered the leader of the
pro-French faction in Greece in the 1840s.

13. *Kondylis, George* (1879–1936) General of the Greek Army, politician, M.P.
and one of E. Venizelos' earlier followers. Held various ministerial posts. In
1926 he overthrew General Pangalos, became Prime Minister and held elections in which he did not take part. Deputy Prime Minister and Prime Minister
(1935), Regent (1935). In October 1935, aided by a rump parliament, he restored
the monarchy and held a confirmatory referendum that brought King George II
back to Greece.

14. *Koumoundouros, Alexander* (1817–83) Leading Greek statesman and political
party leader of the nineteenth century. M.P. from 1853 to his death. Held
numerous ministerial posts and was twice elected Speaker of the House (1855–6,
1875). Prime Minister (1865, 1866–7, 1870–1, 1875–6, 1878, 1878–80, 1880–2).
During his last premiership Thessaly was annexed to Greece.

15. *Koundouriotis, Paul* (1851–1935) Admiral of the Greek Navy. Distinguished
himself at the battles of Elli and Limnos during the First Balkan War (1912–13).
Joined Venizelos' rebellion in Thessaloniki and was a member of the triumvirate
(the third member being General Danglis). On King Alexander's death he
was appointed Regent until the 1920 elections and then again in 1923 when
King George II was obliged to leave Greece. Was elected first President of the
Republic in 1924. Resigned in 1926 and was re-elected in 1929 but soon after
resigned for reasons of health.

16. *Markesinis, Spyros* (1909–) Historian, economist and Leader of the Progressive
Party. M.P., member of an old political family. Held various ministerial posts.
Acting Prime Minister in the absence of Prime Minister Papagos in 1953–4. As Minister of Economic Coordination, responsible for the post-war recovery of the economy, achieved through various measures and a skilful devaluation of the drachma.

17. *Metaxas, John* (1871–1941) Greek General, statesman, Chief of Operations
during the Second Balkan War, Chief of the Army Staff, 1915. M.P. Held
various ministerial posts. In 1921 he founded his own political party. In March
1936 he became Prime Minister and in August of the same year imposed
martial law in Greece, suspended the Constitution and governed until his death

in 1941. Metaxas, one of the most controversial Greek personalities, had brilliantly foreseen the disaster of the Gallipoli campaign as well as the Asia Minor disaster in 1922. His relevant reports are documents of great interest showing the military genius of their author. As Prime Minister he prepared Greece for the coming war, though he did all he could to avoid her involvement. Though unpopular, because of the suspension of the Constitution, he became a national hero, when he refused to succumb to Mussolini's brutal terms and decided to fight Italy. He inspired the nation and gave it its victories against a militarily superior Italian army but soon after died.

18. *Michalakopoulos, Andras* (1875–1938) Diplomat and politician. M.P. Held numerous ministerial posts and as Minister for Foreign Affairs he enjoyed Venizelos' absolute confidence. Deputy Prime Minister (1928–32, 1933). Prime Minister (1924–5). Represented Greece at the League of Nations. As Minister of National Finance he initiated bold social and labour legislation.

19. *Pangalos, Theodoros* (1878–1952) General of the Greek Army, politician. Took part in the 1909 Revolution. Chief of the Army Staff, 1918–20. In 1923 he became Minister of Defence and later Commander-in-Chief of the Army at Evros and was mainly responsible for the reorganisation of the Army after the Asia Minor disaster. His bellicose policy more than once threatened the conference at Lausanne. In 1925 he overthrew the Michalakopoulos Government, became Prime Minister and in 1926 became dictator, only to be overthrown in his turn by General Kondylis in August 1926.

20. *Papagos, Alexander* (1883–1955) Field-Marshal of the Greek Army, Prime Minister. Head of the Army Staff (1936), Commander-in-Chief during the Greek–Italian War, 1940–1. Field-Marshal, 1949. After he had successfully suppressed the Communist uprising he resigned from the army and founded the 'Greek Rally' in 1951. M.P. Prime Minister 1952–5. In 1935, Papagos with army officers obliged Panagis Tsaldaris to resign his Premiership. The Kondylis Government that followed restored the Monarchy in Greece, Papagos became Minister of Defence in the Kondylis Government and in the Demertzis Government that succeeded it.

21. *Papanastasiou, Alexander* (1876–1936) M.P. Held various ministerial posts. Prime Minister (1924, 1932). Papanastasiou was the first leader of a Socialist party in Greece and during his first Premiership the Monarchy was abolished.

22. *Papandreou, Andreas* (1919–) Son of George Papandreou, University Professor, M.P. After a prolonged absence in the U.S.A. he returned to Greece during Karamanlis' Premiership to take up a banking post which was then offered to him. Held two ministerial posts in his father's last Government.

23. *Papandreou, George* (1888–1968) Founder (in 1961) and leader of the Centre Union Party. M.P. Held various ministerial posts. Prime Minister 1944–5, 1963, 1964–5. Papandreou was Greece's leading post-war orator and at the end of his life became highly popular with the electorate.

24. *Plastiras, Nicolaos* (1883–1953) Officer of the Greek Army. Took part in the wars from 1912 to 1922. Following the Asia Minor disaster he became leader of the Revolution and remained in power (with the rank of colonel) until 1923. Following Venizelos' electoral defeat in 1933 he staged an unsuccessful coup and as a result was obliged to reside abroad until 1944 when he returned and became Prime Minister for a short period in 1945. He was also Prime Minister in 1950 and again in autumn 1951 until October 1952.

25. *Rallis, Dimitrios* (1844–1921)   Politician, leader of a political party. M.P. Held various ministerial posts. Prime Minister (1897, 1903, 1905, 1909, 1920–1).

26. *Sophoulis, Themistokles* (1860–1949)   Studied archaeology and later led the Revolution in his own island Samos which proclaimed union with Greece at the beginning of the Balkan wars. M.P. Governor-General of Macedonia, Minister, Speaker of the House, Prime Minister for a brief period in 1924, 1945–6 and again from September 1947 until his death in June 1949.

27. *Stefanopoulos, Stefanos* (1898–)   Politician, leader of a political party, member of an old political family. M.P. 1930–6 and 1946–67. Held various ministerial posts. Deputy Prime Minister 1954–5 and 1964–5. Prime Minister 1965–6.

28. *Stratos, Nicolaos* (1872–1922)   Politician, M.P. Held various ministerial posts. Speaker of the Second Revisional Assembly (1911). Stratos, a good orator and parliamentarian, was executed in 1922 with four others, after being tried by a false military court and allegedly found guilty for the Asia Minor disaster. Ironically, Stratos had always been moderate in his views and his moderation was demonstrated throughout the difficult years of the War.

29. *Streit, George* (1868–1948)   Professor of International Law at the University of Athens, Member of the Academy of Athens. Ambassador in Vienna, 1910–13. Minister of Foreign Affairs, 1914. During the 1914–15 crisis Streit was very close to the King and one of his confidential advisers. His diary, though incomplete, is of great importance and contains valuable information.

30. *Theotokis, George* (1844–1916)   Politician, M.P. Held various ministerial posts. Succeeded Charilaos Trilkoupis as leader of the Trikoupis party. Prime Minister (1899–1901, 1903, 1905–9). During the 1915 crises Theotokis was openly pro-German.

31. *Toumbas, John* (1901–)   Admiral of the Greek Navy, M.P. Held various ministerial posts including that of Minister of Foreign Affairs.

32. *Trikoupis, Charilaos* (1832–1895)   Diplomat and statesman of the nineteenth century. Member of an old political family. M.P. Minister for Foreign Affairs and repeatedly Prime Minister. One of the most outstanding personalities of modern Greek political history. Personally negotiated the acquisition of the Ionian Islands and later as Minister for Foreign Affairs signed the Treaty of Voeslau – the first Balkan alliance directed against Turkey. In 1875 he introduced in Greece principles of orthodox parliamentary government. During his term in office he focused his attention on the internal economic and social reorganisation of the Greek State and the strengthening of the armed forces.

33. *Tsaldaris, Panagis* (1868–1936)   Politician, M.P. Held various ministerial posts. Succeeded D. Gounaris as leader of the Populist Party. Prime Minister in 1932–3 and again from March 1933 to October 1935 when he was obliged to resign following the Papagos–Reppas–Oeconomos military coup (10 October 1935).

34. *Tsirimokos, Elias* (1907–1968)   Politician and party leader, member of an old political family, M.P. During the 1940s he joined various communist guerilla groups, a fact that caused great uproar when in 1965 the King decided to appoint him Prime Minister. Held various ministerial posts. Prime Minister for nearly a month in 1965 but was defeated by the House.

35. *Venizelos, Eleftherios* (1864–1936)   Greek statesman, founder and leader of the Liberal Party. Next to Kapodistrias Venizelos is the best-known political figure in Greece and abroad. Became famous in Crete at the turn of the century when the island was trying to unite with Greece. M.P. Held various ministerial posts.

Prime Minister (1910–15, 1917–20, 1924, 1928–32, 1933). During his second Premiership the 1911 revision of the Constitution was successfully completed; the two Balkan Wars took place and Greece practically doubled her boundaries at the treaty of Bucharest which he personally negotiated. In 1915 he disagreed with the King over Greece's position in the War. He also negotiated and signed the treaties of Sèvres and Lausanne on behalf of his country. During his tenure of office progressive social and labour legislation was enacted. But the quarrel with the King for which he shared responsibility in 1915 led to the 'Greek scission', one of the most tragic and fatal incidents in modern Greek history.

36. *Venizelos, Sophokles* (1894–1964)   Son of Eleftherios, politician, Leader of the Liberal Party. Army officer, M.P. Held various ministerial offices. Deputy Prime Minister and Prime Minister (1944, 1950, 1950–1).

37. *Voulgaris, Dimitrios* (1802–77)   Politician, M.P. Held various offices. Prime Minister (1855–7, 1862–3, 1863–4, 1865, 1866, 1868–9, 1871–2, 1874–5). His rigged elections became proverbial.

38. *Zaimis, Alexander* (1855–1936)   Greek politician, son of Th. Zaimis and member of an old political family. M.P. Held various ministerial posts. High Commissioner in Crete (1906). Speaker of the House (1895–7). Prime Minister (1897–9, 1901–2, 1915, 1917). Prime Minister in the Oecomenical Government (1926–8). President of the Republic (1929–35).

39. *Zaimis, Thrasyvoulos* (1825–80)   M.P. Held various ministerial posts. Speaker of the House (1854–5, 1860, 1874, 1876, 1877). Prime Minister (1869–70, 1871).

40. *Zavitsianos, Constantine* (1879–1946)   Politician, M.P. Speaker of the House and originally one of E. Venizelos' strongest supporters. Minister of Finance, Deputy Prime Minister of Metaxas (1936–7).

41. *Zorbas, Nicholos* (1844–1920)   Lt. General of the Greek Army. Leader of the 1909 Revolution. Minister of Defence, 1910.

APPENDIX 3

Translated articles of various European constitutions

BELGIUM   *Constitution of 7 February 1831*
Art. 71: The King has the right to dissolve the two Houses, either simultaneously or separately. The act of dissolution directs the convocation of the electorate within forty-five days and the meeting of the Houses within two months [of dissolution].

FRANCE   *Constitutional law of 25 February 1875*
Art. 5: With the concurring opinion of the Senate, the President of the Republic can dissolve the House of Representatives before its legal term expires. In this case, the electorate is summoned for new elections taking place within three months.

Constitution of 27 October 1946
Art. 51: If, during a further period of eighteen months, two ministerial crises take place under the conditions contemplated by articles 49 and 50, the dissolution of the National Assembly may be decided by the Council of Ministers, after consulting the President of the Assembly. Dissolution will be pronounced in accordance with this decision by a decree from the President of the Republic.

The arrangements of the previous paragraph apply only after the first eighteen months of Parliament have expired.

Constitution of 4 October 1958
Art. 12: The President of the Republic can, after consulting the Prime Minister and the Presidents of the Assemblies, pronounce the dissolution of the National Assembly.

The general elections will take place not less than twenty days but not more than forty days after dissolution.

The National Assembly will meet automatically on the second Thursday after its election. If this meeting takes place outside the fixed periods of ordinary sessions, a session will automatically be opened for a period of two weeks.

It is impossible to proceed to a new dissolution during the year following these elections.

Art. 16: When the institutions of the Republic, the independence of the Nation, the integrity of its territory, or the execution of its international commitments are endangered in a grave and immediate manner and the regular functioning of the constitutional organs of government is interrupted, the President of the Republic shall take all measures required by these circumstances after consulting the Prime Minister, the Presidents of the Assemblies and the Constitutional Council.

He will communicate the above to the Nation by a message.

These measures must be inspired by a desire to provide the constitutional organs of government with the means of accomplishing their mission in the shortest possible time. The Constitutional Council is consulted about the above.

Parliament is automatically convened.

The National Assembly cannot be dissolved while the emergency powers remain in force.

Art. 19: With the exception of the acts mentioned in articles 8 (paragraph 1), 11, 12, 16, 18, 54, 56 and 61, all other acts of the President of the Republic will be countersigned by the Prime Minister or, should the occasion arise, by the competent minister.

GERMANY   *Constitution of Weimar (1919)*
Art. 25: The President of the Empire can dissolve the Reichstag, but only once for the same reason.

The new election takes place within sixty days of dissolution.

The fundamental law of the Federal Republic of Germany 23 May 1949
Art. 58: Orders and decrees of the Federal President require for their validity the countersignature of the Federal Chancellor or the appropriate Federal Minister. This does not apply to the appointment and dismissal of the Federal Chancellor, the dissolution of the Bundestag under Article 63 and the request under Article 69, paragraph 3.

Art. 63: (1) The Federal Chancellor is elected, without debate, by the Bundestag on the proposal of the Federal President.

(2) The person obtaining the votes of the majority of the members of the Bundestag is elected. The person elected must be appointed by the Federal President.

(3) If the person proposed is not elected, the Bundestag may elect within fourteen days of the ballot a Federal Chancellor by more than one-half of its members.

(4) If there is no election within this period, a new ballot shall take place without delay, in which the person obtaining the largest number of votes is elected. If the person elected obtained the votes of the majority of the members of the Bundestag, the Federal President must appoint him within seven days of the election. If the person elected did not receive this majority, the Federal President must within seven days either appoint him or dissolve the Bundestag.

Art. 67: (1) The Bundestag can express its lack of confidence in the Federal Chancellor only by electing a successor by the majority of its members and by requesting the Federal President to dismiss the Federal Chancellor. The Federal President must comply with the request and appoint the person elected.

(2) Forty-eight hours must elapse between the motion and the election.

Art. 68: (1) If a motion of the Federal Chancellor for a vote of confidence is not assented to by the majority of the members of the Bundestag, the Federal President may, upon the proposal of the Federal Chancellor, dissolve the Bundestag within twenty-one days. The right to dissolve lapses as soon as the Bundestag by the majority of its members elects another Federal Chancellor.

(2) Forty-eight hours must elapse between the motion and the vote thereon.

GREECE   *Article 21 of the Constitutions of 1864, 1911 and 1952*
All powers emanate from the Nation and are exercised in the manner prescribed by the Constitution.

Article 31 of the 1864, 1911 and 1952 Constitutions
The King appoints and dismisses his Ministers.

Article 37 of the 1864, 1911 and 1952 Constitutions
The King convenes Parliament regularly once a year and extraordinarily whenever he deems it necessary; he opens Parliament in person or through a representative and

has the right to dissolve it. But the decree of dissolution, signed by the Council of Ministers, must direct the convocation of the electorate within two months and the meeting of the new Parliament within three months of dissolution.

Article 44 of the 1864, 1911 and 1952 Constitutions

The King shall have no other powers except those explicitly granted to him by the Constitution and the particular constitutional laws.

Article 79 of the 1927 Constitution

The President of the Republic can dissolve Parliament before its legal term expires if he has the concurrent opinion of the Senate. This is obtained on his proposal and by a decision of the absolute majority of its members. If the discussion on the above proposal is not terminated and decision reached within three days of its submission, the proposal is considered rejected.

Two consecutive Parliaments cannot be dissolved for the same reason.

Parliament may decide a self-dissolution by an absolute majority of its members.

The decree of dissolution is always signed by the Council of Ministers and directs the convocation of the electorate within forty-five days and the meeting of the new Parliament within a month of the elections.

Articles 89 of the 1927 Constitution and 78 of the 1952 Constitution

The government must enjoy the confidence of the House. Once formed, it is obliged to seek a vote of confidence from Parliament and it is free to do this whenever it considers it to be necessary. If, when the government is formed, Parliament is not in session, it is convened within fifteen days so as to pronounce its opinion about the government.

Article 46 of the 1968 Constitution

The King may dissolve Parliament after having heard the opinion of the Council of the Nation. However, the Royal Decree dissolving Parliament, countersigned by the Council of Ministers, must direct the convocation of the electorate within thirty-five days and the new Parliament within forty-five days from the elections.

ITALY   *Constitution of 1 January 1948*

Art. 88: The President of the Republic can, after consulting their Presidents, dissolve the two Houses, or even one of them independently.

He cannot exercise this right during the last six months of his tenure of office.

APPENDIX 4

Letters to *The Times*

LORD CHORLEY TO 'THE TIMES', 26 APRIL 1950

In spite of the authority due to his eminence both in law and in politics, I think that Lord Simon is on unsound and dangerous ground when he suggests in to-day's issue of *The Times* (April 24th) that the King might properly refuse to accept the advice of the Prime Minister to dissolve Parliament.

It is in the highest degree desirable that the King should remain au dessus le combat in respect of political manoeuvres not only in actuality but in appearance. By refusing to accept a Prime Minister's advice the King would put the Opposition into office, thereby in effect giving them the opportunity of choosing the occasion for a General Election, which would expose him to criticism. Although such conduct may have been still possible in Victorian times, when it was much debated, I submit that the march of political development has made it no longer justifiable. Moreover, it is very important that in such circumstances the King should be bound by a clear and simple rule which there can be no mistaking, and this is exactly what the convention that he must accept the advice of his Prime Minister provides.

Lord Simon prays in aid the statement of Mr. Asquith made in 1923, which he describes as 'classic'. So far from meriting this adjective, Mr. Asquith's opinion has been strongly criticised. As the late Professor Berriedale Keith said in his book, *The British Cabinet System* (p. 359), 'the assertion was based, no doubt, on the hope that if that occurred (i.e. he was asked for a dissolution) the King would turn to him to form a new Ministry. It is a clear case of sound judgement being obscured by personal feelings, for any serious consideration should have shown that, when the occasion arose, the King would be under every conceivable obligation to allow the Ministry to take the verdict of the country'.

Moreover, the weight of opinion among the constitutional lawyers is with Professor Keith when he adds that 'every consideration of constitutional propriety demands that it (i.e. the request for dissolution) be conceded'. Dicey (*Law of the Constitution*, 8th edn, p. 428 says: 'A Ministry placed in a minority by a vote of the Commons have, in accordance with received doctrine, a right to demand a dissolution of Parliament'. Anson, after quoting the advice of Lord Aberdeen to Queen Victoria to the effect 'that he had never entertained the slightest doubt that if the Minister advised the Queen to dissolve, she would, as a matter of course, do so', expresses his own view 'that the prerogative of dissolution is one which the King exercises on the advice, and at the request, of his Ministers, and that a request is not refused' (*Law and Custom of the Constitution*, I, 326–7).

Of the more modern authorities I may refer to Wade and Phillips (*Constitutional Law*, 2nd ed., p. 126), who say: 'It has for some time been a convention of the constitution that the King will dissolve Parliament at the request of the Prime Minister of the day.' They question whether this convention will survive the growth of three parties, and mention that it has been queried whether the King must grant a dissolution to a Prime Minister 'who had never had a clear majority in the House of Commons, but this view is not generally accepted.' The collapse of the Liberals, however, finally removes this shaky hypothesis.

Finally, Sir Ivor Jennings (*Cabinet Government*, p. 318), after a careful historical analysis of the position which contains a reference to Mr. Asquith's statement, sums up by saying: 'Thus while the King's personal prerogative (i.e., to refuse a dissolution) is maintained in theory, it can hardly be exercised in practice'. Incidentally, it is interesting to observe that he quotes a latter of Sir John Simon to the President of the Spen Valley Liberal Association of October 16, 1935, in which he said: 'The decision whether there shall be an immediate General Election ... rests with the Prime Minister, and until the Prime Minister has decided all anticipations are without authority'. On which Sir Ivor Jennings comments: 'Sir John Simon's statement suggests that the King has no choice but to accept the advice'.

ROY JENKINS TO 'THE TIMES', 26 APRIL 1950

Lord Simon's letter shows that in Mr. Asquith's view – expressed immediately before the formation of the first MacDonald Government and not 'just after', as Lord Simon says – it was the right of the Crown to refuse a dissolution to a Prime Minister defeated in the House of Commons. But it is surely of at least equal importance to remember that this is a prerogative which has been exercised on no occasion since the Reform Bill of 1832; that when Queen Victoria considered exercising it in 1858 she was strongly advised by Lord Aberdeen, whom she consulted informally as a former Prime Minister who was not a supporter of the Government, against taking 'an unusual and, he believed he might say, an unprecedented course'; that when she again considered exercising it in 1886, at a time when she was very prejudiced against the Government of the day, even the Leader of the Opposition warned her of the 'undesirable' consequence that if 'tempestuous times should follow, the responsibility would be thrown on her'; and that in 1924, following upon Mr. Asquith's statement, King George V appears to have had no hesitation in granting a dissolution to Mr. MacDonald, in spite of the fact that this involved the country in its third General Election within two years.

This constitutes a considerable list of precedents. Furthermore, the case for granting a dissolution at present is surely stronger than it was on any of these occasions. Lord Derby, Mr. Gladstone, and Mr. MacDonald were all in a minority – Lord Derby and Mr. MacDonald in very small ones. Mr. Attlee is in a majority, and if he could not secure constant support from the House of Commons, then a fortiori Mr. Churchill, who even in uneasy alliance with the Liberals would command no more than 307 votes, could not do so. He in turn would soon be forced to ask for a dissolution, and the Crown would be placed in the intolerable and dangerous position of granting to a minority Prime Minister what it had recently refused to a majority Prime Minister.

LORD SIMON TO 'THE TIMES', 27 APRIL 1950

The opinion of Mr. Asquith as to the responsibility of the Sovereign in dealing with a Prime Minister's request for a dissolution is not to be dismissed as unfounded so easily as your correspondents of this morning suggest. The insinuation of a learned professor quoted by Lord Chorley, that this view was a judgement 'obscured by personal feelings', will be repudiated by everyone who really knew the qualities of my old chief.

This 'difficult and intricate question' (as Anson called it) cannot be dogmatically answered without considering the circumstances in which it arises. In our constitution, unlike that of the United States, the legislature has not a fixed period of life, but may be brought to an end at any time before five years are up by an exercise of the prerogative. Is it really suggested that, however recent the last General Election may be and whatever its result, the Prime Minister has the absolute right to require the Crown to put its subjects to the 'tumult and turmoil' of another General Election within a few weeks of the last? And, if the result of the second election does not suit him, can he claim a third? On the contrary, I conceive that the Sovereign has the duty, in the case of a freshly elected Parliament at any rate, of considering whether government could be carried on under another head, and that if he thinks that it can, he is acting constitutionally and in the best interests of the country in preferring this alternative. I am not presuming to suggest what might happen at the present time, but I am maintaining an abstract proposition, which I think can be established by taking instances which have actually occurred.

Supposing that, as the result of a General Election, a Prime Minister finds himself left with the support of only a minority in the new House of Commons. He is under no obligation to resign immediately, and his Government may decide to meet the House when it assembles. An amendment to the Address is then carried against them, as happened in 1892. When this happens, can the defeated Prime Minister go to the Sovereign and demand another General Election, and is the Sovereign bound to grant his request? Of course not. But why not? Because there is an alternative Government available, without sending the electorate again to the polls. Or again, supposing that a Government which is normally supported by a majority is defeated by a snap vote, the result of which can be rectified or overlooked. Can the Prime Minister have the right to claim a dissolution, perhaps in the hope of turning his small majority into a larger one? Surely the whole thing depends on the actual circumstances, and the Sovereign, in the discharge of his heavy responsibility, may consider the circumstances; and one relevant circumstance may be that Parliament is only a few weeks old.

Everybody will agree that the King should manifestly remain au dessus du combat, but this result is not necessarily secured in all circumstances by 'taking the advice of a particular Minister to put his subjects to the tumult and turmoil of a series of General Elections so long as he can find other Ministers who are prepared to give contrary advice'. That is what Mr. Asquith said, and it seems to me, with all respect to those who assert the contrary, that the British constitution is not quite so wooden as they suppose. The danger of laying down a universal negative is that it can be upset by instances to the contrary such as the above. It is one of the advantages of having a constitution which is mainly unwritten that its proper working can always be adjusted to the public interest and to common sense. How things might work out in present circumstances is not for your correspondents to decide, or even speculate. But I venture to maintain that the proposition of Mr. Asquith, formulated in words based on almost unrivalled practical contact with constitutional issues, is correct.

'SIR ALAN LASCELLES ('SENEX') TO 'THE TIMES', 2 MAY 1950

It is surely indisputable (and common sense) that a Prime Minister may ask – not demand – that his Soveriegn will grant him a dissolution of Parliament; and that the Sovereign, if he so chooses, may refuse to grant this request. The problem of such a choice is entirely personal to the Sovereign, though he is, of course, free to seek informal advice from anybody whom he thinks fit to consult.

In so far as this matter can be publicly discussed, it can be properly assumed that no wise Sovereign – that is, one who has at heart the true interest of the country, the constitution, and the Monarchy – would deny a dissolution to his Prime Minister unless he were satisfied that: (1) the existing Parliament was still vital, viable, and capable of doing its job; (2) a General Election would be detrimental to the national economy; (3) he could rely on finding another Prime Minister who could carry on his Government, for a reasonable period, with a working majority in the House of Commons. When Sir Patrick Duncan refused a dissolution to his Prime Minister in South Africa in 1939, all these conditions were satisfied: when Lord Byng did the same in Canada in 1926, they appeared to be, but in the event the third proved illusory.

EDITORIAL, 'THE TIMES', 15 APRIL 1969
The right to dissolve

The 'threat of dissolution' is commonly cited as one of the means a Prime Minister possesses for sustaining himself in office. He exacts cooperation from his parliamentary supporters by presenting them with the 'or else' of a general election. The nature of the threat has changed since the nineteenth century, when most was heard of it. Then it hit members of Parliament in their pockets. The expense and general unpleasantness of bribing the electors to return them was something to be undertaken as infrequently as possible. Elections are now inexpensive for the candidates. The threat, in so far as it is still present, takes another form.

In threatening dissolution a Prime Minister is threatening the members of Parliament of his party with loss of their seats, or the end of office for their party, or both. And since these results follow only if the government party is likely to fare badly at an election (the threat vanishes if the party is riding high in popular favour), the Prime Minister's greater ruin is involved in the general debacle. As a deterrent, dissolution has points in common with the hydrogen bomb. The party implementing the threat is included in the massacre. Although this limits the likelihood of the threat actually being carried out, it does not remove it altogether.

In spite of this large element of bluff, governments continue to treat, and backbenchers are deluded into similarly regarding, as votes of confidence a whole range of matters, more or less important, which do not seriously affect the government's general ability to conduct the affairs of the nation.

It is rather like the position of adultery in matrimonial law. One adulterous act is sufficient to bring things to an end. But a better opinion is gaining ground that divorce should depend on a course of misconduct sufficient to confirm the irretrievable breakdown of the marriage. And so in Parliament, one isolated defeat is considered sufficient to dissolve the partnership between the government and the Commons, when a better opinion would be that only the habit of infidelity on the part of its supporters signifies breakdown.

However, according to the present understanding of parliamentary government, defeat in the Commons on so crucial a matter as a Bill to coerce trade unionists would impose on the Government an obligation to resign or seek a dissolution. Alternatively a defeat for the Government's policy in the Parliamentary Labour Party might lead the Prime Minister to want to dissolve. In such circumstances, which presuppose a disunited Labour Party and disunited Cabinet, could the Prime Minister be sure of being granted the dissolution for which he asked?

Constitutional authorities differ about the exact position, and are sensibly reluctant to give rulings concerning imaginary situations. They agree that no Sovereign for more than a hundred years has refused a Prime Minister's request for dissolution, although there have been at least two cases of Governors General refusing the request of Dominion Prime Ministers. They agree also that the Sovereign's personal prerogative in the matter is maintained at least in theory.

Queen Victoria was tempted to refuse more than once. In 1886 Lord Salisbury dissuaded her: to grant the request 'is the natural and ordinary course; it will shield the Queen from any accusation of partisanship'. To grant a dissolution remains the natural and ordinary course, but one can construct situations in which it might be right to depart from it. If a Prime Minister, defeated in Cabinet, unable to carry his policy in the party meeting, were to ask for a dissolution for the apparent purpose of unnecessarily involving his party in his own downfall, the Queen would have ample grounds for refusing him and dismissing him, provided an alternative leader of the majority party was in sight. Perhaps the best solution if a Prime Minister ever asks for a dubious dissolution is for the Queen to follow the nineteenth-century practice of granting dissolution to a Cabinet rather than an individual.

Mr R. G. Paget, Q.C., to 'The Times', 6 May 1969

Sir,—In view of loose talk to the effect that the P.M. might suddenly dissolve Parliament it is perhaps worth while to state the constitutional position.

1. The right to request a dissolution belongs only to a P.M. in office who is in a position to carry on the Government until a new Parliament is elected. This in effect means that he must have the consent of the Cabinet who will share the burden of Government.

2. When a P.M. resigns he ceases to be the Queen's adviser and becomes merely one of a number whom she may consult.

3. When a P.M. resigns the Queen is bound by constitutional precedent to send for the leader of any party who commands a majority in the Commons. Precedents – Baldwin for MacDonald; Chamberlain for Baldwin; Eden for Churchill; Macmillan for Eden; Home for Macmillan; Chichester Clark for O'Neill.

Mr Ian Gilmour to 'The Times', 6 May 1969

Sir,—The Prime Minister's entourage is evidently seeking to bolster his position by suggesting that, if he is defeated on the procedural motion to hold the committee stage of the Industrial Relations Bill on the floor of the House, he will ask the Queen for a dissolution of Parliament. Mr. Wilson's propagandists are of course entitled to peddle any line, however implausible, that is likely to help their boss. But it is surprising that this absurdity should have been taken seriously in sections of the press and elsewhere.

A general election now would virtually annihilate the Parliamentary Labour Party. Whatever Mr. Wilson's faults, he is not insane. He can therefore have no desire to make himself more execrated in his party than Ramsay MacDonald ever was, or to end a disastrous administration with a catastrophic defeat for his party. Nor, unfortunately, is there any reason to believe that he has suddenly become so ready to put country before party that he is anxious to bring Mr. Heath to immediate power.

In sober fact, a threat by Mr. Wilson to ask for a dissolution at this time is no more credible than would be a threat by Britain to make a nuclear strike on the U.S.S.R. unless the Russians released Mr. Brooke immediately. Mr. Wilson is an improbable Samson.

On a similar level of fantasy to the idea of a penal dissolution is the supposition that the vote on the procedural motion could be regarded as a matter of 'confidence', on which a defeat would necessitate the Government's resignation or a request for a dissolution. The Industrial Relations Bill is so important that plainly it should be taken on the floor of the House, whatever the tactical convenience of the Government.

Many Labour M.P.s are passionately concerned about the Bill, and naturally they want to be able to scrutinize and discuss it. Yet it is intimated, with apparent seriousness, that the vote will be one of 'confidence', and that they must therefore deprive themselves of the chance of doing so, and instead vote to send the Bill upstairs to be discussed in safe obscurity in a committee whose membership will be rigged by the Government.

The suggestion that the procedural motion could be a matter of confidence is as trifling as the idea that Mr. Wilson would dissolve Parliament if he was defeated upon it.

Sir Eric Fletcher to 'The Times', 7 May 1969

Sir,—My colleague Mr. R. T. Paget, in his letter on this subject (May 6), mistakes the constitutional position. It has been an established feature of the Constitution for well over a century that the Prime Minister of the day, and he alone – without consultation with the Cabinet – is entitled to ask the Crown for a dissolution.

Such a request has never been refused. It would be a startling innovation for the Crown to depart from a well-established precedent, and would inevitably involve the Crown in undesirable controversy.

Recent illustrations of the Prime Minister's prerogative in this respect occurred in February, 1950, and September, 1951, when Mr. Attlee, against the wishes of some of his Cabinet colleagues, sought and obtained a dissolution.

The timing of any request for a dissolution is a matter for the individual judgment of the Prime Minister based on the political circumstances of the time. It has never been suggested that the Prime Minister's discretion is subject to any veto by his party in the House of Commons (though their wishes are one of the matters a Prime Minister naturally takes into consideration). Historically, lack of parliamentary support has often been the motive and occasion for a dissolution.

The position of a Prime Minister in this respect has been strengthened in recent times by the modern tendency to what is sometimes called a 'presidential' form of general election. In March, 1966, as in October, 1964, the electorate decided that they wished Mr. Harold Wilson to become Prime Minister. Whatever may be Mr. Paget's individual merits (which I do not decry), the electorate of Northampton returned him as their M.P., as in the case of practically every other Labour M.P., because they desired a Labour Government under Mr. Wilson's leadership. Otherwise, Mr. Paget would not have been elected.

LORD SHAWCROSS, Q.C., TO 'THE TIMES', 8 MAY 1969

Sir,—Mr. Paget's view (May 6) of the constitutional position in regard to the dissolution of Parliament is certainly to be preferred to Sir Eric Fletcher's (May 7). It is not an 'established feature' of the constitution that the Prime Minister of the day 'without consultation with the Cabinet' is entitled to ask for a dissolution.

And it is hardly a service to the present Prime Minister to suggest (without the slightest evidence) that he would dream of ignoring the views of his colleagues and the will of Parliament in order to secure himself some imaginary electoral advantage. Neither in 1950 nor 1951 did Mr. Attlee do any such thing.

As a matter of practical politics it is true, as Sir Eric's letter emphasizes, that we are moving closer in many respects to a presidential system: this may present great dangers to the political parties and to parliamentary sovereignty. But constitutionally the Prime Minister remains only primus inter pares and I fancy Sir Eric underestimates the strength of the personal following of some particular members such as Mr. Paget or Mr. Donnelly in their own constituencies.

MR R. T. PAGET, Q.C., TO 'THE TIMES', 9 MAY 1969

Sir,—Nobody disputes that a Prime Minister may ask the Queen for a dissolution at any time. It is equally undisputable that there may be circumstances (although they have not yet arisen in this country) in which the Queen must refuse that request.

To take a hypothetical example: if the Queen had reason to believe that a P.M. was suffering from a mental breakdown or had suffered the sort of mental catastrophe that struck President Wilson, she would certainly have to seek further advice before dissolving Parliament.

The example which I had in mind was where a P.M. had been dismissed from the leadership of the party upon which he had relied. In this case the Queen would have to consider whether the granting of a dissolution conflicted with her overriding duty to see that her Government is carried on. Under our system we cannot spend the weeks between dissolution and the election of a new Parliament without a Government. The Queen must therefore be satisfied that the P.M. asking for a dissolution can govern until a new Parliament is elected, and this in turn means that the Cabinet, whether or not they all agree with the request, must not take their disagreement to the point of resignation or if some do resign, that they can be replaced. It is for this reason that Ramsay MacDonald would not have been entitled to a dissolution in 1931. This is the limitation to the P.M.'s power to dissolve to which I referred.

Sir Eric Fletcher (May 7) goes on to say that we have come near to a presidential system and votes for constituency candidates are really cast for the leader. This is broadly true and it makes it all the more important to those of us who hope to survive, that we should find a leader that our constituents may believe, for there are few who can hope to carry the burden of a leader who has run out of credibility.

In my view, Mr. Harold Wilson, despite the calumny to which he has been subjected in the press, is far and away the best leader this country could have. Constitutional usage entitles him to put that question to an electoral test at a time of his own choosing.

PROFESSOR MAX BELOFF TO 'THE TIMES', 13 MAY 1969

Sir,—Mr. Anthony King in discussing the power to dissolve Parliament (article, May 10) rightly states that 'the Queen must act so as to maintain detachment from the party battle; she must be seen not to be taking sides either between the parties or within them'. But he goes on to propose a course of action which would involve the Queen in doing both, in assisting the Labour Party to stay in power, and in assisting Mr. Wilson's critics to dislodge him from the leadership.

The reason for this is that Mr. King makes the mistake of assuming that political parties are recognized in the Constitution, and that the premiership is an elective office. Neither is true. Mr. Wilson is Prime Minister because, under given circumstances, he was asked by the Queen to form an administration and succeeded in doing so. As her Prime Minister he is entitled to retain the office until he resigns and to enjoy all traditional rights of a Prime Minister, including the right to advise a dissolution if in his view a particular Parliament has outlived its usefulness. It is not for the Queen to inquire into his motives, still less to refuse his advice.

Least of all could the Queen intervene to ensure the survival of a Parliament which has failed to pass an important constitutional measure, and which has by all evidence ceased to represent the majority view of the electorate. The old view that the right to a dissolution is automatic may be simple; it is also the only one that meets the case.

PROFESSOR S. A. DE SMITH TO 'THE TIMES', 14 MAY 1969

Sir,—For one who has, over the years and during the last few days, been obliged to read a number of extraordinary propositions about the Queen's conventional powers, or lack of power, to refuse a Prime Minister's request for a dissolution, it was refreshing to read Mr. Anthony King's article in today's issue.

On two points he may be faulted. In the first place, he indicates that the Queen ought not to refuse a request made by a Prime Minister who is the acknowledged leader of a minority party in the House. But in order to define the Queen's conventional obligations in such a situation one would have to ask a number of questions (e.g. how did the Prime Minister's party come to be placed in a minority; has she substantial grounds for believing that a stable government can be formed without a General Election; when was the last General Election?) before formulating answers.

Secondly, he implies that a Prime Minister ought not to request a dissolution (and presumably the Queen ought to refuse such a request if made), where his motive is to seek a way out of internal party difficulties. Again, much must depend on the particular circumstances. It would be very difficult to support a view that it was constitutionally improper for Captain O'Neill to request a dissolution earlier this year or that the Governor of Northern Ireland acted improperly in granting it.

More generally, Mr. King is surely right to emphasize that there is a range of situations in which Her Majesty has a discretion to refuse a Prime Minister's request. Proponents of the idea that a Prime Minister has an automatic right to a dissolution have used a number of arguments; (*i*) that the modern practice of granting requests for dissolution has mysteriously hardened into a binding convention never to refuse such a request; (*ii*) that the refusal of a request would inevitably prejudice the status of the monarchy; (*iii*) the involvement of the monarch in any degree of political controversy would be the worst of all constitutional evils in any circumstances whatsoever; and (*iv*) that the monarch can never be as well equipped as the Prime Minister of the day to determine what is constitutionally proper. None of these arguments carries conviction.

GENERAL BIBLIOGRAPHY

When two dates are given the first in parenthesis is that of the first edition; the second is the edition or reprint used in the text.

Alexander of Tunis, Field-Marshal Earl, *The Alexander memoirs, 1940–45*, ed. by J. North, London, 1962.

Alexandrakis, M. D., *De l'exercice du droit de dissolution par le pouvoir exécutif*, Paris, 1937.

Alison-Phillips, W., *The War of Greek Independence, 1821–1833*, London, 1897.

Amery, L. S., *Thoughts on the constitution* (introd. G. Marshall), Oxford (1947), 1964.

Amos, Sir Maurice, *The English Constitution*, London, 1934.

Amphoux, J., *Le chancelier fédéral dans le régime constitutionnel de la république fédérale d'Allemagne*, Strasbourg, 1962.

Anderson, M. S., *The Eastern Question*, London, 1965.

Andrews, W. G., 'Some thoughts on the power of dissolution', *Parliamentary Affairs* (1959–60), pp. 286–96.

Constitutions and constitutionalism, 3rd edn, Princeton, 1968.

Anschütz, G., *Die Verfassung des Deutschen Reichs, vom 11 August 1919*. Vierte Bearbeitung, 14 Auflage, Berlin, 1933.

Anson, Sir William, Letter to *The Times*, 10 September 1913.

Law and custom of the constitution, vol. I, 4th edn, 1911; vols II, III, 3rd edn, 1908.

Asquith, the Earl of Oxford and, *The Times*, 18 December 1923.

Fifty years of Parliament, London, 1926.

Memoirs and reflections, 1852–1927, 2 vols, 1928.

Avon (R. A. Eden), 1st Earl of, *Memoirs*, 4 vols, London, 1960–5.

Bagehot, W., *The English Constitution* (introd. R. Crossman), London, 6th imp., 1968.

Baldwin, A .W., *My father. The true story*, London, 1955.

Barthélemy, J., 'Les théories royalistes dans la doctrine allemande contemporaine', *Revue du droit public et de la science politique en France et à l'étranger*, XXII (1905), 717–58.

Barthélemy, J. & Duez, P., *Traité de droit constitutionnel*, Paris, 1926.

Beaverbrook, Lord, *The decline and fall of Lloyd George, and great was the fall thereof*, London (1963), repr. 1966.

Beloff, Max, Letter to *The Times*, 13 May 1969.

Benemy, F. W. G., *The elected Monarch. The development of the power of the Prime Minister*, London, 1965.

Berlia, G., 'La dissolution et le régime des pouvoirs publics', *Revue du droit public et de la science politique en France et à l'étranger* (1956), pp. 130–42.

'Chronique constitutionnelle française', *Rev. dr. pub. et sc. pol.* (1959), pp. 71–86.

'Le President de la République dans la Constitution de 1958', *Rev. dr. pub. et sc. pol* (1959), pp. 71–86.

Birch, A. H., *Representative and responsible government*, London, 1969.

Birkenhead, the Earl of, *Halifax, the life of Lord Halifax*, London, 1965.

Blackstone, W., *Commentaries of the laws of England*, Oxford (1765–9), 7th edn, 1775.

Blake, R., *The unknown Prime Minister. The life and times of Andrew Bonar Law, 1858–1923*, London, 1955.

Disraeli, London, 1966.

Blamont, E., 'La dissolution de l'Assemblée Nationale de décembre 1955', *Revue du droit public et de la science politique en France et à l'étranger* (1956), pp. 105–29.

Blondel, J., *Voters, parties and leaders. The social fabric of British politics*, London, 1967.

Bower, L. & Bolitho, G., *Otho I, King of Greece. A biography*, London, 1939.

Brogan, Sir Dennis, *The development of modern France*, 2nd edn, London, 1967.

Bryce, Lord, *Modern democracies*, 2 vols, London, 1929.

Burdeau, G., 'La conception du pouvoir selon la constitution française du 4 octobre 1958', *Revue française de science politique* (1959), pp. 87–100.

Le régime parlementaire dans les constitutions d'après-guerre, Paris, 1932.

Traité de science politique, 7 vols, Paris, 1949–57.

Cours de droit constitutionnel, 4th edn, Paris, 1964.

Droit constitutionnel et institutions politiques, 14th edn, Paris, 1969.

Butler, Richard Austen, Baron, *The art of the possible: The memoirs of Lord Butler*, London, 1971.

Butt, R., *The power of parliament; an evolutionary study of the functions of the House of Commons in British politics*, London, 1967.

Campbell, E., 'The prerogative power of dissolution; some recent Tasmanian precedents', *Public Law* (1961), pp. 165–79.

Campbell, J. & Sherrard, P., *Modern Greece*, London, 1968.

Campion, Lord (and others), *Parliament: a survey*, London (1952), 4th imp., 1965.

Carter, B. E., *The office of the Prime Minister*, London, 1956.

Cave, G., Letter to *The Times*, 10 September 1913.

Cecil, Lady Gwendolyn, *Life of Robert, Marquis of Salisbury*, 4 vols, London, 1921–32.

Cecil, Lord Hugh, Letter to *The Times*, 26 April 1913.

Chamberlain, Sir Austen, *Politics from inside; an epistolary chronicle, 1906–1914*, London, 1936.

Chapman, B., *British government observed; some European reflections*, London, 1965.

Chateaubriand, F. R., Vicomte de, *De la monarchie selon la Charte*, London, 1816.

Chester, D. N., 'Who governs Britain', *Parliamentary Affairs* (1962), pp. 519–27.

Chorley, Lord, Letter to *The Times*, 26 April 1950.

Churchill, R., *The fight for the Tory leadership*, London, 1964.

Churchill, Sir Winston, *The world crisis. 1911–1914*, 1923; *1915*, 1923; *1916–18*, 1923; *The aftermath*, 1929; *The eastern front*, 1931.

The Second World War, vol. I, 1950; vol. IV, 1954.

Codrington, Sir Edward, *Memoir of the life of Admiral Sir Edward Codrington. With selections from his public and private correspondence*. Ed. by his daughter Lady Bourchier, 2 vols, London, 1873.

Colvin, I., *The life of Lord Carson*, vols II, III, 1934, 1936 (vol. I by E. Marjoribanks, 1932).

Constant, B., *Cours de politique constitutionnelle* (introd. and notes by E. Labouleye), containing: *Principes de politique*, 1815; *Reflexions sur les constitutions et les garanties, avec une esquisse de constitution*, 1814–18; *Des réactions politiques*, 1819; and *De la dissolution de la Chambre de Députés*, Paris, 1820.

Cosmetatos, S. P., *The tragedy of Greece*, 1928.

Cosmin, S. (Cosmetatos, S. P.), *L'entente et la Grèce pendant la Grande Guerre 1916–1917*, 2 vols, Paris, 1926.

Dossiers secrets de la Triple Entente; Grèce 1914–1922, Paris, 1969.

Costin, W. C. & Watson, J. S., *The law and working of the constitution*, 2 vols, London, 2nd edn, 1961–4.

Couzinet, P., *La dissolution des assemblées politiques et la démocratie parlementaire*, Paris, 1933.

Crawley, C. W., *The question of the Greek Independence. A study of British foreign policy in the Near East, 1821–1833*, Cambridge, 1930.

Crick, B., *The reform of Parliament*, London, 1968.

Crossman, R., *Inside view. Three lectures on Prime Ministerial Government*, London, 1972.

Curzon, Lady, *Reminiscences*, London, 1955.

Daalder, H., *Cabinet reform in Britain, 1914–1963*, Stanford, California, 1964.

Dalton, H., *High tide and after. Memoirs. 1945–1960*, London, 1962.

Dareste, F. R. & Dareste, P., *Les constitutions modernes*, 4th edn by J. Delpech and J. Laferrière, 6 vols, Paris, 1928–34.

Debré, M., 'La nouvelle constitution', *Revue française de science politique* (1958), pp. 7–29.

De Gaulle, Charles, 'Discours de Bayeux', *Rev. Fr. de sc. pol.* (1959), pp. 188ff.

De Smith, S. A., Letter to *The Times*, 14 May 1969.

The new Commonwealth and its constitutions, 1964.

Constitutional and administrative law, London, 1971.

Dicey, A. V., Letter to *The Times*, 7 September 1913.

Introduction to the study of the law of the constitution (1885), 10th edn (introd. E. C. S. Wade), 1967.

Driault, E. & Lhéritier, M., *Histoire diplomatique de la Grèce de 1821 à nos jours*, 5 vols, Paris, 1925–6.

Dubois, J., *La constitution de l'empire allemand* (*Weimar*), Paris, 1919 (Greek trans. by P. Thibaios, Leipzig, 1922).

Duguit, L., *Traité de droit constitutionnel*, vols I–III, 3rd edn, 1927–8; vols IV, V, 2nd edn, 1924–5.

Duverger, M., 'Les institutions de la Cinquième République', *Rev. Fr. de sc. pol.* (1959), pp. 101–34.

La Cinquième République, Paris, 1963.

Constitutions et documents politiques, 5th edn, Paris, 1968.

Institutions politiques et droit constitutionnel, 10th edn, Paris, 1968.

Ensor, Sir Robert, *England. 1870–1914*, Oxford (1936), 1966.

Esche, H., *Die Auflösung der Volksvertretung im Deutschen Reich und in seinen Ländern*, 1930.

Esher, Viscount Reginald, *Journals and letters*. Ed. by M. V. Brett, 4 vols, London, 1934–8.

Esmein, A. & Nézard, H., *Eléments de droit constitutionnel français et comparé*, 2 vols, 8th edn, Paris, 1928.

Evatt, H. V., *The King and his Dominion Governors*, London, 1936.

Eyck, E., *A history of the Weimar Republic*, 2 vols, Cambridge, Mass., 1962–3.

Farrer, J. A., *The monarchy in politics*, London, 1917.

Ferrus, E., *Le droit de dissolution*, Bordeaux, 1935.

Finlay, G., *A history of Greece from its conquest by the Romans to the present time B.C. 146 to A.D. 1864*, vol. VII, *The Greek Revolution*, Oxford, 1877.

Fletcher, Sir Eric, Letter to *The Times*, 1 May 1969.

Foreign Relations of the United States, Diplomatic Papers, 1944, vol. V, Washington, 1965.

Forsey, E., *The royal power of dissolution of Parliament in the British Commonwealth*, Oxford University Press (Canadian branch) (1943), 1968.

Forster, E. S., *A short history of Modern Greece 1821–1956*, 3rd edn by D. Dakin, London, 1960.

Frangoulis, A. F., *La Grèce, son statut international, son histoire diplomatique*, 2 vols, Paris, 1926.

Fritz, Kurt von, *The theory of mixed constitution in antiquity*, New York, 1954.

Fusilier, R., *Les monarchies parlementaires. Etudes sur les systèmes de gouvernement (Suède, Norvège, Danemark, Belgique, Pays-Bas, Luxembourg)*, Paris, 1960.

Garvin, J. L., *The life of Joseph Chamberlain*, vol. I, 1932; vols II, III, 1933; vol. IV (by J. Amery), 1951; vols V, VI (by J. Amery), 1969.

Gevirth, A., *'Defensor Pacis' by Marsilius Patavinus* (Engl. trans.), New York, 1951.

Gordon, E., *Les nouvelles constitutions européennes et le rôle du chef d'état*, Paris, 1932.

Gorianow, S., *Le Bosphore et les Dardanelles*, Paris, 1910.

Gouault, J., *Comment la France est devenue républicaine*, Paris, 1954.

Grey, Viscount, of Fallodon, *Twenty-five years; 1892–1916*, 2 vols, London, 1925.

Guizot, M., *Mémoirs pour servir à l'histoire de mon temps*, Paris, vol. 1, 2ème edn, 1858; vols 2–8, 1859–67.

Gwynn, S. & Tuckwell, G., *The life of the Rt. Hon. Sir Charles Dilke*, 2 vols, London, 1917.

Haikal, Y., *La dissolution de la chambre des députées*, Paris, 1935.

Hamon, L. & Mabileau, A., *La personalisation du pouvoir*, Paris, 1964.

Hamson, C. J., *Executive discretion and judicial control; an aspect of the French Conseil d'Etat*, Hamlyn lectures, London, 1954.

The law; its study and comparison, Inaugural lecture, Cambridge, 1955.

Harvey, J. & Bather, L., *The British constitution*, London, 1966.

Hasbach, W., *Die Parlamantarische Kabinettsregierung*, 1919.

Hauriou, M., *Précis de droit constitutionnel*, 2nd edn, Paris, 1929.

Heasman, D. J., 'The Monarch, the Prime Minister and the dissolution of Parliament', *Parliamentary Affairs* (1960), pp. 94–107.

'The Prime Minister and the Cabinet', *Parliamentary Affairs* (1962), pp. 461–84.

'The ministerial hierarchy', *Parliamentary Affairs* (1962), pp. 307–30.

Hertzberg, G. F., *Geschichte Griechenlands seit dem Absterben des antiken Lebens bis zur Gegenwart*, 4 vols, Gotha, 1876–9.

Heuston, R. F. V., *Essays in constitutional law*, London, 1964.

Hinton, R. W. K., 'The Prime Minister as an elected Monarch', *Parliamentary Affairs* (1960), pp. 297–303.

Hogg, Q. (Lord Hailsham), Article in *Sunday Express*, 4 May 1969.

New charter. Conservative and Unionist party publication, 1969.

Hood Phillips, O., *Constitutional and administrative law*, 4th edn, London, 1967.

Reform of the Constitution, London, 1970.

Howard, E., *Theatre of life*, 2 vols, London, 1936.

Impe, H. van, *Le régime parlementaire en Belgique*, Bruxelles, 1968.

Iorga, N., *Histoire des états balkaniques jusqu'à 1924*, Paris, 1925.

Jackson, J., Letter to *The Times*, 27 April 1950.

Jenkins, R., Letter to *The Times*, 26 April 1950.

Mr. Attlee, an interim biography, London, 1948.

Sir Charles Dilke – a Victorian tragedy, London, 1965.

Asquith, Fontana edn, 1967.

Mr. Balfour's poodle; an account of the struggle between the House of Lords and the Government of Mr. Asquith, London, 1968.

Jennings, Sir Ivor, *Cabinet government*, Cambridge (1936), 3rd edn, 1961.

The law and the constitution, 5th edn, London, 1964.

The British Constitution, Cambridge, 5th edn, 1966.

Jones, G.W.,'The Prime Minister's powers', *Parliamentary Affairs* (1964–5), pp. 167–85.

Keir, Sir David Lindsay, *The constitutional history of modern Britain; 1485–1951*, London, 1957.

Keir, D. L. & Lawson, F. H., *Cases in constitutional law*, 5th edn, Oxford, 1967.

Keith, A. B., *Imperial unity and the Dominions*, Oxford, 1916.

Selected speeches and documents on British colonial policy (1763–1917), Oxford, 1918.

Responsible government in the Dominions, 2nd edn, 2 vols, Oxford, 1928.

The King and the Imperial Crown. The powers and duties of His Majesty, London, 1936.

The British cabinet system, 2nd edn by N. H. Gibbs, London, 1952.

Kelsen, H., *General theory of Law and State* (Engl. trans. by A. Wadberg), New York, 1961.

King, A., Article in *The Times*, 10 May 1969.

Laband, P., *Staatsrecht des Deutschen Reiches*, Tübingen, 1876.

Deutsches Reichsstaatsrecht, 7th edn by O. Mayer, Tübingen, 1919.

Laferrière, J., *Manuel de droit constitutionnel*, 2nd edn, Paris, 1947.

Lalumière, P. & Demichel, A., *Les régimes parlementaires européens*, Paris, 1966.

Lascaris, S. T., *La première Alliance entre la Grèce et la Serbie. La traité d'Alliance de Voeslau du 14–26 août 1867*, Paris, 1926.

Lascelles, Sir Alan, Letter to *The Times*, 2 May 1950 (signed: *Senex*).

Laski, H. J., *Parliamentary government in England. A commentary*, London (1938), 1968.

Reflections on the constitution. The House of Commons, the Cabinet, the civil service, Manchester (1951), 1962.

A grammar of politics, London, 5th edn, 1967.

Laubadère, A. de, 'La Constitution française de 1958', *Zeitschrift für ausländisches öffentliches Recht und Völkserrecht*, vol. 20 (1960), pp. 506–61.

Laurence Lowell, A., *Government of England*, London, 1917.

Lavroff, D. G. & Peiser, G., *Les constitutions africaines*, Paris, 1961.

Lee, Sir Sidney, *King Edward VII*, London, 2 vols, 1925–7.

Leeper, Sir Reginald, *When Greek meets Greek*, London, 1950.

Lloyd George, D., *War memoirs*, 6 vols, London, 1933–6.

Locke, J., *Two treatises on government* (introd. P. Laslett), New York, 1965.

Loewenstein, K., 'Réflexions sur la valeur des constitutions dans une époque révolutionnaire, Esquisse d'une ontologie des constitutions', *Revue française de science politique* (1952), pp. 5–23 and 312–34.

Low, S., *The Governance of England*, London, 1914.

Mackenzie, R., *British political parties*, London, 1968.

Mackintosh, J. P., *The British Cabinet*, London, 1968.

Macleod, I., Article in *Spectator*, 17 January 1964.

Macmillan, H. (autobiography), I, *Winds of change*, 1966; II, *The blast of war*, 1967; III, *Tides of fortune*, 1969; IV, *Riding the storm*, 1971.

Maitland, F. W., *The constitutional history of England*, Cambridge (1908), repr. 1965.

Manessis, A., *Deux états nés en 1830; Ressemblances et dissemblances constitutionnelles entre la Belgique et la Grèce*, Bruxelles, 1959.

Marriott, J. A. R., *The Eastern questions: an historical study in European diplomacy*, London (1917), 1963.

The mechanism of the modern state: A treatise on the science and art of government, 2 vols, Oxford, 1927.

Marshall, G., *Constitutional theory*, Oxford, 1971.

Marshall, G. & Moodie, G., *Some problems of the constitution*, 4th edn, London, 1967.

Matter, P., 'La dissolution des assemblées parlementaires', *Etude de droit public et d'histoire*, Paris, 1898.

Maunz, Th., *Deutsches Staatsrecht*, 11th edn, 1962, Munich/Berlin.

Maunz, Th. & Dürig, G., *Kommentar zum Grundgesetz*, I, Munich/Berlin, 1964.

May, Sir Thomas Erskine, *Treatise on the law, privileges, proceedings and usage of Parliament*, 17th edn by Sir B. Cocks, London, 1964.

Mendelssohn-Bartholdy, K., *Geschichte Griechenlands von der Eroberung Konstantinopels durch die Türken im Jahre 1453 bis auf unsere Tage*, 2 vols, Leipzig, 1870–4.

Metternich, Prince de, *Mémoires, documents et écrits divers. Publiés par son fils*, 8 vols, Paris, 1881–6.

Middlemas, K. & Barnes, J., *Baldwin*, London, 1969.

Miller, W., *Greece*, London, 1928.

The Ottoman Empire and its successors, 1801–1927. Rev. edn, Cambridge, 1936.

Mirkine-Guetzévitch, B., *Les nouvelles tendances du droit constitutionnel*, 2nd edn, Paris, 1936.

Les constitutions de l'Europe nouvelle, 2 vols, 10th edn, Paris, 1938.

Les constitutions européennes, 2 vols, Paris, 1951.

Mitchell, J. D. B., *Constitutional law*, Edinburgh, 1964.

Monypenny, W. F. & Buckle, G., *The life of Benjamin Disraeli, Earl of Beaconsfield*, London, 6 vols, 1910–20.

Moodie, G. C., *The government of Great Britain*, London (1964), 1967.

Morgan, J. H., Letter to *The Times*, 10 September 1913.

Morley, J., *The life of William Ewart Gladstone*, 3 vols, London, 1903.

Mowat, C. L., *Britain between the wars, 1918–1940*, London (1955), 1964.

Muir, R., *How Britain is governed. A critical analysis of modern developments in the British system of government*, 4th edn, London, 1940.

Nicolson, Sir Harold, *King George V; his life and reign*, London (1952). Pan Piper edn. 1966.

Oppenheimer, H., *The Constitution of the German Republic*, London, 1923.

Paget, R. T., Letters to *The Times*, 6 May and 9 May 1969.

Petrie, Sir Charles, *The life and letters of the Rt. Hon. Sir Austen Chamberlain*, 2 vols, London, 1939–40.

Pierre, E., *Traité de droit politique, électorale et parlementaire*, Paris, 1902.

Pohl, H., *Die Auflösung des Reichstags*, Stuttgart/Berlin/Leipzig, 1921.

Pollard, A. F., *The evolution of parliament*, 2nd edn, London, 1964.

Prevelakis, E., *British policy towards the change of dynasty in Greece. 1862–1863*, Athens, 1953.

Prevost-Paradol, L. A., *La France nouvelle*, 12th edn, Paris, 1894.

Prokesch-Osten, A. F., *Geschischte des Abfalls der Griechen vom Türkischen Reiche im Jahre 1821 und der Gründung des Hellenischen Königreichs aus diplomatischem Standpuncte*, 6 vols, Wien, 1867.

Radenac, L., *De la dissolution des assemblées législatives. Etude de droit constitutionnel et de législation comparée*, Paris, 1897.

Recouly, R., *Jonnart en Grèce et l'abdication de Constantin*, Paris, 1918.

Redmayne, M., Article in the *Listener*, 19 December 1963.

Redslob, R., *Die Parlamentarische Regierung in ihrer wahren und in ihrer unechten Form*, Tübingen, 1918.

Ries, J., 'Dissolution-sanction et mort du parlement', *Revue socialiste* (1955), pp. 481–93 and 26–37.

Rossi, P., *Cours de droit constitutionnel*, 4 vols, Paris, 1877.

Saripolos, N. N., *Das Staatrecht des Königreichs Griechenlands*, Tübingen, 1909.

Sayles, G. O., *The medieval foundations of England*, 2nd edn, London, 1950.

Schmitt, C., *Verfassungslehre*, München/Leipzig, 1928.

Seton-Watson, R. W., *Disraeli, Gladstone and the Eastern question*, London (1935), 1962.

Seydel, *Constitutionelle und Parlamentarische Regierung*, 1893.

Shannon, R. T., *Gladstone and the Bulgarian agitation 1876*, London, 1963.

Shawcross, Lord, Letter to *The Times*, 8 May 1969.

Simon, Lord, Letter to *The Times*, 24 and 27 April 1950.

Spender, J. A. & Asquith, C., *Life of Herbert Henry Asquith, Lord Oxford and Asquith*, 2 vols, London, 1932.

Stavrianos, L. S., *The Balkans since 1453*, New York, 1961.

Strupp, Ch., *La situation internationale de le Grèce, 1821–1917*, Zurich, 1918.

Sumner, B. H., *Russia and the Balkans, 1870–1880*, Oxford, 1937.

Taron, E., *Du droit de dissolution des assemblées parlementaires spécialement en Belgique*, Paris, 1911.

Taswell-Langmead, T. P. H., *English constitutional history from the Teutonic conquest to the present time*, 11th edn by T. F. T. Plucknett, London, 1960.

Taylor, A. J. P., *English history, 1914–1945*, Oxford, 1965.

Thiersch, F., *De l'état actuel de la Grèce et des moyens d'arriver à sa restauration*, 2 vols, Leipzig, 1833.

Thouvenel, M., *La Grèce du roi Othon*, Paris, 1896.

Vedel, G., *Manuel élémentaire de droit constitutionnel*, Paris, 1949.

Velu, J., *La dissolution du Parlement*, Bruxelles, 1966.

Vermeil, E., *La Constitution de Weimar et le principe de la démocratie allemande*, Strasbourg, 1923.

Victoria, Queen of England, *The letters of Queen Victoria. A selection from Her Majesty's correspondence*, 1st series, 1837–1861, 3 vols, edited by A. C. Benson and Viscount Esher, 1907; 2nd series 1862–1885, 3 vols, edited by G. E. Buckle, 1926–8; 3rd series, 1886–1901, 3 vols, ed. Buckle, London, 1930–2.

Vile, M. J. C., *Constitutionalism and the separation of powers*, Oxford, 1967.

Vinogradoff, Sir Paul, *Common sense in law* (1913), 3rd edn, Oxford, 1959.
  Outlines of historical jurisprudence, Oxford, 1922.

Voinesco, R. P., *De la dissolution des assemblées legislatives en France, en Angleterre et en Belgique*, Paris, 1896.

Voisset, M., *L'article 16 de la constitution du 4 octobre 1958* (Introd. G. Vedel), Paris, 1969.

Wade, E. C. S. & Bradley, A. W., *Constitutional law*, 8th edn, London, 1970.

Waleffé, B., *Le roi nomme et révoque ses ministres*, Bruxelles, 1971.

Walker, L., *The discourses of N. Machiavelli*, 1950.

Walker, P. Gordon, *The Cabinet*, London, 1970.

Walz, E., *Das Staatsrecht des Grossherzogtums*, Baden, 1909.

Wheare, Sir Kenneth, *Modern constitutions*, 2nd edn, Oxford, 1966.

Wheeler-Bennett, Sir John, *King George VI; his life and reign*, London, 1958.

Wigny, P., *Droit constitutionnel*, Bruxelles, 1952.

Williams, F., *A Prime Minister remembers*, London, 1961.

Wilson, G., *Cases and materials on constitutional and administrative law*, Cambridge, 1966.

Wilson, H., *The Labour Government, 1964–1970. A personal record*, London, 1971.

Windsor, H.R.H. The Duke of, *The Crown and the people, 1902–1953*, London, 1953.

Woodward, Sir Llewelyn, *The age of reform*, Oxford, 1962.
  British foreign policy in the Second World War, London, 1962.

Young, G. M., *Stanley Baldwin*, London, 1952.

Young, K., *The Greek passion*, London, 1969.

Zöepfl, H., *Staatsrecht. Gründsätze des Gemeinen Deutschen Staatsrecht*, Leipzig/Heidelberg, 1863.

GREEK BIBLIOGRAPHY

Ἀγγελοπούλου, Θ., Ἡ ἐπί τοῦ ἀγῶνος Α΄ βουλευτική περίοδος (16 Ἰανουαρίου 1822 – 26 Μαρτίου 1823), Ἀθῆναι, 1926.

Ἡ ἐπί τοῦ ἀγῶνος Β΄ βουλευτική περίοδος (26 Ἀπριλίου 1823 – 10 Ὀκτωβρίου 1824), Ἀθῆναι, 1927.

Ἀραβαντινοῦ,Ἰ., Ἑλληνικόν συνταγματικόν δίκαιον, τόμ. ι, 1897, τόμ. ιι, τεῦχος Α΄, 1902. Ἀθῆναι.

Βαμβέτσου, Ἀ., Παρεκβάσεις τοῦ κοινοβουλευτικοῦ πολιτεύματος. Σύμμεικτα εἰς μνήμην Ἀλεξάνδρου Σβώλου, Ἀθῆναι, 1960, σελ. 255 ἑπ.

Βασιλείου, Κ. Ἀ., Ἡ ἀναθεώρησις τοῦ Συντάγματος, Ἀθῆναι, 1912.

Γεωργοπούλου, Κ. Λ., Στοιχεῖα συνταγματικοῦ δικαίου, τόμ. Α΄, Ἀθῆναι, 1968.

Ἑλληνικόν συνταγματικόν δίκαιον, Πανεπιστημιακαί παραδόσεις κατά τό Σύνταγμα τοῦ 1968, τεύχη Α΄ καί Β΄, 1969, καί τεῦχος Γ΄, 1970, Ἀθῆναι.

Δαβῆ, Μ. & Παπαϊωάννου, Γ., Τό ἱστορικόν τῆς ἀναθεωρήσεως τοῦ Συντάγματος καί τά ἐπίσημα κείμενα. Τό νέον Σύνταγμα, Ἀθῆναι, 1911.

Δαγτόγλου, Π. Δ., Ἡ συνταγματική ἐξέλιξις ἀπό τῆς εἰσαγωγῆς τοῦ ἰσχύοντος Συντάγματος μέχρι τοῦ θανάτου τοῦ βασιλέως Παύλου (1952–1964). Ἀνάτυπον ἐκ τῆς Ε.Ε.Ν., Ἰανουάριος, 1966.

Ἡ βασιλική προνομία διορισμοῦ τοῦ πρωθυπουργοῦ κατά τό Ἀγγλικόν συνταγματικόν δίκαιον. Ἐπιθεώρησις Δημοσίου Δικαίου, τόμ. ι (1964), σελ. 244 ἑπ. καί 337 ἑπ.

Δαφνῆ, Γρ., Ἡ Ἑλλάς μεταξύ δύο πολέμων, 1923–1940, 2 τόμοι, Ἀθῆναι, 1955.

Διομήδους-Κυριακοῦ, Ἑρμηνεία τοῦ Ἑλληνικοῦ Συντάγματος, 2 τόμοι, Ἀθῆναι, 1904.

Δραγούμη, Ν., Ἱστορικαί ἀναμνήσεις, 4η. ἔκδοσις, Ἀθῆναι, 1937.

Ζέγγελη, Η. Δ., Τό ἐν Ἑλλάδι κρατοῦν κοινοβουλευτικόν δίκαιον, τόμ. ι, 1906, τόμ. ιι, 1906. Ἀθῆναι.

Ζορμπᾶ, Ν., Ἀπομνημονεύματα ἤ πληροφορίαι περί τῶν συμβάντων κατά τήν διάρκειαν τῆς Ἐπαναστάσεως τῆς 15 Αὐγούστου 1909, Ἀθῆναι, 1925.

Καλλία, Κ. Μ., Εἰσήγησις ἐπί τοῦ χαρακτῆρος τῆς ἐκ τῶν ἐκλογῶν τῆς 31 Μαρτίου 1946 προελθούσης Συνελεύσεως καί ἐπί τῆς ἐκτάσεως τῆς ἁρμοδιότητος αὐτῆς, Ἀθῆναι, 1947.

Κανελλοπούλου, Π., Τά χρόνια τοῦ μεγάλου πολέμου 1939–1944, Ἀθῆναι, 1964.

Καρολίδου, Π., Σύγχρονος Ἱστορία τῶν Ἑλλήνων καί τῶν λοιπῶν λαῶν τῆς Ἀνατολῆς ἀπό 1821 μέχρι 1921, 7 τόμοι, Ἀθῆναι, 1922–9.

Κόκκινου, Δ. Ἀ., Ἡ Ἑλληνική Ἐπανάστασις, 12 τόμοι, Ἀθῆναι, 1956–60.

Κορδάτου, Ἰ., Ἱστορία τῆς Νεώτερης Ἑλλάδος, τόμ. 1–3, 1957, 4–5, 1958. Ἀθῆναι.

Κοτσαρίδα, Ἑλ. Ἰ., Τό χρονικόν τῆς κρίσεως, Ἀθῆναι, 1966.

Κυριακίδου, Ε. Κ., Ἱστορία τοῦ συγχρόνου Ἑλληνισμοῦ (Ἀπό τῆς ἱδρύσεως τοῦ Βασιλείου τῆς Ἑλλάδος μέχρι τῶν ἡμερῶν μας 1832–1892), 2 τόμοι, Ἀθῆναι, 1892.

Κυριακοπούλου, Ἡ. Γ., Τά Συντάγματα τῆς Ἑλλάδος, Ἀθῆναι, 1960.

Χρονικόν τοῦ ἰσχύοντος Συντάγματος. Ἐπιστημονική Ἐπετηρίς εἰς μνήμην Γ. Σ. Σιμωνέτου, Θεσσαλονίκη, 1958.

Ἡ ἐπιρροή τῶν ἀρχῶν τῆς Γαλλικῆς Ἐπαναστάσεως εἰς τό Σύνταγμα τοῦ 1964, Θεσσαλονίκη, 1956.

Λάσκαρι, Μιχ. Θ., Τό Ἀνατολικόν ζήτημα, 1800–1923, τόμ. ι, τεύχη α, β (μέχρι 1878), Θεσσαλονίκη, 1948.

Μάμουκα, Ἀ., Τά κατά τήν ἀναγέννησιν τῆς Ἑλλάδος ἤτοι συλλογή τῶν περί τήν ἀναγεννωμένην Ἑλλάδα συνταχθέντων πολιτευμάτων νόμων καί ἄλλων ἐπισήμων πράξεων ἀπό τοῦ 1821 μέχρι τοῦ 1832, τόμοι ιι: 1–6, Πειραιεύς, 1839, 7–8, Ἀθῆναι, 1840, 9–10, Ἀθῆναι, 1841, ιι, Ἀθῆναι, 1852.

Τά κατά τήν ἀναγέννησιν τῆς Ἑλλάδος ὑπό διαφόρων ἐθνικῶν συνελεύσεων συνταχθέντα πολιτεύματα, Πειραιεύς, 1839.

Μάνεση, Ἀ. Ἰ., Ἡ δημοκρατική ἀρχή εἰς τό Σύνταγμα τοῦ 1864, Θεσσαλονίκη, 1966.

Αἱ ἐγγυήσεις τηρήσεως τοῦ Συντάγματος, τόμ. ι, 1956, τόμ. ιι, 1960–5. Θεσσαλονίκη.

Μαρκεζίνη, Σπ. Β., Ὁ Ἀνώτατος Ἄρχων εἰς τά σύγχρονα δημοκρατικά πολιτεύματα, Ἀθῆναι, 1935.

Ἡ Συνταγματική καί πολιτική θέσις τοῦ ζητήματος τοῦ Δημοψηφίσματος. (Λόγος εἰς τήν Βουλήν 22 Ἰουνίου 1946.) Ἀνάτυπον, Ἀθῆναι, 1946.

Πολιτική Ἱστορία τῆς Νεωτέρας Ἑλλάδος 1827–1920, 4 τόμοι, Ἀθῆναι, 1966–8.

SIR Κάρολος Ντίλκε. Περιοδικόν "Ἱστορία", Αὔγουστος, 1968. Ἀθῆναι.

Παπανδρέου, Γ., Ἡ ἀπελευθέρωσις τῆς Ἑλλάδος, Ἀθῆναι, 1948.

Παπαρρηγοπούλου, Κ., Ἱστορία τοῦ Ἑλληνικοῦ Ἔθνους ἀπό τῶν ἀρχαιοτάτων χρόνων μέχρι τοῦ 1930, 7 τόμοι. 6η ἔκδοσις ὑπό Π. Καρολίδου, Ἀθῆναι, 1932.

Πεσμαζόγλου, Μ. Ἀ., Ἡ νομική φύσις τῆς ὑπό ἐχθρικήν στρατιωτικήν κατοχήν συγκροτηθείσης Ἑλληνικῆς κυβερνήσεως, Ἀθῆναι, 1942.

Πετρακάκου, Δ., Κοινοβουλευτική Ἱστορία τῆς Ἑλλάδος, 3 τόμοι, 1935, 1944, 1946. Ἀθῆναι.

Σαριπόλου, Ν. Ἰ., Πραγματεία τοῦ συνταγματικοῦ δικαίου, 2α ἔκδοσις, τόμοι 5, Ἀθῆναι, 1874.

Σαριπόλου, Ν. Ν., Ἑλληνικόν Συνταγματικόν Δίκαιον, τόμ. ι 3η ἔκδοσις, 1915, τόμ. ιι 4η ἔκδοσις, 1923, τόμ. ιιι 4η ἔκδοσις, 1923. Ἀθῆναι.

Τό σύστημα τῆς κοινοβουλευτικῆς κυβερνήσεως ἐν τῇ νεοτάτῃ αὐτοῦ ἐξελίξει, Ἀθῆναι, 1921.

Ἡ πρώτη Ἐθνοσυνέλευσις καί τό πολίτευμα τῆς Ἐπιδαύρου τοῦ 1822, Ἀθῆναι, 1907.

Σαχίνη, Π. Κ., Περί τῆς διακρίσεως τῶν ἐξουσιῶν, Ἀθῆναι, 1910.

Σβώλου, Ἀ. Ἰ., Συνταγματικόν δίκαιον, τόμ. ι, Ἀθῆναι, 1934.

Ἡ Ἀναθεώρησις τοῦ Συντάγματος, Ἀθῆναι, 1933.

Τά πρῶτα Ἑλληνικά Συντάγματα. Ἐφημερίς Ἑλλήνων Νομικῶν, 1935.

Τό νέον Σύνταγμα καί αἱ βάσεις τοῦ πολιτεύματος, Ἀθῆναι, 1928.

Προβλήματα τῆς κοινοβουλευτικῆς δημοκρατίας (Ἐναρκτήριος λόγος), Ἀθῆναι, 1931.

Σγουρίτσα, Χ., Συνταγματικόν δίκαιον. Ἔκδοσις γ', τόμ. ι, Ἀθῆναι, 1965.

Στρέϊτ, Γ. Ἡμερολόγιον – Ἀρχεῖον, 2 τόμοι: τόμ. ι, 1964, τόμ. ιι, τεῦχος Α, 1965, τόμ. ιι, τεῦχος Β, 1966, Ἀθῆναι.

Συγγροῦ, Ἀ., Ἀπομνημονεύματα, 3 τόμοι, Ἀθῆναι, 1908.

Συμβούλιον Στέμματος, Πρακτικά 1ης καί 2ας Σεπτεμβρίου 1965, Ἀθῆναι, 1965.

Τρικούπη, Χαριλάου, Ἐκ δημοσιευμάτων ἀπό τοῦ Μαΐου 1884 ἐν εἴδει ἡμερο-λογίου, 13 τόμοι: Α', 1907, Β', 1908, Γ', 1908, Δ', 1909, Ε', 1909, ΣΤ', 1910,

Ζ', 1910, Η', 1911, Θ', 1911, Ι', 1911, ΙΑ', 1911, ΙΒ', 1911, ΙΓ', 1917. Ἀθῆναι.

Ἀνάλεκτα ἐκ δημοσιευμάτων ἀπό Ὀκτωβρίου 1862 μέχρι Μαΐου 1884, 3 τόμοι: Α', 1912, Β', 1912, Γ', 1912. Ἀθῆναι.

Τσουδεροῦ, Ἐ. Ἰ., Ἑλληνικές ἀνωμαλίες στή Μέση Ἀνατολή, Ἀθῆναι, 1945.

Φιλαρέτου, Γ. Ν., Σύνταγμα τῆς Ἑλλάδος μετ' εἰσαγωγῆς ἱστορικῆς καί σχολίων κατ' ἄρθρον, Ἀθῆναι, 1889.

INDEX*

* I am grateful to my wife who kindly relieved me of the tedious but important task of compiling the Index.